LATIN AMERICAN CHURCH GROWTH

Church Growth Series

Latin American Church Growth

by

William R. Read
Victor M. Monterroso
Harmon A. Johnson

WILLIAM B. EERDMANS PUBLISHING COMPANY
GRAND RAPIDS, MICHIGAN

FOREWORD

This book is a milestone in Christian research in Latin America. Never before has the Protestant Church there been studied so thoroughly and to such good effect.

Because of rapid social changes and multiplying revolutions, Latin America is very much in the news all over the world. Its Evangelical Churches are also constantly in the Christian news. They are among the most dynamic in the world and as a whole are characterized by a very high rate of growth. The influence of Latin American evangelism is being felt in all five continents.

Latin Americans are beginning to shape their own institutions and their contribution is being sought in wider and wider circles of the Church universal. Some Churches begun by missions are growing larger than their parents overseas and in places are developing more fruitful patterns of reproduction. Within a reasonably short time, the Evangelical community has grown to approximately 15 million and is now generally accepted by the Roman Catholic Church and the community at large as a legitimate part of Latin American Society, with full rights and privileges.

How has this phenomenal growth taken place? What factors have helped or hindered this significant development? What part have missionary structures played in the retardation or acceleration of growth? How have the life, doctrines, and patterns of the founding missionary societies affected for better or for worse the shape of the emerging Churches?

This book is an honest, reliable, and well-documented answer to these and other related questions. Messrs. Read, Monterroso and Johnson, and with them the School of World Mission and Institute of Church Growth at Fuller Theological Seminary, have rendered a great service to the Latin American Churches and especially to the missionary societies working in this area. The information, insights, and analysis presented in this report cannot be found anywhere else today.

To be sure, on minor points here and there, observers may disagree with the findings. Objections can be expected — some well based, some not. A few readers may be disappointed because of the incompleteness of the information and analysis of a particular country or organization of their interest. Thoughtful readers will, of course, understand that in a report that takes the whole of Latin America as its field, all seventeen countries could not be treated exhaustively. The need to keep the report within reasonable limits forced continual winnowing of the material gathered. Much is in the book and many additional data are available in the Latin American archives at Fuller's School of Missions.

It will be a great mistake if minor or even major disagreements with the data or the viewpoints expressed keep us from having "fellowship with the facts." It is high time that we separate fact from fiction and see the facts clearly. The emotionalism that has characterized our overall approach to missions must be seen in all its ugliness and judged by the net results of our labors. Paternalism plagues the missionary enterprise from the cradle to the grave. Accretions to the Gospel must be detected, denounced, and destroyed. After all, it should not be considered so revolutionary for Bible-believing Christians to return to the fresh freedom of Spirit-led, New Testament Christianity!

This report shows that there is a definite relationship between the above (and many other) factors and the degree of success or failure of our efforts as measured by church growth and development. Missionary societies, by definition committed to the numerical growth of the Church, cannot hide behind cliches and platitudes when growth does not accompany their efforts in populations where others are growing greatly. National Churches and missionary societies of all camps can profit much by taking this study very seriously, facing the facts without becoming defensive, and taking appropriate measures to achieve their own objectives.

This report can serve as a focal point for aggressive and creative action on the crucial issues of amalgamation, leadership training, and missionary candidate education and recruiting. It should prove helpful in the quest for an overall strategy for each missionary society and for cooperative efforts by several societies. This document can help educate the homeland constituency on Christian mission. We are beginning to hear much about this task, yet no one seems to know how to go about it. This book should be used in the sending congregations. Let us give them the facts.

There are already encouraging signs. The members of the "Church Growth Research in Latin America" team, now scattered across Latin America, are receiving invitations from groups of nationals and missionaries to share with them additional facts about their specific

vi

situations, and to lead them into fruitful discussions of the data. The publication of *Latin American Church Growth,* in English, Spanish, and Portuguese, will fan such sparks of interest until they become flames of widespread concern for gathering, studying, and implementing church growth data, and for measuring all missionary methods by the criterion of effectiveness in adding members to the Church.

These are days of unprecedented opportunities in Latin America for the fulfillment of the great commission of Christ — that is, for establishing and developing multitudes of Churches. This book is not merely an accumulation of facts as to growth that has already taken place: it is a clarion call for positive action in these favorable days to make Christ known, loved, and believed throughout Latin America. To that end, let us hope, pray, and work!

— J. RUBEN LORES
Assistant General Director,
Latin America Mission
Director,
Office of Worldwide Evangelism-in-Depth

San Jose, Costa Rica

CONTENTS

CONTENTS

LIST OF ILLUSTRATIONS

PREFACE

Christian Mission, come of age, stands at the beginning of its main task — discipling the two billion who have yet to believe — and asks itself, "How are we getting on with the job?" It renders to God an account of its faithfulness in terms, not primarily of hours of labor and sincerity of purpose, but of sheep found and returned to the fold. "How are we getting on with the job?" ask both "Is the Gospel being preached?" and "Is the Gospel being obeyed?" It wants to know both that missionaries are being sent and that on-going churches are being multiplied.

"Feedback" is a term often heard. It means "true, constant light from what is being done, used to improve and guide the undertaking in the future." *Latin American Church Growth* is part of the scientific feedback from the current missionary enterprise. This the Church must have if it is to be faithful to its Lord. It is sure light on how we are getting on with the job.

In an enterprise as vast as Evangelical missions in Latin America, it is inevitable that particular facts, reported to Church Growth Research in Latin America in 1966, were later reported to other publications in slightly different forms. It is also inevitable that, viewing growth on a large canvas, the researchers should pass judgment that a given Church has grown slowly, when its own missionaries or ministers deem the growth gratifying. In short, minor differences of fact and opinion are certain to appear. When this happens, it is well to remember that country-wide and continent-wide trends which this research so clearly establishes are not rendered invalid by a few exceptions.

The CGRILA Study is not a continuing enterprise. The book is not likely to be revised. Extreme care has been taken to discover the facts. As long as the work was in manuscript form, corrections were widely sought and patiently made. Now that the research has been published, we respectfully suggest that readers (a) triple check their own figures before concluding that those given here are in error, and (b) devote their attention to the lessons in mission afforded by every chapter of this monumental study by Read, Monterroso, and Johnson.

xxiii

The book, in English, Spanish, and Portuguese, casts reliable light on how the Gospel is communicated and how it is not, what methods God is blessing to an increase of baptized believers and what methods He is not, and what makes churches multiply and what does not. We trust it will illumine the path of thousands in Latin America — nationals and missionaries — as they press forward, establishing cells of the redeemed and outposts of the Kingdom of God.

Lilly Endowment Incorporated by its generous grant made possible this large pioneer study. Missions are deeply indebted to this Christian foundation for its far-sighted conviction that light on the whole enterprise was worth obtaining. It is now the responsibility of Churches and mission boards to use the light, profit by the feedback, and increase the effectiveness and faithfulness of their operations.

— DONALD McGAVRAN, *Dean*
School of World Mission and
Institute of Church Growth
Fuller Theological Seminary

Pasadena, California

INTRODUCTION

Although the destinies of Latin America and the rest of the Western world have always been intertwined, only in the last few decades has Latin America claimed the active interest of North America and Europe. The success or failure of Latin American countries in meeting the challenges of development and technological advance, furthermore, certainly will affect the future of emergent nations in Africa and Asia.

Thus scholars of every discipline — political science, economics, history, sociology, anthropology, linguistics — are turning their attention to Latin American studies. The Organization of American States, the Alliance for Progress, the United Nations, and other public and private institutions are supplying resources of personnel and capital for the systematic study of Latin American problems. Current research findings thus provide the Churches and missions in Latin America with a background for the study of Evangelical church growth.

The changes which modernity has thrust upon them have led contemporary Latin Americans to investigate radically different patterns of life and thought. Some Latins have sought to find their identity by reaching back into their cultural and historical heritage. At the same time, many non-Christian religious ideologies have arisen, and millions are now Marxists, spiritists, and materialists.

Consciously or unconsciously, Evangelical Churches are involved in the current political and social upheavals as they share in the search for solutions. Indeed, they themselves are the result of change and, in turn, effect social change. The nature and extent of their involvement is a matter for debate among Evangelicals, but all recognize the need to become a real part of the contemporary world.

STUDY OF CHURCH GROWTH DEMANDED

Protestant Churches and missions in the twentieth century have carried on significant missionary work in Latin America, but, particularly in the last few decades, Protestants and Roman Catholics as well have recognized that the spiritual needs of the masses of unchurched, nominal Christians demand increased missionary effort. The result is a concentration of missionary resources (both Evangelical and Roman Catholic) in Latin America. In fact, by 1958, 25

17

per cent of all Protestant missionaries were deployed in Latin America.

The increase of missionary activity in the last three decades, however, has been in the context of revolution. Latin America needs immediate, radical social change in order to solve threatening, even overwhelming problems. The simplistic solutions to Latin American needs which political ideologies of the left and right have offered have been tried, but the problems still remain to be solved.

In the midst of shifting allegiance and rapid change, the Evangelical Churches have grown tremendously. Church membership now numbers millions, even though growth has been very uneven.

The remarkable growth of some Evangelical Churches in Latin America and the lamentable lack of growth of others presents a complicated puzzle. This is particularly true in view of the considerable receptivity of the urban and rural peoples who inhabit Latin America. North American and European Protestant Churches maintain about five thousand missionaries and assist many Evangelical Churches in Latin America. Consequently, they are keenly interested in discovering reasons for growth and non-growth.

CHURCH GROWTH RESEARCH IN LATIN AMERICA (CGRILA)

CGRILA was sponsored by the Institute of Church Growth and School of World Mission of Fuller Theological Seminary under a grant from Lilly Endowment, Inc. (Lilly Endowment made the grant to the Institute of Church Growth in 1964 while the latter was a part of Northwest Christian College, Eugene, Oregon; when the Institute moved to Pasadena, Fuller Seminary became sponsor of the research.) The director of the research was Dr. Donald McGavran, Dean of the School of World Mission and Institute of Church Growth. The advisor on research method was Dr. Alan Tippett, Professor of Missionary Anthropology.

The study was designed to include seventeen republics of continental Latin America, thereby excluding the Caribbean Islands, the Guianas, and British Honduras. Basic objectives were laid down to guide the research:

> To determine the degree and nature of church growth already achieved by Pentecostal and traditional Protestant denominations;
>
> To estimate the degree of responsiveness to the Christian message that the masses in Latin America are likely to exhibit in the years ahead;
>
> To describe the factors which retard and those which accelerate the establishment of soundly Christian churches;
>
> To disseminate this information widely through Spanish, Portuguese, and English to churches in Latin America, the United States of America, and England involved in the Christian mission in Latin America.

The methodology followed the simplified pert charts of the research procedure which accompanies this script (Figures A, B, C). The description thus is set forth in three chronological phases. The first of these synchronized with the Fall Term, 1965 and permitted the researchers to interact with a great variety of missionary leaders from all parts of the world. The second phase of intensive data-collecting on the field lasted ten months for each of the three researchers, or thirty man-months. So many data were collected and so much verification was called for that the third phase was drawn out for twenty months and one member of the team had to remain on for editorial purposes. While this delay in the publication of the work is regrettable, additional verification has provided a more reliable picture of the Evangelical Church of Latin America.

This statement of the methodology will proceed along the following lines:

      First Phase — Preliminary Research
           a. Selection and Preparation of Researchers
           b. Definition of Regional Limits of Research
           c. Preliminary Contacts and Correspondence
           d. Preliminary Statistics
      Second Phase — Field Data-Collécting
           a. How the Team Operated and What It Collected
           b. Interviewing
           c. Informants
      Third Phase — Analysis and Synthesis
           a. Classification
           b. Verification
           c. Writing
           d. Statistics

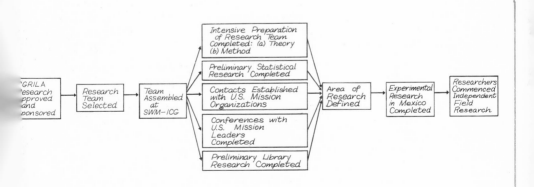

FIRST PHASE: PRELIMINARY RESEARCH

Figure A

First Phase — Preliminary Research

a. Selection and Preparation of Researchers

Dr. McGavran selected his three researchers with great care. He wanted men currently involved in the Latin American situation, men with a wide range of denominational connections, yet men who could work happily together, and who had some spiritual convictions that this kind of project was worthwhile. William Read, of the United Presbyterian Church of U.S.A., was freed from his missionary respon- sibilities in Brazil and supported throughout by COEMAR (Commis- sion on Ecumenical Mission and Relations). He had previously worked under McGavran and had written a book, *New Patterns of Church Growth in Brazil* (1965). He led the research team on the field. Victor Monterroso, though financed from the project, was released by the Latin America Mission, whose support and blessing the team enjoyed throughout. Monterroso is a Guatemalan who was serving in Costa Rica as a seminary professor. Harmon Johnson, a Scandi- navian-American Pentecostal, was released by the Assembléia de Deus in northern Brazil and carried financially by the Independent As- semblies of God. The research could never have been completed without the generous support of their respective organizations. All these men had proved themselves in the Latin American world of Christian mission, had received theological training, and were able to communicate in Spanish or Portuguese.

The three researchers received three months of intensive prep- aration at the School of World Mission and Institute of Church Growth. From Dr. McGavran they were given instruction in church growth principles and theory, and case studies to support them. Throughout the project he was the director of their research and the ultimate authority in all things. They received training in anthro- pology and field data-collecting from Dr. Tippett. They were also involved in basic planning and preliminary data-collecting and did extensive preparatory reading before going to the field.

Their period of preparation was phased out into the field situa- tion by means of a two-week trip to Mexico in the company of Dr. Tippett. The purpose of this trip was to test the response of people on all levels to the approach adopted, and especially to test their methods of interviewing under the critical observation of their ad- visor. This journey was essentially experimental, and Dr. Tippett had an intensive session with each member of the team and a general discussion with them all before the men went their respective ways for field data-collecting.

Charles Bennett, pilot with the Missionary Aviation Fellowship and author of *Tinder in Tabasco* (1968), flew the team to Mexico and shared his valuable knowledge of the country and people. He later conducted a preliminary survey of the Evangelical Churches of Chiapas, Mexico, which provided the basis for the description of the Chol and Tzeltal churches in Chapter Thirteen.

b. Definition of Regional Limits of the Research

Some geographical and ethnic limits had to be set on the survey as neither the personnel nor the budget was regarded as sufficient to cover all South and Central America and the West Indies. The team and advisors discussed this aspect at length and decided to eliminate the Guianas and the Caribbean Islands. This removed all the non-Iberian language areas (unless they were centered in Iberian-speaking lands). It also eliminated those places with the more Protestant background and the colonies which, until recently, were not in the Organization of American States. It is to be hoped that some day may see another survey sponsored to complete the areas the team was compelled to eliminate.

c. Preliminary Contacts and Correspondence

Requests for information were sent to mission boards, executives, and other interested bodies. Two types of communication were used: (1) a form seeking opinion as to the state of the Church, the degree of growth and non-growth, the kind of facts the project should assemble, and the primary object of mission in Latin America; and (2) a form seeking membership statistics over the years, with a standard definition for "member." Both these forms were simple documents to be filled in and returned.

On the whole the response to the first form was good. The information was classified and a long list of critical areas and issues was now before the team. This was used as a basis for discussion when the team and advisors met with selected administrators and technical experts over that preliminary period. Several persons were brought to Pasadena from a considerable distance for these discussions. They were formative sessions. The team had enlarged its list of objectives from ideas expressed by their correspondents. With one item to a line, it ran to thirteen pages. Each item was carefully weighed and the list was reduced to basics. The task was now more clearly defined.

d. Preliminary Statistics

Using the second form the team sought statistics for the last thirty years. As time went on this had to be pushed back as research revealed the great significance of the Panama Conference of 1916. But for the time being, they worked on statistics covering a thirty-year period. These statistics, with others available from records at Fuller, were in the hands of the research team members when they went to the field. They hoped to check them against the archives of the young Churches and to find some dynamic records to set beside the behavior of their graphs of growth. This is a feature of Dr. McGavran's church growth method and the results of this are found in Part II of this book. As the figures took shape, further requests were sent to the organizations concerned so that gaps might be filled. More figures were thus brought to light. This task was pursued with unrelenting persistence.

This information had been collected from some four hundred Churches and missions. Many who did not answer were either small bodies or those which have planted no churches. Some large Churches, unfortunately, keep no records. These posed a serious problem. Some of the indigenous Churches had very inaccurate statistics — another problem which just had to be faced.

Where there were only rough estimates of large Churches, they were tested against samples of congregations, averaging the count and multiplying by the number of congregations known to exist, and thus projecting an estimate. In some cases the team had other aids, e.g., Chile had a census with Roman Catholic, Protestant, Jewish, Moslem and No Religion categories. Here again samples were tested. Various missionary censuses were used and cautiously taken into cognizance. Sometimes, when checking field statistics against the records of the home office, a statistical lag was found. The figures used were thus never merely wild guesses, but even where the team could not guarantee them, they were educated and calculated estimates. The critical testing of statistics commenced in the preliminary period and thus the team was already aware of a number of the problems before they departed for Latin America. Some special attention was paid to this aspect in the experimental trip made to Mexico.

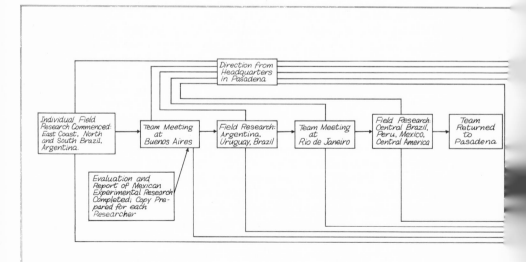

SECOND PHASE: FIELD DATA COLLECTING

Figure B

Second Phase — Field Data-Collecting

a. How the Team Operated and What It Collected

The bridge between the preparatory and field situations was the experimental trip to Mexico. Here the members of the team worked in different ways, sometimes alone, sometimes in pairs, and sometimes in a group. Working with a timetable which had been set up beforehand, they saw how much information might be expected in an hour, a day, or a week in one place. The team met a great variety of responses to the project and began thinking about how best to deal with them. They explored the problems of note-taking. They faced the situation of landing in a town without any contact, and saw that valuable data could be collected even under these circumstances. They began to see the significance of their statistics and the problems of testing them.

Each team member had his own itinerary (Figure D). They were together at Mexico City and then separated to meet again at Buenos Aires and later at Rio de Janeiro. At these meeting places the team re-evaluated its program and problems. Occasionally the researchers kept in touch with each other by correspondence, but more particularly with headquarters in Pasadena. Each man was asked to forward a report every two weeks, and Dr. McGavran replied to each personally.

Each man had his own special interests and developed his own patterns of data-collecting. One made it his practice to start with the archives, libraries, and bookstalls. He located much out-of-the-way statistical and environmental material, local history, and promotional material which opened up areas for investigation and threw light on unsolved problems. He visited tourist bureaus, local associations, and universities and met many important people on various social, economic, and political levels. Thus much expert opinion was added to the collected data, and the information bank received a new dimension. Each member had certain additional resources for working with his own denomination, and often obtained information and had doors opened for the others. One man concentrated on frontier situations and tried to reconstruct phases of church emergence. This man liked to operate from a central location with a telephone, and planned trips from the center. He systematically set out to obtain and classify information from urban centers (a million or more), regional centers (100,000 up), townships (1,500 or so), rural situations with villages (60 to 350 persons), and extended family clusters of four to eight households (about thirty persons). These were his own abstractions and he collected a great deal of information which could not possibly be used in this volume, but would provide the basis for another book. He had material about family structure, migrating communities, and statistics which he related effectively to an ever-growing collection of maps.

Researchers tried to obtain access to church minutes and session books to check against the "behavior" of church statistics. Sometimes these were made available readily; sometimes only after close rapport had been established.

Special attention was paid to church services, where information was collected by both detached and participant observation, and by interviewing both before and after services. Over four hundred Sunday worship services were attended by the team members, and hundreds of week-night services. This made possible interviews with many ordinary people who were church-goers. The degree of participation possible varied according to the nature of the congregation. Some congregations had been pestered by previous investigators and the men had to establish spiritual rapport before there was much cooperation.

Generally the anthropological techniques of observation and interviewing were used more than questionnaires, but there were occasions when use was made of the latter. One researcher spoke at a pastors' conference organized by World Vision International. Here 160 pastors recorded their ideas on a questionnaire.

The researchers were the guests of scores of missionaries of different denominations and appreciated the generous hospitality. Sometimes it influenced the type of information collected, however, and when objectivity was especially desired the researcher involved might elect to stay in a hotel.

b. Interviewing

Behind all interrogation lay the basic questions: What is the Church in this place? How is it structured? Who are its leaders? How does it function? Is it growing? From what part(s) of the community is it growing? Are there any specific patterns in the growth process? Are there opportunities for growth that are not being explored by the Church?

In collecting this kind of information care was taken to differentiate between the opinions of the informant and factual data. Interviews were usually directed for one type of information or the other. Where comparative information was required, a semi-structured interview pattern was frequently used, but mostly they were open-ended. Thus priority was usually given to the basic question: What has this informant to offer me that I cannot obtain elsewhere? This tended to determine the structure of the interviews. Where information was volunteered by informants without a question from the investigator these leads were followed up, often with quite fruitful results. Once a researcher felt he had gained rapport, informants were encouraged to talk and tell things in their own way. This revealed many factors which had not been anticipated. If an informant took a dominant control of the interview and digressed to some irrelevancy, the researcher would feed back some of the informant's own information to regain relevancy.

Informant reliability was tested both by external controls and by internal consistency, and also against both detached and participant observation. The general principles of interviewing had been laid down prior to the Mexico trip and tested in that country. However, from time to time procedures had to be modified to suit problems and circumstances. Interviewing was done in English, Spanish, or Portuguese, whichever seemed effective. Usually all Latin Americans were interviewed in Spanish or Portuguese, and missionaries, also, if a national happened to be present. Some European missionaries were more at home in Spanish than in English and some were not.

Occasionally some instrument had to be devised for obtaining quantitative data. Throughout, the researchers felt free to explore and experiment. Thus the final categories emerged from the research itself and were not predetermined as in some sociological projects. In retrospect, they believe that in this way they achieved a truer picture of the real situation.

On certain occasions and for certain kinds of data-collection, tape recorders were used to obtain more detailed and accurate records, but this was not the usual procedure. It saved some note-taking and correspondence and occasionally permitted them to record speeches.

c. Selection and Distribution of Informants

The research team tried to interview leaders in each type of church, and, as much as possible, they sought an equilibrium of evidence from pastors, missionaries and laymen in each. As each situation was different, the members of the team had to use their discretion in planning and executing the interviews. As they themselves were different in ability and personality, each man had to be free to interpret the opportunity as he saw it. Even so, they concentrated on nationals and lay leaders. Their visits were conditioned by the amount of time that could be spent in each locality. Where time was adequate, interviewing assumed a wider scope. Where time was short, the team was particular to have good contacts with nationals lined up before arrival.

Quite apart from scores of interviews with missionaries on furlough in the United States, some two thousand interviews were executed on the field. A sample of 520 reported interviews with church and mission leaders on the field revealed that 335 were nationals (137, or 26 per cent, leading laymen; 198, or 38 per cent, pastors) and 185, or 36 per cent, were missionaries. This was not a planned distribution and was revealed only by counting the sample. No section of the church community was unrepresented in the range of informants selected for interviewing. Likewise, no type of mission was overlooked: the old-line boards, the faith missions, the Pentecostals, the independents, and the Roman Catholics. The Roman Catholics interviewed were less numerous because they were not primarily the object of this study, and the independents because they were less significant, but the other three types received a roughly equal distribution of interviews. Thus as an Evangelical study, a well-balanced survey was achieved.

As is the case with most researchers, the team met with a few hostile reactions either because the place already had been plagued by too many researchers, or because some who had preceded them had planted problem seeds of which they reaped the harvest. Sometimes people were unwilling to help in any way until they had ascertained the researchers' theological position. The team tried to establish themselves as Evangelicals who were neutral in ecclesiastical politics. Some did not receive the men at all because of a hostility to church growth theory. However, by and large, fine cooperation was given.

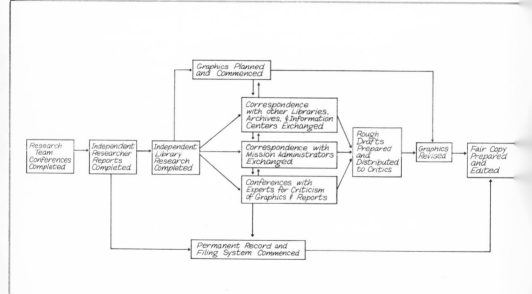

THIRD PHASE: ANALYSIS AND SYNTHESIS

Figure C

Third Phase — Analysis and Synthesis

a. Classification

After the completion of the field work the data collected had to be sorted and classified at Pasadena. Here again the reunited team worked together, interacting and sharing their findings. For some months a daily session of interaction was held by the group and once a week they met with the director for a coordination of the week's work. Each man prepared a set of his own notes for the use of the others and to serve as a basis for discussion.

From time to time prominent missionary leaders from all parts of the country were invited into the group for sharing and criticism. Many subjects had to be verified by library research, especially with respect to statistical and historical dimensions. Information that had been collected from many different places had to be brought together and seen in total relationship. Many missionaries who were themselves engaged in research at Fuller were brought into these discussions.

b. Verification

As much as possible of the library verification was done at Fuller, but other libraries in the Los Angeles area were also used, especially the research library at UCLA. Non-church statistics for critical testing were mostly obtained from the Center for Latin American Studies at UCLA, and for these the team is particularly indebted to Mr. Paul Roberts, editor of the Statistical Abstract produced by that organization. Other essential factual information came from several of the missionary administrators in New York, from the Hispanic Institute at Austin, Texas, from the University of Arizona, and from the Center for Intercultural Documentation at Cuernavaca, Mexico.

c. Preparation of the Manuscript

As a result of this critical analysis the outline of this book emerged, and then, in time, the rough draft. Copies of the rough draft, either in part or whole, were submitted to all manner of critics. The team is much indebted to them for their helpful criticism, and especially for their willingness to struggle through the manuscript while it was yet in the rough. These critics consisted not only of missionaries and administrators, but sociologists, political scientists, anthropologists, and a great many nationals.

The illustrations are the work of Mrs. David Scotchmer, who operated from the CGRILA office and worked with the team. She produced an incredible number of tables, charts, and graphs, which served as a basis for team discussions and were later modified for use in this book.

Figure D

TEAM ITINERARY

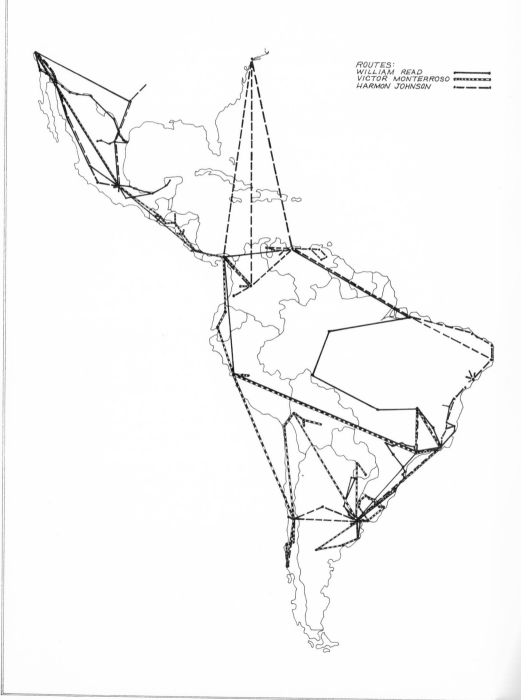

ROUTES:
WILLIAM READ ━━━━━━
VICTOR MONTERROSO ▪▪▪▪▪▪▪
HARMON JOHNSON ▪━▪━▪━

Unfortunately, some planned sections had to be eliminated from this book because of its great length. It is to be hoped that these will appear in the School of World Mission's "Research in Progress Series," which may appear about the same time as this book.

UNDERSTANDING THE BOOK

Latin American Church Growth deals with the growth of the Evangelical Churches of Latin America. Other aspects of Latin America are treated only as they pertain to the growth of the Church. Similarly, this book does not attempt to treat every aspect of Protestant church life in Latin America, but rather only those aspects which relate most directly to the growth of the Churches. For this reason, the subject of church growth has been treated thematically.

The field study and reading of the CGRILA team revealed themes which recurred in every part of Latin America. CGRILA has not been concerned with interesting exceptions and isolated examples, but with those norms which characterize major sectors of the Evangelical Churches. It has been impossible to include all the details; in fact, many interesting and noteworthy things have been omitted that the recurring themes might receive attention. On the basis of the statistical findings these themes have been described and developed.

At times the researchers found the statistical task frustrating because of an attitude of indifference on the part of some missions and Churches toward church statistical record-keeping. Many Churches clearly did not know their numerical strength. Some Churches rounded figures to the nearest ten thousand, and even this rough estimate may have had, it was sometimes suspected, a wide margin of error. On the whole, figures were made available whenever requested, but that is not to say they were of equal value. A conscientious effort was made to verify all information.

The statistics for the Churches of Latin America are, inevitably, incomplete due to the vastness of the field and the partial, inexact nature of membership accounting in most Churches. Even responsible surveys find it impossible to overcome the handicaps of indirect, second-hand, or volunteer data-reporting. The Confederación Evangélica de Colombia, for example, has shown how two other censuses conducted in 1960 differed from their own. The CEDEC census gave a total of 33,156 Evangelical church members. The *World Christian Handbook* (1962) recorded 36,568, and the Evangelical Foreign Missions Association (Taylor and Coggins) listed 25,976. The *Handbook* had omitted three Churches and counted six Churches twice; the EFMA study had omitted fourteen Churches and counted two Churches twice.

Nevertheless, the general trends as demonstrated by the statistics are unmistakable. The cooperation of hundreds of Church and missions leaders has enabled CGRILA to assemble a mass of data which provides the basis for the statistical chapters as well as for the discussions following. The number of members of any given denomination in any given year may be slightly in error, but the graphs of growth are substantially correct.

Every Church and mission must recognize the necessity of keeping a current, accurate record of membership in order properly to care for those for whom they have spiritual responsibility. Good record-keeping is a part of pastoral responsibility, and carelessness in this respect is as bad as carelessness in handling God's money. It is to be hoped that future membership accounting will be conducted more systematically.

One manner of updating the membership records of Latin American Churches would be to publish annually a cumulative graph of growth for each Church. This might well be done by the Documentation Center at Louvain, Belgium, in connection with MARC (Missions Advanced Research and Communication Center) of World Vision International in Monrovia, California. Each denomination or mission would review the published graph and report corrections and additions. Thus, in a few years, each would be assured of a correct growth history as errors of previous years are corrected.

It is not expected that there will be any major corrections of the statistics published in this volume, but error is possible, and any information that will contribute to a refinement of the data will be welcomed. An increasingly accurate record will facilitate better understanding of the growth of Evangelical Churches.

Simplified statistical presentations have been sought for the primary purpose of making the book meaningful to the widest possible audience. The graphs are arithmetic rather than logarithmic. The team chose the type of graphics that seemed most suitable in each case: line graphs, pie charts, bars, or maps, based on the following criteria: (1) the form most suited to communicate meaning, and (2) the form which seemed most accurately to present the data in its completeness (or incompleteness) and in the nature of its contrasts and similarities; that is, to be functionally most honest.

The use of indexes in the general survey of the Evangelical Church today, as presented in the second chapter, was suggested by Harmon Johnson. The team believes this instrument to be most effective and points up some important comparisons, but they ask that it not be used for purposes other than it is intended. Like most statistical tools, it can be abused. It is important, too, that the graphs not be used alone, but that the interpretative text be read with them.

SOME WORDS DEFINED

The word *mission* has been used throughout to refer variously to the sending Church, a denominational mission board, an interdenominational faith mission, the organization of missionaries on the field, or the task of the Church. Usually the context indicates which meaning is intended. If a distinction is not made between two possible meanings, it is because the word is used in this ambiguous fashion in Latin America and therefore the distinction that might be made would be arbitrary.

To speak of the Church Universal and of denominations, the word *Church* has been used; *church* (uncapitalized) refers to a local congregation. When the word is used in a general sense of Latin America it refers to the Evangelical Churches; the Roman Catholic Church is referred to by name.

Evangelical is used in its Latin American sense, referring to all Protestant Churches or, in the plural, to all Protestants. We do not refer to one particular theological viewpoint. The theological consensus in Latin America is such that the use of the word Evangelical rather than Protestants is not confusing.

The expression *church growth* as used in this book refers primarily to numerical increase, especially by conversion from the world. The CGRILA team recognizes that churches also grow qualitatively and organically, and some reference is made to these processes. These kinds of growth, however, are far from being mutually exclusive; it is not always either possible or desirable to differentiate between them.

USE OF THIS VOLUME

Latin American Church Growth, which appears in Portuguese and Spanish as well as English, should be studied as a whole. To be sure, most who begin to read will turn at once to the section where their own Church or mission is described. Yet it has been impossible to mention each mission and the churches it founds, much less each Church which has been formed independently. Each *type* of Church and mission, however, is extensively treated.

We refer readers who wish to investigate any particular aspect of the Evangelical Churches of Latin America which *Latin American Church Growth* describes to study *Protestantism in Latin America: A Bibliographical Guide* by John Sinclair (1967). The *Bibliographical Guide,* which annotates the available literature and to which we refer again on page 373, is available from the Hispanic American Institute, 100 East 27 Street, Austin, Texas.

This research project should be regarded only as a beginning. What is now required is a church growth study in depth for each country, using this basic study merely as a starting point for further investigations. Another survey needs to be done for the areas of Central and South America and the Caribbean not covered herein.

This book has been written for the serious student of the growth of the Evangelical Churches of Latin America. A careful perusal will reveal the major trends of Evangelical mission in Latin America. Executives of mission boards, leaders of Latin American Churches, missionaries, Latin American pastors, and laymen of the sending Churches and of the Churches of Latin America will read *Latin American Church Growth* to see their own part in the growth of the Church. Each Church and mission can learn from the experiences of other Churches while taking a close look at itself. In the context of the entire mission enterprise and of the themes discussed here the growth of each Church will be evaluated.

PART I

DESCRIPTION OF THE CHURCHES

The growth of the Evangelical Churches of Latin America is a striking spiritual and social phenomenon. From a small, persecuted minority doubtful of its own role, the Evangelical Church has grown within the last few decades into a potent force whose influence is felt in all of Latin American life.

Although the progress of the Evangelical Churches diverges from the predominant Roman Catholic heritage, the Evangelical Churches have their roots in Latin American history. The earnest missionary efforts of sacrificial pioneers have resulted in the spread of the Evangelical faith and the planting of Evangelical Churches. The thriving, healthy Churches of today grew out of those early attempts. Now the Evangelical Churches in several countries of Latin America have come of age, and the Churches in other Latin American countries are entering a new period of marked growth.

Chapter One

HISTORICAL BACKGROUND

The first Europeans who arrived in the New World came expecting to find the highly sophisticated civilization of the Orient. Instead they were appalled by what appeared to them to be uncivilized tribes of savages. This first impression has tended to obscure the fact that the noble man of the Americas is the Indian. His flourishing civilizations in Mesoamerica and the Andean Ranges were much older at the time of the European conquest than the civilization of those who overcame them.

The account of the Indian people in recent centuries is both bitterly sad and desperately ignoble. The timeless and dreamful Indian life was suddenly challenged by an enemy with a passion and exactness of purpose. The nonaggressive, ceremonial, hospitable Indian confronted an enemy empowered by lust for gold and religious fanaticism and encouraged by a heroic discipline and hardness toward himself and others. The Indian could comprehend neither what it was the white man wanted nor just what manner of person he was.

Indian institutions soon were adapted to the purposes of the Spaniards: state-required, regulated labor was turned into homicidal enslavement; and the class of honored, tax-exempt artisans were forced to wander from place to place, used without pay for endless services. The Church and State acted as functions of one another: conversion of the savages saved their immortal souls, but "disciplined training" taught them how to live under a European social order.

Colonial society was based on the norms of Iberian culture. Contemporary regional differences and diverse national characteristics have not obliterated the basic expression of the Iberian temperament. Hanke describes the Spanish character as comprised of contradictory elements:

> Spanish character was so fashioned that it can be likened to a medal stamped on each of its two sides with a strong and resolute face. One face is that of an imperialistic conquistador and the other is a friar devoted to God. . . . Neither, when he was most himself, could understand or forgive the other. Yet they were inseparably yoked,

35

sent together into a new world, and together they were responsible for the action and achievement of Spain in America (1949:177-8).

Men like Montesinos, Las Casas, and Victoria raised their voices in fiery denunciation of unjust and un-Christian treatment of the Indians. Perhaps something of the true spirit of Spain can be seen in the lives of these courageous men who were dedicated to the defense of the enslaved Indians.

The Christ of colonial Latin America was the Christ of the crucifix — made of stone, distant and cold, powerless to transform — who could not satisfy the spiritual longings of the Latins. If the Christ whom Ramon Lull had known, the Christ revealed to the great Spanish mystics such as Teresa and Juan de la Cruz, had been brought to Latin America, the result could have been a vital faith and a different type of Christianity. There remained in the heart of the Latin an infinite capacity for spiritual expression. The Evangelical pioneers were to find that, once the barriers of distrust and fear had been removed, Latin Americans could find in the Evangelical faith an avenue of spiritual expression which had been denied them.

Evangelical Beginnings

Protestant advance in Latin America was not to come by political conquest. Attempts by the French Huguenots in the 1550's to establish in Brazil a haven from persecution which would also be a base for Indian evangelization were repulsed by the Portuguese authorities. The Dutch, who had controlled northern Brazil for over thirty years, were also driven out in 1661. By the late 1700's Protestants had, however, secured a foothold on the periphery of South America partly through Dutch, English, and French pirate settlements. It was during this period that the Moravians began missionary work among West Indian slaves; the Congregational and Methodist missionary societies also began in this area and in the Guianas in the early 1800's when the British and Dutch were in control.

Struggle for Religious Liberty

As the countries dominated by Spain and Portugal gained their independence, many discriminatory laws against religion were revised; in some constitutions reactionary statutes were reversed by changing one word. The word *permits,* for example, was substituted for the word *prohibits:* "permits the public exercise of other religions."

Beach's statistics (1900:225) show the direction in which the young churches in South America were growing by 1900.

Dutch and British Guiana	14,376 communicants
Brazil	11,376 communicants
Rest of South America	5,246 communicants

The heaviest concentration of communicants at the turn of the century was found in the Guianas, which the Spanish and Portuguese never occupied. The Moravians, who had arrived in the Guianas about 1738, reported almost 9,000 communicants; the Wesleyan Methodists reported 4,212. In 1900 these Churches in two small Protestant countries constituted close to 50 per cent of the Evangelical communicant membership of South America. The basic reason for Evangelical growth in the Caribbean area in the nineteenth century is that these lands were colonies of Protestant nations. In all Spanish America in 1900 there were only 5,246 communicants and in Brazil only 11,376. The shadow of the Inquisition lay heavy on Latin America: even when the law permitted Protestantism, local public opinion did not, and the Church often pressed persecution long after the legislature had abolished it.

South American countries in the past hundred years have passed through successive stages of progress toward political freedom, and these stages radically affected the climate of religious freedom. Countries with greater political and religious freedom afforded greater opportunity for church growth. By 1900, statements of religious freedom were on the books in the various countries of South America. Real religious liberty, however, lagged decades behind the official pronouncements.

After 1890 Brazil recognized "absolute equality" among the various religious groups. This allowed Evangelicals to establish churches more readily than they could in other South American countries. Legal equality, however, was constantly infringed upon by the Roman Catholic Church. Roman Catholic leaders from all over the continent met in Rome to consider a new policy to check the advance of Evangelical missions. As a result successive waves of persecution struck the Evangelical Churches in Brazil and other Latin American countries. It is worthy of note that even after 1900 Chile, Colombia, Venezuela, Argentina, Peru, Uruguay, Paraguay, Ecuador, and Bolivia opened their doors to Evangelicals with great reluctance, whereas the Evangelical congregations in Brazil were able to multiply three or four times in the next two decades.

Protestant Immigrants

Europeans were induced by offers of free transportation to leave their native lands and begin life again in South American countries — lands of opportunity. Many were able to purchase rich lands there for as little as one dollar per acre! The news spread across Europe, and streams of migrants came from Italy, Germany, Russia, Portugal, Spain, and other European countries. Some were Protestants, zealous in their religious devotion, others were merely nominal believers. Some who had no Protestant background were by no means practicing Roman Catholics.

Argentina, Chile, Uruguay, and Brazil received large numbers of immigrants. Many German Lutherans were in these migrating streams and added their Evangelical heritage to the developing Churches. When Protestant colonists had settled in their newly adopted countries, often the first decade or two would pass in which they received no pastoral visits and maintained no connections with their former Church. Concern for the proper education of their children prompted them to establish schools, but most of these failed to provide adequate religious education. Many became careless in their new environment and were satisfied to continue without the benefits of the Church and religious instruction. Others, however, petitioned their Churches in the homelands to send them ministers.

By 1903 in southern Brazil the 200,000 German colonists had organized 39 churches and had worked out a makeshift lay ministry that was functioning on a hit-or-miss basis (Burgdorf 1925:25). Some German Lutheran pastors had arrived from the Theological Seminary of Witten in the Ruhr. They organized the Synod of the Rio Grande, which by 1925 had 73 ministers, 281 congregations, 21,151 communicants, and a community of 123,616. The La Plata Synod in Argentina was organized at about the same time, but has always been smaller than the German Lutheran Church in Brazil.

Bible Colporteurs

For almost three centuries after the European discovery of the New World the Bible was almost unknown in Latin America. The distribution of Bibles had been forbidden in the colonies by decree of the Pope and the King. The Roman Catholic Church intended to keep Latin America free from the "poison" of the Reformation and the Inquisition backed up its intent.

The Bible, placed in the hands of men and women who were willing to read and receive its message, played a major role in the planting of Evangelical Churches. By 1699 Cotton Mather, who had studied Spanish to prepare himself to minister to Spanish America, had written several evangelistic articles in Spanish. Bernstein says Mather was the first to study Spanish with a view to communicating with Hispanic America (1942:54).

In the early 1800's the first Bibles began to trickle into Latin America. The American and British Bible societies shipped Bibles to merchants who were living in towns along both sides of the continent. The Bible distribution slowly began to accelerate until there were many capable and enthusiastic men devoting full time to Bible colportage work, even though they faced the fury of mobs incited by fanatical priests and were stoned, arrested, and held in prison without trial. Some fought decisive battles for religious toleration and freedom. Men such as Penzotti in Peru and Tonelli in Brazil bore the full brunt of the persecution. Some even paid the price of martyrdom.

One of the most famous pioneers of the early period was the

remarkable James Thomson, who traveled the entire length of the western coast of South America and throughout Central America, Mexico, and the Caribbean. Thomson began his trips in 1817 as an educator with a Bible under one arm. But his gift was that of an evangelist. His letters home to England reveal his genuine concern and holy optimism about the future of the Evangelical Church.

Through such efforts the Bible was placed in eager hands, and eventually its message penetrated receptive hearts. Many stories are told of churches and congregations established solely through the testimony of a Bible reader who had shared with others the reality of his discovery. The Holy Spirit worked in a remarkable manner through the Scriptures to reveal the living Christ to many. Churches sprang up in unusual and unexpected places. Many said that the pattern was clear: first a Bible, then a convert, then a church.

Many attribute the outstanding growth of the Church in Brazil to the long-standing emphasis on Bible distribution and Bible teaching among those receptive to the new message. A pioneer Bible colporteur in Brazil, F. C. Glass, in *Through the Heart of Brazil,* reported:

> In dozens of places where I sold the first copies of the Scriptures the people ever saw, there are strong Evangelical Churches today. ... It was almost invariably the case that the Bible was first in those cases where later came the preacher, except in those cases where the colporteur being also an evanglist, the Bible and the preacher came together. I cannot recall a single case when the Bible came second. Speaking from personal experience I should therefore say that if you want to open up a new area, the first thing to do is to send in someone with a Bible.

Early Church-Planting

Of the early church-planters one of the more famous is Robert Reid Kalley, a Scotch Presbyterian and medical doctor. He has been called the Apostle of Madeira because he established many congregations on that island. He distributed 3,000 copies of the Bible, which prepared the way for a comprehensive church-planting ministry that incorporated education and medicine, along with pastoral visitation, expository preaching, and Bible instruction.

Driven from Madeira by persecution and imprisonment, Kalley went to Brazil in 1855 to begin missionary work. His zeal was unchanged, but persecution had produced greater discretion. The news of the persecution and his flight from Madeira had arrived before him in Brazil to thwart many of his activities, and fanatics attempted to crush his spirit, intimidate him, and neutralize the results of his work (Testa 1963:97). His work in Brazil nevertheless bore fruit from the very beginning. Before leaving in 1876, Kalley had planted churches in Pernambuco as well as some in Niterói and Rio de

Janeiro. The hymnbook *Salmos e Hinos,* still used in many Portuguese services, pays homage to Dr. Kalley, for more than fifty of its hymns were written by him. As Testa has observed,

> The Apostle of Madeira exercised an apostleship of vaster proportions and over an area greater than the confines of an island diocese. The delimitations of his province of Christian witness and service were not determined by geography, but were obliged to coincide with those scattered and distant areas where Portuguese was the spoken language. How great is the spiritual debt owed to one man by people sharing a common language (1963:112)!

By 1900, in some parts of Latin America, quasi-freedom replaced confinement, and Evangelicals could begin to speak more openly. Greater growth became possible in an atmosphere that was relatively free from the former threats of physical harm, incrimination, and bigotry. Unhappy memories plagued believers, but the minority mentality began to change as Evangelists walked cautiously and talked of their faith, breathing the fresh air of a new day.

PRE-PANAMA CONGRESS

The years from 1900 to 1916 marked a new kind of growth for the young Churches. These were years of missionary mobility into the interior of the continent despite isolation, poor communications, bad roads, and primitive living conditions. Heavy responsibilities were placed immediately upon willing, able, and enthusiastic converts, encouraging the emergence of national leadership.

The Swing to Education

Three-fourths of the population of most countries in Latin America was illiterate in 1900. Evangelical schools had been instrumental in removing prejudice against Evangelicals advancing the struggle for religious freedom. Although they never educated more than a fraction of the population, these schools were examples of the newest and finest methods of instruction and were often used as models for new public educational programs. Thus, it was natural for missionary administrators to agree with Bishop Hendrix, who suggested, "The time has come to fortify, and to build colleges is to effect fortifications. . . . A church is no stronger than its institutions of learning" (Tilly 1901:427).

Mission institutions in South America proliferated as traditional Protestant Churches, and missions sought through education to evangelize the upper classes. Latin American leaders anxious to see education develop made their task easier. Such a vacuum existed in the field of education that it would have been impossible for the missionary enterprise not to help correct the fault that had existed under colonial rule for more than three hundred years. Education was the crying need. Was this not the call of God for the period?

Growth from 1900 to 1916

The concentration of Evangelicals located in the Guianas in 1900, due to the work of the Moravians and Methodists, had declined slightly by 1905 (14,000 to 13,000 communicants). The Church in Brazil had grown a little; the rest of South America had doubled in Evangelical communicants. Only nine of the seventeen mission boards reported membership.

Evangelical Churches in Mexico, the country in closest proximity to the United States, reported the largest number of communicants in 1905 (20,832). The two Methodist boards (North and South) reported more than 10,000 communicants — 50 per cent of the Mexican Evangelicals. Methodist stations were located in Monterrey, Chihuahua, Durango, Parral, Torreón, Piedras Negras, Saltillo, and Montemorelos. From these centers the Methodists reached about fifty other places using their traditional circuit plan. The Presbyterian boards (North and South) reported 4,500 communicants, or 25 per cent of the communicants in the country (Dwight 1905).

The Panama Congress (Missionary Education Movement 1917) published the following report of communicants in 1916.

Mexico	22,282
Central America	10,442
West Indies	159,642
South America	93,337

With 49,623 communicants, the Brazilian Evangelical Church towered above Churches in other Latin American countries. The Revolution in Mexico (1912-1914) had adversely affected the growth of Evangelicals in that country (Leslie 1923:120). The 20,386 communicants in Mexico in 1905 had grown to only 22,280 communicants in 1916! Central American Churches, to the contrary, had doubled during the decade. Practically no growth could be seen in Spanish South America, although Argentina and Chile continued in 1916, as in 1905, to have the largest number of Evangelicals.

Pentecostal Beginnings

The Pentecostal Churches of Latin America began at the same time as other Pentecostal revivals of the first decade of the twentieth century elsewhere in the world.

Emilio Conde, a Brazilian Pentecostal leader, states in his history of the Assemblies of God in Brazil that the monumental Pentecostal movement in his country can be traced directly to the Azusa Street revival in 1906 in Los Angeles, California (1960:12). Gaxiola Lopez of the Iglésia Apostólica de la Fé en Cristo Jesus, a Mexican Pentecostal denomination, describes the origins of his Church in the Azusa Street revival (Gaxiola Lopez 1964:17).

Figure 1

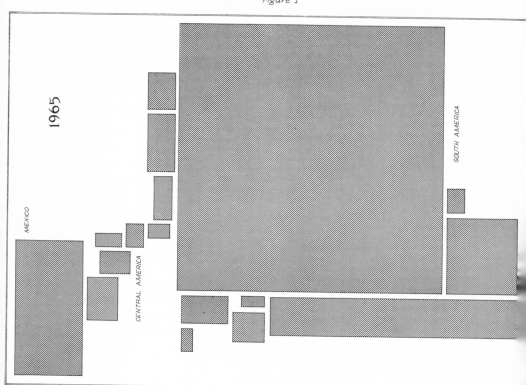

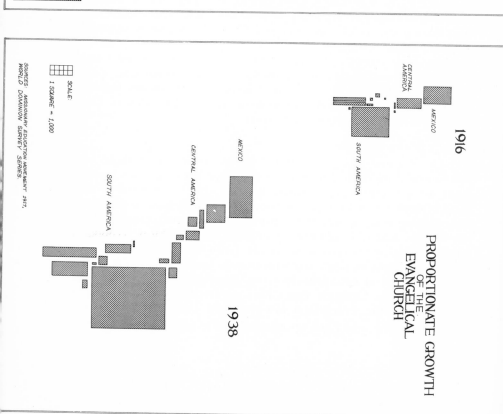

1965

MEXICO

CENTRAL AMERICA

SOUTH AMERICA

1916

CENTRAL AMERICA

MEXICO

SOUTH AMERICA

1938

MEXICO

CENTRAL AMERICA

SOUTH AMERICA

PROPORTIONATE GROWTH
OF THE
EVANGELICAL
CHURCH

SCALE:

1 SQUARE = 1,000

SOURCES: MISSIONARY EDUCATION MOVEMENT, 1917,
WORLD DOMINION SURVEY SERIES.

The Brazilian Pentecostal Church, the Congregação Cristã, also owes its beginnings to the Azusa Street manifestation. In Chicago Luis Francescon received the Pentecostal experience, and he and a companion left for Brazil and Argentina in about 1909. The result of that trip was the establishment of the Congregação Cristã, which was to become the second largest Evangelical Church in Brazil (Read 1965:19). A Methodist minister in Chile, Mr. Hoover, received a letter from an acquaintance in India explaining the effect of this Pentecostal experience on a certain mission station. This connection with the revival was the spark that, according to Mr. Hoover, ignited the Pentecostal fires in Chile (Hoover 1931:9). Other instances reveal similar beginnings among the Pentecostal Churches in Latin America, resulting in a new dimension of church growth. A network of churches developed that reached the masses to an enormous extent.

PANAMA AND AFTER

Missionary leaders setting up the World Missionary Conference in Edinburgh in 1909 limited attendance to the boards and societies working in "pagan" countries. Because its people were at least nominally Roman Catholic, Latin America was not considered as a mission field. Some German and British societies refused to permit an Edinburgh representation from boards working in Latin America.

During the Edinburgh Conference, North American delegates decided that a special meeting should be held to consider the unique missionary problems of Latin America. Careful preparation was made for the Panama Congress which was held in 1916. A total of 304 delegates from forty-four mission boards and societies in the United States; one from Canada; two from Jamaica, and three from Great Britain met with 204 auditors in Panama. The Congress included missionaries, ministers, and laymen from national Churches in Latin America, as well as many special guests.

Reports of the Congress

The Panama Congress fulfilled the expectations of those who had prepared its eight different study sections. In fact, it set a precedent: never before had a conference dealt with so extensive a field in so intensive a manner. Latin American missiologists value highly the resulting reports, which constituted the first comprehensive survey of the material, physical, political, moral, ethical, economic, social, and religious conditions of the Latin American countries at this crucial point in time. Many missionary leaders divide the period of the Evangelical enterprise in Latin America into the "pre-" and "post-" Panama Congress eras. This conference proved to be a watershed for the Evangelical Movement in Latin America.

The *Review and Findings* of the historic meeting indicate that the orientation was definitely that of the missions and boards, since out of the 304 delegates only twenty-six were Latin Americans. The Panama Congress Report is weighted by a missionary mentality regarding problems and plans:

— Division of territory.
— Cooperation in literature production.
— Publicity bureau to be established.
— Joint educational survey to be made.
— Annual inter-mission conferences planned.
— Formation of rules of comity.
— Cooperative evangelism promoted.
— Campaigns among educated classes.
— Fraternal relations.
— Training of candidates in cooperation.
         (Missionary Education Movement 1917.3:102-103)

Generally, the Panama Congress created a spirit of expectancy. When the delegates returned to their fields these fresh insights grew into plans for advance.

The survey of statistics, facts, and data found in the appendix of the Report is a significant historical milestone. It gives the most accurate picture available at that point, being the first statistical summary for all Evangelicals of Latin America. It can be used, therefore, as a fixed point of reference to measure church growth before and after 1916. Figure 1 is based in part on the Panama Congress Report.

The Second Congress — 1925

The war years between 1914 and 1919 had been lean ones for missionary replacements, but following the First World War a stream of new missionaries entered Latin America. Lay leaders and young national pastors began to play a more important role in the advancing missionary enterprises, but they needed orientation. In some cases, growing leadership and finances made possible the transition to autonomous national Churches. The move toward independence came earlier in Brazil because of the rapid growth of the churches there, but the same process was beginning in Mexico, Argentina, and Chile, though at a slower rate.

In 1925 the second Congress of Christian Work in South America was held in Montevideo. This time more than half of the delegates at Montevideo were representatives of national Churches. In Panama the language spoken had been English and the planning, initiative, and leadership had been in the hands of mission administrators. All of this was changed in Montevideo. South Americans were leading this conference; the official language was Spanish and the President of the Congress was a Brazilian. Most significant was the fact that this conference was an expression of Latin American Evangelical Christianity. New questions were asked in 1925 since some of the older issues of 1916 had been forgotten, or were no longer relevant. Arthur J. Brown observed:

> The fact that such a representation of the national churches of that great continent could assemble for a conference and that the national delegates were men of marked intelligence and ability was, in itself, an eloquent testimony to the progress that had been made in the nine years since the Panama Congress (1936: 785).

Remarkable progress and accelerated growth had occurred in a short decade. The statistical table published in the Montevideo report indicated that in almost every case the communicant membership in the Evangelical Churches had at least doubled. Outstanding missionary and national leaders had laid foundations for even greater future growth.

Educational Advance

In 1926 the Committee on Cooperation in Latin America (CCLA) began an ambitious program called "Educational Advance in South America."

> All the boards concerned joined in the campaign, which was vigorously conducted. A total of approximately $1,000,000 was secured, of which about a fourth accrued to our Presbyterian work. Later, an additional $500,000 was contributed for the schools included in the campaign, of which $200,000 was assigned to Presbyterian institutions (Brown 1936: 786).

Education in South American republics had been given highest priority in missionary strategy. Evangelistic advance and responsibility for church-planting, while still a concern of missions, were relegated to a less important role. It was taken for granted that the Churches would assume the evangelistic and pastoral work at the congregational level. Some did, especially in Brazil; but most lacked the numbers, leadership, and spiritual momentum to carry the load of evangelism without the help of mission boards and thus could not achieve the maximum quantitative and qualitative growth possible in the period. The missions were preoccupied with the task of "reaching" the middle and intellectual classes of South America. In order to do this they felt the need for a larger network of educational institutions. Emphasis shifted, therefore, to what was called indirect evangelism through schools.

The period of heavy institutional work which began after 1925 continued intermittently for at least three decades. In mission after mission the yearly meetings were conducted in an atmosphere of tension as opinions differed concerning the priorities given to different types of work. Mission reports reveal this push-and-pull between the programs for educational advance and the programs for evangelistic advance. (Both programs were said to be evangelistic, one direct and the other indirect.) In any case, new institutions were established and those already in existence continued to grow. Debates were lively and heated when the distribution of the yearly budget was voted each year. In many missions, institutions began to acquire more and more of the finances and personnel. Such missions did not and could not adequately evangelize their fields, but this was not discovered for years.

From time to time emphasis on education recorded a setback. The Mexican Revolution, specially after 1926, wrote many laws into the Mexican Constitution, attempting to abolish the tyrannical control of the Church. These applied equally to Protestants and Roman Catholics. In 1934 the pressure became so great that the Presbyterian Board approved the action taken by its Mexican mission: to seek new areas of service not under the restrictions of the governmental decrees. During these years all Evangelical educational work was at a standstill in Mexico. In 1935 the Presbyterian Mission USA in Mexico adopted this new emphasis:

> We are convinced that from now on we must depend upon personal seeking of souls for Christ, and upon personal dealing with Christians to strengthen and build them up, more than upon institutions or special plans of work. Our institutions have a rather uncertain existence at present, but the opportunity for personal evangelism and personal comradeship is greater than ever. We need to search for new ways of making contacts, and then make these truly effective in clinching souls for the Saviour (Brown 1936:819).

Entrance of Faith Missions

In Latin America as a whole the institutional emphasis was given priority in most traditional missions, but other missions (and Churches) began to move into South America with a single-minded evangelistic approach.

World War II had far-reaching effects on church growth in Latin America for several reasons. Lindsell points out that North America began to send many more missionaries, and missions began to act defensively amid the rising nationalism and international antagonism (1962:190). In addition, the enormously powerful position of Communist Russia after World War II and her plan for fomenting revolutions in every land, encouraged the dispossessed in Latin America to greater demands and spurred the ruling oligarchies to provide more lest violent revolution overwhelm them. Industrialization, urbanization, mechanization, education, migration, and revolution turned more and more of the common people responsive to new ideas — and to the Evangelical position.

In the early 1930's, missions which practiced "faith principles of support" began to arrive in larger numbers. Some of these had been in existence for many years, but the largest number were begun during and after World War II. Lindsell attributes their growth to three predominant religious movements at work in the U.S.A.

> The first is the development of independent churches, the second the rise of the Bible School movement, and the third the development of anti-denominational missionary spirit within denominational churches and among individuals.

> These movements produced a constituency of eight million people who were supporting faith missions by 1960 to a tune of twenty million dollars (1962:198, 202).

The post-war decades were characterized by unusual activity on the part of faith missions in Latin America.

In 1958 the total number of missionaries from all Churches and missions throughout the world came to 20,970. Of these, 5,431 missionaries, or 25 per cent, were working in Latin America. Out of this 25 per cent (5,431) 3,182 represented faith missions. Approximately 60 per cent of all missionaries in Latin America in 1958 were sent out by societies affiliated with the International Foreign Mission Association (IFMA) or the Evangelical Foreign Missions Association (EFMA).

In 1960 the Wycliffe Bible Translators officially withdrew from the IFMA. This took nearly 550 missionaries from the ranks of the IFMA, but by 1962 there were, nevertheless, 3,518 missionaries working in Latin America whose missions were associated with the IFMA and EFMA, plus almost 600 Wycliffe Bible Translators in the category of "non-affiliated."

Chapter Two

STATISTICAL OVERVIEW: EVANGELICAL GROWTH IN LATIN AMERICA

A never ending controversy rages as to whether it is possible or proper to speak of Latin America as an entity. Many experts who are themselves known as Latin Americanists maintain that it is fallacious and dangerous to consider Latin America as a whole. The wide diversity of cultures and the strong antagonism between Latin American nations tend to emphasize the differences and minimize the similarities. Everyone involved in the study of Latin America or who seeks a solution to Latin American problems must adopt a position in regard to the basic question of the validity of the concept of "Latin America."

For better or worse, all countries of Latin America share a common heritage so strong as to be determinative. The similarities are basic and permanent, the differences superficial and passing. The solutions for which Latin America is groping will be solutions which meet the needs of the whole continent.

Most of the mission-related Churches are administered on a continent-wide level. The Churches themselves, whether or not they are mission-related, tend to think of themselves as part of the great community of Evangelical believers of Latin America. Chapters Three to Eight describe the variety and diversity from country to country as growth patterns of the Evangelical Churches are outlined. First, however, a look at Evangelical growth in all of Latin America is in order.

COMMUNITY

Of the seventeen countries included in this study, the total *communicant membership* of 4,915,477 in 1967 must be distinguished from the number of *Evangelicals* (Figure 2) in these countries. In addition to communicant members there are large numbers of unbaptized believers (mostly the result of pre-conversion marital entanglements) as well as non-communicant children of Christians (the

Figure   2

EVANGELICALS IN LATIN AMERICA

COUNTRY ◊	EVANGELICALS			◊ POPULATION**		◊
	1967 COMMUNICANTS (Thousands)	ANNUAL GROWTH RATE 1960–1967	INDEX OF RELATIVE SIZE*	MID-1968 TOTAL (Millions)	CURRENT ANNUAL GROWTH RATE	
ARGENTINA	249.5	5.0 %	107	23.4	1.5 %	
BOLIVIA	45.4	11.5	116	3.9	2.4	
BRAZIL	3,313.2	11.0	375	88.3	3.2	
CHILE	441.7	8.5	485	9.1	2.2	
COLOMBIA	73.9	12.0	38	19.7	3.2	
COSTA RICA	14.2	7.0	89	1.6	3.5	
ECUADOR	12.6	15.0	22	5.7	3.4	
EL SALVADOR	35.8	5.5	109	3.3	3.7	
GUATEMALA	77.2	9.0	158	4.9	3.1	
HONDURAS	18.8	8.5	75	2.5	3.5	
MEXICO	429.9	11.0	91	47.3	3.5	
NICARAGUA	19.8	3.0	110	1.8	3.5	
PANAMA	37.5	5.5	268	1.4	3.2	
PARAGUAY	15.2	11.0	47	2.2	3.2	
PERU	61.9	6.5	48	12.8	3.1	
URUGUAY	21.8	7.0	78	2.8	1.2	
VENEZUELA	46.9	14.0	48	9.7	3.6	
TOTAL	4,915.4	10.0 %	204	240.4	3.0 %	

* INDEX OF 100 EQUALS 1.00% OF POPULATION.
** POPULATION REFERENCE BUREAU 1968.

immediate families of church members) who are a part of the Evangelical community.

At the present time it is impossible to state exactly the size of the Evangelical community in Latin America. Such factors as the size of the average family (which varies widely among regions and among social classes), the number of unbaptized believers (which largely depends upon prevailing social conditions), and the effectiveness of a given Church in integrating its community into the life of the Church, all affect the ratio of community to communicants.

The difficulty in establishing one ratio of community to com-

Figure 3

TOTAL COMMUNICANT MEMBERSHIP BY COUNTRY

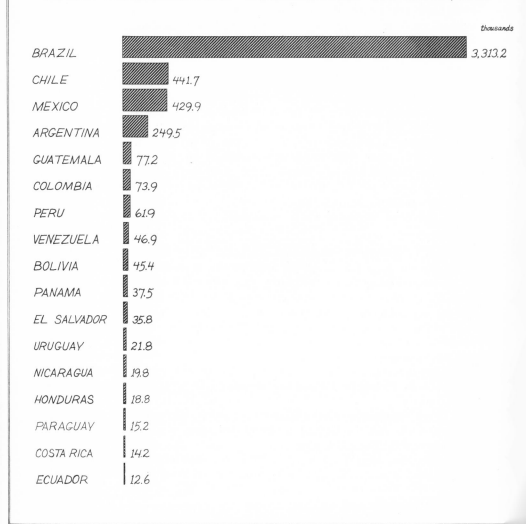

thousands

BRAZIL	3,313.2
CHILE	441.7
MEXICO	429.9
ARGENTINA	249.5
GUATEMALA	77.2
COLOMBIA	73.9
PERU	61.9
VENEZUELA	46.9
BOLIVIA	45.4
PANAMA	37.5
EL SALVADOR	35.8
URUGUAY	21.8
NICARAGUA	19.8
HONDURAS	18.8
PARAGUAY	15.2
COSTA RICA	14.2
ECUADOR	12.6

municants in all of Latin America is easily seen. Studies in northern Brazil suggest that for some Churches the ratio ought to be calculated at five Evangelicals to every one church member. This agrees with the ratio used by the Evangelical Council of Chile to calculate relief services for the Pentecostal Churches of that country. Other Churches, however, are noted for their low ratio of community to communicants. The Disciples of Christ in Mexico, for example, have reported a very small community.

The various ratios used in Evangelical censuses in Latin America have been arbitrarily chosen. The Evangelical census of Guatemala used a ratio of five Evangelicals to each communicant member. Similarly, the 1960 census of the Evangelical Confederation of Colombia calculated community on a ratio of five Evangelicals to one communicant member. In 1966, however, the ratio was decreased to four to one, and the 1967 census utilized a ratio of three to one. Any of these ratios may be correct. The problem is that no adequate objective standard has yet been devised by which community can be measured. To use the conservative ratio of two to one probably understates the size of the Evangelical community, but certainly does not overstate community in any of the cases which we studied. We can affirm, then, that there are at least ten million Evangelicals in Latin America — but there may be even fifteen or twenty million. In these totals we have not included those in the larger sphere of influence which represents the mission field of each Church.

RELATIVE SIZE OF THE EVANGELICAL CHURCH

Since the total communicant membership represents only a part of the total Evangelical community (the exact size of which is not known) in each country, we have chosen to show (Figures 2 and 4) the communicant membership as an index of its relative size, rather than as a percentage of general population. These indexes measure the Evangelical impact in Latin America. They do not indicate which segments of society are being reached nor which Churches have grown most, but they do measure the results of the combined efforts of *all* Evangelical Churches compared to total population in each country.

When expressed graphically, these indexes present an interesting pattern. Chile has the highest index of 485, then Brazil at 375 and Panama at 268. These countries have the highest ratio of Evangelicals to population. After Guatemala at 158, six countries are clustered around 100. The remaining seven countries are lower than 100, the lowest being Ecuador at 22.

The Mexican and Chilean Evangelical Churches, for example, are approximately the same size numerically (429,877 and 441,698, respectively). When the ratio of Evangelicals to population is expressed in terms of the index of relative size, the Chilean Church is seen to be about five times larger than the Mexican Church. This is because the population of Mexico is many times that of Chile. In a similar way, the numerical totals for Guatemala and Colombia are approximately the same (77,239 and 73,937, respectively). However, the Evangelical Church in Guatemala *compared to population* is four times as large as the relative size of the Evangelical Church in Colombia.

Annual Evangelical Growth Rate

The annual average growth rate can be seen in proper perspective only as comparison is made with the relative sizes of the Churches. For example, although the Churches of both Mexico and Brazil have been growing at an average annual rate of 11 per cent, Brazil's index of 375 as compared with Mexico's index of 91 indicates that the **Evangelical Church in Brazil is four times as large as that in Mexico**

Figure 4

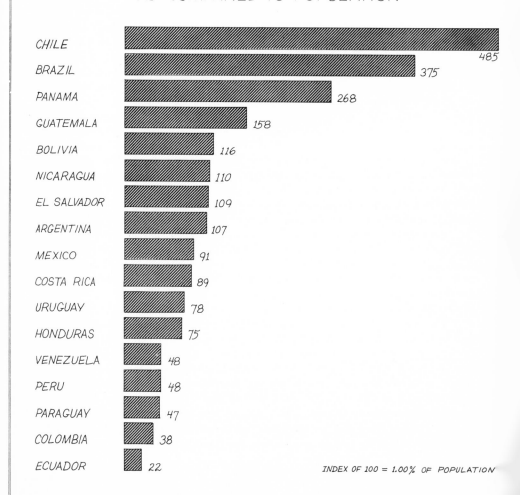

RELATIVE SIZE OF CHURCHES BY COUNTRY
AS COMPARED TO POPULATION

CHILE — 485
BRAZIL — 375
PANAMA — 268
GUATEMALA — 158
BOLIVIA — 116
NICARAGUA — 110
EL SALVADOR — 109
ARGENTINA — 107
MEXICO — 91
COSTA RICA — 89
URUGUAY — 78
HONDURAS — 75
VENEZUELA — 48
PERU — 48
PARAGUAY — 47
COLOMBIA — 38
ECUADOR — 22

INDEX OF 100 = 1.00% OF POPULATION

— when compared with the populations of the two countries — although numerically the Brazilian Church is almost eight times as large.

The comparison of growth patterns country by country is significant for our understanding of Evangelical Church growth, whether they are expressed as average annual rates (Figure 2) or as total growth percentages for 1960 to 1967 (as in Figure 5). This method of comparison does not show which specific Churches have grown nor which segments of society are responding, but it does show the growth trend for all Evangelical Churches in each country. This can be interpreted as either the responsiveness of the particular country or the effectiveness of the Churches.

By itself, Figure 5 does not give a clear picture of Evangelical growth. Its meaning is understood only when this percentage of growth is compared with the index of relative size, with the total communicant memberships, and with the growth rate of population.

The phenomenal growth rate (179 per cent for the period) of the Evangelical Church in Ecuador, for example, must be seen in relation to its infinitesimal size as compared with the population of the country. If the Churches of Ecuador continue to grow at the same rate, it will be more than twelve years before they reach the total membership that the Churches in Guatemala have reached already. Added to this is the fact that the growth in Ecuador is not the result of one Church that has achieved notable growth. Rather, it is made up of many small Churches representing considerable investments of time and money. To reach the level of growth of the Evangelical Churches in other countries, Ecuadorian Churches will have to maintain for many years their present high growth rate. For a country whose population is more than 5,000,000, a total Evangelical communicant membership of only 12,551 is small indeed.

Venezuela is another example of rapid growth (154 per cent for the period) in Churches that are still quite small. Bolivia, on the other hand, which also more than doubled over the seven-year period, is a larger Church in comparison with the Bolivian population. Mexico, roughly comparable to Bolivia in relative size, also grew more than 100 per cent during the period.

The Churches low in terms of relative size but large in total membership also showed remarkable vigor in a sustained rate of growth. The Evangelical Churches of Chile grew at a commendable rate of 80 per cent for the seven-year period. The Brazilian Churches, which totaled 3,213,252 communicant members in 1967, achieved a growth rate of 104 per cent from 1960 to 1967.

The Evangelical Churches in seven of the 17 countries grew at a rate of more than 100 per cent during the period. Their vigor and effectiveness have helped to compensate for the many small, non-grow-

Figure 5

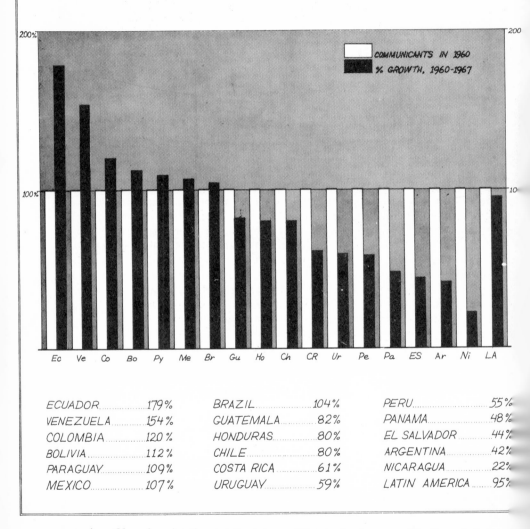

TOTAL PERCENTAGE GROWTH OF CHURCHES. 1960-1967

COMMUNICANTS IN 1960
% GROWTH, 1960-1967

ECUADOR	179%	BRAZIL	104%	PERU	55%
VENEZUELA	154%	GUATEMALA	82%	PANAMA	48%
COLOMBIA	120%	HONDURAS	80%	EL SALVADOR	44%
BOLIVIA	112%	CHILE	80%	ARGENTINA	42%
PARAGUAY	109%	COSTA RICA	61%	NICARAGUA	22%
MEXICO	107%	URUGUAY	59%	LATIN AMERICA	95%

ing Churches in the total picture. The inclusion on this list of the Brazilian, Chilean, and Mexican Churches, which together comprise 84.9 per cent of the Evangelical communicant membership of Latin

Figure 6

ANNUAL GROWTH RATES

ANNUAL EVANGELICAL GROWTH COMPARED TO ANNUAL POPULATION GROWTH

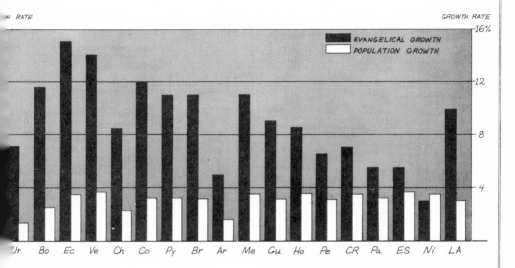

COUNTRY	CURRENT EVANGELICAL GROWTH RATE	CURRENT POPULATION GROWTH RATE	RATIO OF EVANG./POP. GROWTH RATES
URUGUAY	7.0 %	1.2 %	5.83
BOLIVIA	11.5	2.4	4.79
ECUADOR	15.0	3.4	4.41
VENEZUELA	14.0	3.6	3.89
CHILE	8.5	2.2	3.86
COLOMBIA	12.0	3.2	3.75
PARAGUAY	11.0	3.2	3.44
BRAZIL	11.0	3.2	3.44
ARGENTINA	5.0	1.5	3.33
MEXICO	11.0	3.5	3.15
GUATEMALA	9.0	3.1	2.90
HONDURAS	8.5	3.5	2.43
PERU	6.5	3.1	2.10
COSTA RICA	7.0	3.5	2.00
PANAMA	5.5	3.2	1.72
EL SALVADOR	5.5	3.7	1.49
NICARAGUA	3.0	3.5	.86
LATIN AMERICA	10.0 %	3.0 %	3.33

RATIO OF EVANGELICAL GROWTH RATE TO POPULATION GROWTH RATE

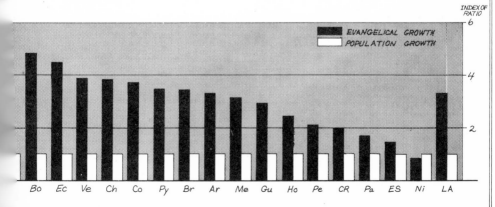

America, has produced a growth rate of 95 per cent from 1960 to 1967 for combined Evangelical Churches in Latin America.

Population Growth Rate

The growth rates of the Churches must also be compared with the growth rates of the populations among which they work. The Nicaraguan Churches, for example, which grew at an annual rate of only 3 per cent, were actually losing ground, since at the same time the population of the country was increasing at an annual rate of 3.5 per cent. Similarly, though the Churches in Mexico and Paraguay both grew at an annual rate of 11 per cent, the Paraguayan Church was actually growing faster because the population rate was only 3.2 per cent as compared with 3.5 per cent in Mexico.

When the growth rate of the Evangelical Churches is expressed as a ratio to the growth rate of the population by country, the relationship is clearly seen as shown graphically in Figure 6. In order

Figure 7

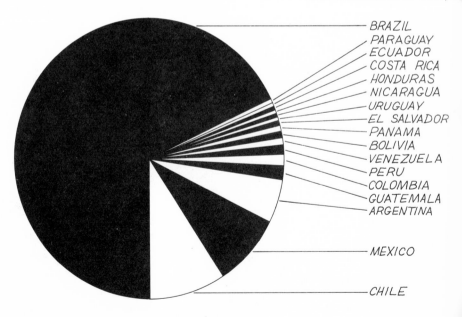

RESPECTIVE SIZES OF CHURCHES BY COUNTRY

TOTAL COMMUNICANTS: 4,810,700

BRAZIL
PARAGUAY
ECUADOR
COSTA RICA
HONDURAS
NICARAGUA
URUGUAY
EL SALVADOR
PANAMA
BOLIVIA
VENEZUELA
PERU
COLOMBIA
GUATEMALA
ARGENTINA

MEXICO

CHILE

Figure 8

TYPES OF CHURCHES: MISSIONARIES AND MEMBERS

A) COMMUNICANT MEMBERS    B) MISSIONARY DEPLOYMENT

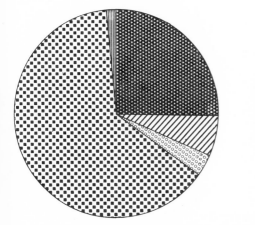   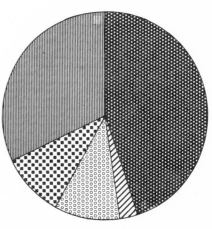

|||||||| *FAITH MISSIONS*
PENTECOSTAL CHURCHES
NEWER DENOMINATIONS
ADVENTIST CHURCHES
TRADITIONAL DENOMINATIONS

to show the ratio more clearly, the population growth is standardized and compared again.

Respective Sizes of the Evangelical Churches

It would naturally seem that the Churches in the larger countries tend to be larger numerically, and the Churches in the smaller countries tend to be smaller numerically — but there are notable exceptions. Chile is seventh in population but second in the number of Evangelicals; Panama is seventeenth in population and tenth in the number of Evangelicals.

We do not propose to deal with the Evangelical Churches of

Latin America according to their respective sizes. Brazil does not occupy two-thirds of the book although more than two-thirds of the Evangelical membership of Latin America is in Brazilian Churches.

Types of Churches

We have classified the Churches of Latin America as five basic types. The Churches which are related in a direct manner to the faith missions constitute one type. The Pentecostals are a second type. The third type we have classified as newer denominations. These include the non-Pentecostal indigenous Churches as well as the Churches related to newer denominations abroad. By reason of the unique Adventist growth pattern, we have classified the Seventh-Day Adventist Church separately. The fifth classification is composed of the Churches of the traditional denominations.

Though this classification is admittedly arbitrary, it does provide a measurement of what kind of growth is occurring and where. In Chapters Three to Eight this classification is used to analyze the growth of the Evangelical Churches in each country of Latin America.

Using these classifications, then, we calculate that in 1967 there were 74,394 communicant members in the Churches related to faith missions in Latin America, or 1.5 per cent of the total membership. In the Pentecostal Churches of Latin America there were 3,104,535 communicant members in 1967, or 63.3 per cent of the total membership. In the traditional Churches there were 1,252,434 communicant members in 1967, or 25.5 per cent of the total membership.

The missionary deployment for the same five categories provides a startling contrast. Missionaries of the faith missions constitute 32.4 per cent of the total although the Churches related to the faith missions comprise only 1.5 per cent of the total communicant membership. Pentecostal missionaries make up 9.8 per cent of missionaries in Latin America, while Pentecostal Churches have 63.3 per cent of communicant membership. The newer denominations have 10.3 per cent of the missionaries and 3.4 per cent of the communicant membership. Adventists have only 2.7 per cent of the missionaries and 6.3 per cent of membership. The missionary deployment of the traditional denominations amounts to 44.8 per cent of the total while membership comprises 25.5 per cent.

Figure 9 shows the relationship of communicant membership and missionary deployment of the non-Pentecostal Churches.

Adventist Growth Pattern

Adventists work in Latin America as an international Church emphasizing the importance of local autonomy. There is no Seventh-Day Adventist mission board, as such. When the Church within a country grows sufficiently, it is recognized as a "national" Church. Based on its size, the national Church is classified as an "association"

Figure 9

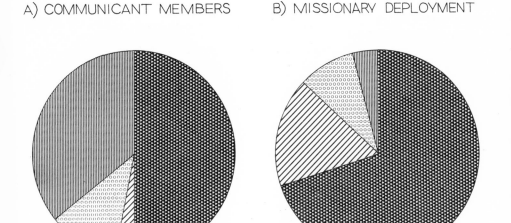

NON-PENTECOSTAL CHURCHES: MISSIONARIES AND MEMBERS

A) COMMUNICANT MEMBERS   B) MISSIONARY DEPLOYMENT

FAITH MISSIONS
NEWER DENOMINATIONS
ADVENTISTS
TRADITIONAL DENOMINATIONS

or "union." All unions, of which there are many in the world, belong to the General Conference. This type of organization is free from the grip of paternalism. The Adventists are among the most *Latin* and the most *national* of all Evangelical groups in Latin America.

Different forms of medical and social work are included in church activities, yet Adventists do not allow their institutional activities to stifle their zeal for evangelism. The Church makes good use of evangelistic campaigns, employing local pastors and seminary students as well as outside help. The membership is dedicated; laymen are trained to teach, witness, and win others. Some conduct as many as twenty Bible classes per week. Adventists claim that an average of 20 per cent of those taught in this vast network of classes are eventually baptized.

As different levels of leadership are cultivated, the national Church becomes an increasingly effective and responsible force working for the enlistment and instruction of others. High-quality educational materials help lay people to teach more effectively in the thousands of branch Sabbath schools. Correspondence courses are promoted, and organized colportage teams regularly distribute religious and scientific books as well as Bibles. Adventist seminaries are also subject to steady academic improvement. Radio programs of high quality are broadcast on secular networks. Because of the Adventist emphasis on education, all Adventists can receive free elementary school training in the comprehensive Adventist program. Due to the widespread thirst for education in Latin America, the balanced educational emphasis of the Seventh-Day Adventist Church is contributing to steady church growth.

PART II
DIVERSITY OF THE CHURCHES

A statistical study of the Evangelical Churches country by country serves to emphasize the cultural, social, and religious diversities of the countries, especially in the light of the varied rates of growth of denominations or missions in varied national settings. Part II describes the circumstances of special significance in each country and gives a statistical picture of the Churches.

To list the membership of Churches and missions within each country for a particular year (1967), however, is not sufficient. In order to apprehend clearly the nature of the Churches it is necessary to consider the rate of growth for individual cases over an extended period. In Chapters Three to Eight these rates of growth are illustrated by means of a series of graphs for the seventeen countries included in this study.

The largest denominations (for which we have compiled historical communicant membership records) appear on the line graphs. Occasionally a smaller denomination has been included to illustrate a particular point. The difficulty in obtaining statistical data for all Churches in a given year is obvious; when the goal is to present a reasonably accurate picture for a half century, the difficulty is compounded. Thus, the number of Churches presented in the line graphs is limited.

The use of the line graph also has a distinct disadvantage — namely, that the multitude of small Churches and missions is not seen. The larger countries of Latin America each have from 40 to 200 missions and Churches whose adherents number only a few hundred and in many cases less than a hundred. Were these to be included on the graphs, the lower portion would be a solid mass of lines.

In order to include these groups in the contemporary picture, bar graphs are presented for each country which show the growth of types of churches (as introduced in Chapter Two) from 1950 to 1965, and the relative sizes of denominational groupings in 1967. This multitude of small enterprises taken together *constitutes a substantial portion of Evangelical growth in Latin America.*

Chapter Three

BRAZIL

The vast nation of Brazil, larger than the continental United States, has experienced remarkable growth in spite of political problems resulting from unmet social and economic needs. The building of cities, the migrations into new lands, the advancing coffee booms, and the development of modern industrial complexes, especially iron and steel, have provided the context for the continuous growth of the Evangelical Churches. National growth has, indeed, opened the way for evangelization.

MISSIONARY DEPLOYMENT IN BRAZIL

A recent study published by the Missionary Information Bureau in Rio de Janeiro (1967:1, 2) reported more than 2,600 missionaries serving in Brazil, and that 79 per cent are from North America and 21 per cent are from Europe. The greatest number of missionaries is found in the four southern states (the city of São Paulo has 328 missionaries), where 40 per cent of the missionaries are working among 36 per cent of the nation's population. Goiás, Mato Grosso, and Brasilia have nearly 12 per cent of the missionaries, yet only 5 per cent of the population. Work in the interior has attracted 15 per cent of the missionaries to the North, yet here live only 4 per cent of the population. In the East, 19 per cent of the missionaries work among 34 per cent of the population, and in the Northeast, 14 per cent of the missionaries serve 21 per cent of the population. The report also stated that missionaries are engaged primarily in "evangelization" (60 per cent) and educational institutions (25 per cent).

These data, however, can be significant only when correlated with the records of growth achieved. We must know what part of the 60 per cent engaged in evangelization are successfully planting churches and where these churches are being planted. Where are these missionaries working and how well do they speak Portuguese? What is their relationship to their Brazilian Church? How long were they in Brazil before they became effective church-planters? Do they train Brazilian leadership? How do they choose areas of work? Do they regard high-potential areas? When we find answers to some

Figure 10

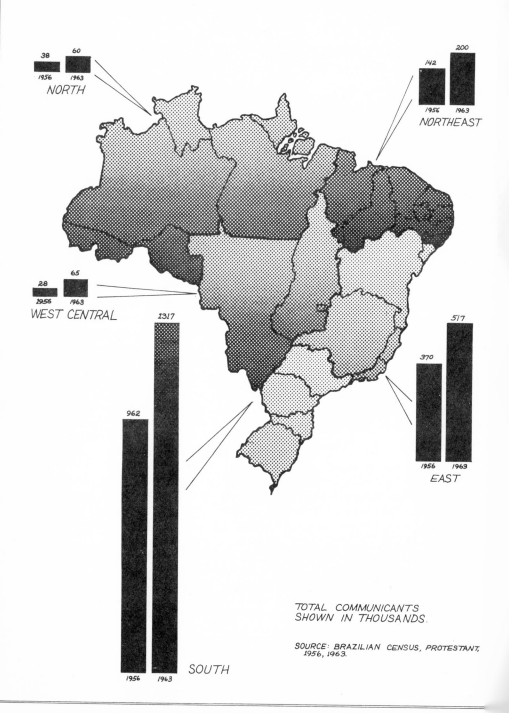

BRAZIL: GROWTH BY REGION
1956–1963

NORTH
38 — 1956
60 — 1963

NORTHEAST
142 — 1956
200 — 1963

WEST CENTRAL
28 — 1956
65 — 1963

SOUTH
962 — 1956
1317 — 1963

EAST
370 — 1956
517 — 1963

TOTAL COMMUNICANTS
SHOWN IN THOUSANDS.

SOURCE: BRAZILIAN CENSUS, PROTESTANT,
1956, 1963.

Figure   11

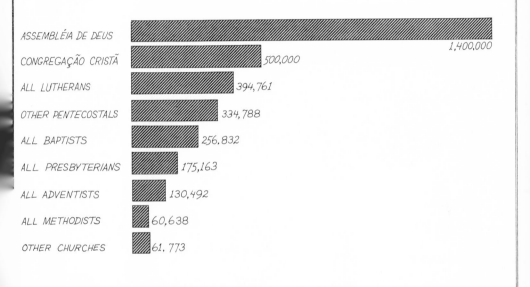

BRAZIL: COMPARATIVE SIZES OF CHURCHES
1967 COMMUNICANT MEMBERSHIP

ASSEMBLÉIA DE DEUS 1,400,000
CONGREGAÇÃO CRISTÃ 500,000
ALL LUTHERANS 394,761
OTHER PENTECOSTALS 334,788
ALL BAPTISTS 256,832
ALL PRESBYTERIANS 175,163
ALL ADVENTISTS ... 130,492
ALL METHODISTS .. 60,638
OTHER CHURCHES .. 61,773

of these questions, then we are beginning to understand the Evangelical Church as it is developing in Brazil.

THE EVANGELICAL CHURCHES

Since the beginning of the current decade, the growth of the Evangelical Churches has surged forward. Many Brazilians are looking for new frameworks of thought and new dimensions of living. Will the Evangelical Churches, however, meet this challenge fast enough? Great opportunity faces every Evangelical Church and mission in Brazil.

The Evangelical Churches have grown in every part of the land, as indicated by the data in Figure 10. The particular Churches, however, have grown in this highly responsive atmosphere in *very different measure*. A glance at Figure 11 reveals the situation.

When we classify total communicant membership according to

Figure 12

BRAZIL: TYPES OF CHURCHES
DISTRIBUTION OF GROWTH: COMMUNICANT MEMBERS, 1950–1965

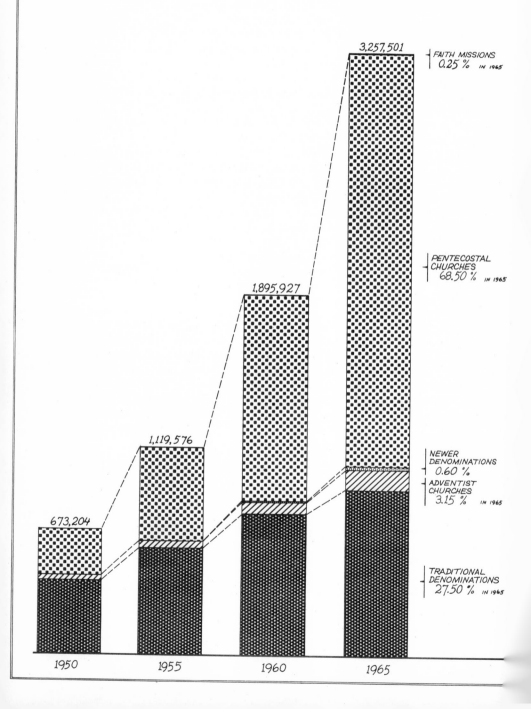

the five types of Churches as introduced in Chapter Two, an interesting pattern emerges. The growth pattern for the period 1950 to 1965 is seen in Figure 12.

A comparison of percentages shows that the Churches related to the faith missions are only one-sixth as large in Brazil as in Latin America as a whole. Similarly, the Churches of the newer denominations constitute only 0.6 per cent in Brazil as compared with 3.4 per cent for all of Latin America. The Adventist Church is about one-half as big in comparison with all of Latin America. The Pentecostal and traditional Churches are both slightly larger.

It must be emphasized, however, that the growth rate of the Churches of the faith missions, newer denominations, and Adventists is not slower in Brazil than it is elsewhere in Latin America. Their small *relative* size must be seen in comparison with the huge Pentecostal and traditional Churches which were at work in Brazil long before the arrival of the faith missions and newer denominations. Even the total for the Seventh-Day Adventist Church is 109,392 communicant members. This is larger than almost every Evangelical Church in Latin America outside Brazil.

The Pentecostal Churches of Brazil in 1965 reported a total of 2,230,144 communicants — that is, 68.50 per cent of all Evangelicals in Brazil. If the Pentecostals maintain their current index of growth (nearly 10 per cent annually), the total Pentecostal membership of Brazil will constitute 70 per cent of Brazilian Evangelicals by 1970.

Pentecostal Churches

The growth of the Evangelical Church so often referred to in mission literature arises largely — although *not* solely — through the amazing multiplication of Pentecostal congregations and denominations. The Pentecostal Churches of Brazil fall into four main classifications: The Assembléias de Deus (Assemblies of God), 62.6 per cent; the Congregação Cristã (Christian Congregation), 22.3 per cent; independent Pentecostal Churches, 12.8 per cent; and mission-related Pentecostal Churches, 2.3 per cent.

Assembléias de Deus

Beginning in 1911 a large number of consecrated laymen began to plant churches (without financial assistance from outside Brazil) in main centers on the coast from Belém to Recife, and finally down to Rio de Janeiro and Pôrto Alegre. Within fifty years the Assembléias had established churches in every state in the Republic, eventually becoming the largest Church in most states. It is the largest Evangelical Church in Latin America, having 1,400,000 communicant members.

More than 200 large "mother church complexes" are located in

chief cities all over Brazil. From these mother churches radiate networks of smaller churches, congregations, and house churches. The
mother churches are known as *ministerios* (ministries) and range
upward in size from 500 members. The Madureira Church in Rio
de Janeiro claims more than 40,000 members; the mother church
in Pôrto Alegre more than 25,000; in Belém, 30,000; in Recife, 22,-
000; and in São Paulo, 30,000. The members of every congregation
within each geographic area belong to and answer to the mother
church, a practice which has been a significant feature of the Assembléias' growth in Brazil. Decentralization is continuously in
process, as smaller mother churches break away, forming new ministries. Thus, restructuring often occurs as new dynamic leaders
emerge and sometimes clash with the older leaders.

Emphasis on Bible institutes for the training of ministers and

Figure 13

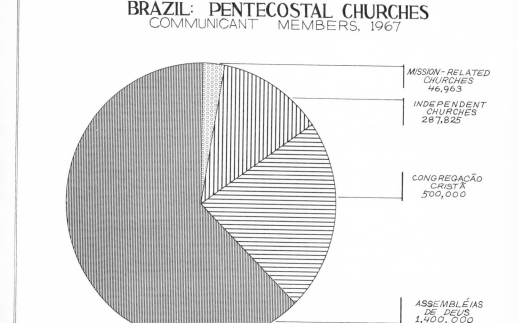

BRAZIL: PENTECOSTAL CHURCHES
COMMUNICANT MEMBERS, 1967

MISSION-RELATED
CHURCHES
46,963

INDEPENDENT
CHURCHES
287,825

CONGREGAÇÃO
CRISTÃ
500,000

ASSEMBLÉIAS
DE DEUS
1,400,000

lay leadership has recently begun in the Assemblies of God of Brazil. Seven institutes are now functioning and more are to be established. Many missionaries cooperate with the Assembléias of Brazil, including those sent by the Assemblies of God in the United States, the Svenska Fria Missionen (The Swedish Free Mission), the Independent Assemblies of God, and the Norske Pinsevenners Itremisjon (Norwegian Pentecostal Mission). The ratio of missionaries to communicant members is approximately one to 27,000.

Congregação Cristã no Brasil

The original and central church of the Congregação Cristã is located in one of the industrial sections of São Paulo (see Chapter Thirteen). The annual rate of increase of membership exceeds 10 per cent. Almost 60 per cent of the baptisms each year occur in the State of São Paulo and 30 per cent in the State of Paraná. The membership (communicant) now stands at 500,000. That the pattern of growth before 1945 differed from the pattern of succeeding decades is shown in Figure 83.

The denomination had grown so rapidly by 1966 that some elders of the central church spoke of enlarging their building. Others felt that additional churches, each seating 5,000 and built in other districts of the city, could better care for the large numbers of converts. The result is a service one night a week which everyone attends at the central church.

Tithes and offerings are used for the construction of new churches. Indeed, each year more than fifty (and sometimes as many as seventy-five) churches are constructed by means of a unique central budgeting plan. The Congregação Cristã had constructed 777 church buildings in this way by 1962, and by 1967 the number of churches constructed exceeded 1,000. This is the most effective church-construction program to be found in Latin America (Read 1965: 31).

Although funds are solicited for the construction of new churches, the ministry of the Congregação Cristã is unpaid. Leaders from every church are expected to be present at the annual meeting of the denomination held at Easter. During this time prayer sessions are scheduled, and through special inspiration the new elders, deacons, and helpers are selected. They are subsequently ordained by the laymen — for life. Each year the number of leaders of the entire Church increases to correspond with the growth achieved during that year. The oldest elder automatically becomes president at this yearly meeting.

Independent Pentecostals

The independent Pentecostal Churches are of four categories: (1) those belonging to the Confederation of Independent Pentecostal Churches located in São Paulo; (2) those which have separated from larger Pentecostal mother churches and do not wish to remain identified with their former denomination; (3) those which have arisen within non-Pentecostal Churches and cannot be identified with their former denomination, and (4) those that are completely autochthonous — they began and still grow without any help from or connection with other Churches or missions.

The two largest independent Pentecostal Churches are the Brasil Para Cristo (Brazil for Christ) with over 100,000 communicants and the Cruzada Nacional de Evangelização (National Evangelization Crusade) with over 30,000 communicants. Both of these Churches have emerged within the last two decades — a significant feature of the Pentecostal surge in Brazil. Some other independent Pentecostal denominations, however, constitute single congregations with less than 150 members. Some have less than five churches totaling 1,000 members. The Igreja da Restauração (Church of the Restoration) located in Rio de Janeiro has nine organized churches, 60 congregations, 5,000 communicants, 15 pastors, 40 evangelists, and 20 more evangelists in preparation!

Some new and growing denominations are composed of Christians who, when they receive the Pentecostal experience and spiritual gifts, leave their former denominations (such as Baptist or Presbyterian). The Renovação Espiritual (Spiritual Renewal), one such denomination, has churches in Recife, Ilheus, Conquista, Vitória, Belo Horizonte, Brasília, Goiánia, São Paulo, and Rio de Janeiro.

At least thirty other independent Pentecostal Churches exist in Brazil, totaling no less than 100,000 communicants (which is a conservative estimate). Because of their locations, exclusive tendencies, and cultural adaptations, their statistics are commonly unreported.

Mission-Related Pentecostal Churches

Approximately ten Pentecostal missions (other than those working with the Assemblies) have work in Brazil. These include the Pentecostal Church of God in America, the Pentecostal Assemblies of Canada, the Church of God, the Pentecostal Church of Christ, and the United Pentecostal Evangelical Church. The largest is the Evangelho Quadrangular (International Church of the Foursquare Gospel), which reports 26,172 communicants — half the number of communicants which come under this classification.

Traditional Churches

Communicant members of traditional Churches constitute 27.5 per cent of the total number in Brazil. Furthermore, 24 per cent of the total communicants are Lutherans, Baptists, Presbyterians, or Methodists.

Figure 14

BRAZIL: GROWTH OF CHURCHES
1910-1970

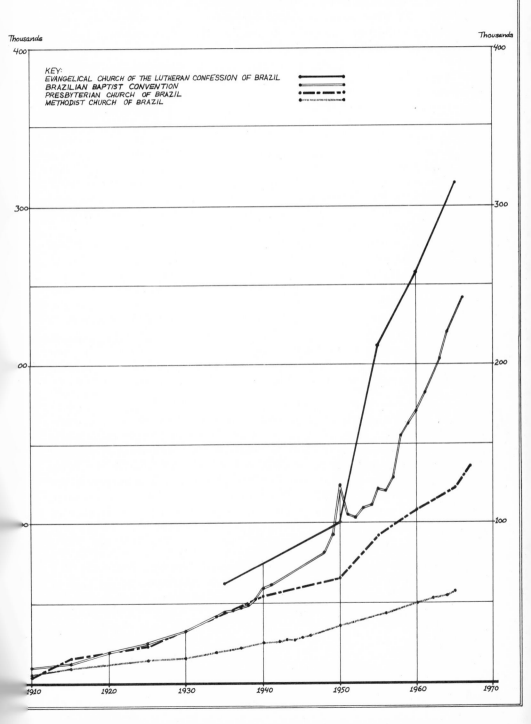

Lutherans

Heavy concentrations of Lutherans are found in Rio Grande do Sul, Santa Catarina, and Paraná. The combined total of 394,761 Lutheran communicants (Figure 11) actually represents a community of more than 800,000 in southern Brazil. The Igreja Evangélica Luterana do Brasil (Evangelical Lutheran Church of Brazil) is related to the Missouri Synod Lutheran Church and records 79,461 communicants. The Igreja Evangélica de Confissão Luterana do Brasil (IECLB, the Evangelical Church of the Lutheran Confession of Brazil), constituted mostly of German Lutherans, has included since 1964 the work of missionaries from the American Lutheran Church and in 1967 recorded 315,000 communicants.

The plotted line of the IECLB (Figure 14) illustrates the registered increase when children of church members continue within the church. The Lutheran rate of growth exceeds that of the Baptists and Presbyterians (which suggests that the Baptists and Presbyterians are losing large numbers of their youth), and itself is exceeded only by the Pentecostal growth. The reasons, however, that Lutheran youth remain in the Church seem to be largely ethnic (see "Immigrant Churches" in Chapter Thirteen). As the German Lutherans become acculturated, much erosion through marriage and secularization can be expected, unless an awakening occurs among them.

The city of Joinville, Santa Catarina, has 4,500 Lutheran families, which represent a community of more than 25,000 in the local churches. Yet, on any given Sunday, only 10 per cent of this Lutheran community attend the worship services conducted by the four Lutheran pastors in the city. Baptisms, confirmations, marriages, funerals, and other pastoral duties keep the pastors so busy that they have no time to create in this community a passion for Christ and a certainty of salvation. As a result, growth is purely biological and many members of the Joinville churches are only nominal Christians.

A new emphasis on evangelism and stewardship education in some larger Lutheran churches in southern Brazil may result in steps toward renewal. In 1963 the IECLB invited the missionaries of the American Lutheran Church to cooperate in a partnership. The American Lutheran missionaries had come to Brazil in 1953 and since then had planted seven small congregations. A complicated pattern of educational institutions, however, had demanded increasing funds and personnel. The missionaries saw that if they continued to follow the ineffective traditional lines of many Evangelical Churches in Brazil, it would take at least twenty-five years for their churches to develop adequately.

The invitation from the IECLB opened a new opportunity to the American Lutheran Church — one given to no other mission in the history of Brazilian Evangelicalism. If, through a process of spiritual renewal and revival, German Lutherans could be won, these able young missionaries could reach out to all Brazilians. Since 1964, even more of the American Lutheran missionaries have been working with the German Lutheran Church in southern Brazil, seeking to impart the riches of the gospel and seeking to create within this Church whole congregations of active Christians in living contact with their Lord, engaged in vital evangelism among the masses.

The decision of the American Lutheran missionaries displayed mobility and flexibility in a willingness to move into high-potential areas. They were aware of the urgency of the time, appraised their own growth honestly, and faced their commitments realistically, knowing that they would lose their identity as a mission. One of these missionaries working in the IECLB, looking back on his first year of work, felt that the results of his present ministry had been beyond his most extravagant dreams. He had seen gratifying outcomes in his evangelistic endeavors and his teaching ministry was being used effectively to help nominal Lutherans claim the dynamics of their Christian heritage.

The Lutheran Churches of Brazil have an important role to play in the future development of the Evangelical community. In 1967, the President of the Rio Grande Synod of the Evangelical Lutheran Church was elected President of the Evangelical Conference of Churches, the largest inter-Protestant organization in Latin America. Every case of revitalization increases the prospect that the resources in the Lutheran community will become available to the Evangelical cause.

Baptists

The combined total of Baptist communicants in Brazil is 256,832. The Convenção Batista Brasileira (Brazilian Baptist Convention) represents by far the majority of this total, recording 242,452 communicants (Figure 14). The Foreign Mission Board of the Southern Baptist Convention began work in Brazil in 1881 and organized the Convenção in 1907. Other mission boards presently cooperating with the Convenção are the Baptist General Conference, North American Baptist Conference, the Baptist Missionary Society, and (in southern Brazil) the Conservative Baptists. The remaining 14,000 Baptist communicants represent the Örebromissionen (a Swedish Independent Baptist Missionary Society) with 7,944 communicants, as well as five other Baptist missions.

Plan of Cooperation. The mission board of the Southern Baptist Convention works with the Convenção in a "Plan of Cooperation" that utilizes the resources of both Churches. Currently 277 missionaries are assigned to Brazil; of these, 42 are in Rio de Janeiro and 30 are in Recife, the locations of the largest Baptist seminaries. The

Baptist publishing house is also located in Rio de Janeiro. The other missionaries work in strategic urban centers all over Brazil.

The Southern Baptist Convention invests nearly three million dollars each year in the missionary work in Brazil — one of the most complete patterns of service found in Latin America. Of the 1,982 churches, however, 1,585 are self-supporting. Dedicated church-planting evangelism is largely responsible for the growth shown in Figure 14. In 1938 the Convenção reported fewer members than the Presbyterian Church of Brazil. Yet, in 1966, the Baptists had nearly twice as many members as the Presbyterians, despite slow growth between 1948 and 1956.

A nationwide evangelistic campaign held in 1965 well illustrates the Baptist zeal. In 1966 the Convenção recorded 242,452 communicants — an increase of 22,363 over the previous year. This increase included many who came to Christ in the 1965 campaign, in which nearly 100,000 made decisions. The year 1967 also saw fruit from the great campaign.

Although the campaign contributed much, Baptist growth in Brazil is largely due to the steady work of missionaries and national pastors. In São Paulo we visited many laymen, pastors, and missionaries who were engaged in church-planting labors. A missionary living in Presidente Prudente, a commercial and transportation hub with 55,055 population, was in the process of establishing three churches in that center. The Foreign Mission Board of the Convenção also maintains missionaries in Paraguay and Bolivia.

The Paulista Convention. The Convenção Batista Paulista administers all church-planting activities in the State of São Paulo, which has more than 277 churches and 200 pastors. The Paulista Convention is divided into eleven associations. The goal is to locate a missionary within each association to provide effective mobile evangelization, teaching, pastoral support, lay leadership training, and consultation.

The cooperative plan at the level of the Paulista Convention involves the careful use of subsidy from the mission board. The percentage of the budget which is subsidized varies according to the total funds received from the 277 local churches. One-third of the budget for cooperative work in November and December of 1965, for example, came from the United States. The Paulista Convention grants use of subsidy in priority situations, according to agreements made with the local churches. Churches receiving subsidy in 1966, furthermore, would receive less funds the following year.

In the Sorocaba Association (one of the eleven in the Paulista Convention), the towns of Ourinhos, Presidente Epitácio, Teodoro Sampaio, Rencharia, and Paraguaçu Paulista were on the priority list in 1965 and were to receive help in church-planting. From 1961 to 1964 the number of members in the 17 churches of the Sorocaba Association had remained at about 1,500. In 1965 an evangelistic campaign in all of these churches brought 190 persons to baptism and lifted the membership to 1,750.

The Sorocaba Association is faced with the problem of providing adequate pastoral oversight for both the churches already established and the ones to be planted. Ministerial candidates are desperately needed. Evangelism, stewardship education, and lay leadership training cannot be neglected.

The Paulista Convention is growing at the rate of 12 per cent per year. Of the eleven associations, two have reached a plateau and two are losing members — a fact which is concealed when we look at the total growth. Furthermore, all are receiving transfer growth from other parts of Brazil; this hinders proper evaluation of growth in the Paulista Convention.

The development of the Brazilian Baptist Convention reflects their enthusiasm for church growth, yet perhaps they should take even more action in the areas of high receptivity. It is not enough just to locate in areas which have the potential for accelerated growth. Fields must be carefully analyzed to determine ways in which more sound and more rapid church growth can be achieved, especially in those areas which are losing members.

Presbyterians

The combined total for all Presbyterians in Brazil (Figure 14) is 175,163 communicants. This total includes the Igreja Presbiteriana do Brasil (Presbyterian Church of Brazil) with 136,195; the Presbiteriana Independente (Independent Presbyterian) with 32,000; and the Presbiteriana Fundamentalista (Fundamental Presbyterian) and Presbiteriana Conservadora do Brasil (Conservative Presbyterian Church of Brazil).

The Presbyterian Church of Brazil and Cooperating Missions. The Igreja Presbiteriana do Brasil (IPB) is the sixth-largest Church in Latin America and is also one of the oldest (1859). Yet it is impossible to understand the development of the IPB without recognizing the unique contributions of the field mission organizations of the United Presbyterian Church in the U.S.A. (UPUSA, New York office) and the Presbyterian Church in the United States (PCUS, Nashville office).

Since 1917, according to the Brazil Plan (Read 1965:84-116), the IPB has purposed to utilize the efforts and resources of the cooperating missions in a church-planting program. The Brazil Plan officially ended in 1954, but the practical partnership continues operating through an Inter-Presbyterian Council which assigns fields on the frontiers to the five mission organizations. The Central Brazil

Mission (UPUSA); the North, East, and West Brazil Missions
(PCUS); and the Junta Missões Nacionais (JMN, the Board of
National Missions of the IPB) all work to establish churches and
pastor them until developed. The churches are then transferred from
the missions to the national Church (IPB).

The continual establishment and transference of churches and
members is indicated in Figure 15. The year following a transfer,
the membership for that mission is reduced. In 1960, for example,
the JMN transferred churches in Teofilo Otoni, Nanuque, and other
places to the IPB. The pastors thus released were transferred to new
fields in Paraná, São Paulo, and Rio Grande do Sul. The result was
that JMN showed fewer members in 1961, but the IPB showed
that many more. In 1961, the Central Brazil Mission transferred three
presbyteries (including buildings, properties, and housing for pastors) in Mato Grosso, Goiás, and North Minas Gerais to the IPB.
In 1962, the North Brazil Mission transferred to the IPB a group
of churches totaling nearly 3,000 communicant members.

Such a partnership plan can work effectively if a solid basis

Figure 15

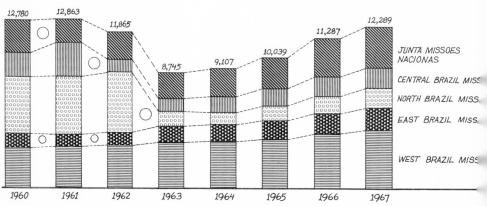

TRANSFER OF MEMBERS: MISSION BOARDS TO NATIONAL CHURCH
PRESBYTERIAN CHURCH OF BRAZIL

NOTE: THE NATIONAL CHURCH IS NOT SHOWN. ON
MEMBERSHIP OF CONGREGATIONS YET
UNDER THE DIRECTION OF THE FIVE
MISSIONS ARE SHOWN.

○ CIRCLE INDICATES TRANSFER OF MEMBE
TO NATIONAL CHURCH.

Figure 16

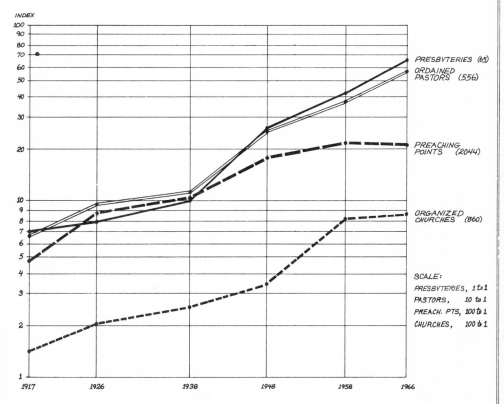

GROWTH OF PRESBYTERIAN CHURCH OF BRAZIL,
1917–1966

NOTE: THE LOGARITHMIC SCALE IS USED IN ORDER TO COMPARE THE RATES OF CHANGE — NOT TO COMPARE NUMERICAL DIFFERENCES.

of understanding is maintained and if a continuing evaluation based upon adequate statistics is made. One factor which has contributed to the success of the Brazil Plan in its last decade has been the excellent work of Harold Cook, Secretary of the Department of Statistics of the IPB. No other Church in Latin America has as complete a statistical record of all phases of its growth and development. Unfortunately, the IPB has not yet utilized these resources to indicate the most fruitful mission areas in its long-range planning.

Growth of the IPB. The excellent statistics of the IPB make possible a brief study of its development from 1917 to 1967 in terms of churches and leadership (Figure 16). The period of greatest growth, 1938 to 1958, coincides with the demographic and social changes of Brazil. The increase in number of ordained pastors represents graduates from the two Presbyterian seminaries after 1940. A third seminary has been established in the Espirito Santo area, resulting in five times as many ordained pastors in 1965 as there were in 1938. The increase in number of preaching points indicates the degree to which the IPB is establishing new contacts in society. This is also an indication of the size of the lay leadership, since 85 per cent of these preaching points are served by laymen. The number of presbyteries indicates the extent of high-potential areas and the ecclesiastical structure of the Church.

The growth of communicant membership also reflects the changes since 1938 (Figure 14). Yet from 1958 to 1968, the annual rate of increase has been 3.5 per cent, hardly more than the population growth rate, 3.1 per cent. The communicant membership in 1967 (136,195) carries potential for much more increase. In 1963, J. P. Ramos revealed his alarm at the static situation of his Church. Ramos pointed out that in 1962 the entire IPB showed a net gain of only 630 new members. Additional statistical evidence forced him to conclude that *insignificant evangelism* and *petty evangelistic strategy* had produced such a condition (Ramos 1963:7).

The Presbyterian Churches of Brazil are located where there is great potential for growth, but this growth is not being achieved. We wonder how long these Churches will continue to bring only a few sheaves out of these ripe Brazilian fields.

Methodists

The combined total for the Methodist Churches is 60,638 communicants. The Igreja Metodista do Brasil (Methodist Church of Brazil) constitutes 58,363 communicants. The other 2,000 communicants are members of the Irmandade Metodista Ortodoxa (Orthodox Methodist Brotherhood) and the Igreja Metodista Livre do Brasil (Free Methodist Church of Brazil).

The Methodist Church of Brazil dates its missionary beginnings as early as 1835 (Read 1965:181). After slow growth in the early years, the national Church was organized in 1930. In 1940, about 25,000 communicants were reported; in 1960, 48,387 communicants (Figure 14). In the five-year period from 1960 to 1965 the net gain was 9,369 communicants (the total of new members was 18,446). This was an annual increase of about 4 per cent; yet the goal set by the General Council in 1960 was 10 per cent per year.

At the meeting of the General Council in 1965, a statement was published which urged all members and leaders of the Methodist Church of Brazil to intensify, during the 1966 to 1970 period, the spiritual life of the Church. In this way, new opportunities in geographical frontiers could be gained and the news of redemption through Christ could be spread to more and more people (Igreja Metodista 1965:47, 48).

In the western area of São Paulo, for example, there are thirteen towns between Bauru and Andradina, a distance of 170 miles. In nine of these towns, the Methodist membership totals more than 3,264 communicants — one of the larger Churches. These churches lie along an artery of transportation, close to the mighty Urubupungá hydroelectric development on the Paraná River. New industry will soon invade the area and the highway south from Brasilia will pass through one of the towns. The Methodists are strategically located for development and growth, as this booming area has every indication of being responsive and open to change, yet these churches gained only thirty-six members from 1960 to 1964, an average of one member per year per church. The most plausible reason for non-growth is the rush of people into the city of São Paulo; yet other Evangelical Churches were growing rapidly in these same towns.

The recommendation of the Methodist General Council in 1965, calling for a deeper spiritual life and more active participation of laymen in the mission of the Church, certainly applies to this section of Brazil. Years ago as São Paulo's western frontier moved out to the Paraná River, the Methodists planted effective churches; but now they seem powerless to multiply even in a more favorable population. Strategic locations in Pôrto Alegre, São Paulo, Rio de Janeiro, and Belo Horizonte indicate the *potential* for future Methodist growth.

Chapter Four

THE RIVER PLATE REPUBLICS: ARGENTINA, PARAGUAY, AND URUGUAY

Argentina, Paraguay, and Uruguay are united by a river and by traces of a common Spanish heritage and subsequent struggle for independence. Yet here the resemblance stops, since each has developed its peculiar concepts of democracy, economy, and religion. Each country, then, presents a unique opportunity for Evangelicals.

ARGENTINA

Not only is Argentina one of the most cosmopolitan countries in the world, it has become the most economically advanced country in Latin America. Buenos Aires, furthermore, constitutes the third largest metropolis in the hemisphere and one of the world's largest ports, having an easy access to shipping lanes on the Atlantic. Most internal migration has been to Greater Buenos Aires; in fact, the city's population of seven million accounts for more than a third of the national total. The Argentine urban centers together contain about three-fourths of the population — the highest urban concentration in Latin America.

The fertile plains of the Chaco in the north and the central Pampas — the economic heart of the country — supply more than enough food for the people. Agriculture and cattle provide the economic base, although industry is developing rapidly. At the same time government spending causes prices to rise more than 25 per cent annually (*World Business* 1967.4:5) since the country is still recovering from the Perón dictatorship.

Not unlike North America, Argentina has been a melting pot for many European elements: Italians, Spaniards, Portuguese, Germans, etc. Most have become tradesmen rather than agriculturalists. Today Argentines are predominantly white, especially in the capital and surrounding province. The Argentine self-image described by Mafud (1965: 368-69) has evolved from interaction between European and frontier settlements, rather than from a European and Negro or European and Indian confrontation. Even so, the complexity of

80

the Argentine population has prevented the emergence of the "typical Argentine," since too many think of themselves as Italians, Germans, Chileans, or Slovaks, and not as Argentines.

THE EVANGELICAL CHURCHES

The lack of national identity and paucity of integration have affected the Argentine morals, value judgments, social expressions, and the fulfillment of personal and national destinies. These also affect the formation of church organizations, evangelical preaching, and thus the growth of the Evangelical Churches.

In a recent study, Dr. Luis Villalpando states that the seventy Evangelical denominations in Argentina register a membership of 414,000 communicants and a Christian community of 800,000 (1966:

Figure 17

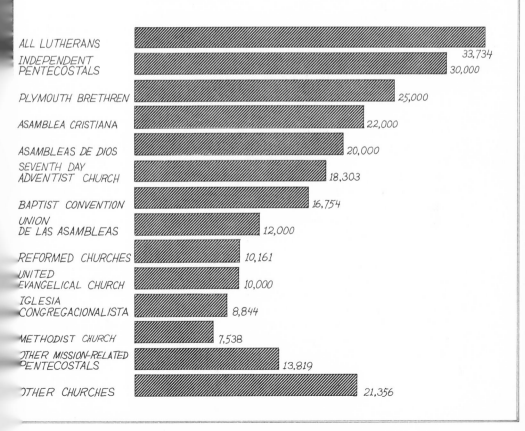

ARGENTINA: COMPARATIVE SIZES OF CHURCHES
1967 COMMUNICANT MEMBERSHIP

ALL LUTHERANS	33,734
INDEPENDENT PENTECOSTALS	30,000
PLYMOUTH BRETHREN	25,000
ASAMBLEA CRISTIANA	22,000
ASAMBLEAS DE DIOS	20,000
SEVENTH DAY ADVENTIST CHURCH	18,303
BAPTIST CONVENTION	16,754
UNION DE LAS ASAMBLEAS	12,000
REFORMED CHURCHES	10,161
UNITED EVANGELICAL CHURCH	10,000
IGLESIA CONGREGACIONALISTA	8,844
METHODIST CHURCH	7,538
OTHER MISSION-RELATED PENTECOSTALS	13,819
OTHER CHURCHES	21,356

1). Statistics available to us total only 249,509 communicants, the major groupings of which are shown on Figure 17.

Ethnic Churches

Many contingents of European immigrants brought their churches with them, resulting in a number of ethnic Churches, some of which do not conduct services in Spanish, and most of which do not try to evangelize the Spanish-speaking people who surround them. Unfortunately, the younger generations in these Churches tend to forget the mother languages and lose their faith as well.

In speaking of ethnic Churches in Argentina, a clear distinction must be made between Churches made up of descendants of immigrants who came to Argentina as Evangelicals, and Churches whose members became Evangelicals after their arrival in Argentina as part of ethnic groups. The Lutheran, Reformed, Mennonite, Waldensian, Presbyterian, and Armenian Churches came with their respective immigrants. In contrast, the Asamblea Cristiana (Christian Assemblies), the Asamblea Cristiana Cultural (Cultural Christian Assemblies), the Russian and Slavic Assemblies, and the Chilean Pentecostal Church all began by evangelization of immigrant groups (although many Chileans arrived as Pentecostals).

MEMBERSHIP OF THE ETHNIC CHURCHES OF ARGENTINA

Swiss Reformed Church	—
Hungarian Reformed Church	—
Armenian Congregational Church	40
Armenian Evangelical Church	55
Armenian Brethren Church	96
French Reformed Church	100
Slavic Gospel Association	250
Norwegian Lutheran Church	300
Synod of Evangelical Lutheran Churches	550
Swedish Lutheran Church	600
Mennonite Board of Missions and Charities	820
Russian and Slavic Assemblies	1,500
Scotch Presbyterian Church	1,600
Christian and Reformed Church	1,850
Dutch Reformed Church	2,000
Asamblea Cristiana Cultural	2,000
Danish Lutheran Church	3,000
United Evangelical Lutheran Church	4,800
Chilean Evangelical Pentecostal Church	5,000
Waldensian Church	6,461
La Iglésia Congregacionalista	8,844
German Lutheran Church	14,875
Evangelical Lutheran Church	13,245
Asamblea Cristiana	22,000

Immigration declined after the 1930's, and now less than 10

Figure 18

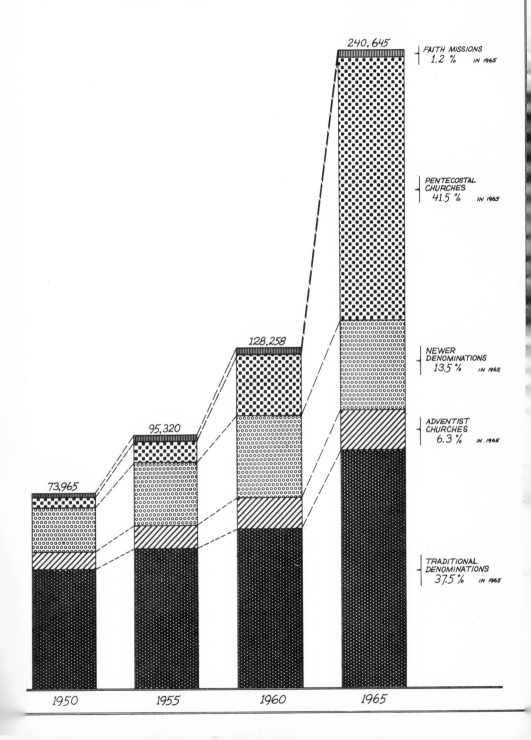

ARGENTINA: TYPES OF CHURCHES
DISTRIBUTION OF GROWTH: COMMUNICANT MEMBERS, 1950-1965

240,645   ⌐ FAITH MISSIONS
             1.2 %   IN 1965

           ⌐ PENTECOSTAL
             CHURCHES
             41.5 %   IN 1965

128,258   ⌐ NEWER
             DENOMINATIONS
             13.5 %   IN 1965

95,320   ⌐ ADVENTIST
             CHURCHES
             6.3 %   IN 1965

73,965   ⌐ TRADITIONAL
             DENOMINATIONS
             37.5 %   IN 1965

1950   1955   1960   1965

per cent of the Argentine population is foreign born. Eventually these disparate elements will melt into one Argentine race. The present situation, however, challenges the Evangelical Churches to win a larger proportion of the first and second generation immigrants.

The Churches which are ethnic, linguistic, and racial in character must also break out of their cultural pockets and evangelize the Argentines who surround them. A pastor of the Dutch Reformed Church in Platanos (Province of Buenos Aires) is trying to do just this. He already has a large number of *criollos* (those of European or Spanish ancestry) attending evangelistic meetings and is close to breaking through this cultural barrier.

Plymouth Brethren

The Brethren constitute the largest Church in Argentina at the present time. Church statistics from the Brethren are very difficult to secure, but reliable data have been obtained from Brethren leaders in Argentina (Enns 1967:186) upon which we base a chart of growth (Figure 19). The chart is substantially correct in showing the steady growth of this denomination from about 1,000 in 1910 to more than 25,000 in 1967.

Early Brethren churches flourished along the railways built by the British. Both the freedom of railroad employees to believe biblical truth and the communities settled by these British believers in Argentina were factors in the growth of the Brethren congregations. Lay ministries and Christian fellowship are characteristic of the Brethren — the laymen start churches wherever they go. Teaching the Scriptures and preaching are not done by ordained men, but rather by the laymen.

We found considerable evidence, however, that Brethren churches may be entering a plateau of slower growth. They are identified with the British in a day when Britain is unpopular. They also have prospered and are now part of the middle class — a fact which cuts them off from the most responsive segments of society. Considerable friction exists among the leaders of the congregations, since the old missionaries have gone and new ones have not yet arrived. It will be interesting to see whether this gifted Evangelical Church will, indeed, slow down or whether it once more will move forward to great propagation of the gospel.

Adventists

Argentina was the first country in South America entered by Adventist missionaries, beginning in 1891. Since that time, the Adventists have emphasized Bible colportage work and active lay participation. Their rate of growth has been steady and is now increasing, due to their strong emphasis on evangelism and radio and correspondence ministries. The Seventh-Day Adventist Church is now fifth

Figure 19

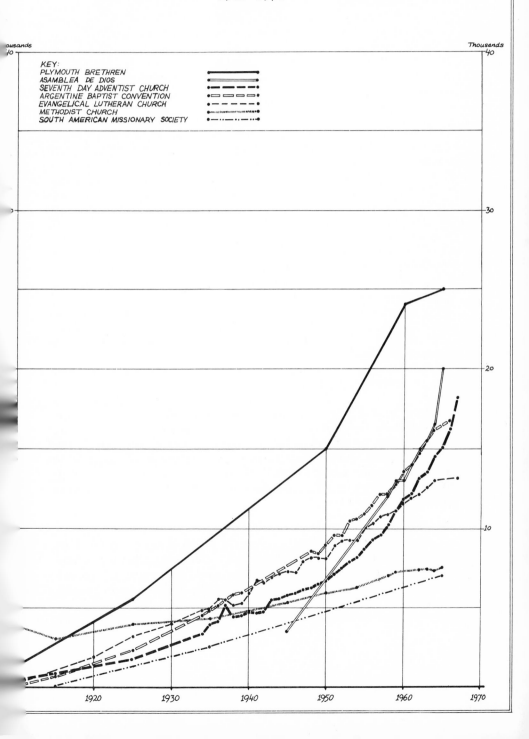

ARGENTINA: GROWTH OF CHURCHES
1910-1970

KEY:
PLYMOUTH BRETHREN
ASAMBLEA DE DIOS
SEVENTH DAY ADVENTIST CHURCH
ARGENTINE BAPTIST CONVENTION
EVANGELICAL LUTHERAN CHURCH
METHODIST CHURCH
SOUTH AMERICAN MISSIONARY SOCIETY

in size (compared with the other Churches of Argentina) and reported 18,303 communicants in 1967.

Baptists

Baptist work in Argentina began as early as 1903; since that time it has expanded to include nearly every section of the country. About 100 missionaries from the Southern Baptist Convention and other Baptist missions presently work with the Argentine Baptist Convention. The 170 national pastors and the 188 self-supporting (out of 214 total) churches in the Convention provide a good basis for church growth and reflect a solid Argentine leadership. The missionary distribution, however, leaves much to be desired, since at least forty are located in Buenos Aires where the churches are not recording much increase. Most of the other missionaries are also working in major Argentine cities.

In 1966 only one Buenos Aires Baptist church showed growth; the others apparently were marking time. One Baptist seminary professor suggested that a rising standard of living gives the Argentines a sense of satisfaction causing them to be somewhat nonresponsive to the gospel. Furthermore, members were depending on the pastors to do everything, thus forfeiting the increase Baptists usually can attribute to their active lay ministry. A mission-Church crisis culminated in 1964. Because the leaders have agreed on a new working relationship tension has decreased since that time.

Baptist growth has been noteworthy and steady, although not necessarily commensurate with the growth potential of churches in Argentina. A ten-year plan of the Argentine Convention calls for increased membership by 1975. Interviews with both missionary and national leaders, however, indicate that they are encountering difficulties. The membership recorded for 1966 is 16,754 communicants.

Anglicans

Through the South American Missionary Society, the Anglican Church has carried on work among the Indians in the Chaco of northern Argentina, including the translation of the New Testament into two Indian languages. The Indian communicant membership now numbers more than 3,000. A number of Indian pastors have received theological preparation and ordination and have assumed leadership roles among their people.

The Anglican Church has historically restricted missionary activity in Latin America to evangelization of Indian tribes, on the grounds that the Roman Catholic Church was already ministering to all the people, and that, therefore, any similar effort by Anglicans would be proselytization. The Lambeth Conference of 1958 reversed this position. Bishop Tucker, recently arrived in Argentina from England, has emphasized this new attitude in his call for Anglicans to evangelize all of Latin America. He has outlined a threefold plan of advance for Anglican work in Argentina. First, they will continue the growing Indian work among the Matacos and other tribes located between the Pilcomayo and Bermejo Rivers. A new phase of this work opens as the Indians migrate to nearby towns. Second, Anglicans have begun church-planting evangelization among Spanish-speaking Argentines in several towns in northern Argentina. Third, theological education is now available to the Anglican ministerial candidates in cooperation with the Union Theological Seminary in Buenos Aires. The Anglicans in Argentina, both Indian and English-speaking, total approximately 7,000 communicants.

Lutherans

The Lutheran Churches entered Argentina primarily by way of the European immigrants from Germany and Scandinavia. The combined total of all Lutherans represents the largest single group (Figure 17) in the country — that is, 33,734 communicants. Of this total, the Evangelical Lutheran Church (related to the Missouri Synod Lutherans) reports 13,029 communicants; the United Lutheran Church (related to the Lutheran Church in America), 2,430 communicants; the German Evangelical Lutheran Church, La Plata Synod, 14,875 communicants; the Danish Lutheran Church, 2,000 communicants; the Swedish Church, 600 communicants; the Synod of Evangelical Lutheran Churches, 550 communicants; and the Norwegian Church, 300 communicants.

The speaking of European mother tongues is diminishing in the Churches of ethnic origin. Many of the second and third generation are now living in the urban centers of Argentina and are speaking fluent Spanish. Many churches are changing to Spanish services through the efforts of the younger pastors who are also trying to minister to the surrounding Spanish communities. The Lutheran Churches must provide ministers for several stages of integration into Argentine society of these ethnic groups. Lutheran growth as yet is almost entirely biological; therefore, as these churches and German communities become less isolated from Argentine culture, the Lutherans will marry Roman Catholics and leave the Church of their fathers. At the same time, increased integration brings these churches new opportunities. The flame of a new spiritual life, which once kindled among Lutherans in Germany a great spread of the biblical faith, could have the same effect in Argentina.

Iglésia Congregacionalista

The Iglésia Congregacionalista is made up of Russian-Germans and their descendants, who belong to the German Pietist movement. In 1963, the Iglésia Congregacionalista had 8,424 communicant members and a constituency, according to their own estimate, of approximately 19,000. The Iglésia Congregacionalista began in Argentina in 1924. By 1938, the membership totaled 2,757. The average annual growth rate slightly exceeds the growth rate of the Argentine population as a whole. There are churches in the provinces of Entre Rios (where the Iglésia Congregacionalista is strongest), Buenos Aires, Missiones, Chaco, Formosa, Santa Fe, and Corrientes, i.e., the areas where there is the greatest concentration of Argentines of German descent.

The seminary at Concordia, Entre Rios, which trains ministers for the Congregationalist churches in Argentina and Brazil, teaches all courses in German. The young people of the churches, however, are assimilating rapidly with the Latin culture. There are twenty parishes served by nineteen nationals and one North American missionary.

Methodists

Methodist work in Buenos Aires began in 1836, the first permanent Protestant missionary work in Argentina. Yet the graph line of their growth history (Figure 19) shows little growth. The increase of 3,000 members in 56 years indicates that the 4,000 communicants in 1910 have increased at the annual average rate of 1 per cent, or 54 persons per year. This Church has lost most of her own children and has won few converts. During this last half century she has been assisted by a good force of missionaries, ample mission funds, and a large corps of highly educated nationals. Such slow growth may have been necessary before 1910; since 1910, however, such small increase has not been necessary. The Methodists could have grown as greatly here as they have in the Philippines and many other lands. Yet, most churches in the greater Buenos Aires area neither expect nor experience growth. Forty-three Methodist churches experienced no growth at all in 1966.

In addition to the 7,500 communicants, there are more than 2,500 members in stages of preparation, so that the actual total is more than 10,000 members. The Methodists estimate their constituency, which includes children in church school, sympathizers, and other persons under the influence of their Church, to number more than 40,000. However, this aura of influence beyond the communicants exists for all Evangelical denominations! If 7,500 Methodists have a constituency of 40,000, then the Brethren and the Asamblea Cristiana each have a constituency of about 150,000. The comparison of communicant figures is far more objective than conjectures about a supposed aura of influence.

The president of the Evangelical Theological Seminary in Buenos Aires, Dr. José Miguez-Bonino, advocates a thorough study of the Methodist congregations which have grown consistently throughout the past decade, so that other Methodist congregations will profit. We trust his suggestion will be put into practice and enlarged to include a study of non-growing Methodist congregations, as well as growing congregations of other denominations.

We have seen a growing desire among Methodists for authentic communication of the gospel to today's Argentines in the totality of their social environment. The Australian evangelist, Alan Walker, visited Methodist churches in Argentina in 1967 in a series of leaders' training institutes for the purpose of awakening among these churches an appreciation for the centrality of evangelism and the need to call modern man to place his faith in Jesus Christ. Fletcher Anderson, Executive Secretary of the Committee on Evangelization in the Methodist Annual Conference in Argentina, has said,

> The Methodist Church has been interested in Christian education, in social service, in the preparation of an educated ministry, in ecumenics. I believe that this has been a most necessary part of our witness and faithfulness and that we helped to awaken other churches to these concerns. But perhaps this diversification of our concern has impeded the single-minded concern for evangelism which has enabled other groups to forge ahead more in numerical growth (1967).

Churches not only in Argentina, but all over Latin America, have suffered from such *diversification of concern,* which has severely damaged their effectiveness. A "single-minded concern for evangelism" *will* advance social justice and other important phases of the Church's ministry. If social justice and involvement in all of life is the only goal, the Churches will neither grow nor achieve the desired social justice.

Pentecostals

Compared to the size of the Brazilian Pentecostal Churches, the four largest Pentecostal Churches in Argentina are indeed small. The Assemblies of God (Swedish and Norwegian Pentecostals) number about 20,000 communicants (Figure 17); the Union of the Assemblies of God (including the American Assemblies' and Canadian Assemblies' mission work) number about 13,000 communicants; the Asamblea Cristiana (Italian Pentecostals) number about 22,000 communicants; and the Church of God mission work, about 10,000 communicants.

The Chilean Pentecostals in Argentina (Iglésia Evangélica Pentecostal) share the same sense of enthusiasm and evangelistic zeal which characterize their churches on the other side of the Andes. They are also just as opposed to statistical records, consequently no one knows exactly how many communicant members they have. We estimate a conservative total of 5,000, although Enns calculates 10,000

(1967:113). It is also possible that there are as many as 17,000 communicants in the Chilean Church, since they have established churches in all the major cities of Argentina. These churches are naturally the strongest where the largest numbers of Chilean immigrants are located, such as Rio Gallegos, San Julean, Bahia Blanca, Neuquen, Buenos Aires, and the provinces of the Patagonia region below the Rio Negro.

The Pentecostal Churches in Argentina began quite slowly — even slower than the Baptists! The event that changed their growth pattern was, according to Pentecostal leaders, the Hicks campaign in 1952. Enns describes the difficulties in organizing a campaign of such magnitude. Contrary to the organizing committee's plans, Hicks himself insisted that they rent a stadium which would seat at least 28,000 — more than ten times the size they had considered adequate. Permission for such a request was quite difficult to secure, and it was only after an unusual and miraculous healing of a presidential guard and supposedly of the President himself that Perón granted full permission for the meetings. (The fact that Perón's relationship with the Roman Catholic Church was far from cordial at the time was certainly a decisive factor.) In addition, radio and press coverage were secured, providing a real breakthrough for the Evangelical Churches in Argentina. The results were realized almost immediately — in fact, the Assemblies of God began five churches in 1955 alone. "The intangible but nevertheless solid result of the campaign was a new spirit of faith and spiritual optimism which pervaded the entire Evangelical community, even beyond the limit of the officially cooperating body of Churches" (Enns 1967:107-108).

Since the Hicks campaign, the Pentecostal Churches in Argentina have had rapid growth. There are at least twenty-five Pentecostal denominations with a total communicant membership (conservative estimate) of 100,000 — 80 per cent of which have been added since 1955. We estimate that the Pentecostal Churches in Argentina have an annual rate of increase of more than 8.0 per cent. By 1970, 50 per cent of the Evangelicals in Argentina may well be found within the Pentecostal family of Churches.

Other Churches and Missions

There are more than thirty Churches and missions with less than 2,000 communicant members; at least 60 percent of these Churches and missions have had little or no growth. Some of the leaders now face their church-planting responsibilities with a measure of desperation. A missionary whose mission has been working in Argentina since about 1900, and whose static churches report a total membership of less than 1,000, expressed to us an opinion widely held by his colleagues: "If we are not able to grow by 1970, we may as well quit." Dissatisfaction was causing them to evaluate old fields, projects, and methods, and to begin searching for new solutions. To "pull out," however, is not necessarily the solution here, since some Churches are obviously growing in the Argentine situation.

URUGUAY

Among the Latin American nations, Uruguay has enjoyed much success in developing and preserving democratic institutions. Its citizens take much pride in their welfare state which provides free education, public housing, medical care, and old-age pensions. The country is known for its gentle climate, fine grazing land, ease of communications, and progressive laws; yet Uruguay is faced with a serious problem of increasing inflation approaching bankruptcy.

Half of the 2.7 million Uruguayans live in the small "old world" metropolis of Montevideo, and 90 per cent of the population is white,

Figure 20

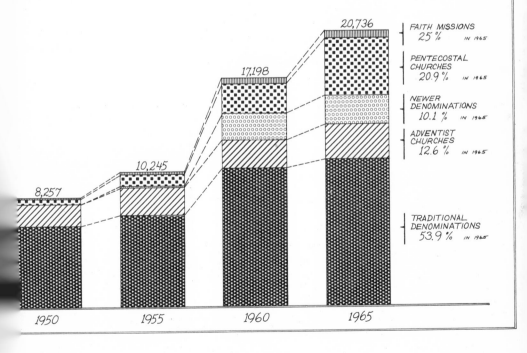

URUGUAY: TYPES OF CHURCHES
DISTRIBUTION OF GROWTH: COMMUNICANT MEMBERS, 1950-1965

Figure 21

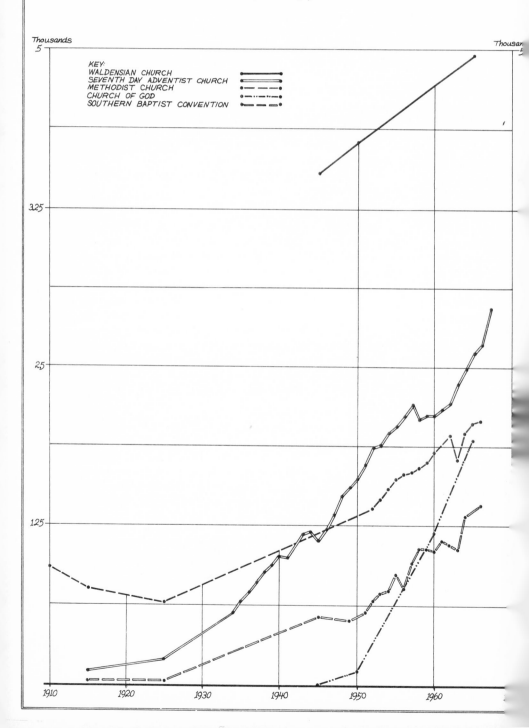

URUGUAY: GROWTH OF CHURCHES
1910–1970

KEY:
WALDENSIAN CHURCH
SEVENTH DAY ADVENTIST CHURCH
METHODIST CHURCH
CHURCH OF GOD
SOUTHERN BAPTIST CONVENTION

due to heavy European immigration. The country surrounding Montevideo is devoted to sheep and cattle ranches, upon which depends the economy of the country. Unfortunately, the *latifundias* (vast land holdings) are owned and operated by only a few.

It is not surprising that Uruguayans tend to become bored with a too comfortable and too uneventful life. They are free thinkers and positivists. The political domination of the earlier Batlle party and the reforms following 1910 brought atheism into the schools, creating antagonism toward religious endeavor, both Roman Catholic and Protestant. Church and State are completely separated and the former antagonism has given way to a new religious tolerance.

The Evangelical Churches

The growth of the Evangelical Churches in Uruguay has been minimal, as seen in Figures 20 and 21. The total number of communicants, which has not surpassed 25,000, makes up less than 0.8 per cent of the population.

Waldensians

The largest Evangelical Church in Uruguay, the Waldensian Church, is ethnic in origin (Italian colonists). The Waldensians celebrated their centennial year in 1958. In 1966 the Church reported 4,962 communicants, over 3,000 families, and a community of more than 13,000. Unlike their sister Church in Argentina, the Uruguayan Waldensians make little effort to evangelize the surrounding population. Pastors are trained at the Union Theological Seminary in Buenos Aires and spend a final year of study in Europe. Montevideo has only one large Waldensian church; the rest are located south and west along the River Plate. Perhaps an aggressive evangelistic endeavor can be promoted by the Waldensian Church in cooperation with other members of the World Presbyterian Alliance.

Mennonites

One of the earliest ethnic colonies in the country was comprised of Mennonite refugees from Poland and Russia. Although the group has kept to itself culturally and socially, some members of the churches are beginning evangelistic work in the city of Montevideo. The Mennonite Brethren, General Conference Mennonites, and Mennonite Board of Missions churches together total 1,012 members.

Methodists

The work of the Methodist Church was established in Uruguay in 1841; the membership in 1966 was reported as 2,072 communicants. The central church in Montevideo is also the largest — a beautiful Gothic structure which houses a congregation of about 700 members who come from all over the city. They are predominantly middle and upper class — doctors, lawyers, professors — and their influence in the affairs of the city is probably more than the membership would suggest. The Methodists in Uruguay have emphasized work in education and medical care. Their leaders have been active in many of the cooperative Evangelical causes in all of Latin America. The Methodist Bishop for Uruguay and Argentina is Dr. Sante U. Barbieri, the outstanding thinker, writer, and authority on Latin American affairs and also one of the past Presidents of the World Council of Churches.

Church of God

During the 1940's two Italian Christians from Montevideo visited the Church of God in Buenos Aires and subsequently invited the pastor to return the visit, and a church was established with eight members (Conn 1959:164-166). By 1949 this tiny congregation had expanded into two churches with 105 members. Growth since 1949 has not been spectacular, but it has endured. In 1958, Conn reported 25 churches and missions in Uruguay with 1,204 members. The *World Christian Handbook* (1967) records 1,923 communicants as the latest figure.

The Assemblies of God and the Swedish Pentecostals have also experienced growth in the last fifteen years, reporting 1,532 and 1,605 communicants, respectively. The greatest need of the Uruguayan Pentecostals at this time is to supply the demand for pastors. Some

Figure 22

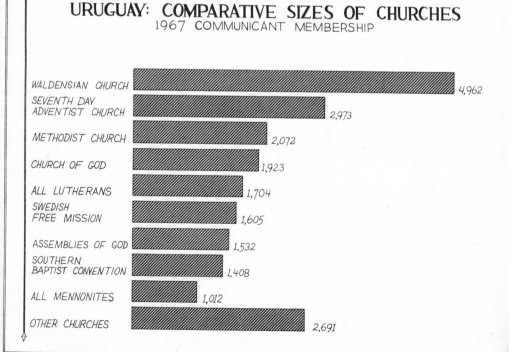

URUGUAY: COMPARATIVE SIZES OF CHURCHES
1967 COMMUNICANT MEMBERSHIP

WALDENSIAN CHURCH — 4,962
SEVENTH DAY ADVENTIST CHURCH — 2,973
METHODIST CHURCH — 2,072
CHURCH OF GOD — 1,923
ALL LUTHERANS — 1,704
SWEDISH FREE MISSION — 1,605
ASSEMBLIES OF GOD — 1,532
SOUTHERN BAPTIST CONVENTION — 1,408
ALL MENNONITES — 1,012
OTHER CHURCHES — 2,691

leaders say they could establish twenty-five new churches in one year if they could provide adequate pastoral care.

Other Churches and Missions

The graph line of the membership of the Seventh-Day Adventist Church (Figure 21) follows a remarkably similar pattern to that of the Methodist Church, with few variations. The Adventists overcame a thousand-member lead, however, and now number 2,973 communicants, compared with the 2,072 communicants reported by the Methodist Church. Both Churches have emphasized the importance of education, but perhaps the Adventists have been more intent on evangelization than the Methodists.

The Baptist Convention in Uruguay has only 1,408 members, although they have been working here since 1911. Of the twenty-four churches, six are self-supporting: ten of the twenty-four missionaries are working in Montevideo. There are also twenty Baptist national pastors; they, however, are suffering because of the inflation. The Convention is facing the problems encountered when growth does not provide for the normal stages of development.

The Nazarene Church began in Uruguay in 1949. After a slow start, problems developed in missionary-national relationships. Church membership has not advanced beyond 200, and the missionaries are examining the situation in light of a planned concentration in Montevideo as a center for expansion.

It is difficult to assess the growth of the Evangelical Churches in Uruguay. The annual growth rate of the Churches is five times that of the population, but then the population growth rate is one of the lowest in Latin America. If Uruguayans are providing leadership in other areas of Latin American affairs, and even within the Latin American Evangelical Churches, then it seems only fair to suggest that the Uruguayan Churches themselves must respond to great challenges of church expansion.

PARAGUAY

When compared to Buenos Aires and Montevideo, Asunción is little more than a provincial capital. Civilian life is slower, simpler, more friendly, and more leisurely. European immigration has also remained a mere trickle when compared to Argentina and Uruguay; in fact, most of the people are partly of Guarani descent. The country, historically, has been remote and isolated from main transportation lines and world markets.

Recent road construction may be the means for economic improvement. An asphalt road from Asunción into Brazil, as well as the first stage of the Trans-Chaco highway from Asunción to the

Figure 23

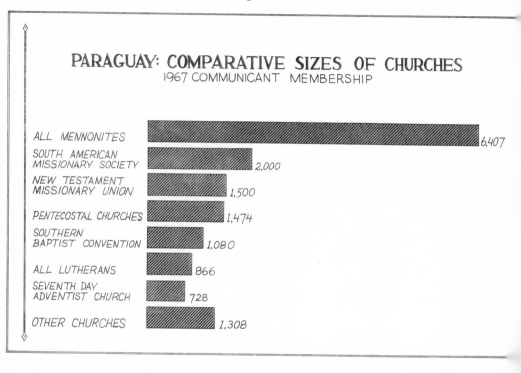

PARAGUAY: COMPARATIVE SIZES OF CHURCHES
1967 COMMUNICANT MEMBERSHIP

ALL MENNONITES	6,407
SOUTH AMERICAN MISSIONARY SOCIETY	2,000
NEW TESTAMENT MISSIONARY UNION	1,500
PENTECOSTAL CHURCHES	1,474
SOUTHERN BAPTIST CONVENTION	1,080
ALL LUTHERANS	866
SEVENTH DAY ADVENTIST CHURCH	728
OTHER CHURCHES	1,308

Bolivian border (providing access to a cattle-raising and lumbering area) have been completed.

THE EVANGELICAL CHURCHES

The general attitude of the Evangelicals in Paraguay is discouragement; they expect little church growth. As Figures 23 and 25 show, there are good reasons for their discouragement. Most Evangelical denominations have between 400 and 700 members, and the four largest denominations report not more than 2,000. The types of churches and their growth since 1950 are shown in Figure 24.

Mennonite Brethren

The Mennonite Brethren have fraternal work among the German Mennonite settlements and also missionary work among the Indians and *mestizos*. The communicant membership has grown from about 250 in 1959 to 1,265 in 1966, of which about 1,100 are Indians. The Indian mission stations are located in Boqueron among three tribes —

Figure 24

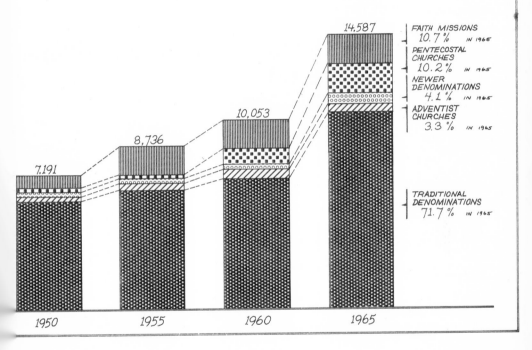

PARAGUAY: TYPES OF CHURCHES
DISTRIBUTION OF GROWTH: COMMUNICANT MEMBERS, 1950–1965

FAITH MISSIONS
10.7 % IN 1965

PENTECOSTAL CHURCHES
10.2 % IN 1965

NEWER DENOMINATIONS
4.1 % IN 1965

ADVENTIST CHURCHES
3.3 % IN 1965

TRADITIONAL DENOMINATIONS
71.7 % IN 1965

14,587

10,053

8,736

7,191

1950   1955   1960   1965

the Lenguas, Chulupi, and the Guaranis — and most recently among the Moros.

New Testament Missionary Union

The New Testament Missionary Union has a number of churches in the Departments of Central, La Cordellera, Paraguari, Guiara, and Caaguazu, as well as five in Asunción itself. The total communicants reported to the *World Christian Handbook* in 1957, 1962, and 1967 were 1,500 members.

Baptists

The line of growth for the Baptists (Figure 25) shows many

Figure 25

PARAGUAY: GROWTH OF CHURCHES
1910-1970

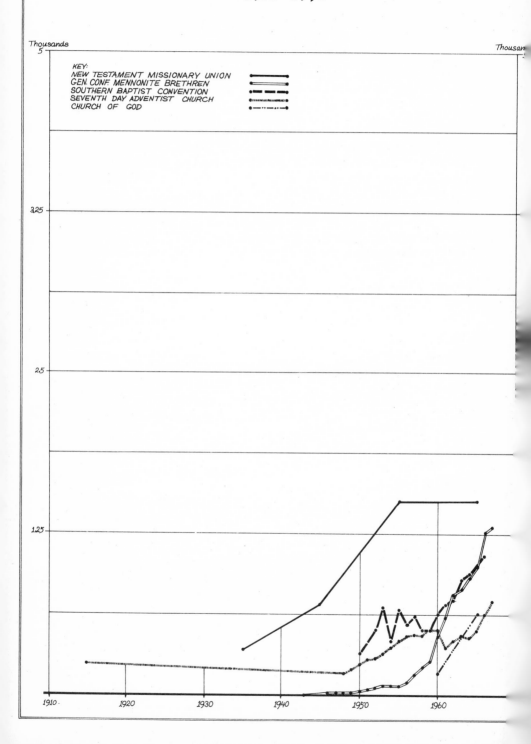

KEY:
NEW TESTAMENT MISSIONARY UNION
GEN. CONF. MENNONITE BRETHREN
SOUTHERN BAPTIST CONVENTION
SEVENTH DAY ADVENTIST CHURCH
CHURCH OF GOD

breaks between 1953 and 1959, but the Church began to grow more steadily after this time. The Southern Baptist Convention reports 1,080 communicants in Paraguay in 1966. Of the twenty-two missionaries from the Convention, twenty are working in Asunción with the churches, hospital, and educational institutions. Of the eleven Baptist churches, only five are self-supporting. Fourteen national pastors, some of whom come from Argentina, are in charge of the churches. The Baptists may find it difficult to establish churches unless they are heavily backed by institutions.

Paraguay, which has the smallest population of any country in South America, also has few Evangelical communicants (14,587). On the other hand, the annual rate of growth of the Evangelicals is 11 per cent since 1960. This unusual growth rate has been achieved by pouring in large numbers of missionaries and by building large institutional bases. Such growth has a low ceiling, since missions can add another church and another fifty members every time they build another social center, hospital, or school — but the extent to which missions have funds to do this is limited. The Churches in Paraguay are still very closely related to foreign mission boards and have not yet developed a dynamic national leadership.

Chapter Five

THE ANDEAN REPUBLICS:
CHILE, BOLIVIA, AND PERU

In the Andean world the vitality of an emerging civilization is seeking to prove itself politically, economically, socially. The differences between the coastal desert, the mountains, and the inland jungles are as extreme as the heights of the mountains themselves. The Andes are second only to the peaks of the Himalayas of Asia. The differences of race, heritage, and outlook are strengthened and sustained by the mountains, which have shaped domestic politics, interregional prejudices, foreign policies, economics, folkways, and the character of the people.

The major part of the Andean population — the Indians — live in the highlands. They are agricultural people by heritage and instinct, but the agricultural resources are meager, forcing the people into perpetual misery and hunger. Consequently the Indians are poor and uneducated, but they are at the same time infinitely enduring. The Quechua language gives them unity greater than loyalty to their individual countries. The traditional view of the Indians as an inert human mass, silent, withdrawn, and passive, is changing as they begin to experience their own self-determination. The Indian population is destined to be given genuine citizenship and included at last in the Andean societies.

The solution to the economic and political disunity, however, lies in the building of roads. Each of these countries is making valiant efforts at road construction. An international highway on the eastern slopes of the Andes will eventually connect with crossroads to the Pacific and also with Brazil's road system. Air transportation and radio communications are also increasing unification among the people who have been traditionally isolated and separated by the cordilleras.

Nowhere in Latin America is the aspiration for social progress more evident than in the Andean countries. Perhaps the difficulties of national and regional jealousies, internal fragmentation, land ownership and use, political instability, and social inequality will be relieved, or at least improved, by the revolutionary forces which are rational in Chile, vehement in Bolivia, and expanding in Peru.

CHILE

Although the Andes and coastal highlands comprise from one-third to one-half of the land of Chile, the *chilenos* are united by the mountains rather than divided, as in Peru and Bolivia, since the people all live on the same side. The rainless, hot desert of the north, the fertile heartland (where the majority of the population resides), and the cold, rainy forests of the south, plus the narrow width of the country itself, result in problems of communication and food production. Land use is poor and land owners are few; agriculture is limited to the valleys between the coastal and inland mountain ranges.

The racial diversity is far less than in most countries. The influence of immigrants has been far larger than their actual numbers. The *chilenos* are an orderly and self-reliant people; the middle class is substantial. Over one-half of the population is concentrated in the central valley (less than 15 per cent of the land area), especially in Santiago, Valparaíso, and Concepción.

THE EVANGELICAL CHURCHES

Our calculation as to the number of Evangelicals in Chile is based on the 1960 Chilean government census. At that time 411,530 Chileans identified themselves as Evangelicals to census-takers. Exactly what Evangelical community the census measures is debatable. Two-fifths of the Evangelicals counted in the census were persons under fifteen years of age (about the same proportion as in the population at large), so the census includes more than adult communicant members, probably representing members and their immediate families.

If the Evangelical Churches have continued to grow at an annual rate of 6.5 per cent since 1960 (which is a conservative estimate), then at mid-1967 there were approximately 649,500 Evangelicals (or 6.9 per cent of the population). We estimate the annual growth rate to be 6.5 per cent because from 1930 to 1940 the Evangelical growth rate was 6.45 per cent; from 1940 to 1952, 6.62 per cent; and from 1952 to 1960, 6.6 per cent. Our estimate of an Evangelical community that totals 6.9 per cent of the population is low compared to other estimates which run as high as 20 per cent.

Pentecostal Churches

The indigenous Pentecostal Churches constitute most of the Evangelical Church of Chile, as shown on Figure 26. Most Pentecostal leaders, however, are unwilling to take a census of their congregations. This may be due to a certain fear of knowing the facts, to a general indifference toward statistics, or to the lack of facilities with which to carry out a census. The same leaders are usually willing to make a guess as to their own membership, but anyone who takes these guesses to be accurate statements is bound to come to strange conclusions.

Therefore we are forced to base our calculations for the Pentecostal Churches on indirect indications, such as the average size of their congregations, the number of churches, their voting strength in the Chilean Evangelical Council, the publications of the various Churches, and the estimates of each group or denomination. We have found it impossible to construct graphs of growth history, as statistical records do not exist. Furthermore, the growth has been so tremendous that the graph line would bear no resemblance to

Figure 26

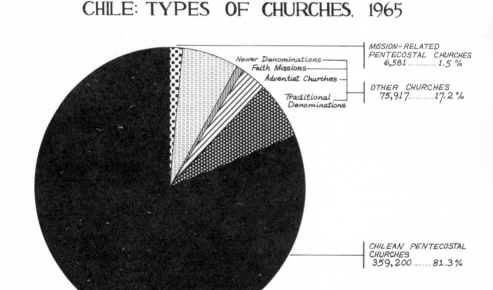

CHILE: TYPES OF CHURCHES, 1965

MISSION-RELATED PENTECOSTAL CHURCHES
6,581 .... 1.5 %

Newer Denominations
Faith Missions
Adventist Churches
Traditional Denominations

OTHER CHURCHES
75,917 .... 17.2 %

CHILEAN PENTECOSTAL CHURCHES
359,200 .... 81.3 %

TOTAL COMMUNICANTS: 441,698

that of the traditional Churches. A reconstructed picture of the starting dates and present size of the Pentecostal Churches is shown in Figure 27.

It is difficult to measure which of the 125 or more Pentecostal

Figure 27

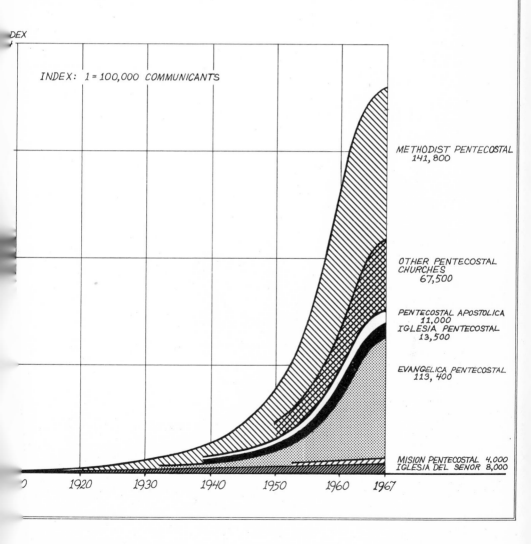

CHILE: GROWTH OF NATIONAL PENTECOSTALS, 1910-1967

INDEX: 1 = 100,000 COMMUNICANTS

METHODIST PENTECOSTAL 141,800

OTHER PENTECOSTAL CHURCHES 67,500

PENTECOSTAL APOSTOLICA 11,000
IGLESIA PENTECOSTAL 13,500

EVANGELICA PENTECOSTAL 113,400

MISION PENTECOSTAL 4,000
IGLESIA DEL SEÑOR 8,000

1920   1930   1940   1950   1960   1967

Figure 28

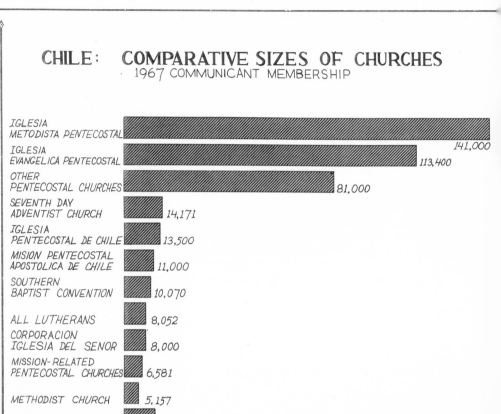

CHILE: COMPARATIVE SIZES OF CHURCHES
· 1967 COMMUNICANT MEMBERSHIP

IGLESIA METODISTA PENTECOSTAL — 141,000
IGLESIA EVANGELICA PENTECOSTAL — 113,400
OTHER PENTECOSTAL CHURCHES — 81,000
SEVENTH DAY ADVENTIST CHURCH — 14,171
IGLESIA PENTECOSTAL DE CHILE — 13,500
MISION PENTECOSTAL APOSTOLICA DE CHILE — 11,000
SOUTHERN BAPTIST CONVENTION — 10,070
ALL LUTHERANS — 8,052
CORPORACION IGLESIA DEL SENOR — 8,000
MISSION-RELATED PENTECOSTAL CHURCHES — 6,581
METHODIST CHURCH — 5,157
OTHER CHURCHES — 11,638

denominations grows fastest at any particular time. Lalive d'Epinay, the Swiss sociologist who made a study for the World Council of Churches, states as axiomatic that the newer the group, the faster the growth (1965-66:25). He may be right, as several growth factors support his opinion.

The influence of strong personalities vying for leadership has produced a proliferation of Pentecostal groups and denominations. The dynamic force behind a newborn Church creates a certain spiritual momentum that results in growth. It is for this reason that the splintering foreseen by Browning (1930:31) did not arrest the Pentecostal expansion, but rather led to greater growth. Some of the emergent leaders left the older Pentecostal Churches because of dissatisfaction with moral and ethical standards. Others were forced out because of their own lack of standards, and others moved out to find greater opportunities for themselves. Whatever their motivation, many of them were strong leaders to whom followers rallied. Those whose leadership qualities were not strong enough saw their groups dwindle and in some cases disappear.

In the Pentecostal movement, allegiance is given essentially to the personality of the leader and not to the denomination. When Pentecostals move to a new residence, they seek out the congregation which seems to be closest to their former church, although it may not be of the same denomination. Thus, all Pentecostal Churches are made up of converts, of members who have transferred from elsewhere, and of some who have been pried away from other Churches. This constant transfer of members may have value, but it distorts the growth picture. Because of this and because there exists an essential unity of doctrine and practice among Christian Pentecostals, we treat the movement as a statistical whole in Figure 26.

Since the beginning of the Pentecostal revival in Chile, Pentecostals elsewhere have been disturbed by the isolation of Chile from the rest of the worldwide movement. Unlike most Pentecostals, the Chileans have practiced infant baptism. Over this issue, Willis Hoover, the pioneer of Chilean Pentecostalism, separated from the worldwide Pentecostal movement.

The Swedish Pentecostals, the North American Assemblies of God, the Church of God of Cleveland, Tennessee, and the Church of the Foursquare Gospel all volunteered to assist the Chilean Church. They disagreed vigorously, however, with the national Pentecostals over the nature of supernatural manifestations and the mode of baptism. Thereby, they estranged themselves but remained to found their own denominations in Chile.

The Swedish Pentecostals arrived in 1938 and have been moderately successful in planting churches. They numbered 1,900 communicants in 1966 and, despite their small membership, are enjoying a current annual growth rate of 10 per cent, which promises well for the future. Though some of their Chilean leaders come from the national Pentecostal Churches, they have grown by evangelizing the unconverted. Their churches are known as the Autonomous Assemblies of God.

The North American Assemblies of God, which began work in Chile in 1942, have only 1,110 communicant members. They have been plagued by missionary-national tensions and, along with other mission-related Pentecostal Churches, have reacted against the extremes of the national Pentecostal Churches. As a result, they have chosen not to identify themselves as Pentecostals in Chile. This has

Figure 29

CHILE: GROWTH OF CHURCHES
1910 - 1970

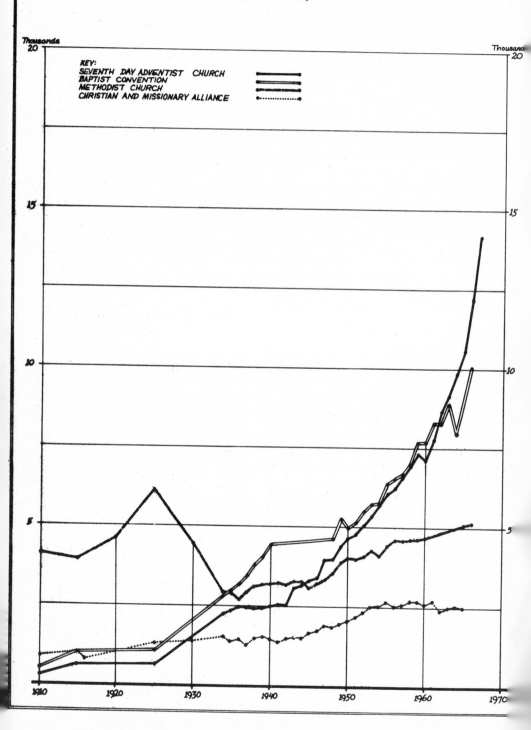

lost for them the very dynamic which produces growth among the less inhibited indigenous Pentecostal Churches.

The Foursquare Church and the Church of God came in much later. They took over small national Pentecostal groups which were looking for spiritual and financial aid. The Foursquare Church has 2,209 members and the Church of God, 1,362 members. It is too early for either to have a distinctive growth pattern. The same reaction against extreme Pentecostalism may prevent these Churches from evangelistic effort of the kind to which Chileans will respond. Despite being Pentecostal, the secret of great increase has so far escaped all four of these mission-related Churches.

Traditional Churches

For the traditional Protestant Churches of Chile, we base our calculations on churches' minutes and records. One of the larger non-Pentecostal Churches not included in Figure 29 is the Iglésia Alemana (the German Lutheran Church), an immigrant Church which does not evangelize. Growth in this Church is biological, i.e., it consists of incorporating into the Church the children of members. The total of 8,052 communicants shown in Figure 28 is the estimate reported by the Church. Annual totals have not been kept.

An outstanding example of growth among non-Pentecostal Churches in Chile at the present time is the expansion of the Adventist Church since 1960. Adventist communicants numbered 12,171 in 1966. Remarkably parallel to the Pentecostal method of lay participation, though within their own ecclesiastical pattern and on a much more sophisticated level, the Adventist Church has discovered the way to appeal to Chileans. Their excellent seminary in Chillán is producing men who are growth-conscious; their utilization of lay evangelists shows the way for other Evangelicals.

The growth of the Baptists began about the time that they initiated a program to stimulate and encourage Christian stewardship among their churches. Mission subsidy was not diminished but redirected to allow churches to grow. The study topics chosen for their annual conferences in 1964 and 1965, "Conserving the Results of Evangelism" and "The Growth of Chilean Baptist Churches," reflect the emphasis on church growth. Some leaders think their chief problem is a lack of pastors; but unless they find some way to involve more lay people in church-planting, they will find it difficult to reach their goal of growth.

The Methodists, Presbyterians, Christian and Missionary Alliance, Salvation Army, and Gospel Mission of South America have not grown in spite of large investments of personnel and money. We observed little evidence that their growth pattern will change since they are all committed to the present sterile methods and approaches.

Many other denominations have begun work in recent years.

Attracted by Pentecostal increase, they all seem to feel that what Chile needs is their own particular variety of Protestantism.

BOLIVIA

Most of the Bolivians live in the Altiplano, the high, bleak, southwestern corner of the country. The fact that the nation is landlocked and also divided by the mountain ranges has impeded economic development. The revolution of 1952 forever separated Bolivians from their feudal past. The highlanders are now beginning to migrate from the Altiplano to the frontier regions of the eastern mountain valleys and lowlands where the economy is developing. Those living in the Santa Cruz area are more neighborly with Brazil and Argentina, though, than with their own highland countrymen.

Figure 30

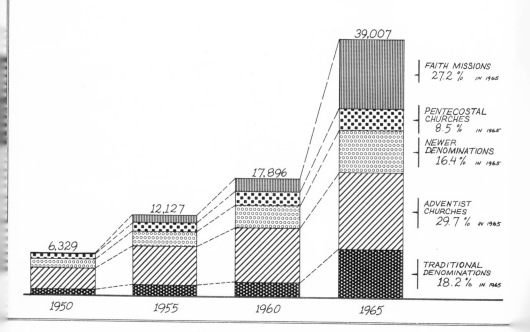

BOLIVIA: TYPES OF CHURCHES
DISTRIBUTION OF GROWTH: COMMUNICANT MEMBERS, 1950-1965

Figure 31

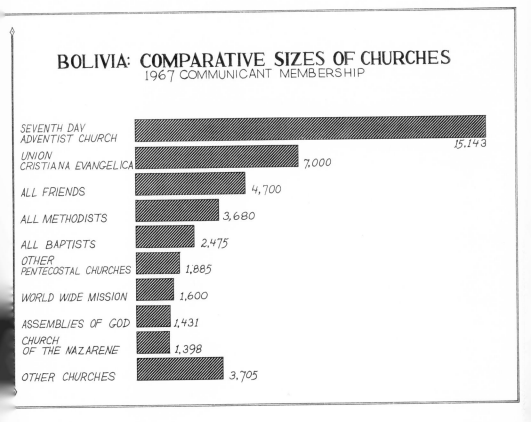

BOLIVIA: COMPARATIVE SIZES OF CHURCHES
1967 COMMUNICANT MEMBERSHIP

SEVENTH DAY ADVENTIST CHURCH	15,143
UNION CRISTIANA EVANGELICA	7,000
ALL FRIENDS	4,700
ALL METHODISTS	3,680
ALL BAPTISTS	2,475
OTHER PENTECOSTAL CHURCHES	1,885
WORLD WIDE MISSION	1,600
ASSEMBLIES OF GOD	1,431
CHURCH OF THE NAZARENE	1,398
OTHER CHURCHES	3,705

This may change soon since this is the fastest-growing area in the country.

THE EVANGELICAL CHURCHES

Perhaps the outstanding feature of the church growth picture in Bolivia is the overall growth since 1950. The 7,000 communicants of that year had grown to 20,000 by 1960, and again to 43,000 by 1967. Some Evangelical leaders in Bolivia, however, would estimate a total communicant membership of 60,000 as more accurate.

Adventists

The Adventist Church in Bolivia is spread throughout the country, although the density is greatest around the La Paz and Lake Titicaca areas. A people movement occurred within the Adventist Church among the Aymara Indians around Lake Titicaca between 1915 and 1934 (Hamilton 1962:47). The decrease in membership

Figure 32

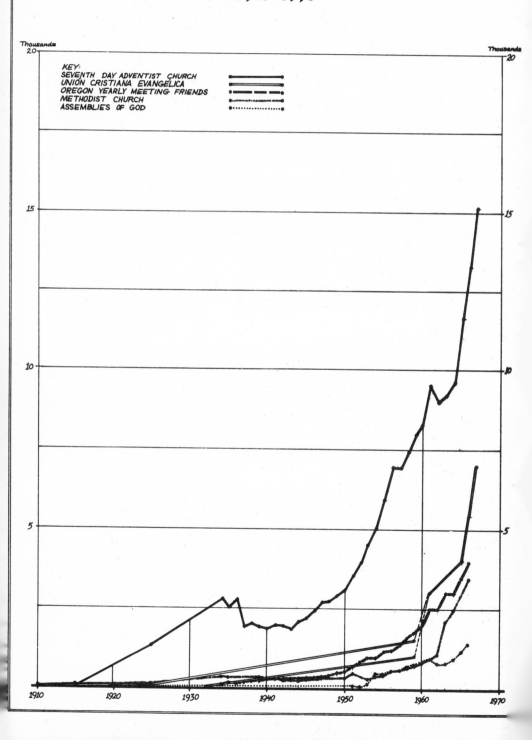

BOLIVIA: GROWTH OF CHURCHES
1910-1970

KEY:
SEVENTH DAY ADVENTIST CHURCH
UNION CRISTIANA EVANGELICA
OREGON YEARLY MEETING FRIENDS
METHODIST CHURCH
ASSEMBLIES OF GOD

following that time (Figure 32) might have been due to the depression, emigration of members to coastal Peruvian cities, or even loss of membership among the Indians. Since the revolution in 1952 the rate of growth has again increased. This Church is now the largest in Bolivia.

The Adventist pattern of growth, so firmly anchored to their school system, will probably prevent any further people movement among the Quechuas and Aymaras. These schools are heavily subsidized by foreign funds, yet they contribute directly to the planting of churches. Many schools are located alongside organized churches, but many begin in new areas where no congregation exists. Within a short time the ministries of the teachers in and outside the school become the means whereby believers begin to function as a new congregation. As long as this pattern continues, growth will be slow, though in comparison to other slowly growing Churches it may appear to be rapid.

Methodists

In the early 1960's, the Methodists assessed their Bolivian Church, under the leadership of Paul McCleary, and came to the conclusion that they had overemphasized the institutional work at the expense of church-planting. Keith Hamilton, who had studied at the Institute of Church Growth, was placed in a leadership position connected with evangelistic responsibility. This new emphasis accounts for the increase of growth as shown on Figure 32 after 1962.

Hamilton (1962:30, 31) records 1,400 communicants in 1960, of whom 800 were Aymara and 600 Spanish. In 1967, the Methodists had about 3,500 members, of whom 2,100 were Aymara and 1,400 *mestizos*. The increase of 2,000 in seven years points up the possibilities existing among both *mestizos* and Indians. The responsiveness of the Aymaras also is stressed by Hamilton. Other missions are now recognizing the Aymara as one of the most fruitful populations in Bolivia at the present time.

Unión Cristiana Evangélica

The Andes Evangelical Mission and the Evangelical Union of South America cooperate with the national Church, the Unión Cristiana Evangélica. The Unión, since 1966, has been an autonomous body.

The mission of the Andes Evangelical Mission (formerly the Bolivian Indian Mission) has been to carry the gospel to the rural people of Bolivia. Crisologo Baron, a Bolivian convert, and George Allan, pioneer missionary, were responsible for the translation of the Quechua New Testament which was completed in 1920, thirteen years after the mission began its activities.

The mission later expanded to work among other Indian tribes.

By 1935, the first Spanish institute for lay workers was conducted. The mission began to concentrate greater effort on the towns and cities of Bolivia.

The Unión has shown healthy growth, particularly since 1954, when the mission began to seek closer ties to other Churches, strengthened the leadership training program, and concentrated on preparing the national Church for autonomy. There is considerable ambiguity as to the correct number of members at present. The Unión has always had a large number of unbaptized believers. Apparently the Unión is in the process of redefining membership. In 1966, there were 7,000 communicant members.

Other Churches

The Pentecostal Churches in Bolivia are growing very slowly. The Assemblies of God represent the general pattern (Figure 32) for the several small Pentecostal denominations, indicating the error in assuming that Pentecostals always grow in Latin America.

The Oregon Friends have established more churches among the Aymaras than have any other Church except the Adventists. The revolution of 1952 and the land reform which followed made Bolivians more receptive to the gospel. The growth of the Friends began in the early 1950's. The Friends' efforts met with notable success in the Yungas, the high valleys leading down the east side of the Andes which have recently opened for settlement.

In addition to the denominations shown on the line graph, about fifteen other denominations have membership of less than 1,000 communicants. Their very slow growth shows that growth is not automatic here. However, what was once a very resistant country for Evangelical church-planting is now becoming very responsive. Problems exist on every side, but they are problems of growth, not of stagnation.

PERU

The majority of the population of Peru, much like in Bolivia, is Amerindian and lives in the highlands of the Andes. One-fifth of the Indian population speaks only Quechua, Aymara, or other indigenous languages. Cultural disparity is one of the major obstacles to programs of development.

THE EVANGELICAL CHURCHES

Evangelicals have had a difficult struggle in Peru trying to establish solid bases upon which they can build. Adventist growth contrasts remarkably with the growth of other Evangelical Churches. The same factors which have hindered economic development have also hindered the growth of the Churches. Total communicants in 1966 numbered about 60,000, nearly half of which are reported by the Adventist Church (Figures 33 and 34).

Figure 33

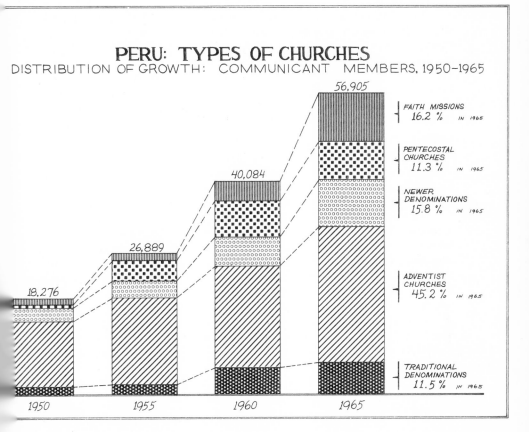

PERU: TYPES OF CHURCHES
DISTRIBUTION OF GROWTH: COMMUNICANT   MEMBERS, 1950-1965

56,905

FAITH MISSIONS
16.2 % IN 1965

PENTECOSTAL
CHURCHES
11.3 % IN 1965

40,084

NEWER
DENOMINATIONS
15.8 % IN 1965

26,889

ADVENTIST
CHURCHES
45.2 % IN 1965

18,276

TRADITIONAL
DENOMINATIONS
11.5 % IN 1965

1950   1955   1960   1965

Adventists

As in Bolivia, the Adventist Church is the largest Evangelical Church in the country, although in Peru it comprises nearly half the Evangelical communicants. Peru and Bolivia together form the Inca Division of the South American Seventh-Day Adventist work. The Adventist church-planting which began initially among the Aymaras around Lake Titicaca has spread north into Peru and south into Bolivia. This Aymara people movement, which accounts for 50 per cent of the Peruvian Adventist membership, is a major factor in the denomination's growth. Another factor is the network of schools similar to those in Bolivia. A large Adventist normal school in Lima trains teachers for their comprehensive school program. Because of the widespread thirst for education in Peru and Bolivia, the Church's emphasis on education is paying off in steady growth.

Figure 34

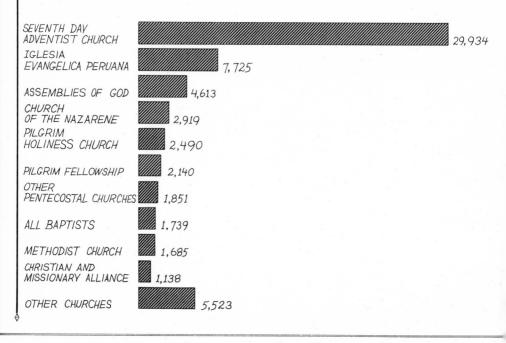

PERU: COMPARATIVE SIZES OF CHURCHES
1967 COMMUNICANT MEMBERSHIP

SEVENTH DAY
ADVENTIST CHURCH — 29,934

IGLESIA
EVANGELICA PERUANA — 7,725

ASSEMBLIES OF GOD — 4,613

CHURCH
OF THE NAZARENE — 2,919

PILGRIM
HOLINESS CHURCH — 2,490

PILGRIM FELLOWSHIP — 2,140

OTHER
PENTECOSTAL CHURCHES — 1,851

ALL BAPTISTS — 1,739

METHODIST CHURCH — 1,685

CHRISTIAN AND
MISSIONARY ALLIANCE — 1,138

OTHER CHURCHES — 5,523

Some Adventist groups have broken away from the Seventh-Day Adventist Church. The largest group is known as Israelitas, one congregation of which is found in the department of Junin in the vicinity of San Ramón. Here close to 1,000 communicants, led by priests with long beards and white robes imitating the priesthood of Aaron, organize their lives around sacrificial worship similar to that found in the Old Testament. Another group, the Reformed Adventists, are known for their legalistic observances. Little other information is available concerning this denomination, although it is believed that they have no more than 500 communicant members.

Iglésia Evangélica Peruana

Founded by John Ritchie through the Evangelical Union of South America, the Iglésia Evangélica Peruana (Evangelical Church of Peru) has developed into a denomination of 150 to 200 churches

Figure 35

PERU: GROWTH OF CHURCHES
1910-1970

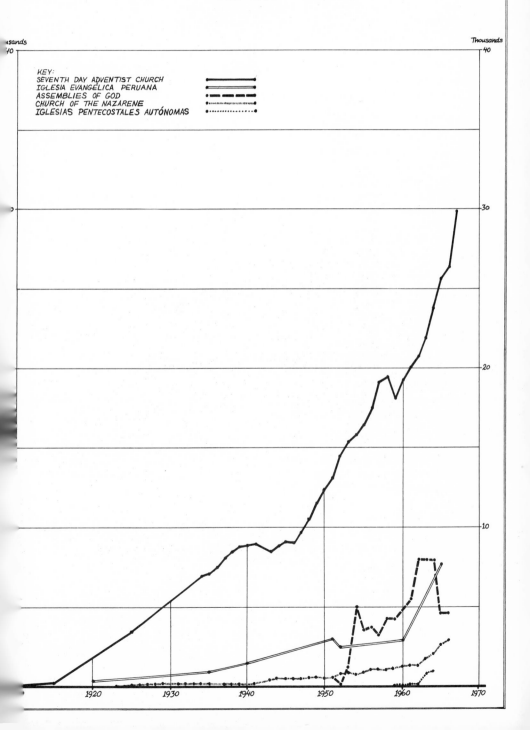

KEY:
SEVENTH DAY ADVENTIST CHURCH
IGLESIA EVANGÉLICA PERUANA
ASSEMBLIES OF GOD
CHURCH OF THE NAZARENE
IGLESIAS PENTECOSTALES AUTÓNOMAS

with approximately four thousand communicants in the center of Peru, and an additional 150 churches and two thousand communicants in the south. Today there are only seven national pastors, although the national leadership tends to fall to these men. The reason, in part, for few pastors within the Church is due to John Ritchie's view of the ministry. He feared the "professionalism" of the ministry and therefore stressed the need for itinerant preachers who would not settle down so readily into professional status.

In its initial stages Ritchie had the key to an indigenous, rapidly expanding Church, but due to a failure to develop a systematic and comprehensive training program, what might have developed into the churches' strength has now become their weakness. The Christian and Missionary Alliance entered Peru in 1923 and began to cooperate with the Evangelical Union of South America in the formation of the Iglésia Evangélica Peruana. Following the principles already established by Ritchie, the churches in that area grew into three presbyteries. Later, in 1937, the Independent Board for Presbyterian Foreign Mission joined the other two missions in the IEP. But in 1944 the Independent Presbyterians split the Church because they felt that the Church was not truly presbyterian, and took with them the presbytery established in the Ayacucho area. Almost ten years later, the Church experienced another split when the Christian and Missionary Alliance separated over the need for ordination and a more defined concept of the ministry.

Prior to this, however, the Alliance had withdrawn from the Lima Bible Institute, which had been initiated as an independent school in conjunction with the Union and the Free Church of Scotland. In 1946, the Alliance initiated its own Bible school in Huanuco. This means that they can more effectively train their leadership within the geographical and cultural boundaries of their Huanuco church. Church growth figures seem to prove the wisdom of their policy.

As has been mentioned, the Achilles' heel of the Iglésia Evangélica Peruana is its training policy. It has fallen to the Lima Bible Institute to train the necessary leadership, but it has not effectively carried this load. The Institute has trained leaders for the *mestizo* culture of the coastal churches or the *mestizo* towns in the highlands, but it has not met the needs of the thirty preachers who itinerate among the Indian churches. At the present time, none of the itinerate preachers has had any serious systematic training. This accentuates the Church's desperate need for serious ministry.

Nazarenes

The Church of the Nazarene has worked in the northern part of Peru only, although two Lima congregations function in the southern border of the district. Most of the membership is among the *mestizos* in the lower socio-economic level. The churches on the coast are generally in a static situation, but the mountain churches are growing, although patterns of social organization make evangelization of a community very difficult. When one extended family comes into the church, other families are reluctant to become Evangelicals.

In 1965 the Nazarenes acknowledged thirty organized congregations, all self-supporting, with a membership of 2,919 and an additional 1,000 probationers. The largest Nazarene congregation is located in Chiclayo, a commercial and agricultural center in the northern coastal region. Eighteen missionaries serve the mission, including four in pastorates. Most are engaged in institutional work or serve as supervisors of a mission-established network of zones. An acute shortage of Peruvian leadership is apparent, since only forty-two national workers and lay leaders were reported in 1965, and only six ordained ministers were on the active list.

Other Churches

The Pentecostal Churches are beginning to grow, although slowly as in Bolivia. The erratic line of growth (Figure 35) of the Assemblies of God is due both to faulty statistics and losses caused by splits.

Chapter Six

GRAN COLOMBIA: ECUADOR, COLOMBIA, AND VENEZUELA

The Republic of Gran Colombia was formed at the time of independence in 1819 under the leadership of Simon Bolívar, who then became President. Although Venezuela and Ecuador seceded in 1830, the republics still reflect common bonds which were forged during their struggle for independence.

Ecuador, Colombia, and Venezuela are united by the rugged northern reaches of the Andes; Colombia and Venezuela are as two sisters looking out over the Caribbean together.

ECUADOR

A double ridge of the Andes divides this small country into three major geographical regions. The Sierra, constituted by the highland valleys framed by the mountains, contains most of the population as well as the capital, Quito. The low, forested Oriente, containing many of the headwaters of the Amazon, is largely unexplored and contains few inhabitants. The Coast is dominated by Guayaquil, Ecuador's largest city. Strong migration from the Sierra to the Coast is making the latter a fast-developing area.

THE EVANGELICAL CHURCHES

The growth of the Evangelical Churches in this Andean country has been very slow. It must be remembered, however, that Ecuador was one of the last Latin American countries to be open to Protestant work, due to a strongly entrenched Roman Catholic Church. The landed aristocracy did not intend to permit Evangelicals to subvert the people. Since most of the Indians were located on haciendas and thus firmly under control of their feudal lords, the chief populations open to the Evangelical movement were the Spanish-speaking citizens of *mestizo* towns, yet these were firmly under control of the Roman Catholic Church. Migration to the cities, industrialization, settlement of new lands, and other factors which would help the Evangelical cause all came late and in small quantity. As a result, while many

118

missionaries have located in Ecuador, the growth of the Evangelical Churches has been small.

Approximately 360 Evangelical missionaries were working in Ecuador in 1967 among twelve thousand Evangelical communicants. Even if the missionaries working with radio station HCJB were deducted from this total, the ratio of missionaries to communicant Evangelicals is one to fifty — one of the highest in Latin America. If the missionaries at HCJB are included, the ratio rises to one missionary to thirty-four communicants. No other country in Latin America has such a high concentration of missionaries for such a small evangelical membership — or such large resources for so little church growth.

The people movement of the Aymara Indians within the Seventh-Day Adventist Church which occurred about 1920 around Lake Titicaca accustomed the Indians in southern Peru and Bolivia to the thought of becoming Evangelicals; nothing close to this has occurred in Ecuador. The Indians have, for the most part, remained unresponsive to Evangelical work. Very few of the missionaries have become fluent in Quichua and have conducted their work in Spanish instead.

Figure 36

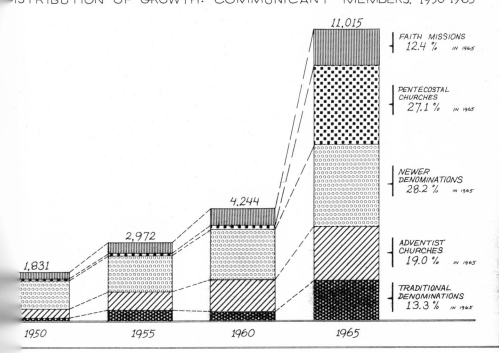

ECUADOR: TYPES OF CHURCHES
DISTRIBUTION OF GROWTH: COMMUNICANT MEMBERS, 1950-1965

11,015

FAITH MISSIONS
12.4 %   IN 1965

PENTECOSTAL CHURCHES
27.1 %   IN 1965

NEWER DENOMINATIONS
28.2 %   IN 1965

ADVENTIST CHURCHES
19.0 %   IN 1965

TRADITIONAL DENOMINATIONS
13.3 %   IN 1965

4,244

2,972

1,831

1950   1955   1960   1965

Figure 37

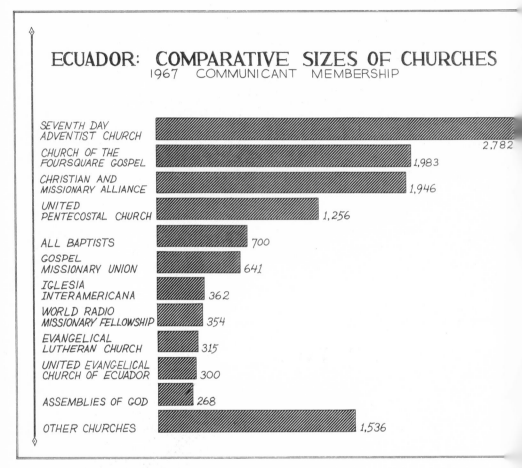

ECUADOR: COMPARATIVE SIZES OF CHURCHES
1967 COMMUNICANT MEMBERSHIP

SEVENTH DAY ADVENTIST CHURCH — 2,782
CHURCH OF THE FOURSQUARE GOSPEL — 1,983
CHRISTIAN AND MISSIONARY ALLIANCE — 1,946
UNITED PENTECOSTAL CHURCH — 1,256
ALL BAPTISTS — 700
GOSPEL MISSIONARY UNION — 641
IGLESIA INTERAMERICANA — 362
WORLD RADIO MISSIONARY FELLOWSHIP — 354
EVANGELICAL LUTHERAN CHURCH — 315
UNITED EVANGELICAL CHURCH OF ECUADOR — 300
ASSEMBLIES OF GOD — 268
OTHER CHURCHES — 1,536

The growth of the Evangelical Churches from 1950 to 1965 is shown in Figure 36.

World Radio Missionary Fellowship

Perhaps the most widely known Evangelical ministry in Ecuador is that of radio station HCJB, which has been located in Ecuador since about 1935. The broadcasts from high in the Andes to all of Latin America have probably paved the way for church-planting in other countries.

About 100 missionaries are involved in the work of station HCJB, resulting in a heavy concentration of foreign personnel in Quito. A few churches have been established by them; in 1966 they reported seven churches, seven church schools, and 354 communicant members. A strong literature program and correspondence program

Figure 38

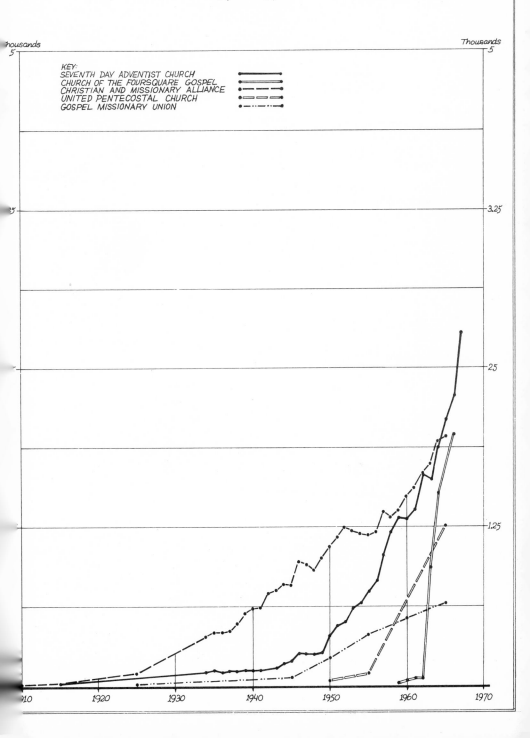

ECUADOR: GROWTH OF CHURCHES
1910-1970

KEY:
SEVENTH DAY ADVENTIST CHURCH
CHURCH OF THE FOURSQUARE GOSPEL
CHRISTIAN AND MISSIONARY ALLIANCE
UNITED PENTECOSTAL CHURCH
GOSPEL MISSIONARY UNION

Thousands

5

3.25

25

1.25

1910   1920   1930   1940   1950   1960   1970

in Bible have been established, which would indicate that a department designated for the planting and nurture of churches could also be established. Missionaries and nationals working at the station and living suitably dispersed throughout Quito and its environs could thereby become responsible for planting many small congregations. (The Latin America Mission in Costa Rica faced a similar problem, for many years having only one church, the Templo Bíblico in San José. They began to urge their eighty or so missionaries to plant churches throughout the city, resulting in about a dozen churches fathered by missionaries of the Latin America Mission.)

Pentecostal Churches

The comparison by total size of the Pentecostal Churches and non-Pentecostal Churches is shown in Figure 37. Like most Evangelical work in Ecuador, the churches are young. The growth of the Pentecostal Churches is best illustrated by the graph line of the Church of the Foursquare Gospel (Figure 38). Missionary work was begun in 1957, and by 1962 two churches in Guayaquil and El Milagro were organized, reporting a total membership of 70 communicants. In that same year Pedro Aguirre, a United States citizen of Mexican descent, visited Ecuador and organized a city-wide campaign in Guayaquil, urging all other Evangelical missions and Churches to participate. The preacher was Roberto Espinoza, and the ministry of healing attracted thousands. Newsmen publicized the unusual events and the meetings were broadcast to all parts of the country. Attendance reached 35,000. The campaign resulted in the addition of 600 new members to the small congregation in Guayaquil. The church had to move from the small building to an open lot where a simple roof was erected until a central church could be built. In 1965 this congregation had grown to 900 members with a church school of 600 as well as twelve other congregations in the city.

The United Pentecostal Church has grown in a similar way. Both Churches are young and have grown so fast that seasoned leadership has not developed, however. The lay people are enthusiastic and witness openly to their experiences. The Pentecostal success in Guayaquil is due partly to the accelerating migration from the high country. The population of Guayaquil was approaching 600,000 by 1966.

Gospel Missionary Union

The Quichua Indians of Ecuador are supposedly dull, withdrawn, and resistant. Many missionaries have held this particular opinion mainly because their approach has been through the Spanish language. When this error is corrected, perhaps then missions will find a receptivity among the Indians. The Gospel Missionary Union has begun work among the Quichua and Jivaro Indians; two primary schools have been established. Forty missionaries assist in the work, which includes a bookstore in Guayaquil, a hospital, two clinics, and three small radio stations, two of which are used for the hospital. The communicant membership reported in 1961 was 650, with 31 churches and six national pastors. Only nine of the churches, however, have more than 20 members. The historical and ethnological factors of Evangelical work among the Quichuas has been thoroughly treated by Donald Dilworth in his thesis, "The Evangelization of the Quichuas of Ecuador" (1967).

Other Churches

The Christian and Missionary Alliance began work in Ecuador in 1897, only one year after the Gospel Missionary Union. By 1935 they reported 400 communicant members. In 1966 they reported 1,945 communicants, comprising the third largest Church in Ecuador.

The Oriental Missionary Society has fathered a group of small churches, the Interamerican Church, which began in 1954 with a city-wide evangelistic campaign. In 1955 the first church was organized with five communicant members. Membership has grown since that time to 362 communicants in nine churches.

The martyrdom in 1956 of the five missionaries who were attempting communication with the Auca Indians in the Oriente still remains a vivid memory in the minds of those who have an active interest in the growth of the Evangelical Church in Ecuador. The epilogue to the Auca tragedy is the victorious entry into the Auca tribe by other missionaries and the subsequent acceptance of Jesus Christ by some of these Indians. The power of the gospel to reach Auca, Quichua, and *mestizos* in Ecuador is real. Walls of hate, prejudice, and idolatry are falling as Ecuador finds itself in the midst of rapid social change. Mighty movements among the Quichua Indians should be increasingly possible as land reforms are instituted. Evangelicals are unanimous in their belief that the current situation constitutes a day of change for Ecuador. The past decade of growth supports this conviction.

COLOMBIA

The great plains which are parched and flooded each year in turn and the rain forests of the Amazon, which together constitute a major part of the land of Colombia and Venezuela, are quite unhospitable to the people. As a result, the bulk of the Colombians live in the mountain valleys of the Andes, and economic activity is confined to the long valleys nourished by the Magdalena and Cauca Rivers which provide access to the Caribbean Sea. The mountain barriers hinder east-west communication and result in isolated human islands.

The majority of the population, estimated in mid-1967 to be

18.8 million, is found in a network of towns and cities of the highlands. Since 1950 rural to urban migration has produced major changes in the Colombian scene. The 65 per cent of the population which lived in highland rural areas in 1940 has decreased to less than 50 per cent in 1966. Urban networks have formed around Bogotá; Medellin, the industrial and coffee center; Cali, in the Cauca Valley; and Barranquilla, the fluvial port. Ten other cities now have more than 150,000 inhabitants each.

La Violencia

The growth and development of the Evangelical Churches in Colombia must be seen in the light of the historic political struggle which lasted from 1946 to 1961: *La Violencia*. The liberal party provided the ignition spark in 1946 when they accused the conservatives of unfairly using the police force for their own gains. By 1948 riots had disrupted public services in the Departments of Valle and Santander and the cities of Cali and Bogotá. Leaders of capital and labor were pitted against each other in what appeared to be the beginning of a revolution. In that same year the popular leader of the liberal party, Gaitan, was assassinated in the streets of Bogotá, and the riots and arson which followed left few public buildings undamaged.

Violence soon spread over the entire country, angry mobs defacing or burning schools, churches, and convents, and attacking priests, political leaders, and Evangelical pastors. Whole villages engaged in guerilla warfare, and many were wiped out in the process. During this period thousands of farmers from devastated areas fled to towns and cities for protection. Some even crossed into Venezuela seeking safety.

After 1950, during the administration of the conservative Gomez, all liberals were considered communists, bandits, and lawbreakers. This stirred up much religious hatred, since most Protestants were followers of the liberal party. Fanatical elements within the Roman Catholic Church, including many priests, took advantage of *La Violencia* to persecute the Evangelicals. Most suffering occurred in the highlands from Santander to the Cauca Valley and in the upper regions of the Magdalena Valley.

Acts of violence began to decrease in 1958; thereafter, control was gradually exercised by the National Front, a new political organization acting within the conservative party, which transferred rule from the military to an elective government. After 1959 the number of deaths due to political feuding and banditry dropped from 10,000 each year to only a few hundred. Many guerilla chiefs, who during the Violence had flourished on highly organized systems of extortion and blackmail operating behind legal fronts, returned to their homes to assume prominent political leadership.

The national anguish uprooted thousands of people, cut traditional family ties, and effected serious changes in the social classes, public and private institutions, political affairs, and the customs and cultures of the Colombians. If we are to understand the state of the Evangelical Churches in Colombia today, we must keep in mind this period of turmoil and suffering.

Some observers suggest that *La Violencia* gave the Evangelicals much "free publicity." People who never thought about the Evangelical Church soon became aware of its position. Converts of this period had to be sincere, since conversion was a costly business. Open evangelistic meetings were impossible, so laymen became evangelists.

Figure 39

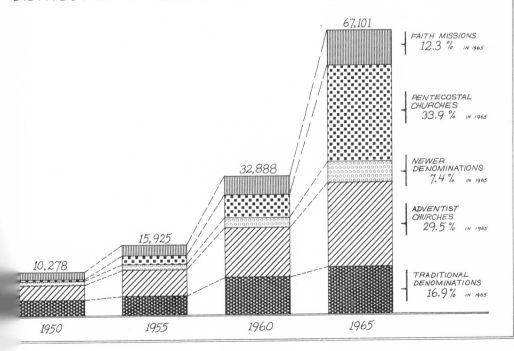

COLOMBIA: TYPES OF CHURCHES

DISTRIBUTION OF GROWTH: COMMUNICANT MEMBERS, 1950-1965

67,101

FAITH MISSIONS
12.3 % IN 1965

PENTECOSTAL CHURCHES
33.9 % IN 1965

32,888

NEWER DENOMINATIONS
7.4 % IN 1965

ADVENTIST CHURCHES
29.5 % IN 1965

15,925

10,278

TRADITIONAL DENOMINATIONS
16.9 % IN 1965

1950   1955   1960   1965

Figure 40

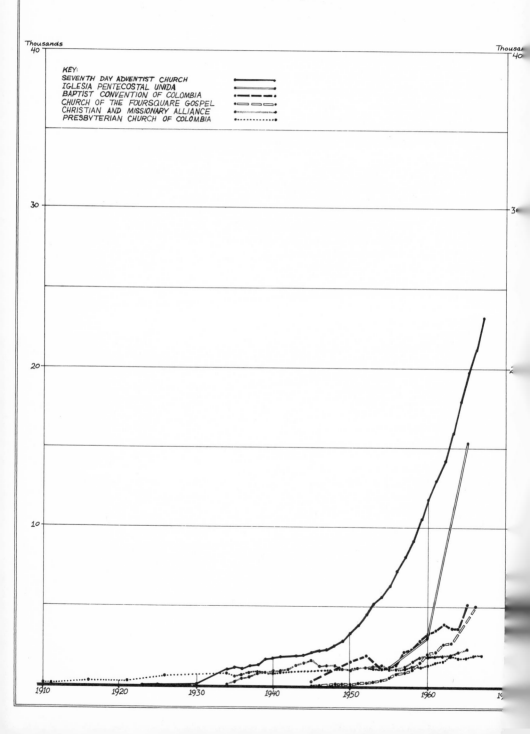

COLOMBIA: GROWTH OF CHURCHES
1910-1970

KEY:
SEVENTH DAY ADVENTIST CHURCH
IGLESIA PENTECOSTAL UNIDA
BAPTIST CONVENTION OF COLOMBIA
CHURCH OF THE FOURSQUARE GOSPEL
CHRISTIAN AND MISSIONARY ALLIANCE
PRESBYTERIAN CHURCH OF COLOMBIA

The missionary spirit engendered in the days of persecution has continued in many churches and coincides with a new wave of receptivity among certain elements of the population.

THE EVANGELICAL CHURCHES

The total number of communicants reported for 1967 was over 70,000 — seven times the total for 1950. Growth of the various types of churches is illustrated in Figure 39; the rate of increase for individual Churches and missions can be seen in the following table, the data for which were reported by the Evangelical Confederation of Colombia in 1966.

RATE OF GROWTH OF THE
EVANGELICAL CHURCHES OF COLOMBIA, 1960-1966

	Communicants		Increase
	1960	1966	%
Alianza Cristiana y Misionera Colombiana	1571	1988	26.5
Asambleas de Dios	159	596	274.8
Asociación de Iglésias Evangélicas del Caribe	914	1200	23.9
Asociación de Iglésias Evangélicas del Magdalena	361	304	-15.8
Asociación de Iglésias Evangélicas Interamericanas	588	849	44.4
Congregaciones Independientes	...	158	...
Convención Bautista de Colombia	3422	4021	17.5
Cruzada Hispanoamericana	164	675	311.6
Embajadores Cristianos de Colombia (Asambleas de Jesucristo)	100	275	175.0
Federación Luterana Mundial, Comisión para America Latina	1380	936	-32.2
Hermanos Menonitas	202	350	73.3
Iglésia Adventista del Séptimo Día	11866	19213	61.9
Iglésia Bautista Independiente	9	25	177.7
Iglésia Cruzada Evangélica	692	1000	44.5
Iglésia Cristiana del Norte	125	220	76.0
Iglésia de Dios	219	775	253.9
Iglésia de Dios Pentecostal	....	282	....
Iglésia Episcopal	1105	1272	15.1
Iglésia Evangélica Cristiana, Independiente	....	35	....
Iglésia Evangélica Cristiana, Casa de Oración	....	80	....
Iglésia Evangélica Cuadrangular	1524	3620	137.5
Iglésia Evangélica Luterana	500	890	78.0
Iglésia Fundamental Trinitária	30	...	....
Iglésia Hermanos Cristianos	50	408	716.0
Iglésia Pentecostal Unida	3000	15352	411.7
Iglésia Presbiteriana Cumberland	859	833	-3.0
Iglésia Presbiteriana de Colombia	1684	1882	8.2
Misión a las Tribus Nuevas	300	2900	866.7
Misión Alianza Evangélicas	665	623	-6.3
Misión Evangélica de Colombia	57	57	0.0
Misión Indígena de Sur America	132	156	18.2

| | Communicants | | Increase |
	1960	1966	%
Misión Menonita Colombiana	143	205	46.2
Misión Metodista Wesleyana	191	387	102.6
Misión Panamericana	105	862	720.9
Misiónes Mundiales	....	30	....
Sociedad de Amigos	....	30	....
Sociedad Misionera Suramericana	207	...	....
Union Church de Bogotá	196	225	14.8
Unión Misionera Evangélica	764	1096	43.5

(CEDEC 1966)

Christian and Missionary Alliance

Alliance churches are located in the economically depressed south-west rural areas, and the greatest concentration of the churches falls in an area of former violence which still continues sporadically. Emigration to the cities makes it difficult for the congregations to support paid pastors unless radical social change and land reform should occur. Note the peak of 1945, and then the decline and pla-teau which ended in 1957 (Figure 40). It was not until 1959 that the Christian and Missionary Alliance surpassed the total for 1945.

Other factors may have contributed to the decline of the Alliance churches since 1945: (1) a rigid adherence to "indigenous" principles without suitable adaptation to changing circumstances (at the peak of the Violence, for example, the mission reallocated 25 per cent of the subsidy to a building program, but then held the Church re-sponsible for continuing all former programs which had been financed by subsidy, a decision which the Church still does not understand); (2) maintenance of an inadequate ministerial training program; (3) churches which lean on the mission, requesting missionaries to act as pastors; (4) insufficient sharing of authority with nationals. Con-sequently national leaders have charged that they are not permitted to solve their own problems or direct their work. Certainly much is to be said for the side of the mission, yet unless nationals have the opportunity of planning, solving problems, making mistakes, and administering, they have little interest in the enterprise. It is not surprising that, even after the Violence subsided, the Alliance has shown only moderate growth.

Gospel Missionary Union

The Violence had drastic effects on the work of the Gospel Missionary Union: twenty-four out of thirty-two churches were lost within two years. The 1,060 communicant members reported in 1948 had declined to less than 300 in 1955 and only twelve churches remained. Churches in the Departments of Cauca, Valle, Caldas, and Chocó had lost over 500 communicants. This year (1955) was the turning point, and by 1960 the Union reported 28 churches with

949 communicants. By 1966 the Union had 1,096 communicants, having spent eighteen years regaining the members lost during the Violence.

Distinct problems resulting from these years of Violence must be faced by the mission: (1) members who moved to the cities to escape persecution found no churches of their own denomination, so they joined new churches and have remained in them; (2) many pastors were lost in the same manner; (3) the mission lacked organization; (4) missionary-national tensions increased; and (5) resources have been fed into low-potential areas. A major problem for this mission is its ties to narrow indigenous principles: a church must succeed on its own or die. The Union does not spend funds on church-planting, but it does emphasize a network of schools. This heightens the tension that exists between missionaries and underpaid national pastors. Churches founded by a missionary prosper until he leaves, taking his equipment, money, and influence with him. A national pastor following the missionary has great difficulty.

Despite these obstacles, the Gospel Missionary Union has shown great courage and dedication. A new hope and optimism prevails within the Union, an indication of their willingness to take drastic steps leading to the solution of their growth problems.

Mennonite Brethren

The Mennonite Brethren began work in the humid tropical plains of the Cauca and San Juan rivers in 1945. After fifteen years, their Church reported 200 communicants and thirteen missionary couples were working among them. Many of the believers were moving to Cali, so in 1957 some of the missionaries decided to move with their converts to the city. This eventually led the mission to change its emphasis from jungle activity to church-planting in the city. The new growth of the church is indicated by their yearly record of baptisms from 1960 to 1965: 56, 42, 89, 74, 69, and 96. In 1966, after a complete relocation of their work, the Mennonites reported 350 communicants; this number has increased to 423.

In 1965 the Mennonites decided to begin twelve new churches; already seven of these have been established. The mission matches funds for evangelism with the Church. Although they planted a church in a middle class district in Cali, they have been unable to attract converts from this middle class. Instead their members are from the lower class living in the surrounding *barrios*. This one church has now planted four daughter congregations in the *barrios*. The Mennonites find themselves in a responsive population open for planting churches.

Other Churches

Four other Churches show increase in spite of the Violence.

The Adventists grew from 2,000 to 11,000, and the United Pentecostal Church and the Foursquare Church both show an uninterrupted pattern of growth (Figure 40). The New Tribes Mission working in the jungle lowlands immediately after the Violence, shows a fantastic increase from 300 to 2,900 between 1960 and 1966.

High-potential areas do not mean automatic growth. They do show, however, that Evangelicals with vision, aggressive plans for evangelism, courage to shift resources and manpower, and spiritual dynamic are likely to see the multiplication of churches.

VENEZUELA

The development of a huge oil industry in Venezuela has re-

Figure 41

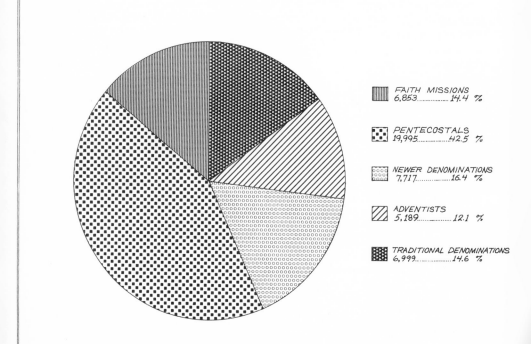

VENEZUELA: TYPES OF CHURCHES. 1965

FAITH MISSIONS
6,853..............14.4 %

PENTECOSTALS
19,995..............42.5 %

NEWER DENOMINATIONS
7,717..............16.4 %

ADVENTISTS
5,189..............12.1 %

TRADITIONAL DENOMINATIONS
6,999..............14.6 %

placed estate agriculture as the basis for economy, resulting in one of the healthiest economies of Latin American countries, and also one of the highest standards of living. Unfortunately, the proved oil reserves of Venezuela are limited. In 1959 a study by the International Bank for Reconstruction and Development estimated that at the current rate of output, proved reserves would be depleted by 1977 (Department of the Army 1964: 383).

The oil revenues, however, are wisely being used to diversify and broaden the economic base. Even if no more oil is found, Venezuela will continue to enjoy prosperity. The pattern of economic development has resulted in a series of migrations from rural areas to urban and industrial centers. The exploitation of oil, first in the west and later in the east, and the growth of the industrial complex in the general area of Caracas have attracted large numbers of workers. This trend is likely to continue as the east develops. The Venezuelan government is encouraging investment in the industrial development of the rich natural resources of the Guayana region. The Guri Dam on the Orinoco River is the hub of the largest hydroelectric project in the world.

THE EVANGELICAL CHURCHES

Venezuela was one of the last countries of Latin America to be evangelized. It was not until the early part of this century that missions began to arrive in force. The first missionaries arrived at a time of strong anti-foreign feeling. This feeling was the result of the German and British blockade of Venezuelan ports in 1902. President Cipriano Castro had tried to curb the power of foreign business interests in the country. The blockade was in retaliation for his action.

To an extent not found anywhere else in Latin America, mission work in Venezuela has been conducted on a mission compound basis. This isolationism on the part of the missionaries began as a reaction to anti-foreign sentiments of the Venezuelans, and has increased with the passing of time. Isolation from society has hindered church growth, however.

At present there are approximately 47,000 communicant members in the Evangelical Churches in Venezuela. Except for the Apure Church under the direction of Aristides Dias, most of them are found in the area of Venezuela which has seen the greatest economic development and where there is the greatest concentration of population.

Plymouth Brethren

The largest Evangelical denomination in Venezuela is the fellowship of Plymouth Brethren churches. Stephen Adams, one of the first Brethren missionaries, arrived in 1910. Though the Brethren missionaries participated in the original comity arrangement, they have since lived in almost total isolation from the rest of the Evangelicals. They have experienced almost uninterrupted progress since they began. In the early 1950's the growth accelerated, and from a total of 2,000 members in 1955 they have grown to 7,000 in 1967.

Because the Brethren churches exist in isolation from other churches, most Evangelicals in Venezuela are unaware of the phenomenal growth they have enjoyed. The Evangelical Churches would do well to study the Brethren pattern of evangelism through lay witness and the emphasis the Brethren place on incorporating converts into the life and activity of the church. Their strong teaching program prepares their members effectively to communicate the gospel.

Adventists

Although the growth pattern of the Seventh-Day Adventist Church (Figure 43) shows several short declines, it is overall one

Figure 42

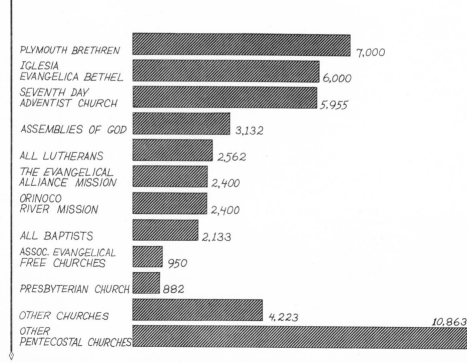

VENEZUELA: COMPARATIVE SIZES OF CHURCHES
1967 COMMUNICANT MEMBERSHIP

PLYMOUTH BRETHREN	7,000
IGLESIA EVANGELICA BETHEL	6,000
SEVENTH DAY ADVENTIST CHURCH	5,955
ASSEMBLIES OF GOD	3,132
ALL LUTHERANS	2,562
THE EVANGELICAL ALLIANCE MISSION	2,400
ORINOCO RIVER MISSION	2,400
ALL BAPTISTS	2,133
ASSOC. EVANGELICAL FREE CHURCHES	950
PRESBYTERIAN CHURCH	882
OTHER CHURCHES	4,223
OTHER PENTECOSTAL CHURCHES	10,863

Figure 43

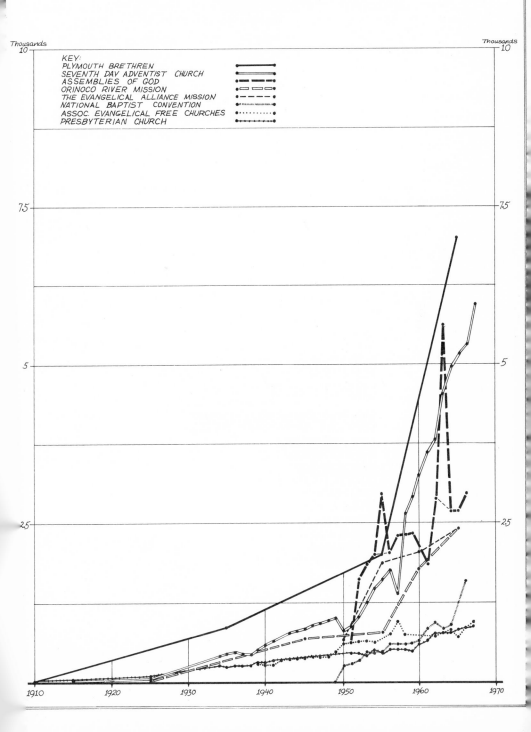

VENEZUELA: GROWTH OF CHURCHES
1910-1970

KEY:
PLYMOUTH BRETHREN
SEVENTH DAY ADVENTIST CHURCH
ASSEMBLIES OF GOD
ORINOCO RIVER MISSION
THE EVANGELICAL ALLIANCE MISSION
NATIONAL BAPTIST CONVENTION
ASSOC. EVANGELICAL FREE CHURCHES
PRESBYTERIAN CHURCH

of constant and accelerating growth. The Adventist Church has grown from 1,400 members in 1957 to 5,955 communicants in 1966. This is one of the best growth rates of Churches in Venezuela, although the Adventist Church has little contact with other Churches.

Orinoco River Mission

This faith mission arrived in Venezuela in 1918 in the person of Van Eddings, the first missionary. The present communicant membership total is 2,400 in 66 churches, an average of 36 members per congregation, typical of Venezuela. Another 1,400 Evangelicals in eastern Venezuela belong to churches which were once affiliated with the Orinoco River Mission in the Asociación de Iglésias Evangélicas en el Oriente, but which are now independent.

The plateau on the growth curve between 1948 and 1956 may be explained by the breakaway of churches and by migration of church members to other parts of the country. The comity agreement hindered the mission's providing pastoral care to these members in their new locations. The current industrial development of eastern Venezuela, with its attendant demands for a large labor force, provides the opportunity for increased church growth. The Churches affiliated with the Orinoco River Mission may be able to recoup what they have lost to other areas.

Evangelical Alliance Mission (TEAM)

The first missionaries arrived in 1906, and since then the work has been concentrated in the western part of the country. TEAM headquarters are located in the city of Maracaibo, which is the center of the western oil fields.

The membership totals for the churches affiliated with TEAM reached about 2,400 in 1966, an average of 45 members per missionary. This mission has suffered more than most in Venezuela due to breakaways to other denominations. There are more than 25 churches which were begun by TEAM and now belong to other denominations. The plateau on the growth curve (Figure 43) reflects this.

Evangelical Free Church

Independent Free Church missionaries began work in Venezuela in 1898, and in 1920 the work was taken over by the mission of the Evangelical Free Church in North America. In sixty years, it has grown to 950 communicants; its twenty-three churches and sixteen national pastors are all located in central Venezuela, in the general area assigned to them by comity agreements.

Until 1956 national pastors were heavily subsidized. However, over a period of several years these subsidies were gradually diminished in size. By 1966, the mission was no longer providing any pastoral support. This achievement was due in large part to a reduction of pastors' income, rather than to increase in the amount of money raised by the churches. The affairs of the Evangelical Free Church in Venezuela are decided at joint meetings of Church and mission, at which the influence of the mission predominates.

In the decade between 1953 and 1963, eight new churches were established, but two larger churches broke away from the association. This latter loss of membership is shown by the drops in the graph line (Figure 43). The missionaries are concerned that the new churches they are founding should be turned over to national leaders, but such leaders are not available. Other missions face this same leadership problem, which is at least partially a result of a lingering paternalism and cultural isolation.

Presbyterians

Theodore Pond, the first Presbyterian missionary, arrived in Caracas in 1897. Yet, after seventy years, the Presbyterian Church reports a communicant membership of only 882, while other Churches have achieved much greater growth.

The emphasis of the Presbyterian mission in Venezuela has been education. The Colegio Americano in Caracas absorbed the time and attention of the missionaries for many years. Educational projects such as this were maintained at the expense of an effective evangelism program.

In 1910, a group of recently arrived Armenian immigrants appealed to the Presbyterian missionaries for evangelistic and pastoral assistance. Their request was turned down because of lack of funds and personnel for this "extra work." This represents one of the greatest missed opportunities in Evangelical history in Venezuela. The group was lost to the Evangelicals permanently as a result. A sizable colony of active Evangelicals which was in the process of integrating into national life might have been just the thing to spark a rapid increase in church membership.

For many years, the Presbyterian Church in Venezuela was hampered by the lack of a national clergy. The churches called pastors from other Latin American countries. Only in the last few years has the situation changed. In recent years two Venezuelans were ordained into the ministry. There are several other candidates who are preparing themselves for the ministry. The improvement in this area promises to change the growth pattern of the Church.

Baptists

Southern Baptists came to Venezuela in 1950 and began their work by taking over a number of existing Evangelical churches. The extreme form of congregational polity which has characterized most of the missions at work in Venezuela has created an atmosphere in which denominational ties are comparatively loose. The phenomenon of a church breaking away from one denomination to join another or to become independent is not uncommon.

The 1950 Baptist membership of 273 had grown to 1,605 by 1966, at which time there were twenty-one churches, eleven national pastors, and five missionaries serving as pastors. Some of the national Baptist pastors were trained at the Bible institute operated by Orinoco River Mission and TEAM. This is in contrast to the pattern in other Latin American countries: usually the Southern Baptists have begun their missionary work by establishing a seminary. The Baptists feel that they ought to train their own men rather than entrust them to other Churches. In keeping with this feeling they are now sending Venezuelan pastoral candidates to their International Seminary in Cali. They plan to establish a Baptist seminary in Venezuela.

One of the gravest problems for the Baptists in Venezuela is that the churches pastored by missionaries tend to grow more than churches pastored by nationals. This may be due to the greater resources at the command of the missionaries; to a lack of know-how on the part of the nationals; to overriding missionary-national tensions which dissipate the energies of the nationals, or to a feeling on the part of the nationals that they have no real stake in the growth and progress of their Church. Whatever the explanation, this problem must be solved if all Baptist churches are to enjoy a healthy rate of growth.

Other Churches

Four of the largest denominations in Venezuela are not included in the line graph (Figure 43) because their growth histories are not available. These are the Iglésia Evangelica Bethel (Bethel Evangelical Church), the Iglésia Ebenezer (Ebenezer Church), the Unión Pentecostal Venezolana (Venezuelan Pentecostal Union), and the Lutheran Church (Figure 42).

The Bethel Church was begun by Aristides Dias, a *mestizo* cattle buyer who found a Bible and was converted by reading it. From his evangelistic efforts has grown a group of over 150 churches, most of which are in the State of Apure in southern Venezuela. This Church has developed without outside guidance or aid. A historical, statistical record of the growth of these churches does not exist. In 1966, this Church was estimated to have approximately 6,000 communicant members.

The Iglésia Ebenezer is a group of Pentecostal churches, some of which formerly belonged to other denominations. They are the results of the campaigns conducted in Venezuela by the North American evangelist, A. A. Allen. Annual membership totals do not exist for these churches, but estimates place membership at 5,000.

The Unión Pentecostal is a split from the Assemblies of God and is presently receiving aid from the Disciples of Christ of Puerto Rico. Present membership is estimated at 2,800; annual growth totals are not available.

The first missionary of the Assemblies of God arrived before 1910. Since then the Assemblies have grown to a total of 3,132 communicants in 1966. They are at present the third largest Evangelical Church in Venezuela.

The Lutheran Church in Venezuela attempts to provide pastoral care for Lutheran immigrants. The 1966 membership total of 2,618 represents the size of the Lutheran colony rather than the result of growth by conversion from the world.

Chapter Seven

PANAMA AND CENTRAL AMERICA: PANAMA, COSTA RICA, NICARAGUA, EL SALVADOR, HONDURAS, AND GUATEMALA

For many years dismissed as the "banana republics," the tapering land mass separating Mexico from South America has always been one of the least-known areas in the new world. The difficult terrain has been an obstacle to the development of commerce and sense of unity. The social structure of the area is far from uniform: Costa Rica's citizens are largely of European stock; Guatemalans are mainly Indians, and Negroes are concentrated in the hot, coastal areas. The cities are small and most of the people live in the rural areas. The recent development of the Central American Common Market, however, not only is advancing the economy of the whole area, but also is producing stronger political ties.

PANAMA

The population of Panama — 1.2 million — is small indeed compared with most Latin American nations. In the twentieth century, Panama has been the focus of world attention to a degree much greater than the size of the country might indicate. In order to build the Panama Canal, the United States engineered a revolt by which Panama separated from Colombia and became a separate nation. By the terms of the ensuing treaty the United States has exercised a dominant role in the internal affairs of the country. The Canal Zone, fifty miles long and ten miles wide, is under the jurisdiction of the United States.

Panama is also divided linguistically. The older West Indian Negroes still prefer English although the younger generation is integrating into the Spanish-speaking culture. In addition there is a large English-speaking population in the Canal Zone. In order for church membership totals to be meaningful, these homogeneous units must be recognized and recorded separately.

The Evangelical Churches

The Canal Zone and the Republic of Panama together total 37,000 communicants and will be considered as a statistical whole. The growth of the types of churches can be seen in Figure 44.

The largest Church in Panama is the Foursquare Gospel, which began in 1928 with the arrival of the Edwards. By 1930 there were at least 250 believers in the Church at Frijoles. In 1937 property was purchased in Panama City where the Foursquare Church today has a membership of more than 500 members. Lay preachers played a decisive role in the Church's growth, and by 1964 churches had been established in all of the provinces in Panama except one (Butler 1964:60). The Church has 163 national workers, 128 churches, 65 meeting places, 10,276 baptized members, two Bible schools, and a program of brief training institutes. The membership is 95 per cent Spanish speaking.

Figure 44

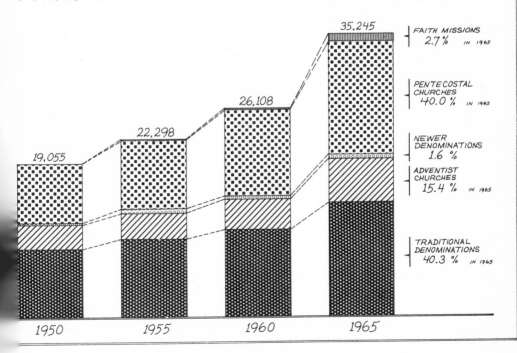

PANAMA: TYPES OF CHURCHES
DISTRIBUTION OF GROWTH: COMMUNICANT MEMBERS, 1950-1965

Figure 45

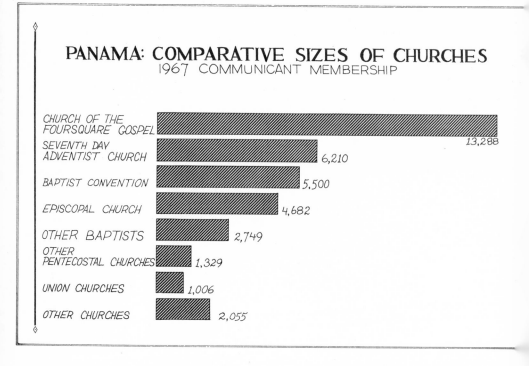

PANAMA: COMPARATIVE SIZES OF CHURCHES
1967 COMMUNICANT MEMBERSHIP

CHURCH OF THE FOURSQUARE GOSPEL — 13,288
SEVENTH DAY ADVENTIST CHURCH — 6,210
BAPTIST CONVENTION — 5,500
EPISCOPAL CHURCH — 4,682
OTHER BAPTISTS — 2,749
OTHER PENTECOSTAL CHURCHES — 1,329
UNION CHURCHES — 1,006
OTHER CHURCHES — 2,055

The Episcopal Church is composed of about 3,000 West Indian Panamanians and about 700 citizens of the United States, a small section of the large North American population found in the Canal Zone. The transient population accounts for the large fluctuations which occur from year to year, typical of Churches in Panama.

The Seventh-Day Adventist Church has been able to achieve steady growth. It is composed of West Indian Panamanians (40 per cent) and of Indians (20 per cent).

The Baptist Convention after two decades of slow growth beginning in 1940 has been growing rapidly. One-third of its membership is West Indian, one-third Indian, and the rest is found among the Spanish-speaking Panamanians and the North Americans in the Canal Zone. The past few years have seen some encouraging advances among the Indians, and optimism concerning church-planting is running high among Baptists.

The Church of God of Cleveland, Tennessee, has shown notable growth between 1955 and 1966. This Pentecostal Church has not grown as rapidly as the Baptists, but has increased fourfold since 1950.

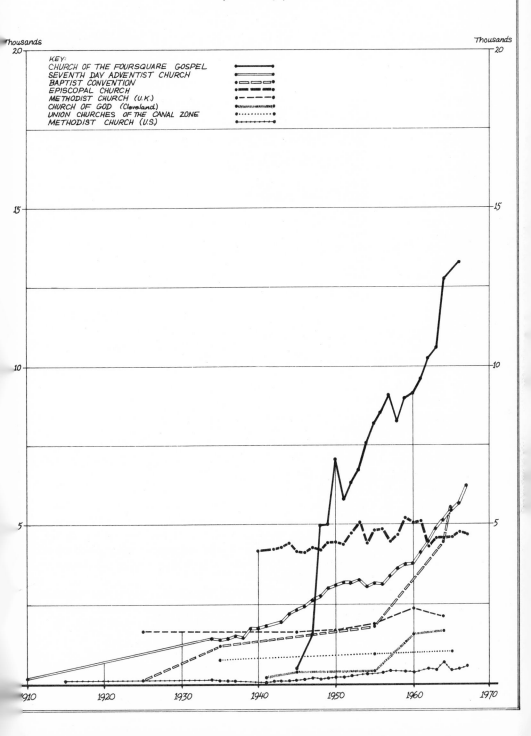

Figure 46

PANAMA: GROWTH OF CHURCHES
1910 – 1970

KEY:
CHURCH OF THE FOURSQUARE GOSPEL
SEVENTH DAY ADVENTIST CHURCH
BAPTIST CONVENTION
EPISCOPAL CHURCH
METHODIST CHURCH (U.K.)
CHURCH OF GOD (Cleveland)
UNION CHURCHES OF THE CANAL ZONE
METHODIST CHURCH (U.S.)

Methodist Churches both from the United States and from Great Britain have shown a smaller increase in recent years, even though the British Methodists minister primarily to Spanish speakers. The American Methodists have examined their work and have found a master plan lacking and little interest in church-planting (Butler 1964:48). In 1962 their church membership rose to 500 in eleven organized churches and sixteen preaching points.

In 1964, the Evangelical communicants were divided as follows: 14,102 Evangelicals were Spanish-speaking Panamanians; 10,564 West Indians; 3,752 Indians, and 3,559 United States citizens (Butler 1964: 118). It is the Spanish speakers who comprise the great majority of the population of Panama, and it is to these that the Churches must begin to minister effectively.

Figure 47

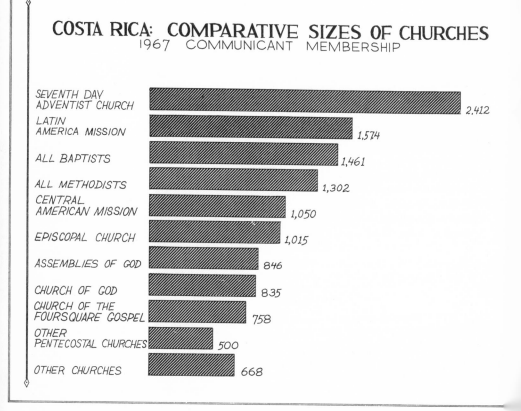

COSTA RICA: COMPARATIVE SIZES OF CHURCHES
1967 COMMUNICANT MEMBERSHIP

Church	Membership
SEVENTH DAY ADVENTIST CHURCH	2,412
LATIN AMERICA MISSION	1,574
ALL BAPTISTS	1,461
ALL METHODISTS	1,302
CENTRAL AMERICAN MISSION	1,050
EPISCOPAL CHURCH	1,015
ASSEMBLIES OF GOD	846
CHURCH OF GOD	835
CHURCH OF THE FOURSQUARE GOSPEL	758
OTHER PENTECOSTAL CHURCHES	500
OTHER CHURCHES	668

Figure 48

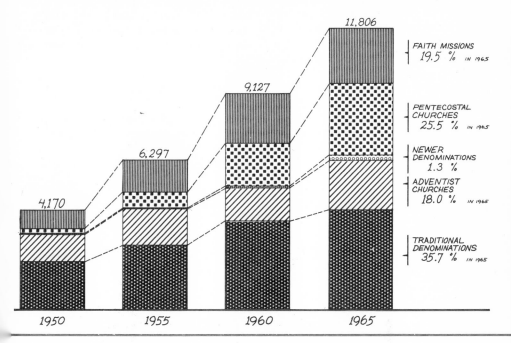

COSTA RICA: TYPES OF CHURCHES
DISTRIBUTION OF GROWTH: COMMUNICANT MEMBERS, 1950-1965

11,806

FAITH MISSIONS
19.5 % IN 1965

9,127

PENTECOSTAL
CHURCHES
25.5 % IN 1965

6,297

NEWER
DENOMINATIONS
1.3 %

ADVENTIST
CHURCHES
18.0 % IN 1965

4,170

TRADITIONAL
DENOMINATIONS
35.7 % IN 1965

1950   1955   1960   1965

Costa Rica

Costa Rica is mainly Iberian in culture and dependent economically upon agriculture. Two-thirds of the population is concentrated in the central plateau, where the people are self-supporting,
small landowners. Although there are a few Indians in the interior
of the country, as well as some Negroes elsewhere, there has been
almost no intermarriage between them and the predominant Spanish
peoples. The educational level of the country is one of the highest
in Latin America, with less than 16 per cent illiterate in 1965. At
the same time, the rate of population growth per year, 4.3 per cent,
is the highest in Latin America.

The Evangelical Churches

The Roman Catholic Church has had great power in Costa Rica.
Unfortunately, during the fifty years when an anticlerical government was in power (1890-1940) Evangelical missions did not stress
church-planting. The bar graph (Figure 47) reveals the small size
of the Evangelical Churches in Costa Rica. In 1930 only three missions were at work, and the churches they had established had a
combined membership of less than 500. In 1940 this figure had

Figure 49

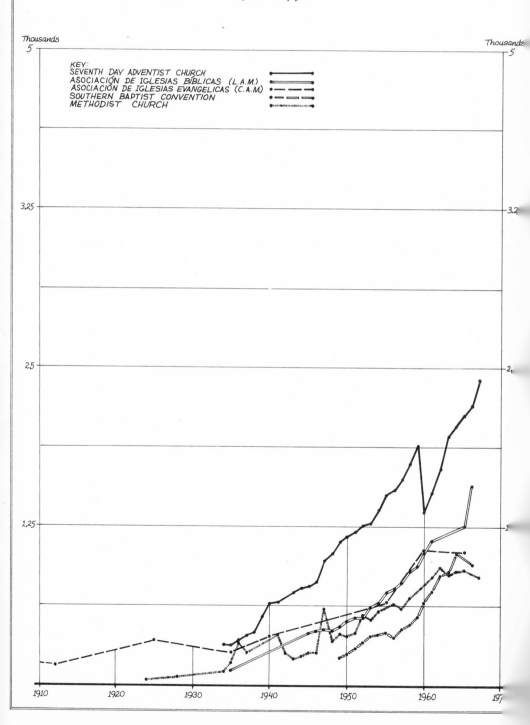

COSTA RICA: GROWTH OF CHURCHES
1910-1970

KEY:
SEVENTH DAY ADVENTIST CHURCH
ASOCIACIÓN DE IGLESIAS BÍBLICAS (L.A.M.)
ASOCIACIÓN DE IGLESIAS EVANGELICAS (C.A.M.)
SOUTHERN BAPTIST CONVENTION
METHODIST CHURCH

grown to six churches with 2,000 communicants, and in 1950 more than twelve Churches had a combined membership of almost 4,500 communicants.

Some of the reasons for slow beginnings have been suggested by Wilton M. Nelson (1963) of the Seminário Bíblico in Costa Rica. (1) Central America was the most neglected part of all Spanish America. (2) The early Evangelical movement endured heavy attacks from the Roman Catholic clergy. (3) Much broadcast "seed-sowing evangelism" took place in the early years, without the accompanying organization of churches. (4) The task of mission was misinterpreted in the light of the second coming of Christ. (5) There was an inadequate concept of the Church, with little importance given to visible churches and great emphasis placed on the invisible Church. (6) The resurgence of Roman Catholicism in mid-twentieth century without the defense of a dynamic political liberalism has slowed Evangelical growth since 1946. (7) Costa Rican people are very individualistic.

The Central American Mission, which reported 1,050 communicants in 1966, has the distinction of being the first mission to enter Costa Rica, arriving in 1892. It proclaimed the gospel widely, but established few churches. Indeed for forty-five years, until 1937, it had less than 300 members. Growth between 1937 and 1940 was more than negated by a church split which took the membership down to 250. The average annual growth rate of 17 per cent from 1952 to 1964 is commendable and is roughly paralleled by the Latin America Mission, Methodists, and Baptists (Figure 49). The marked plateau in church membership graphs since 1960 may be nothing more than a failure to report statistics, although on observing that the Baptists and Methodists also lost numerically, it could be that the Central American Mission simply failed to grow.

The Latin America Mission, with 1,574 communicants in 1966, began work in 1927 with the primary purpose of conducting great campaigns of evangelism in Central America. When the converts of the Costa Rica campaign of 1927 numbered 400 believers who did not desire to affiliate with either the Central American Mission or the Methodist churches, the Latin America Mission established a Church of its own, now known as the Asociación de Iglésias Bíblicas. The mission then turned to theological education for Central America, started a hospital, a book shop and press (now called Editorial Caribe), an orphanage, and a radio station, and began an evangelistic ministry in Peninsula de Nicoya, a rural section of Costa Rica which lies about 150 miles west of San José. A large staff of missionaries (eighty-one were reported by the *World Christian Handbook* in 1957) staffed the institution while only two were assigned to church-planting in the Peninsula de Nicoya.

In about 1952, the mission decided to emphasize church-planting in the capital city. Since that time it has begun about a dozen congregations which have a membership of fifty or more. The graph line of growth (Figure 49) shows clearly the effect of church-planting policies. Had it not been for Evangelism-in-Depth, the Latin America Mission with its large staff might have very little church growth to show.

Before 1950 even strong missions were doing little by way of church-planting. After that, membership figures for almost all missions show vigorous growth.

NICARAGUA

The Churches of Nicaragua, like those of Honduras, can be divided into those whose members are chiefly West Indians and those whose members are Spanish speaking. We have not yet been able to separate all the strands of memberships, but until this is done and growth of each strand considered by itself, a true picture of these Churches cannot be obtained. The brief account presented is based on undefined total membership.

Figure 50

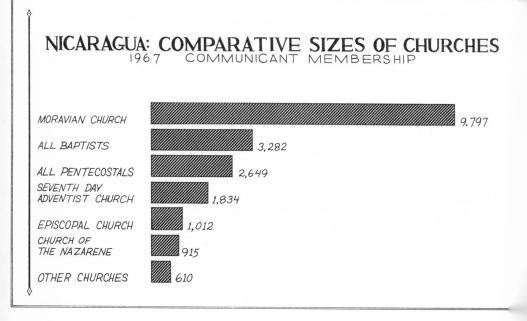

THE EVANGELICAL CHURCHES

The largest denomination in Nicaragua is the Moravian Church, which is located among the Protestant West Indian laborers on the banana plantations. In 1967 a total community of more than 25,000 and a communicant membership of 9,797 were reported. As Figure 50 shows, the Moravians are as numerous as the other Churches put together. Nevertheless, the Moravian Church does not dominate the scene in Nicaragua as the graph might indicate. It is confined to the coast and has little to do with the Spanish-speaking Churches. Because the Moravians are dark-skinned Christians, speak English, live on the plantations separated from the Spanish population, and for the most part practice a pattern of marriage which bars them from vigorous Christian life, they have slight influence on the further spread of the gospel in Nicaragua. The same can be said for the Episcopal Church with 1,000 members and for the English-speaking sections of the Baptist and Adventist denominations.

The Central American Mission began work in this country through the visit of its founder, Dr. C. I. Scofield. Its work, which is largely among Indians, remained at a plateau of about 700 members from 1925 until 1952, at which time it dropped still more, as can be seen in Figure 51. Although the Central American Mission has emphasized self-support and self-propagation, the Church has obviously not been successful at self-propagation. Neither has the mission granted self-government fast enough to suit its congregations, so that by 1955 eleven of the twenty-two churches declared themselves independent, a fact which explains the drop in the graph line of growth. In 1965 several of the remaining congregations left to form the Asociación Misionera Evangélica Nacional. This Association has no connection with any mission. Its leaders told us, "Our work is carried forward by laymen. Tithing is emphasized. Lay pastors earn their living outside the Church. Church buildings are only big enough for 200 members, and when they are filled a new congregation is started." If this breakaway has spiritual depth and emphasizes evangelism, these characteristics will help it grow.

The Nazarene Church assisted by its mission has a good, though small, growth pattern except for the 1957-1963 plateau (Figure 51). The Church increased from 238 members in 1950 to 915 in 1966. It has 31 small organized and 14 unorganized churches.

The American Baptists in Nicaragua have also grown steadily, doubling between 1940 and 1960 from 1,422 members to 2,760. In 1966 their membership declined to 1,834. Their emphasis on institutional work has been heavy and many valuable resources have been poured into seminary, school, and hospital work.

The Southern Baptists, whose churches form the Baptist Con-

Figure 51

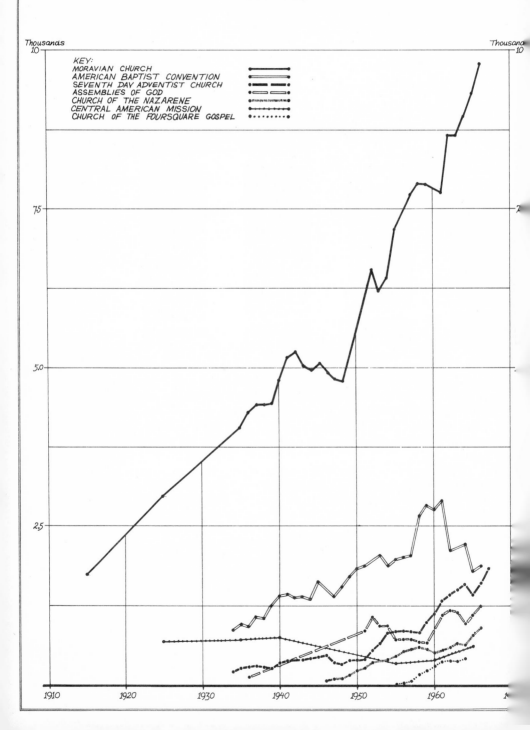

NICARAGUA: GROWTH OF CHURCHES
1910 – 1970

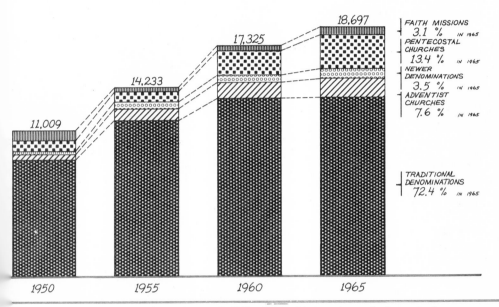

NICARAGUA: TYPES OF CHURCHES
DISTRIBUTION OF GROWTH: COMMUNICANT MEMBERS, 1950-1965

vention, have had their share of difficult problems since their arrival in 1935. The Baptist Convention has been practically static, with 1,400 members since 1950. Missionary-national tensions have plagued them for years. The problems raised by too much subsidy, mission control, and the like, have been detrimental to the growth of the Baptist Church in Nicaragua.

The graph line of growth for the Seventh-Day Adventists (Figure 51) is unusual for this denomination. The Adventists had less than 400 members for many years prior to 1952, then after a brief spurt of growth a plateau of 800 was reached in 1955, at which time level membership stayed for five years. In 1958 the Church started to grow again, reaching a membership of 1,834 in 1966.

Pentecostal Churches have been growing more slowly in Nicaragua than in other Central American countries. The Assemblies of God, which started in 1936, reported 1,249 in 1966; the Church of God, 989 in 1966; the Foursquare Church began in 1955 and reported 411 in 1966.

El Salvador

El Salvador, the smallest republic of the American continent, is also the most densely populated, having nearly six times the average of other Central American republics. More than 90 per cent of the land is under cultivation. Because of El Salvador's overdependence on agricultural production, the Central American Common Market is advancing industrialization faster here than in the rest of the area.

The Evangelical Churches

The growth of the Evangelical Churches in El Salvador presents a very encouraging picture when the totals are compared by five-year periods (Figure 53). The rapid growth was achieved by the Pentecostal Churches, while only moderate growth was realized by the older traditional Churches during the same period.

Figure 53

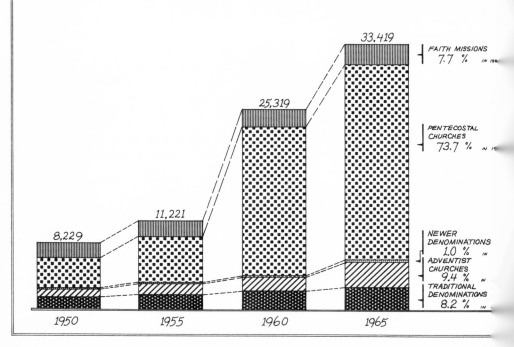

EL SALVADOR: TYPES OF CHURCHES
DISTRIBUTION OF GROWTH: COMMUNICANT MEMBERS, 1950–196

33,419

FAITH MISSIONS
7.7 %   IN 196

25,319

PENTECOSTAL
CHURCHES
73.7 %   IN 19

11,221

8,229

NEWER
DENOMINATIONS
1.0 %   IN
ADVENTIST
CHURCHES
9.4 %   N
TRADITIONAL
DENOMINATIONS
8.2 %   IN

1950   1955   1960   1965

Figure 54

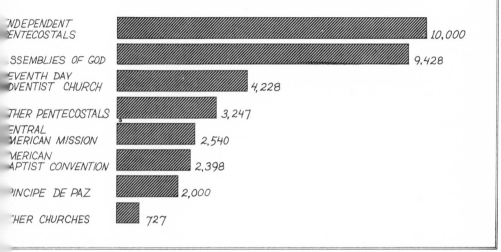

EL SALVADOR: COMPARATIVE SIZES OF CHURCHES
1967 COMMUNICANT MEMBERSHIP

INDEPENDENT PENTECOSTALS — 10,000
ASSEMBLIES OF GOD — 9,428
SEVENTH DAY ADVENTIST CHURCH — 4,228
OTHER PENTECOSTALS — 3,247
CENTRAL AMERICAN MISSION — 2,540
AMERICAN BAPTIST CONVENTION — 2,398
PRINCIPE DE PAZ — 2,000
OTHER CHURCHES — 727

In 1966 the Pentecostals represented almost 70 per cent of all Evangelicals in El Salvador (Figure 54). Melvin Hodges describes this surge of growth as a result of a revival that broke out within the Assemblies of God churches after ten days of prayer and fasting in the Bible school. This revival spread because of the active participation of large numbers of laymen and young people who established preaching points, house churches, and a large network of church schools.

A Southern Baptist missionary executive, James D. Crane (1961), noted the following characteristics of the Assemblies' growth: (1) the leadership is Latin American; (2) the churches are self-supporting; (3) the structure includes a large community coming into the churches (whose average size is 48 members) and very large church school attendance; (4) the churches have applied New Testament principles such as simplicity of approach, immediate teaching of the converts, emphasis on the baptism of the Holy Spirit, and a commitment to indigenous church principles.

The American Baptist Convention has been working in El Salvador since the early 1900's, but the growth of its churches has

Figure 55

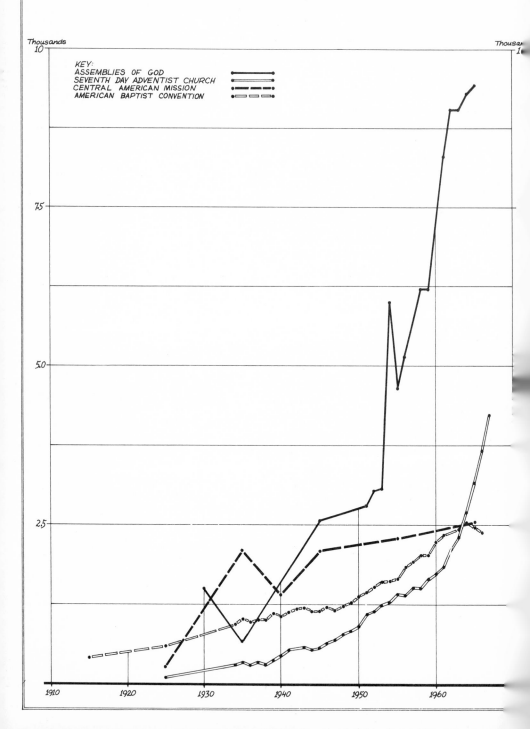

EL SALVADOR: GROWTH OF CHURCHES
1910–1970

KEY:
ASSEMBLIES OF GOD
SEVENTH DAY ADVENTIST CHURCH
CENTRAL AMERICAN MISSION
AMERICAN BAPTIST CONVENTION

been slow. After a series of struggling years between 1935 and 1950, a small margin of increase begins to show on the graph (Figure 55). Perhaps the chief weakness of the Baptists is the lack of an emphasis on ardent evangelism.

The same pattern can be seen in the line of growth of the Central American Mission. The drop in 1937 coincides with the beginning of the National Baptist Convention. It took the Central American Mission seventeen years (until 1954) to recoup these losses. Slow gains are recorded after 1955. The Central American Mission should study seriously its small growth in a land where great growth is clearly possible, as is shown by Churches as different as the Assemblies of God and the Seventh-Day Adventists.

A look at the bar graph (Figure 54) illustrates the present comparative size of the Evangelical Churches of El Salvador. Independent Pentecostal Churches and the Assemblies of God constitute 60 per cent of the total Evangelical communicants, each having a membership of about 10,000. Apart from the Seventh-Day Adventist Church, with 4,228 members, the remaining Churches have fewer than 3,000 members.

HONDURAS

Forests of pine and broad-leaf timber cover more than 50 per cent of Honduras, Central America's most mountainous country. The recently completed Canaveral hydroelectric station has increased the energy potential of the country to twice its present need. Nevertheless lack of roads (only 250 miles paved and 2,500 miles unpaved) prevents any very extensive development of its economy. In spite of the mountainous terrain, Honduras is famous as a "banana republic," with most of the modern banana plantations developed by the United Fruit and Standard Fruit Companies located on the Caribbean coast.

New development of Honduran industry accounts for almost 20 per cent of the gross domestic product and is concentrated mainly in the San Pedro Sula region. A steel mill and paper pulp plants are being proposed for the Bajo Aguán Valley, as well as new ventures in crop diversification and grain and livestock improvement. The Central American Common Market is playing a major role in the change from a feudal plantation system to an industrial economy. Large migration to the cities has not begun, but with the new emphasis on industry, such migration is sure to occur. The government hopes to resettle many in the Bajo Aguán Valley region to work in the paper and steel mills there.

The complexity of Honduran church growth is reflected in Figure 56. Sudden declines indicated purging of rolls, statistical redefinition, or shifting populations within the plantations. The largest church

Figure 56

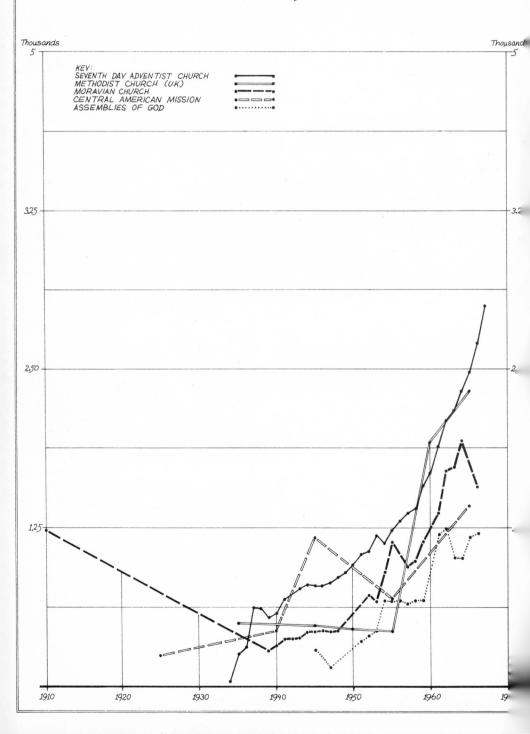

HONDURAS: GROWTH OF CHURCHES
1910–1970

KEY:
SEVENTH DAY ADVENTIST CHURCH
METHODIST CHURCH (U.K.)
MORAVIAN CHURCH
CENTRAL AMERICAN MISSION
ASSEMBLIES OF GOD

Thousands
5
3.25
2.50
1.25

Thousand
5
3.2
2.
2.

1910   1920   1930   1940   1950   1960   19

Figure 57

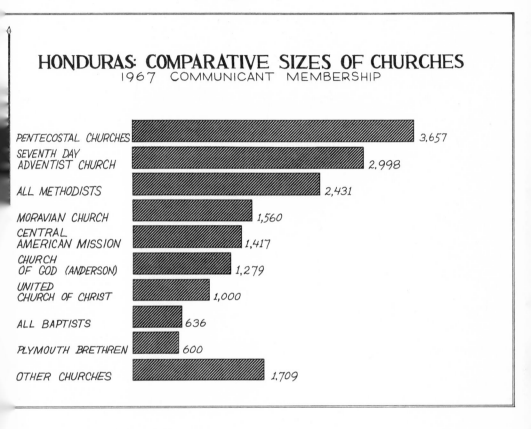

HONDURAS: COMPARATIVE SIZES OF CHURCHES
1967 COMMUNICANT MEMBERSHIP

PENTECOSTAL CHURCHES — 3,657

SEVENTH DAY ADVENTIST CHURCH — 2,998

ALL METHODISTS — 2,431

MORAVIAN CHURCH — 1,560

CENTRAL AMERICAN MISSION — 1,417

CHURCH OF GOD (ANDERSON) — 1,279

UNITED CHURCH OF CHRIST — 1,000

ALL BAPTISTS — 636

PLYMOUTH BRETHREN — 600

OTHER CHURCHES — 1,709

membership is only 2,998. The Churches and missions not shown on Figure 56 have less than 600 members each.

Protestant Churches in Honduras are growing in two distinct and mutually exclusive populations: the dark-skinned, English-speaking West Indians who labor on the plantations and in coconut groves on the islands off the coast, and the light-skinned, Spanish-speaking people who now comprise 80 per cent of the labor force on the banana plantations, but who generally live in the valleys and towns of the highlands. The West Indians came to Honduras as Protestants. Most of the rest of the population (more than 95 per cent) is nominally or actively Roman Catholic.

The greater percentage of the Protestant missions in Honduras have arrived since 1946 and are still passing through the exploratory stage of missions. Their churches are small and heavily dependent on the mission; some are sealed off from the community they serve by a mission-station approach. Most of the larger missions have their own leadership training programs composed of men with some secondary school education, although few are high school graduates.

Despite exploratory beginnings and small membership, the graph lines on Figure 56 indicate good trends for the future of the Evangelical Churches in Honduras. The growth of the Churches from a total of 4,000 in 1950 to more than 18,000 in 1967 constitutes a fourfold increase in seventeen years.

THE EVANGELICAL CHURCHES

The English Methodist and Episcopal Churches, together with a few others, are English-speaking denominations. When disease invaded the banana plantations with the result that thousands of workers were

Figure 58

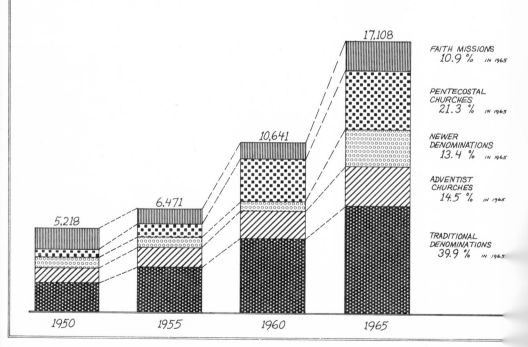

HONDURAS: TYPES OF CHURCHES
DISTRIBUTION OF GROWTH: COMMUNICANT MEMBERS, 1950–1965

17,108

FAITH MISSIONS
10.9 % IN 1965

PENTECOSTAL CHURCHES
21.3 % IN 1965

NEWER DENOMINATIONS
13.4 % IN 1965

ADVENTIST CHURCHES
14.5 % IN 1965

TRADITIONAL DENOMINATIONS
39.9 % IN 1965

10,641

6,471

5,218

1950   1955   1960   1965

dismissed and returned to Jamaica and the islands, the membership of these Churches declined. This accounts for some of the past fluctuations on the graph (Figure 56).

The line of growth of the Seventh-Day Adventists would imply that the Adventist system produces steady growth among both Spanish speakers and West Indians. Thorough indoctrination, a sense of separateness, careful selection of members (each must promise to tithe before being accepted), and unceasing evangelism have created a Church which grows steadily. The Adventist growth is especially significant in view of the fluctuating lines of growth of other Churches.

As a Church or mission develops a strong base upon which it can build, the advance into new phases of work becomes a possibility. By 1970 some Churches in Honduras will have this necessary base. The health of the Evangelical enterprise in Honduras must be measured by its Spanish-speaking membership. If the Churches and missions of Honduras will concentrate on the Spanish-speaking population, learn all they can about church-planting in towns and cities, and develop strong national leaders, a period of notable expansion lies before them.

GUATEMALA

Guatemala, the third largest of the Central American countries, is the most populous. Only about one-half of the land is populated. Most of the people live in the basins of the volcanic highlands.

Guatemala has two distinct major cultures, the *ladino (mestizo)* culture dominated by the Western values and commercial economy of Guatemala City, and the self-supporting indigenous culture of the Indian communities. The 1964 census showed an Indian population of over 50 per cent of the total.

The Evangelical Churches of Guatemala have a current annual growth rate of 9 per cent. In 1967, the Evangelical Churches had a total of 77,000 communicant members.

THE EVANGELICAL CHURCHES

Presbyterians

The oldest Evangelical Church in the country is the Presbyterian Church, which reported 11,500 communicants in 1967. Its churches, made up of Indians and *ladinos* (known as *mestizos* in most of the rest of Spanish America), are located in the capital city and the central and southwest parts of the country, both in the fast-growing Pacific coast area and on the central plateau of Guatemala which contains one-tenth of the land area and 30 per cent of the population.

Since the outstanding demographic fact of this area of Guatemala is the predominance of Indian tribes which do not speak Spanish, many churches include both Indians and *ladinos*. While the Indians predominate in the country, the *ladinos* predominate in the church.

Figure 59

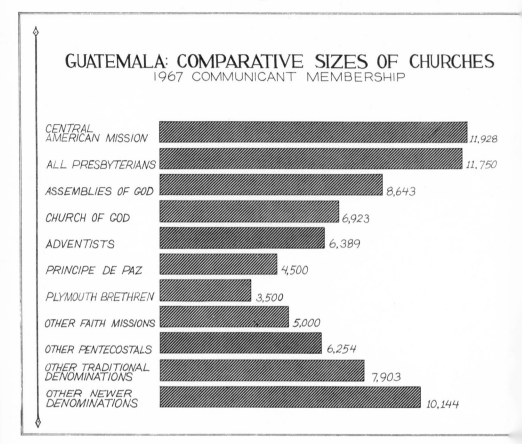

GUATEMALA: COMPARATIVE SIZES OF CHURCHES
1967 COMMUNICANT MEMBERSHIP

CENTRAL
AMERICAN MISSION — 11,928

ALL PRESBYTERIANS — 11,750

ASSEMBLIES OF GOD — 8,643

CHURCH OF GOD — 6,923

ADVENTISTS — 6,389

PRINCIPE DE PAZ — 4,500

PLYMOUTH BRETHREN — 3,500

OTHER FAITH MISSIONS — 5,000

OTHER PENTECOSTALS — 6,254

OTHER TRADITIONAL
DENOMINATIONS — 7,903

OTHER NEWER
DENOMINATIONS — 10,144

The Presbyterians have many congregations whose members speak the Mam and Quiché languages. The Church operates the Mam Bible Institute for the training of Mam Indian leaders and the Quiché Bible Institute in San Cristobal for training leaders in the Quiché churches. The latter institute is operated in cooperation with the Primitive Methodists.

The large majority of the Presbyterian churches are located in rural areas. Consequently rural ministerial students were either out of their element in the capital city or, if they adjusted to city life, never wanted to return to the needy rural churches. The few city pastorates that existed became competitive jobs, while the many rural churches were left without pastors. To deal with this problem the seminary in the capital was moved to San Felipe and began a theological training program to prepare pastors within their own environ-

Figure 60

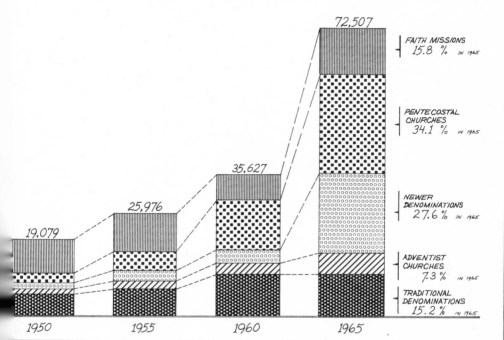

GUATEMALA: TYPES OF CHURCHES
DISTRIBUTION OF GROWTH: COMMUNICANT MEMBERS, 1950-1965

72,507

FAITH MISSIONS
15.8 % IN 1965

PENTECOSTAL
CHURCHES
34.1 % IN 1965

NEWER
DENOMINATIONS
27.6 % IN 1965

ADVENTIST
CHURCHES
7.3 % IN 1965

TRADITIONAL
DENOMINATIONS
15.2 % IN 1965

35,627

25,976

19,079

1950   1955   1960   1965

ment. This program has now passed the experimental stage and is discussed in Chapter Twenty-two.

The Presbyterian Church of Guatemala is the first to become national by her own decision. The full integration of mission and Church took place in 1961. Under the new system the missionary from outside the country has chosen to work under the ecclesiastical jurisdiction of the national Church. As in most well-established Churches, missionaries are rarely pastors and do not participate in the basic ecclesiastical structure of the Church. They are primarily advisory and do not return to Guatemala following furlough unless invited. The Presbyterians call a missionary in this kind of Church a "fraternal worker." He serves under the direction of the Church, often in one of its institutions. The funds beyond missionary salaries

Figure 61

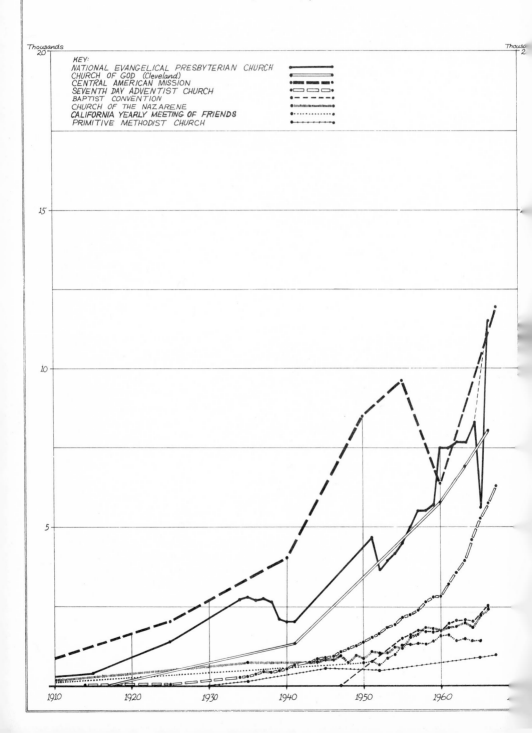

GUATEMALA: GROWTH OF CHURCHES
1910-1970

KEY:
NATIONAL EVANGELICAL PRESBYTERIAN CHURCH
CHURCH OF GOD (Cleveland)
CENTRAL AMERICAN MISSION
SEVENTH DAY ADVENTIST CHURCH
BAPTIST CONVENTION
CHURCH OF THE NAZARENE
CALIFORNIA YEARLY MEETING OF FRIENDS
PRIMITIVE METHODIST CHURCH

which come from the United States are not used to pay national pastors nor to build church buildings but primarily sustain the programs of the institutions. Even so, the institutions are administered through the Church.

In regard to institutions, one of them, the mission hospital, was sold after being nationalized, since it became clear that neither the previous mission nor the new national administration could bring it to the place where it did not require substantial annual subsidy. The new owners include two Protestant doctors, and the hospital is now successfully self-supporting. Even with the sale of this institution, however, some national pastors feel that through integration of the Church and mission the Church has acquired certain church-related institutions which are also too large to administrate effectively.

The curious humps and valleys of the Presbyterian growth curve (Figure 61) represent discrepancies in the handling of statistics. It would have to be said, however, that despite two very small splits, the Church has increased definitely but not spectacularly since the formal ceremony of integration turned over the reins of control to the national Church in 1962. Solid growth had preceded this event. The fact that United States funds have not been used for either pastors' salaries or church buildings has been true for over thirty years. During that time there was neither financial dominance nor even ecclesiastical dominance by the missionaries since their "votes" have always been few in number (though perhaps somewhat weighty). In regional and national presbyteries and synods the voting foreigners were never more than four to six, but the votes of the national delegates increased from thirty to seventy.

Central American Mission

The Central American Mission in 1940 had 4,000 communicant members and increased to 9,000 in 1954. The reported total for 1967 was 11,928. The mission has three Bible institutes in Guatemala, two of which are specifically for Indians and one for their churches throughout Central America. Their well-known Central American Bible Institute in Guatemala City is at the present time adding a seminary level to its training program.

The Evangelism-in-Depth campaign gave many new members to the Central American Mission churches in Guatemala. Unfortunately these new converts were not given adequate nurture, as is so often the case. Nevertheless, no other mission has had comparable success in Guatemala with the Indian element that makes up more than one-half of the population.

Other Churches

The Nazarene Church has one *ladino* Bible institute in Coban and two Indian Bible institutes for lay leaders. Church-planting has been chiefly among these ethnic groups. At the present time there are fourteen self-supporting churches and about fifty ministerial candidates in the institutes. The mission gives the churches no subsidy for pastoral support. Every church must construct its own building with mission help, which in some cases is up to 60 per cent of the cost of land and construction.

The California Friends are based in Chiquimula and areas close by. After more than a half century of work they have some excellent schools, a Bible institute, and a solid, high-quality membership. They combine a holiness type of theology with the Quaker tradition in regard to sacraments, and thus do not have a "communicant" membership as such. We understand that the size of their movement would be represented more fairly if the data plotted on our graph were multiplied by five. Although they have been relatively weak in evangelistic outreach, along with the other older Churches, and have been plagued with slow growth even after 1945 when many other Churches started to grow more rapidly, their Church has produced outstanding ministers and laymen who have not only served them well but have undertaken important roles in many other Churches and agencies throughout the country. Their progressive outlook is reflected in new projects that range from economic development to an adaptation of the Presbyterian Seminary's extension system of local leadership training.

The Baptist Convention in Guatemala grew to more than 2,500 communicants in 1965 after remaining on a plateau for three years. The Southern Baptist missionaries have increased from six in 1961 to more than twenty in 1965. In 1961 there were only three self-supporting churches, but in 1965 these numbered more than eighteen. In 1943 a Southern Baptist missionary, Paul Bell, rebaptized 300 people who were former members of the Independent Evangelical Church of Guatemala, and these new Baptist members became the nucleus for the Baptist Convention organized in 1946. Since this time, through steady evangelistic zeal, this Church has enjoyed a better than average growth.

Another aspect of the Evangelical Churches in Guatemala is that of the Primitive Methodist work. Their field is 95 per cent Indian. The reported membership is just above 1,000. The Primitive Methodist churches are located in the western mountains except for a few churches on the coast and in the capital city. Together with other Churches scattered among the twenty-one subtribes of Guatemala, the Primitive Methodists have invited Wycliffe Translators to assist them. That, plus the outreach of the Quiché Bible Institute, should mean more church-planting among the Quichés.

The Pentecostal Churches as a group are growing rapidly in

Guatemala. The Assemblies of God, for example, have grown from 850 in 1950 to more than 8,000 in 1967, effectively using their *ladino* Bible school in Guatemala City and their Cakchiquel institute to develop men who plant churches. The Foursquare Church began work in 1955 and has grown to 2,000 members. Similarly, the Church of God of Prophecy has grown from 350 in 1950 to 3,000 in 1967. The Church of God has had a more rapid growth like that of the Assemblies, growing from 1,100 in 1950 to 6,923 in 1967. A completely indigenous Pentecostal Church known as the *Principe de Paz* has had really phenomenal growth, when you take into account its small base: it has grown from 100 to 4,500 in the seventeen years between 1950 and 1967. A great deal of this growth has occurred through the use of radio.

Several Pentecostal denominations in Guatemala give no statistical reports, but two matters are noteworthy. The Pentecostal Churches made fastest strides in the urban areas and have leaned heavily on the older Churches for their members. However, they have not merely drawn members from the older Churches. They have engaged in concerted evangelism and have been part of the stimulation which has enabled the older Churches to move forward substantially despite such losses.

Chapter Eight

MEXICO

A great diversity of climate and topography characterizes Mexico, including the arid North and West, the great central plateau bounded by mountains, and the tropical rain forests of the Southeast. Uneven rainfall makes it impossible to utilize more than 1 per cent of the land without at the same time providing for either drainage or irrigation. Extensive irrigation projects now under construction will soon utilize water from the mountains in the States of Sonora, Sinaloa, Durango, and Nayarit. More than 500,000 acres have been irrigated since 1960, including the rich Mexicali Valley where the Colorado River flows. The section of the country next to the Texas border contains many agricultural and industrial centers and therefore attracts many immigrants from the South.

The heavy concentration of inhabitants around the Federal District indicates that more than 50 per cent of the total population is living in only 15 per cent of the land area of Mexico. The Federal District (consisting of Mexico City and its twelve adjoining communities) has more than six million people and is now one of the largest modern metropolitan areas in the world. The government has plans in the near future to move some inhabitants of the overpopulated central plateau to Campeche, Quintana Roo, and other well-watered lands in the Southwest.

THE EVANGELICAL CHURCHES

The 1960 census of Mexico reported that 578,515 people were affiliated with Protestant Churches. The census figures are given for individual states and also for the areas around Mexico City within the Federal District. We estimate that the 1970 census will show an increase of approximately 100 per cent over the 1960 figures. A Roman Catholic study of the Evangelical Churches in Mexico, *Instituciones Protestantes en Mexico* (Rivera 1962:25-27), gave the total number of Protestant adherents *(adeptos)* for that year as 645,145, consisting of 41 Protestant denominations, 2,420 organized churches, 1,622 congregations, 2,470 Sunday Schools, and 2,452 missionaries (both foreign and national). Rivera claimed that more than

164

200,000 of these 645,000 Protestants live in the Federal District; more than 100,000 in the State of Vera Cruz; more than 50,000 in each of the States of Chiapas, Tabasco, Puebla, Tamaulipas, Nuevo Leon, Coahuila, and Chihuahua; having less than 25,000 each in Yucatán, Campeche, Oaxaca, Guerrero, Michoacán, Mexico, Hidalgo, and San Luis Potosi.

Totals of communicants for 1960 and 1966 show an increase of 224,827 in just six years. The Pentecostal Churches constitute more than 50 per cent of this increase. The most conservative estimates from Mexican Pentecostal leaders have been used.

Figure 64 shows the growth of the Pentecostal Churches whose yearly statistics were available. It was not possible to include on this graph growth information concerning Churches whose statistics covered only certain geographical areas.

Pentecostal Churches

Iglésia Apostólica de la Fé en Cristo Jesus

From its beginning in 1914, the Iglésia Apostólica (Apostolic

Figure 62

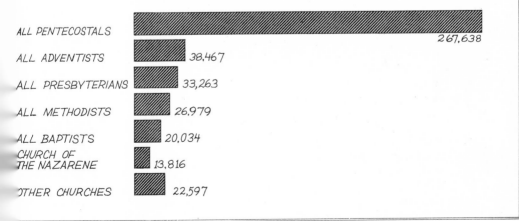

Church) has been an indigenous Church. Communicants number 16,500, while the community is estimated to be five times as large, or about 80,000. This Pentecostal Church baptizes by immersion and in the name of Jesus only. Its governmental system is episcopal, using bishops and superintendents much like the Methodists. The Iglésia Apostólica has thirteen districts in Mexico and churches in every state except Puebla. In 1967 there were 13 bishops, about 70 presbyters (superintendents), 350 pastors, 55 assistant pastors, 325 ordained deacons, 237 unordained deacons, and 1,050 preachers. The Iglésia Apostólica has congregations and branch congregations in 1,067 towns throughout Mexico, but most of its strength is in the North and Northwest. Each of the 425 fully organized churches has its own separate field with its own preaching stations.

A home mission organization of the Iglésia Apostólica plants and nurtures churches in pioneer areas. Foreign missions are also carried

Figure 63

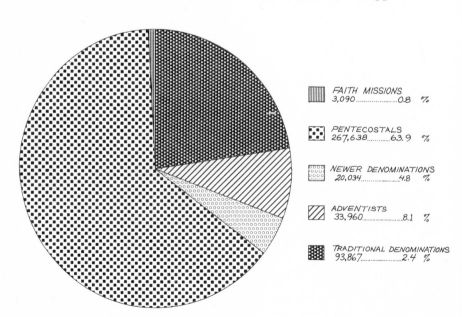

MEXICO: TYPES OF CHURCHES, 1965

FAITH MISSIONS
3,090 .... 0.8 %

PENTECOSTALS
267,638 .... 63.9 %

NEWER DENOMINATIONS
20,034 .... 4.8 %

ADVENTISTS
33,960 .... 8.1 %

TRADITIONAL DENOMINATIONS
93,867 .... 2.4 %

Figure 64

MEXICO: GROWTH OF CHURCHES
1910-1970

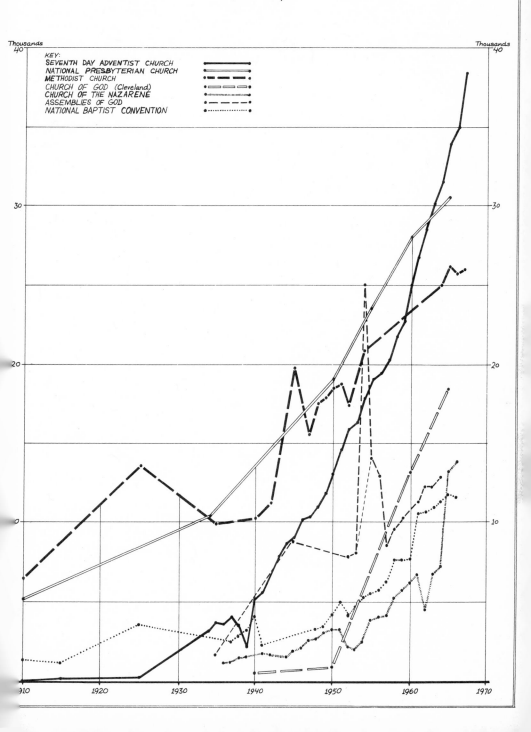

KEY:
SEVENTH DAY ADVENTIST CHURCH
NATIONAL PRESBYTERIAN CHURCH
METHODIST CHURCH
CHURCH OF GOD (Cleveland)
CHURCH OF THE NAZARENE
ASSEMBLIES OF GOD
NATIONAL BAPTIST CONVENTION

on in Guatemala, where there has been rapid growth since 1949, as well as in El Salvador and Nicaragua. In the latter, growth has been so encouraging in the past two years that the missionary feels these churches will gain their independence by 1969.

Many members of the Apostólica have migrated into Baja California and Sonora, where they have planted churches in the Mexicali Valley and the large border towns of Mexicali, Tijuana, San Luiz, and Ensenada. Migration into the United States has enabled establishment of more than fifty Spanish-speaking Apostolic churches in the State of California alone!

The growth of the Iglésia Apostólica has been as high as 20 per cent per year, at times, but now its annual rate of increase is less than 10 per cent. Church extension in pioneer areas is not producing the results it once did, but the spontaneous growth of past years is being replaced by deliberate church-planting. As a result the Church now faces the problem of financial support for its ministers and missionaries. Leaders who see the Iglésia Apostólica shifting from a rural base to an urban base are reappraising the situation in which the Church finds itself. They seek to face realistically the problems of educating and conserving the younger members. They try to send as many as possible of the children to secondary school and to the university.

Their strategy calls the church to concentrate its efforts in Mexico City and in other urban centers. At the present there are only five churches in the Federal District, but more are needed to serve members who move there from rural areas and to spread the gospel among the responsive urban population. Six young pastors have begun training for urban church-planting.

The Apostólica has proven its capacity to reach into Mexico's developing middle class. Its solid organization and evangelical fervor give it great potential for accelerated growth.

Assemblies of God

A Pentecostal Church of equal size to the Apostólica is the Assemblies of God. Its line of growth, shown on Figure 64, rose in years following 1935 only to level off until 1954. After a surge (which looks like a changed definition of membership), the Church declined in 1958 and then slightly accelerated in growth until 1966. The Asamblea in Mexico has 300 ordained pastors, 400 licensed pastors, and 100 ministers in preparation. It has 600 churches and over 300 preaching stations. The most effective church-planting has been in the States of Tamaulipas, Coahuila, Nuevo Leon, Distrito Federal, Chihuahua, and Sonora; few Assembly of God churches are found in southern Mexico. The Asamblea and Apostólica are the only Pentecostal Churches in Mexico which train their workers in Bible institutes. The Asamblea operates seven of these institutes.

Other Pentecostal Churches

The Fraternal Association of Pentecostals in the Republic of Mexico, a rather unstructured association, claims a total membership of 200,000 adult communicants, and lists the following movements and denominations as members.

> Asamblea de Dios
> Iglésia de Dios de la Republica Mexicana
> Iglésia de Jesus Cristo Interdenominacional (Portales)
> Iglésia Cristiana Bethel
> Unión de Iglésias Independientes
> Movimiento Libre Pentecostales
> Iglésia Evangélica Cuadrangular
> Iglésia Pentecostales de Dios
> Iglésia Apostólica Pentecostales Independientes
> Iglésia Berea de Pentecostales
> Iglésia Gideon Cristiana
> Communidad Iglésia Pentecostales Libres
> Iglésia Evangélica Independiente
> Iglésia de Dios Independiente

More than 100 other Pentecostal Churches are not members of this Association. The total membership of all Pentecostal Churches is estimated at 267,638, but could be as much as 300,000 (Figure 62). There is not much question that the accelerated growth of the Pentecostal family of Churches in Mexico deserves special study (see Chapter Twenty-one).

Traditional Churches

Presbyterians

The Presbyterian Church began work in Mexico in 1872 and soon will celebrate its centennial year. As the second largest Evangelical Church in Mexico (see Figure 64), and also the second largest Presbyterian Church in Latin America, it has three synods, 14 presbyteries, 170 organized churches, 500 congregations, 375 missions, and a total of 755 church buildings, as well as 150 ordained ministers, 575 elders, 400 deacons, and 34,479 communicants.

The greatest concentration of members is found in southern Mexico. The *mestizo* and Indian churches of the State of Chiapas have at least 9,000 members. These churches, begun by Presbyterian pioneers Coffin and Lango, have greatly increased because of the people movements among the Chols and Tzeltals which have brought multitudes to responsible membership in Christ's Church. Presbyterians in Tabasco number more than 5,000 hardcore communicants, and in Yucatán more than 4,000. Thus the 19,000 members in southern Mexico (Synod of the Gulf) comprise nearly two-thirds of the entire Church. The Central Synod, which includes Mexico City and the

Federal District, has 6,000 communicants; the First Synod in Northeast Mexico has 5,000 members.

The line of growth of the Presbyterian Church, as shown in Figure 64, is gradual and steady. Because statistical summaries were given at long intervals for the entire Church, the graph shows an evenness which is illusory. The inadequacy of using the field totals is evident here. There is a need for expertise in gathering data for statistical reports. This Church is large enough to be able to have a trained secretary for statistics who would make a yearly report of accurate data for each church and presbytery. In this way Presbyterian leaders could become aware of areas of rapid growth and areas of non-growth, and therefore could take the proper steps to assist congregations and presbyteries to fulfill their mandate.

Methodists

The Methodist Church has an excellent annual statistical record of its growth in Mexico. The line of growth as seen on Figure 64 includes the healthy five years (1942-1946) in which 6,000 members were added to the Methodist churches in Mexico! A study made by Robert H. Conerly of the Commission of Church Extension of the Methodist Church in Mexico, gives us a picture of growth of more than 90 per cent for the decade 1950-1960. It is interesting to see how certain churches sprang to life between 1940 and 1950, especially during the years of the Second World War. The following list is a sampling of those which grew the most.

Church	Communicants:	1940	1950
Alamo, Ver.		85	158
Leon, Gto.		57	100
Pachuca, Hgo.		187	267
Valle de Santiago, Gto.		35	124
Zimapan y Jiliapan		13	68
Zacualtipan, Hgo.		0	57
Mixquiahuala, Hgo.		0	67
Acozac, Pue.		90	208
Hueyotlipan, Pue.		89	146
Matamoros, Pue.		60	109
Papalotla, Tlax.		47	88
Teotlalcingo		33	90
Anahuac, D.F.		307	681
Aztecas, D.F.		255	364
Balderas, D.F.		346	739
Gante, D.F.		1063	1722
Jujutla, Mor.		126	221
Peralvillo, D.F.		59	190
Tacubaya, D.F.		91	135
San Agustin, Mex.		25	103
		2968	5637

Growth such as this could happen again. But to bring this about church and mission administrators need to know which churches are growing and why.

Baptists

Mexico was the first country in Latin America to be entered by the Southern Baptist Convention (1880). The Mexican Baptist Convention was organized in 1903. The Convention now has thirteen districts, as shown in the following list of communicants by field for 1965:

1.	Central Field	3,500
2.	Chihuahua	1,469
3.	Coahuila	1,086
4.	Laguna	1,050
5.	Jalisco	831
6.	Michoacán	721
7.	Guerrero	699
8.	Sonora	521
9.	Chiapas	519
10.	Sinaloa	375
11.	Yucatán	326
12.	Durango	310
13.	Guanajuato	309
		11,716

For many years the Southern Baptists did splendid mission work in Mexico, but very little church-planting. The line of growth on Figure 64 maintains a plateau from 1925 until 1952 when a definite policy of advance was adopted, and evangelism and church-planting were emphasized.

At the same time, for reasons the Southern Baptists could not have anticipated, the field became more receptive. Many thousands suddenly became responsive to the gospel because of their experience in the United States under the *bracero* program. This began during World War II and at its peak recruited 400,000 Mexican men to serve as agricultural laborers, returning them each year to Mexico. While in the United States they worked on farms belonging to Protestants, where they were treated fairly and became increasingly able to "hear" the gospel. Sometimes they visited Protestant churches where they heard the gospel, and sometimes Evangelicals visited them in their migrant camps and gave them New Testaments in Spanish. Where their receptivity was met by ardent evangelism, churches arose of every Evangelical denomination.

Evangelistic work done by Baptist circuit riders in southern Texas affected church growth in Mexico (Taylor 1962: 49). A striking correlation can be seen between the density of church members in each of the thirteen Baptist areas of Mexico and the density of *bracero* population in that area. Taylor shows that Baptist church membership has grown in the areas in which also reside the greatest number of *braceros*. Baptist and other missionaries have reported case after case of members in their churches who have made one or more trips to the United States under the *bracero* program, and who first found Christ as their Savior while attending an Evangelical Church in the States.

Baptists face opportunities as well as difficulties in their work in Mexico. Although only fifty-five of their 190 churches are now self-supporting, they face the decade ahead with evangelistic zeal and Baptist optimism.

Nazarenes

The Nazarenes also are indebted to the movement of Mexican migrants across the border. A group of young men from Mexico were converted in Texas and studied in the Nazarene Bible Institute in San Antonio. Upon their return to Mexico they became the leaders of a generation of church-planters who have established one of the most vigorous Churches in Mexico. The line of growth (Figure 64), which begins in 1936, rises slowly, suffers a period of decline after 1950, then makes a sizable advance by 1961. From 1962 to 1966 the membership doubled — an occurrence which is unique in Mexico.

The Nazarene Church has little missionary assistance. Leadership is Mexican and the Church is growing along indigenous lines. Its effective use of lay leaders is exceptional. The growth of the Nazarene Church in Mexico is much greater than its growth anywhere else in Latin America. Is this because here it is more free from guidance and control by missionaries?

THE MEXICAN BORDER

Every state adjacent to the border is among the ten Mexican states having the largest number of Evangelical Churches:

			Church buildings
	1.	Distrito Federal	329
Border	2.	*Tamaulipas*	242
	3.	Vera Cruz	214
Border	4.	*Coahuila*	193
Border	5.	*Nuevo Leon*	186
Border	6.	*Chihuahua*	178
	7.	Yucatán	163
Border	8.	*Sonora*	158
Border	9.	*Baja California*	147
	10.	Sinaloa	118

This concentration of Evangelical Churches is verified by the results of the 1960 census, which shows that the ratio of Evangelicals to

population is higher in the border states than in the other states
of Mexico. The border states exhibit the following ratios of Evangelicals to the total population (Mexican census 1962) :

Sonora	1 Evangelical — 62 inhabitants
Chihuahua	1 Evangelical — 46 inhabitants
Nuevo Leon	1 Evangelical — 42 inhabitants
Baja Calif.	1 Evangelical — 41 inhabitants
Coahuila	1 Evangelical — 40 inhabitants
Tamaulipas	1 Evangelical — 30 inhabitants

Evangelicals have had less success in establishing churches in the
heartland of Mexico. The States of Zacatecas, Aguascalientes, Jalisco,
Colima, Queretaro, Guanajuato, and Michoacán, are centers of traditional Roman Catholicism. According to the 1960 census, the areas
of Mexico in which the Evangelical Churches have grown most rapidly have been the northern and southern border states, the Federal
District, and Morelos.

Professor John Huegel of Union Theological Seminary (1963:2)
disagrees with Evangelicals who believe that for them Mexico City
is *the* "bridge into Mexico ... [to which] people come from all over
the country in search of good jobs." He believes that, quite to the
contrary, "the most effective bridge into Mexico's heartland is precisely the northern border area." His reasons are as follows: (1) the
seasonal migration, past and present, to and from the United States;
(2) drought and economic pressure which push people in large numbers into the dollar economy along the border; (3) the influence of
the northern states upon Mexico's heartland, and (4) the growth of
nine major urban centers along the border (c1963: 2).

We also believe in the strategic importance of the border land
for the future growth of Evangelical Churches (Read 1967b: 2-5).
A more biblical concept of mission should lead to the fervent belief
that God wills a great harvest of the receptive common people of the
northern tier of states. "Doing a little for these poor Mexicans" must
give way to "doing a lot for these fine people for whom Christ died"
— and the "lot" will include, first of all, leading them to personal
knowledge of the Power and Wisdom of God.

THE PARADOX

It has proved impossible to secure a complete list of Protestant
missions and denominations in Mexico. Our tabulation listed 89 of
these, but we are confident that more exist. A true picture of church
growth in Mexico would include many groups of Protestants — one
can scarcely call them denominations — ranging in membership from
10 to 1,000 and showing little growth.

These slow-growing groups are part of the picture in Mexico and
other Latin American countries. The responsiveness of a country

seems to make little difference in its rate of growth. Whether located in the fertile border land, the liberal metropolis, or the resistant highlands, these churches do not grow. Missionaries attached to them continue doing what does not communicate the Evangel, seemingly quite content with merely mission work, no matter whether it is effective or not. Possibly they do not know how to work so that their faith is transmitted. The paradox of Latin America is that in the same area and at the same time one can find both Churches of great growth (those presented on Figure 64) and Churches of little growth.

PART III

VIGNETTES OF
CHURCH GROWTH

Our survey now passes from statistical data to the dynamic events which are flesh and blood to the statistical bones. We have tried to reflect this transition by changing our literary style for this section.

The rich diversity of the Latin American Evangelical Churches and the variety of environmental situations in which these Churches live and work represent a complex picture, difficult to describe. The examples which follow reflect this complexity. This method has been used because important principles of Latin American church growth can be illustrated more clearly in this manner than is possible through other methods.

Of the thousands of churches, missions, and individuals observed, only a few representative cases have been chosen, typical of Latin American church growth and non-growth. The examples are not fictional, even though real names have not been used. The examples are descriptive of similar cases, exemplifying the kind of church growth problems and opportunities found in many locales, Churches, and missions.

We have retained the colloquial, conversational tone as much as possible. In each case, positive and negative growth factors are present. In every Church and mission, often side by side and apparently inextricably intertwined, some factors tend toward the growth of the Church and other factors militate against growth.

These sketches of Evangelical church life in Latin America give specific, concrete examples in order to illuminate the theory of growth with which this book deals. The Evangelical whose church situation corresponds to any of the cases may see a parallel and evaluate his own situation.

Chapter Nine

CHURCHES

1.

"If you can be here before seven o'clock, I'll try to get someone else to go with you," the pastor said. "It takes an hour by bus from here, so you must leave by seven. They will be expecting you to lead the meeting, so don't disappoint them. They are only new converts and this will be the first service in their home, so be patient with them. If we can win their friends and neighbors now, we will have a church there within six months."

This was Eduardo's first assignment to lead a service on his own. He would have preferred to begin in one of the established congregations. He had spoken in the open-air services and in the central church, but had never had occasion to take charge of the meeting without supervision. Now he had no one on whom he could depend.

When Eduardo arrived at the church shortly before seven, he found Carlos waiting for him. Eduardo felt relieved. "Do you want to lead the meeting, Carlos?" Carlos had had much more experience in the work of the Lord than he.

"No, Eduardo. The pastor asked you to take charge. I will do anything I can to help you. If you are to go to the Bible Institute in the fall you must learn how to do things for yourself. You can be proud that the pastor would send you to conduct a service in a new place."

The neighbors of the new converts were all crowded into the small living room when Eduardo and Carlos arrived. Eduardo wished he could conduct the meeting outdoors where the air was fresh and more people could hear, but he wisely let them sit where they were. As the service began, Carlos was amazed at the poise Eduardo showed in teaching them simple gospel choruses.

When everyone was relaxed and happy, Eduardo invited Carlos to give his testimony. Then the family of new converts each spoke briefly about their salvation. In as few words as possible, Eduardo explained to the crowd how they, too, could receive salvation, and when he asked how many wanted to accept the Savior, seventeen neighbors raised their hands.

Tired but happy, Carlos and Eduardo took the last bus back to the church. The pastor's vision of another new church was already being fulfilled.

2.

Josué had been visiting Marçaça one weekend a month for a long time. Every time he held a service there the attendance was good, but no one ever responded to the invitation. This time Antonio, in whose house the services were held, told him, "Don't bother to ask people to raise their hands here. The things you are telling us are new. Be patient with us. When we have made up our minds about this matter, we will let you know. Please continue to come as often as you can to tell us all that you know about the way of the believers."

For four more months Josué continued to visit Marçaça. Each time he would hold two services and preach the gospel at both services, never giving another invitation. Finally, when he was beginning to wonder if there ever would be results for his labors, Antonio said to him as he came up the trail to the settlement, "Tonight you should ask people to raise their hands."

That night Josué gave an invitation and Antonio and his wife and two daughters raised their hands. The next evening seven more responded to the invitation. Within a few weeks over seventy persons had made a public profession of faith in Christ.

Antonio continued to be the leader of the group. He was the one who suggested that the new congregation ought to be baptized. Under his direction the group chose a plot of ground on which to build a chapel. He led the committee of new converts to ask the governor to supply a teacher for the school that they had begun in their new church building.

Antonio never sought the limelight. He patiently sidestepped the politicians who now swarmed around him looking for his support, saying, "I don't want to be used by anybody." He told the congregation, "We have a good community here since the gospel came. We owe it to each other as neighbors and as brethren in the Lord to stand together against any disruptive influence."

At last, over 80 per cent of the population in the settlement was Evangelical. Everyone in the area called it "Marçaça of the believers." Josué's patience had paid off.

3.

Joan was leaving for the interior on the mission plane that afternoon. Meanwhile, though, she had a few free hours while she waited for her husband Ron to finish buying the supplies. While she waited, she sat and talked with Ellen, whom she hadn't seen for months.

"What's happening up there where you are, Joan? I saw a news item in the mission letter last month that said you were starting a congregation in a new town."

"Oh, that was about six months ago. We already have twenty-two baptized members. That's more than we had in our last congregation after four years of work. What are you doing down here? We don't see your work mentioned in the mission letter."

Ellen sighed. "It's more of the same old thing here. Pete is still pastoring the church since there is no national pastor. With all the usual church activities, he's so busy he can't get out to the other towns around here. It is almost like pastoring a church back in the States."

"What about the Lopez and Gonzalez families from our area who moved down here to the coast?" queried Joan. "Are they as active in the Church here as they were at home?"

"We never see them any more. Mrs. Gonzalez said that things were so different here, and there was no connection with their old church. They lost interest and the children don't even come to Sunday School now. We hated to see it happen because the group is so small here anyway."

"Do you ever see any of the other missionaries? We're so far from the rest of the field that no one ever visits us."

"It isn't much better here," said Ellen. "We see them when they come back from furlough and when they go again. I wish our work would allow us to get together once in a while."

"There doesn't seem to be much fellowship between the churches either, does there? They don't seem to feel the need of mutual aid and encouragement. What do you think we could do to bring them closer to each other?"

4.

The paper was entitled "The Growth of Our Church." It represented the work of the denomination's leading pastors and missionaries. As it was read to the annual conference, everyone could feel the excitement rising.

"We are on to something big," declared a young pastor. "This shows us where to begin to increase our growth. We have been worrying about stewardship, ministerial training, ministerial prestige, church buildings, and a dozen other church matters — everything except growth! If we had begun to look at the reason for our growth ten years ago, we could have solved the other problems, too."

The paper had not just happened. It was born in mission planning a year before. The missionaries had discussed among themselves the best way to emphasize the necessity of church growth. They finally decided that the best plan would be to prepare carefully a paper for the whole conference to discuss.

Now their plans were coming to fruition. The positive reaction far exceeded their expectations. Fortunately the missionaries who taught in the seminary and those who were involved in the boarding school and in the day schools were all at conference. They, too, caught the enthusiasm that gripped everyone else. It was going to be necessary to deploy missionaries differently and to change the emphasis of the seminary.

"How can we transmit this new insight to our students?" asked the seminary director. "Can we get them involved in planting new churches before they graduate from seminary? The pattern of preparing pastors for static churches just does not work on the mission field. These candidates for the ministry must be prepared to found churches.

"I am sure that in years to come we will mark the beginning of our real growth in this country from the presentation of this church growth paper. If we do not grow, the fault will be ours. Everything is propitious for immediate growth."

5.

Tom slammed shut the tailgate of the station wagon and walked around to the front door. A group of new converts pressed around the car, urging him to come back as soon as possible. He started the motor and waved to them, promising that someone would be back the following week to hold another service.

Once underway he began to chat with the two lay preachers who were traveling with him. "How many people bought New Testaments? Was the man who raised his hand at the invitation the same man we sometimes see in our services in town?" he wanted to know.

As they drove along, they discussed the response to the gospel. One of them carefully wrapped the phonograph records they had played.

"Before we go out again next week, we'll have to replenish our stock of tracts. Everyone in town must have taken one!"

They had to push on to reach the next town before dark. Here they planned to show a gospel film and hold another open-air evangelistic rally. They discussed the subject of the evening sermon and worked out the evening program. Their discussion of the sermon topic led them into a Bible study of the letter to the Hebrews. The kilometers sped by.

They planned to spend the night in the next town. In fact it would be Friday before they reached home. They felt encouraged to know that three other teams also made up of a missionary and a few lay workers were out doing the same kind of work at the same time. The evangelistic force was quadrupled in the shared ministry of missionary and lay preacher. Already six churches had been started in just this way. Living and traveling together was the best possible kind of training for both missionary and national. This was a Church that would never be faced with the problem of indigenization. It was from its inception the happy result of combined mission and national effort.

6.

It was the last night of the Church's annual conference. The Bishop had presented an inspiring message reminding everyone of the victories of the past year. Now at the end of the service it was time for the ordination.

"Our brother Jorge has asked to go to Argentina as a missionary. He has been a faithful worker in the Church ever since he was converted fifteen years ago. He enjoys our confidence and respect. We know that he will be used of God in carrying our message to the Chileans who have gone to Argentina looking for work. There are also many Argentines in need of salvation."

As the Bishop and the senior ministers gathered to lay hands on Jorge, one of the veteran pastors spoke a prophetic word. He told how God had promised to bless His Word to the ends of the earth. He bestowed a special blessing on the new missionary.

The next morning at the Bishop's home, Jorge received all the money which he was to receive from the sending Church — a one-way ticket to Buenos Aires. "If you are in difficulty, remember that God will help you," promised the Bishop. "We hope that you will be able to come back in time for next year's conference to report how things have gone. Remember always that you go as the official representative of this Church, and that everything you do reflects in some way on those who send you. Be sure that the believers in Argentina are aware of their fraternal tie to the brethren in Chile. Brother Pedro is already in Bahia Blanca. He will help you to get started. Don't forget, though, that you are the minister, and that Pedro was not sent by us. If you keep the upper hand he will be a good helper. It's good that you know him well. With your family and his, you have the beginning of a church."

7.

Ben rang the bell and then walked up the steps into the chapel. Everyone was already seated waiting for the meeting to begin. As his eye ran over the congregation, he counted to himself. All the pastors from the field were there except the three from the other side of the mountains. They would be there by morning.

That meant the largest conference ever. Twenty-seven pastors would be gathered for a week of study and prayer. He noticed that none of the other missionaries had arrived as yet. He hoped that they would come to help with the Bible studies. He would rely on the national pastors for the evening evangelistic messages.

For the opening hymn he called for the hymn of welcome his own son had written in Spanish and set to a plaintive indigenous tune. Even the newcomers were soon singing the simple words to the old familiar melody. Once they started singing, they sang song after song. It was almost two hours later when Ben stood to welcome them to the conference. He made special mention of the new workers who were attending for the first time.

Most of these men were his sons in the faith. For eighteen years he had been wandering over these same hills. When he arrived he found only one man who was an Evangelical. This man had accepted the Lord while working in the United States as a boy. That first Christian had died five years ago, but now there were thousands of believers. Nobody knew exactly how many there were, but Ben estimated between 7,000 and 9,000 members, besides their families.

The conference had been an annual affair from the first year. Those first believers were now the veteran pastors to whom the younger ones looked for leadership. The conference was the time for renewed enthusiasm and faith. Every year Ben had presented a fresh challenge to which the pastors never failed to rise. This year would be no exception. Before the week was over, Ben would call on them to cross the mountain range into the next valley where they already had a small toehold. He did not know where their work would finally end because beyond that valley lay another, and beyond that yet another.

8.

Mel heaved the box of supplies onto the table. As he opened it and began to set up the medicines, the rest of his team scattered to their posts. Someone set up the portable dentist's chair and started the generator to provide power for the drill. Another set up a table for registration of all the patients. A line had formed outside Mel's temporary dispensary. He made a quick mental calculation. If so many were already waiting, he would be busy all morning and most of the afternoon.

Behind him women were gathering in the empty schoolroom for the hygiene class. Maria, who taught the course, unfolded her easel and began to talk. The women waiting by the dispensary began to fidget. They did not want to miss their class.

From his vantage point on the steps, John watched the various activities get underway within a few minutes. Soon eleven classes were in progress in the small settlement. People were busy studying everything from mosquito control to potato planting.

As the day wore on, the tempo of activities stepped up. The excitement was contagious. The sun was hot, but no one seemed to care.

Finally, as the shadows lengthened, people began to congregate in the plaza. Mel packed away the medical supplies in the truck and took out the two accordions which John and he played. Everyone sang familiar gospel choruses as more villagers gathered around. When almost everyone was there, Maria told the story of the prodigal son with colorful flannelgraph figures. After the story Pedro preached a short message and gave an invitation for those who wanted to receive the Savior. Seven people responded.

After the service everyone gathered around the truck. "This week we received permission from the authorities to build our chapel. By the time you come next month we should have the walls up," they told Mel.

"Pedro has suggested that we have our next baptismal service when we dedicate the chapel. We want you to be here for that."

Chapter Ten

LAYMEN

1.

Manuel turned off his taxi signal as he opened the back door to let out his passenger. He had been on the street since six that morning and had had a good day. If he were to take one more fare, he would miss the evening service. Even a passenger for the north side would make him late for church. Just then, he spied Brother José, waiting for the bus with his Bible under his arm.

"Are you going to church? Come, ride with me. You'll be late if you wait for the bus."

All the way to church they talked about Sunday's services. José described how he had given his testimony in an open-air service in the plaza.

At the end of the service, eight persons had responded to the invitation. "Counting all six street services, there were forty-two who accepted salvation. I can't think of anything more exciting than to see people come forward in response to an invitation."

When they arrived at the church building they found it crowded. They had to stand in the side doorway because there were no seats left. After three enthusiastic songs by the congregation and a fervent united prayer, the pastor spotted Manuel in the crowd.

"Now we will hear a word from Brother Manuel. He has invited the church to come to his house for a special service of thanksgiving."

As Manuel began to speak, tears came to his eyes. "This week makes it one year since I stopped outside this church for the first time. I was on my way to a party where I had planned to meet my friends, but the music caught my attention. I stayed to listen to the rest of the service. At the close I came forward to pray.

"Since then, everything has been different. My wife has come back to me, and she too has found salvation. I still drive the taxicab, but now I use it for God's glory. Everyone who rides with me receives a gospel tract. Everything I have belongs to God, including my time."

As the choir rose to sing following Manuel's testimony, he walked

from the platform with a big smile on his face. The choir was singing the song that had first caught his attention. Now he knew all
the words and could have sung along with them.

2.

Samuel maintained his membership in the Evangelical Church
by paying an annual subscription. It was no longer any social lia-
bility to be an Evangelical. Besides, his wife would make a scene if
he dropped out altogether. Nevertheless, one religious person in the
family was enough.

He stopped at the door of the church to talk to the pastor.
Most of the congregation had already left.

"I just wanted to explain why the church hasn't seen very much
of me lately. My business takes me out to the provinces about one
week a month. I seem to be busy every Sunday. I encourage my wife
to be here when she can, although she would rather not go to
church alone."

"We miss you when you are not here, Sam. I hope you continue to come when you can. I am glad you don't drop out completely. Every man needs the church."

As Samuel and his wife drove away, he remarked to her, "I
don't know why I keep going back. What is happening in church
has nothing to do with the rest of my life. If only our church would
concern itself with vital social and political issues. The church should
be more concerned with social justice and political reform than with
merely theological themes."

"Well, I like church. I enjoy the choir music and the pastor's
sermons are very comforting. One can hardly expect more of the
church. It is not as if it were our whole life. I am sure that we
both have long since outgrown childish ideas about religion. It is
just a part of life for us now, the way it should be. As long as the
church makes no undue demands on us, we should continue to attend
services. Besides, if we were to drop out now, we would have to
find a new circle of friends."

3.

Jorge hurried off the bus in downtown Santiago and across the
square to catch the jitney. It was time for the service to start, and
he still had a ten-minute ride ahead of him to get to the church.
It had been a long day. He had had to forego his *once* (the traditional
afternoon snack) to go directly from work to school. And now going
on to church would mean that it would be several hours yet before
he would be able to eat dinner.

He was excited because several of his old friends from the
national students' organization had promised to be in church that
evening. He had been telling them of the joy and enthusiasm in the

services, and hoped that they would find the same satisfaction he had found in committing himself to Christ.

The damp, cold night had not discouraged anyone from coming to church. The long hall was full. The orchestra of guitars and accordions was playing the Chilean hymns they all loved to sing, while the rafters rang with their exuberance. The many songs were interspersed with comments by the pastor and brief greetings from visitors.

The text that night was from the fourteenth chapter of John's Gospel. Jorge hardly noticed how the pastor developed his theme. From where he was sitting he could see the expression of his friends' faces. He wondered what they thought of the preacher's rustic Spanish. He need not have worried. They were too intent on the message about loving Christ and doing His commandments to worry about niceties of grammar.

After the service Jorge went with his friends to a nearby restaurant. As they sat waiting for their order, his friends began to question him.

"What motivates these Evangelicals? They have evidently found something that satisfies them. What dedication they show! What did the pastor mean when he said that the gospel they preach will change Chile? Does he think that religion will solve Chile's problems before the revolution?"

For more than an hour Jorge sat and talked with them concerning spiritual things. When he finally rose to leave, they all said they would like to visit the church again. "Whatever it is that you people have, we would like to experience it."

4.

"To think it was in that old plaza that the gospel first came to us!" Julio eased the pack from his back and gazed down the hill two kilometers to the square at the center of the market town. Tonight would be the second annual fiesta at the Evangelical church, and he hoped to sell his beans and fruit early in order to return in time to plane the last of the new benches before the evening service.

As he hefted the pack again and started down the hill, Julio thought back two years to the time when he had first heard the *evangelicos* sing. That morning about eleven o'clock, when he had sold almost all his merchandise, what sounded like the gringo music the dance halls played had begun on the other side of the square. He had wrapped his wares and joined the crowd around four men who were singing without accompaniment. In their exuberance the performers did not seem to miss the guitars or drums.

One of them was obviously an *outlander,* but Julio thought he recognized the other three as former neighbors who had moved to the lowlands to find work. After they sang for a long time the three former mountain men began to talk.

They told how they had heard the story of God and then came to experience a new kind of life. At the close, Julio had gone over to them. "Are you the brothers who lived near us?"

"Julio! We remember you. We have come back up here to share the news of what happened to us. We will stay until our people here have experienced the same thing. Then we will return to our families in the lowlands."

Julio now trudged on down the hill. What a difference two years had made. Now he and all his neighbors had accepted the evangelical faith. Old pagan practices had given way to new Christian experiences. At the annual fiesta there was spiritual fellowship and Bible study. To think that it all started in the market place!

5.

The guard at the police check point waved the car on through, but the driver pulled over and beckoned. As the officer approached the car, he recognized the driver as his pastor.

"I didn't know you had a car."

"It isn't mine. The church bought it to help me evangelize. How are things here, João? You've been stationed here about three months, haven't you? How long will it be before you are transferred back to town?"

"I may stay here permanently. I never saw a place where it is so easy to win souls. In every service at least two or three want to become Evangelicals. There are no church members here, so I have to do all the preaching. They are learning all the songs in the song book."

"How can I help you, João? It looks as if you have everything under control here."

"Not really, pastor. I can't begin to teach these people. Can you send someone out on Sundays to give them doctrine? I can get them started on this way of the believers, but someone else will have to lead them along."

"We'll send someone out this Sunday. How many new converts do you have?"

"About thirty-five. Most of them live within a kilometer or two of the crossroads. So far, we are meeting twice a week. We have to vary the days when we have services because I work different shifts different days."

"Can we send you some Bibles for these people?"

"It would not be of much help, really. Only three of them know how to read, and I already sold them their Bibles and song books.

If some of those bright young folks from town could come out to teach these people to read, then maybe we would get somewhere."

"I'll be on my way then, João. God bless you."

"Greet the church for me. Ask them to pray for me."

6.

Sergio closed the shutters of his house. The whole town was silent with the quiet of an afternoon siesta. Outside, the hot sun beat down on the street, but inside, the house was cool. Usually Sergio and his wife took a siesta after lunch, but today was different. Their son Arturo had just arrived home that morning. They had too many questions to ask him to think about sleeping now.

"The big city life must agree with you, Arturo. You look much healthier and happier now. Is life in the city that much better, son?"

"Not really, mother. There are better opportunities to get ahead there, but life in the city is very fast. If you don't rush the same way everyone else does, you won't get ahead there, either. It is expensive to live, too, because there you must buy everything."

"How come you look so good then, son?"

"It is because I have found a new kind of life. Do you remember how afraid we always were of the Protestants? I had never seen one, but I knew they must be terrible. It was only when I arrived in the city that I saw a Protestant for the first time. There, they call them believers."

"That is terrible, son."

"No, no, Dad. Do you know who was the first believer I met? It was Raul, your sister Maria's oldest boy. He helped me find work when I arrived in the city, and later when I knew him better he helped me to find God, too. Now I am also a believer."

"You mean that you are a Protestant? What a shame for our family!"

"But both of you remarked about how well and happy I look. It was this new life of faith that did that for me. Before I was nervous and mean all the time. Since I became a believer, I am relaxed and happy. The reason I came back home to visit you is to tell you about what happened to me and to tell you how you can experience the same thing yourselves. Before I go back to the city, I want to help you to become believers."

7.

Pedro placed twenty pesos on the counter and accepted the house keys with a beating heart. There was a new threshold to cross in this way of freedom and obedience, but he was happy.

Anna, his wife, was not so sure. "But our own house in the port-city is much more up-to-date. Pedro! O Pedro, are we doing the right thing?"

"Anna," he said, "you know we can live comfortably here, or at least make ends meet, on that one hundred and twenty pesos the city property brings us each month. Now we can evangelize this town. What more could we ask of our Lord?"

At the village market place the next morning neither of them was so sure. No one responded to the invitation to accept Christ as Savior and Lord.

"People have come here preaching that religion before," the man at the general store said, "but they only visit here on market days. It isn't enough to have religion only one day a week."

"It will be different now," Pedro replied. "You will see. My wife and I are living in that pink house one street away."

The next market day three men decided to follow Christ. Then they gathered at Pedro's home and drank coffee together. The following week four more responded to the invitation. With the group of seven Pedro began a full schedule of services: a church school and an evangelistic rally on Sundays, a prayer meeting on Thursday nights, an evangelistic meeting on Friday nights as well as the open-air services in the market.

By the time reports of Pedro's activities reached the church in the port-city, the village lay preacher had gathered thirty-eight new believers who were requesting baptism.

"Anna," Pedro said several months later on rent day, "the Lord has proved to us that He wants us to give our lives to winning others for Him."

Chapter Eleven

MISSIONS

1.

"Mission meetings were never like this in the old days, were they, Bob?"

"They sure weren't. Why, now we can get through our business in a day and a half."

"I think we could cut the meeting to one day if we tried. Most of our business now is only internal housekeeping. We could take care of more of it by correspondence."

"It's a good idea to get together like this at least once a year," commented Bob. "Now that we aren't all on every committee, we'd never see everybody if we didn't have our annual meeting. We live so far from each other and keep so busy that we can never get together."

John laughed. "The only time I saw Joe this whole year was when we both went to the seminar in Buenos Aires. I had to leave the country for a chance to have coffee with the same fellow I used to see at least twice a month.

"Remember how Joe thought we were doing ourselves out of our jobs by turning everything over to the nationals? When we were together in Buenos Aires, he told me that now he knows what it's really like to be a missionary. He had never realized how many projects were left unfinished before. Now that he doesn't have to leave to attend all the committee meetings, he can give full time to his field.

"I'm going to take his suggestion for training lay preachers, Bob. Now that I can stay closer to home, I'll be able to meet with them every week. I think Tuesday will be the best night for us."

Bob looked thoughtful. "You know, many of the new ideas we're trying out would never have had a chance under the old setup. Already in this first year, we missionaries have started forty-three new congregations!"

"The national Church is thriving, too. I think we made the change at the right time."

190

2.

The field conference was almost over. Johnson, the board secretary, was pressing to wind things up. His plane was due to leave in three hours. He had hoped for time to answer an urgent letter from the Japan field committee before plane time, but he now saw that this would be impossible.

This year the distribution of the field budget had been no problem because the mission was in the middle of the three-year plan it had adopted two years before. No one was completely satisfied with the outworking of the plan, but everyone was content to let it ride for another year.

Field assignments had proved to be especially difficult this year. The national Church was requesting more missionary personnel for institutions. To agree would have meant moving missionaries out of the pioneer fields. The mission had finally agreed on an unhappy compromise. Two missionary couples were being reassigned to the board school, and other missionaries had doubled up on the pioneer assignments.

The question on the floor now was the routine matter of furlough times. It looked as if the proposed new project of apartment house evangelism would have to be tabled for another year because there were not enough missionaries to go around. Besides, the mission still had to vote on whether the national Church should be urged to assume greater responsibility for its own administration.

Johnson was relieved when an unexpected motion to continue the present furlough time schedule was passed without further comment. As discussion began on the literacy seminar he thought to himself, "If I can prevent the coffee break from dragging out for half an hour, I may get to that letter."

Now that the end of the week-long session was in sight, everyone was beginning to relax. All the committees had been chosen and the dates for the next meeting agreed upon. No one but the board secretary was in any particular hurry, as everyone was planning to stay in the city for an extra day to do some shopping. After the hard week, everyone wanted a change of pace before getting back to work.

3.

"No new missionary has been able to complete a term on that field for the past ten years. I don't know if the problem is in the kind of young people we've been sending out, if it's the peculiar nature of our work there, or if it's the fault of the field administration."

The home board had gathered for its annual meeting. The routine reports had been read. In an informal session before the afternoon's business session, board members were airing their views on mission problems.

"I don't think the problem is in the kind of personnel we are sending to this field. Some of them have been reassigned to other Latin American fields and have made excellent missionaries. It's as if there were something about this field that prevented them from fulfilling their potential."

"It isn't the field administration either. Richards is one of the best missionaries we have. I never will forget the presentation he made at our last missionary convention. Everyone was deeply challenged with the need of his field."

"No, I am sure it is not the fault of the field director. I wish all our men were as well qualified as he."

"The problem can't really be the field, either. Even though our churches aren't growing very much, other Evangelical missions in the same area are seeing phenomenal growth. There is no reason why our work should lag behind the others."

"We have no way to tell for sure what is wrong. Even the veteran missionaries there don't seem to know what needs to be changed. I'm glad they don't give up in discouragement. We must encourage them to continue their work. Surely the time will come when the seed they are sowing will bear fruit."

4.

Dear Dan:

I enclose the monthly statement of gifts that have come in for you here, along with the record of office expenses. I sent receipts to everyone. The bank deposit was very small this time. It must be time to send out another letter asking for financial support.

I'm sure that everyone would like to hear about the congregation you mentioned in your last letter. Do you have a picture of yourself and Mary with the group? It would be better not to have to use the picture we used last time.

Everyone here is wondering if you are going to participate in the evangelistic campaign in your town. The Community Church wrote asking specifically. If you do, they won't continue to support the mission. They feel it would compromise their doctrinal position if you participated. I'm sure you can write and put them at ease on this point. I know you don't want to get mixed up in anything like that.

Do you still plan to come home next February? If so, how long do you plan to stay? In your last letter you mentioned that you would have to leave the church untended while you are home in the States, so I guess you won't be able to stay here very long. If you will let me know which churches you want to visit, I'll contact them for you.

There are so many missionaries traveling among the churches now that we need to set up an itinerary as soon as possible.

Pastor Jones plans to visit your area this summer. Can you put him up? It would be good if you could show him your work. If he gets interested in the mission, his church could be a big help. The more time you can spend with him the better. I'll write again as soon as I have the dates of his trip, so that you can contact him.

Your brother,
Jim

5.

Ken opened the morning service with a brief prayer. That Sunday they were celebrating the twelfth anniversary of their church, and the chapel was full. Over half the day school students were there, and by themselves filled six benches. The members of the church sat in the last three rows.

All six missionaries were present. Jean played the organ, while the others sat on the platform in honor of the occasion. Each participated in turn. They recounted how they had chosen the mountain town because there was no church of their denomination in the vicinity. They reminisced about raising the money in North America to build the chapel and school. They told of the help they had received from other Evangelicals in town, and how the church had finally started to grow.

Now there were thirty members, counting the missionaries. Their church was still the smallest of the sixteen Evangelical churches in town, but each one who spoke emphasized that numbers weren't everything and that quality was more important than quantity.

The missionaries all agreed that it would be some time before they would be ready to start other congregations. Between serving in the clinic and in the school, they were all kept busy during the week. On Sunday they were needed in the church to teach Sunday School, conduct the services and alternate in preaching.

This morning, Ken, the pastor of the church, preached the sermon. As senior missionary he was the most experienced of the group and able to speak with the greatest authority. The theme of his message was obedience to the Great Commission. His conclusion was a ringing call to sacrifice.

"We must be willing to continue to work even though we see little fruit for our labor. It is our lot to be called to a hard place. Perhaps if we had more missionaries we would see greater growth."

6.

All the missionaries were in chapel. Jack had put off his trip to the hills until the following day so as not to miss the service.

The morning speaker was the Rev. John Jones, the well-known North American pastor. He was on the last lap of a trip around Latin America.

His theme was the new role of the missionary. He referred to the missions he had visited and the missionaries with whom he had spoken. He spoke of the dangers of communism and nationalism and of the need to safeguard the Church against contamination with the world.

After chapel everyone gathered around the speaker. "That is our situation exactly," they told him. "Nothing seems to be safe any more. All we can do is continue to serve the Lord in the best way we know. If others misunderstand us, we can't help it. This is a hard field, and it seems that suspicion and misunderstanding are our lot. We don't know how much longer the door will remain open, but as long as it does, we will continue to work."

"Can you stay over an extra day to visit our church in the hills?" asked Jack enthusiastically.

"I'm sorry but I have another speaking engagement tomorrow night, so I must catch the morning plane. This afternoon I'm going to see the facilities here, and tonight I'll be having dinner with the Johnson's, who are from our Church in the States. I would have enjoyed getting out a little bit."

"Our church up there is small but very solid. We've been visiting this hill town for twelve years. We built a little chapel where the group meets every Sunday. The congregation can't support a pastor yet, so we missionaries take turns going on Sundays. Once a month I go up to celebrate the Lord's Supper with them."

7.

"Can you come to help us? We want to hold a city-wide evangelistic campaign in November."

"Have you asked the cooperation of the other churches? Who is sponsoring the campaign?"

"We have already spoken to some of the pastors and they are willing to cooperate. We hope to involve all the Evangelical Churches. We'll assume responsibility for the campaign, but it will be publicized as an interdenominational effort."

"Why do you want to have it in November? Would any other time of the year be better?"

"We settled on November because by that time the rainy season is over and everything is back to normal."

"Fine. To have a campaign in November you'll have to begin preparations immediately. The special prayer services, the pre-campaigns in every church, the advertising and preparation all take time."

"We're ready to begin today. All we need is the word from you."

"What kind of help do you want from our organization?"

"What kind of help can you give us?"

"We can supply personnel for specialized tasks such as music, speaking, and training counsellors, or we can coordinate the whole campaign for you."

"If you supply the speaker and train counsellors for us, could we handle the rest of it?"

"You probably could, but we wouldn't recommend it. If you're interested, the best way would be for us to direct the campaign. There are so many aspects that only an overall plan can ensure that everything is done on time."

"What do we do first?"

"Let's begin by setting up a meeting where everyone can come together to discuss the campaign. The campaign may well double the number of Evangelicals in the city. It will certainly be the beginning of new congregations. We need to know where we are going so that we are not caught unprepared when we reach the end of the campaign and have the responsibility of caring for a much larger Evangelical community."

Chapter Twelve

MISSIONARIES

1.

Harold dismissed the class. He had an hour to catch his breath before his next class. His teaching load was doubled this year because Bob was home on furlough.

Practical theology wasn't really his field. He had come to the seminary to teach systematic theology. Edwards resigned the following year, and Harold had had to step in. There weren't enough qualified men on the faculty to take care of every subject, so everyone had doubled up on assignments. If it weren't for the part-time instructors, the seminary could not continue to function.

Some of the courses were simple to teach. He still had all his own seminary notes for his homiletics course, and he could use the books from the seminary library to fill out what he would teach. Also he had a psychology minor from college, which gave him enough background to teach the introductory course in counselling.

Other courses were proving more difficult. These young men were not going to pastor congregations whose members had been brought up in the Church. They would have to minister to first generation Evangelicals. Though they themselves had been educated in church schools they seemed to recognize that they were called to be pioneers, to claim new territory.

Harold's own background had not prepared him for such a ministry. Every day was a challenge. It was exciting to see the students respond to his teaching. He saw now that he had been forced by circumstances to develop new approaches and new ideas. If his training had been in practical theology, he probably would never have gone beyond transmitting a carbon copy of his own education.

Harold was confident that his students would prove successful in the ministry. Already they were finding ways to put into practice what he was teaching. With his help they had already begun three new congregations. When they were asked to minister, they did not do it as an academic exercise nor as playing church. They were actually communicating with others.

2.

"NATIONAL DELEGATE ELECTED PRESIDENT OF IN-
TERNATIONAL BANKING ORGANIZATION," read the morn-
ing headlines. John put the paper down as Herb entered his office.

"Now that you've spent two months with us in the capital, Herb,
I think you are ready to take up your duties at the Bible Institute."

"I'm anxious to go, sir. Ever since I finished language school
I've been looking forward to this."

"If you move up to the hills now, you'll still have a month
to get ready for the new school term. I'm sure you'll enjoy your
work. You're catching on to the language quite quickly."

"Tom wrote that they're expecting seven students this year."

"Yes, the number is down. Last year we had eleven. Four years
ago we had eighteen."

"What is happening? Aren't there as many candidates for the
ministry any more?"

"Oh, the people here just aren't leaders. We can't get them to
take responsibility. I don't know how many of our young men
have chosen to go to other kinds of schools these last few years.
We missionaries end up having to do everything."

"Do you think it's because of the low salaries our pastors receive?"

"Not really. For their level of education, they aren't earning
bad salaries. Besides, to be a success in the ministry a man ought
to be willing to sacrifice a bit."

"To get back to the subject of my move to the Bible Institute.
Is the new missionary house finished? If it isn't I'd better leave the
family here for the time being."

"You don't need to worry about that. Tom has been there to
make sure that the job gets done. By next week everything will be
set. I'm sure you'll find the house to your liking."

3.

Tim closed his office door. The whole student body was in the
auditorium for the opening address of spiritual emphasis week, but
he was taking a few minutes out in his own study.

Spiritual emphasis! Tim still didn't know what the school was
seeking. Most of the students were from non-Evangelical homes, and
the school was firmly opposed to offending anyone on questions of
race or creed. In practice this meant the gospel was never overtly
mentioned in chapel or out of it. There seemed to be an unuttered
assumption that true Christianity consisted in performing good deeds
in the name of the Lord.

How this interpretation had come about no one knew. The
preaching of the Churches in the mission was certainly clear concerning the nature of the gospel. But the school existed independently

of the denomination, by the preference of the school administration.

The administration had never asked for an indication of his own Christian commitment. His professional standing as an experienced teacher and his proven ability to minister cross-culturally had landed him the job without difficulty.

Now he was confused. He had hoped that in service to the Church he would find fulfillment. But this had turned out to be just another teaching assignment. Surely there should be something more to missionary service than that. How could the school give spiritual emphasis without spiritual content? Religious relativism that found everything to be good would lead the students into a cynicism that denied all good. If only the school did not pretend to provide spiritual help.

The bell rang, marking the end of the service. Tim waited until everyone had time to leave the auditorium. Then he opened the door and stepped out to mingle with the crowd.

4.

From where he stood behind the counter, Gene could see a young man on the sidewalk gazing at the Bible in the window. This was not the first time the young man had stopped. Gene knew from experience that eventually he would come in to talk.

The customer Gene was helping was an evangelist from the interior. He came in about once a month. Every time he came Gene could count on his staying in the bookstore all morning. On each visit, he bought a supply of Bibles and Testaments and a dozen hymnbooks. After making his purchases, he would browse through the new books. His ride back home did not leave until after lunch. He enjoyed talking to the people who came into the store. Sometimes he would meet a colleague in the ministry or an old friend from the church in town.

Gene tried to encourage the Evangelicals to use the bookstore as a place to meet. Since the beginning, the policy of the store had been to stock literature for all Evangelical Churches in the area. As a result, the bookstore had proved to be a unifying factor. Gene always kept a pot of coffee on the hotplate at the back of the store. Many a cooperative venture had been born over coffee as Evangelicals shared their experiences in the back room.

The mission was making plans to expand the store into a combined bookstore and publisher's outlet. So many Evangelical Churches were springing up in the area, all needing supplies, that the present setup was inadequate. They would need space for storage, a man to take care of shipping, and an improved bookkeeping system. The increased sales volume had not provided more funds because the low-profit margin had been used to pay for a sales assistant.

The number of churches had increased only in the last five years. Gene had remarked to his wife just that morning how exciting it was to be at the hub of an expanding network of new churches. From behind his counter in the store Gene was watching the Church grow.

5.

It was Monday morning and the telephone was ringing as John opened the office door. "Looks like another busy week," he thought to himself as he picked up the receiver. The currency exchange was on the line with the day's rate. He jotted it down and made a mental note to buy a few hundred extra dollars' worth of pesos. The way the market was fluctuating, it was impossible to tell what to expect these days.

He glanced at the memo pad. Dave was scheduled to come in to begin processing his visa for leaving the country. John checked to make sure all the necessary forms were in the file.

We would have to deposit the pesos for the national Church's building fund this week, too. Harry would know how much more was in the national church budget.

Last year's statistical reports from the missionaries were not in yet, although almost all of the churches had reported. He would have to send another reminder. The home board was asking for field totals, but how could he send them until everyone had reported?

He checked the calendar. Today his own family was coming back from the country. He phoned the American School and was assured that the children's school registration was in order.

When he put the telephone down, it rang again. This time it was Pastor Wood of the Union Church. "Can you tell me how to contact your wife, John? We are hoping she'll be able to take charge of the youth choir again."

"She's not arriving till later this morning. Why don't you call her this afternoon at home? I'm sure she'll be glad to help."

John decided to wait to fill out the monthly report until Roberts came in after lunch. John had never visited the fields in the interior and had no idea which name went with which church. All the names were so alike anyway. Now that things were slowly being turned over to the national Church, his own job would surely get easier. Soon he would give all his time to the business affairs of the missionaries alone.

6.

"For seven years we have been working on a modern system of teaching illiterates. We took the best features of three existing methods and developed our own. We have solved most of the problems involved. Now we are ready to go."

It was the opening meeting of a city-wide literacy campaign. The speaker was Art, the literacy expert from the capital. This was to be the pilot project in a nationwide series of campaigns.

"Our mission has decided that because of the high rate of illiteracy in this country, literacy campaigns should take precedence over every other type of mission activity. We have had to cut back other activities to make this possible."

"Since this program is designed to serve the whole community, it is not confined to Evangelicals. We will try to draw teachers from all religious groups and from other community organizations. Participation in this program is not restricted to professionals, but is open to anyone and everyone who is interested in community improvement."

"Where will the classes meet?"

"We have decided not to use Evangelical church buildings nor even other church facilities, so as not to give the wrong impression. We are asking for the loan of other quarters for classes. That way we can remain neutral."

"If non-professionals can teach, how can you maintain the necessary high standards?"

"We have assigned nine qualified missionaries who will act as administrators of the program. They will seek out competent supervisors who will choose the teachers. We are confident that this system will enable us to maintain high quality on every level.

"By this time next year we will be ready to evaluate the program. By then enough people will have completed the course for us to know if your approach is effective. If it works here, we plan to invest more men and money as we expand to other cities."

7.

"If the Christians themselves had not begun to reach out with the gospel and to do missionary work, I don't know what would have happened," Bernie thought to himself as he steered the truck around a pothole and pressed the accelerator. He wanted to get home before the storm broke. The last hill would be treacherous in the rain.

It had been a good trip. The teams of lay evangelists were functioning smoothly. There were eleven congregations now instead of the original two, and in each of them new converts were receiving instruction in winning others. "Now," Bernie thought, "all I have to do is visit them to see what God is doing, encourage them a little, and keep up the supplies of literature. At this rate every town in the region will be reached by the end of next year."

The truck was traveling light. Bernie calculated that there was over a ton and a half of literature deposited along the way, most

of it with the colporteurs who depended on him to keep them supplied. The record player, the projection equipment, the loudspeaker
and his own luggage were all that remained in the truck. They
were strapped to the sides and bolted down with the special fasteners
he'd made for these back-country roads.

He revved the engine and shifted to low gear for the descent
from the last hill. The rain was beginning to fall and obscure the
trail, but Bernie was on home ground. It would be good to settle
in with the family and wait out the rainy season. Two months were
just long enough to prepare the next series of Bible studies. Then
he must be back on the road with more books and supplies, to find
out once again how the Christians had been at work for the Lord.

PART IV
CONTEXT OF GROWTH

The growth of the Evangelical Churches in every country of Latin America must be seen in the broad social context of regional settlement patterns; class divisions; religious practices; economic, social, and political development; and demographic shifts currently in process.

> *To place the development of Protestants (or any other religion) in the context of a particular culture is to assume that the questions of why, where, how, and when Protestant denominationalism arose are tied in with what has been happening to institutions and customs which, at first glance, seem unrelated to religious behavior (Willems 1967. a:v).*

The growth patterns which have been described in Part II reflect environmental effects on the Evangelical Churches.

The Evangelical Churches, in turn, are changing Latin American society through their exerted influence. The field of activity of the Churches must be determined by the locality of change and the attitude of the people concerning change. Not only is the growth of the Church unavoidably linked to the social context itself; the extent of growth is also determined by the manner in which the Churches meet the challenges of that context.

Chapter Thirteen

ETHNIC STRUCTURES

The Evangelical Churches of Latin America comprise an ethnic cross-section of the population including all major culture groups. The Churches in which these are found differ greatly even though in some cases the denominational affiliation remains the same. For example, there is little basis for comparison of a Mennonite congregation in the Chocó in Colombia and a Mennonite immigrant church in Paraguay. Furthermore, the attention given by Churches and missions to these groups is neither in direct proportion to their numerical size nor to their relative influence within society.

In considering the ethnic makeup of the Evangelical Churches of Latin America, the idea of "social race" as developed by Charles Wagley helps one to see the ambiguities of classification:

> Such terms as Negro, White, Indian, or Mulatto do not have genetic meanings in most American societies; they may in one society be classifications based on real or imaginary physical characteristics; in another, they may refer more to criteria of social status such as education, wealth, language, and even custom; while in still another they may indicate near or distant ancestry (1965: 531).

Despite this complexity, a rough and perhaps overly generalized classification of the ethnic groups is essential as a backdrop for this study. With this in mind, we present the six groupings suggested by Butland (1960).

1. *Indians.* (A more accurate term would be "Amerindians" so as to distinguish this group from natives of India.) There are some 35 million Indians who have not mixed with the other peoples who came to the New World beginning in the sixteenth century. The majority of Latin America's Indians are descendants of the great mountain civilizations of the Aztecs (Mexico), Mayas (Yucatán), and Incas (Ecuador, Peru, Bolivia). Their distribution (but *not* their population density) is indicated in Figure 65. Much less significant are the marginal Indian tribes which roam the jungles of the Amazon Basin. For example, Brazil reports only 136,000 Indians in a total population of 86 million. However, the Indian group con-

Figure 65

PREDOMINANT ETHNIC COMPOSITION
OF LATIN AMERICA

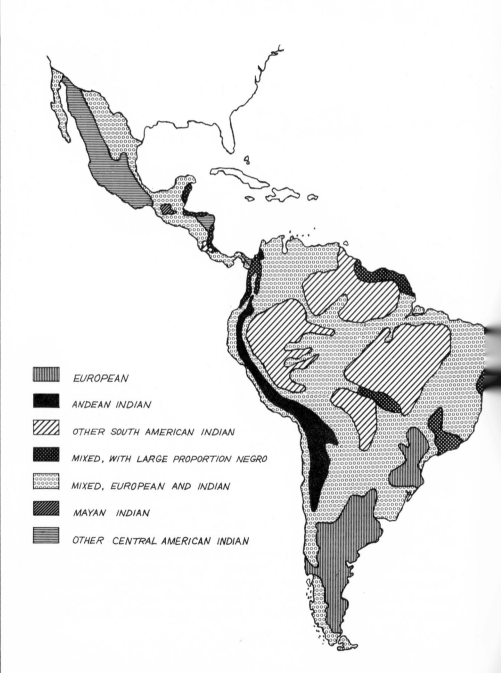

EUROPEAN

ANDEAN INDIAN

OTHER SOUTH AMERICAN INDIAN

MIXED, WITH LARGE PROPORTION NEGRO

MIXED, EUROPEAN AND INDIAN

MAYAN INDIAN

OTHER CENTRAL AMERICAN INDIAN

Figure 66

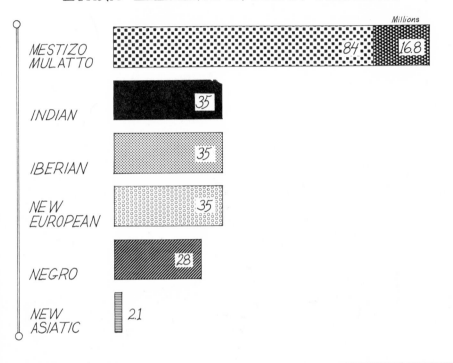

ETHNIC ELEMENTS IN LATIN AMERICA

Millions

MESTIZO
MULATTO
84   16.8

INDIAN
35

IBERIAN
35

NEW
EUROPEAN
35

NEGRO
28

NEW
ASIATIC
2.1

stitutes the majority of the population in Guatemala and Bolivia (Figure 67).

2. *Iberians.* Racial intermarriage has been the rule for Iberians in the New World, but it is estimated that there are some 35 million of "pure" Iberian descent. Argentina and Uruguay together contain about one-third of the Iberian population.

3. *Negroes.* Brought to the New World from Africa by slave traders, Negroes now number about 28 million in Latin America. They are significant in northeast Brazil, the West Indies, and in all countries which have a Caribbean coastline.

4. *Mixed Elements.* Three basic mixtures in Latin America are derived from many degrees of ancestry: (a) *mestizos,* a mixture of Indian and Iberian, constitute one-third of the total population, or some 84 million; (b) *mulattoes,* an Iberian-Negro cross, are found in countries with significant Negro population and number about 16.8

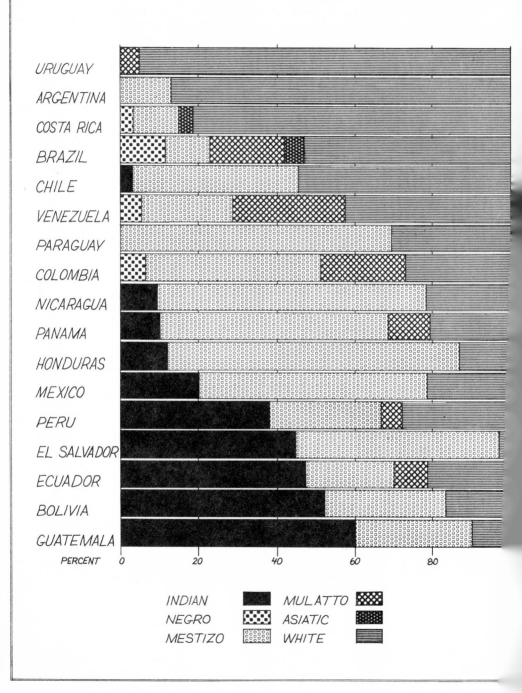

Figure 67

million; (c) *zambos* or *cafusos* are an Indian-Negro cross, and are not significant demographically.

5. *New Europeans.* Immigration from European countries, other than the Iberian Peninsula, has been increasing since the independence movements of the early 1800's, especially in the last hundred years. These immigrants have not mixed freely with others. Italians form the largest group, followed by Germans, Poles, Swiss, and others. The band of territory from São Paulo south through Uruguay and most of Argentina has become home for most of the 35 million Europeans.

6. *New Asiatics.* The tide of immigration from Asia has been increasing throughout the twentieth century. A large colony of Japanese has settled in Brazil. Recent Asian immigrants throughout Latin America number 2.1 million.

Racial prejudice exists in certain pockets of Latin America such as Guyana, where East Indians and Negroes battle for political power. But, in general,

> The complexity of this ethnic distribution is increased by the widespread scale of the racial mixture which has taken place. As a result there are few racial antagonisms of any significance. The differences which do occur are largely the outcome of social classes, based on economic, educational, and cultural distinctions. Latin America is thus singularly fortunate in being relatively free of the racial problems which beset much of the world (Butland 1960: 7).

The ethnic structure of the Latin American population manifests itself in two kinds of churches: (1) the ethnic Church or denomination which draws its membership from one ethnic group; and (2) the Church or denomination which itself reflects the great ethnic and racial mixture that is Latin America. Most Latin Evangelicals belong to Churches of the latter type and thus share in the variegated cultural values of Latin American society. Most of the generalities concerning the Evangelical Churches in Latin America also refer to these racially mixed congregations. Indeed, we might say that most of this report concerns them, for upon them depends the future of the Evangelical cause. It is into this larger fellowship that the strictly ethnic churches are becoming integrated.

Having said this, we will consider in this chapter the ethnic Churches, since they represent some of the gravest problems as well as greatest opportunities for church growth. Their relationship to each other and to society as a whole directly affects the evangelization of Latin America.

Foreign Colony Churches

At the one end of the Protestant spectrum are foreign Churches composed of temporary residents. Several denominations which are now more inclusive began thus among the foreign residents of Latin America before the days of religious liberty. Among these were the Presbyterian Church in Chile and the Anglican Church wherever there were groups of British subjects. Very few of the congregations of the foreign colonies, however, succeeded in transmitting their faith to the native-born of those countries so that Spanish or Portuguese churches could be planted. The foreigners were so transient and so removed from the surrounding culture that they developed neither the ability nor the desire to propagate the faith outside their own colony.

These foreign colony Churches have a curious relationship to the other Evangelical Churches of Latin America. While they are numerically a very small percentage of the total membership of the Churches, they often have disproportionate influence because of the wealth and social standing of their members. The foreign churches, among which we include the various Anglican, Baptist, Lutheran and Union Churches which use English or other European languages, appear to fall into a few broad categories irrespective of denominational affiliation.

The first common type concerns itself primarily with the social life of its members. It is difficult to determine whether this institution functions more as a church or a social club. Social work, which many foreigners in Latin America feel conscience-bound to promote, is frequently conducted along the same lines as a North American club. Members are encouraged to maintain an active social life with others of the congregation. The result is a real, if unintended, isolation from national life. Although most foreign commercial companies at work in Latin America encourage their employees to participate in authentic community activities, this seems to be easier said than done. In addition, most of the foreigners' children study together in special schools, further isolating not only them but their parents as well. The impression is thus created among nationals that the only foreign Protestants interested in their spiritual welfare are the missionaries — professionals who are paid to be interested.

A second type of foreign colony Church shows a much healthier attitude toward Latin American society. This Church channels willing members directly into activities which aid the country socially and spiritually. These have included literacy, literature distribution, and in many places direct financial aid to national churches or to various social services.

A third type works in direct partnership with the national Church, supporting the programs and activities of local congregations. Most often this type of cooperation is not along denominational lines.

Even at best, however, these foreign Churches have little evangelistic or pastoral impact outside their own circles. The outsiders they do reach are usually persons who are trying to improve their English or who have some direct social tie to the foreign community.

IMMIGRANT CHURCHES

Unlike the foreign Churches, the immigrant Churches draw their membership from permanent settlers. The German and Scandinavian Lutherans in Chile, Argentina, Brazil, Venezuela, and Uruguay; the Mennonite colonies in Mexico, British Honduras, Bolivia, Uruguay, Paraguay, and Brazil; the Waldensians; and the members of the Japanese Holiness Church in Brazil were already Protestants when they emigrated to Latin America. Each group has tended to live in isolation from the mainstream of Latin American Protestantism, having practiced endogamy and maintained the language and customs of its country of origin.

These isolationist practices are disappearing as the younger generation marries outside its group and drifts away from ethnic identification. Because these Churches have been closely tied to foreign culture-values, when acculturation of the youth causes the foreign patterns to give way, the Churches lose their reason for existence. During the three months we spent in Chile, over three-fourths of the marriages of German Lutherans listed in the Santiago newspapers were to Chilean Catholics. The ceremonies were usually performed in the Roman Catholic Church, clearly showing which way the tide is moving.

When the statistics of the immigrant Churches are combined with the totals of all Evangelical Churches an impression of receptivity is created. Their lack of growth can so lower the figures as to conceal the evangelistic effectiveness of neighboring Churches. In Chapters Three and Four we have dealt with this problem as it occurs in Argentina and Brazil.

The isolation until recent times of the immigrant Churches from the rest of Latin American Protestantism is explained by the fact that their members did not come as missionaries but as colonists. The German Lutherans in particular have stated that they consider Latin America to be Catholic by tradition and that it is necessary to respect that tradition by not proselytizing (Vergara 1962: 33). Their purpose is to provide spiritual care for the German colony, and pastors for their Churches are supplied from Germany.

The ethnic Lutheran Churches which are growing in Latin America are mostly those with North American ties. The Lutheran Church of America in Argentina, the American Lutheran Church missionaries in Brazil, and the Missouri Synod Lutheran Church in both of these countries are seeing hopeful signs of renewal and some growth as they associate more with the national Churches.

Rigid nationalistic feelings which have tended to isolate the ethnic Churches from society at large are beginning to disappear.

This should produce a climate propitious for church growth. As the ethnic Churches strengthen their ties with national Churches and begin to relate more meaningfully to the rest of society, they should be able to reach out and bring men into the Church. This will require a shift in thinking, a new spiritual dynamic, and a sense of mission such as will produce evangelistic fervor. Many are seeking ways to solve the problem of isolation (Jensen 1965).

NEGRO CHURCHES

The West Indian Churches of Panama, Costa Rica, Nicaragua, and Honduras are made up of English-speaking Negroes whose ancestors had migrated to Central America to work on fruit plantations and had brought their church structures with them. These Anglicans, Methodists, and Moravians now make up a sizable part of the Evangelical Church in Central America. In Costa Rica, for example, over one-third of all Evangelicals are members of Negro Churches even though West Indian Negroes constitute only 2 per cent of the total population (Nelson 1963: 67, 256, 257). West Indians in Panama constitute 14 per cent of the population (Butler 1964: 30), yet membership in their Churches also accounts for one-third of all Evangelicals. The disproportion arises in each case because the Negro population is overwhelmingly Evangelical.

The Protestantism of the Negro, however, is for the most part nominal; great numbers are Protestant only by tradition. The Church here has narrowly conceived its task as merely caring for its own. Yet its teaching program has failed not only to integrate the children of church members into the life of the Church, but even to hold them in the Church.

The problem of church membership is further complicated by the West Indian pattern of common-law marriage, which keeps most of the men and women between the ages of sixteen and forty-five in a series of temporary unions. As a result, although most of the laboring people consider themselves Protestants, they are not eligible for church membership. Consequently, the congregations are composed of the relatively few who have married and thus attained the status symbol of the older and more successful (McGavran 1962:41-76).

Isolation of Negro Churches has been heightened by the inability of their members to speak Spanish, the tongue of their adopted land, and also by the lack of roads from the coastal areas inland. Lack of industry has kept the standard of living at a low level, causing most West Indian Negroes to be tied to the economy of the plantations. Poor economic conditions, however, have driven many young people to the cities, where they are forced to integrate into the national life. In an effort to participate more fully in this national life, the younger generation tends to speak Spanish and attempts to emulate Spanish culture.

Acculturation represents a combination of danger and opportunity for the Negro Churches. On the one hand, acculturation produces an indifference toward the Evangelical Church because of its image as a part of the old isolated life. On the other hand, this same process can lead the youth into vital Christianity through contacts with other Evangelicals in Spanish-speaking society who enjoy a more dynamic spiritual life.

We saw encouraging signs of vitality among the Moravians in Nicaragua. The graduates of their Bible institute who have gone on to the Seminário Bíblico in San José, Costa Rica, for a final year of schooling have returned to the Negro Nicaraguan churches as a revitalizing force. Evangelism-in-Depth has helped these churches to forge ties with other Evangelical Churches, providing a path for spiritual renewal. The Moravian Church is seeking new ways to win the nominal Christians of its own community and to teach the young people in such a way as to keep them in the Church. The future of their Church rests on the success of these efforts.

ITALIAN-AMERICAN CHURCHES

The Congregação Cristã (Christian Congregation, Brazil) and the Asamblea Cristiana (Christian Assemblies) and Asamblea Cristiana Cultural (Cultural Christian Assemblies, Argentina) are not immigrant Churches in the sense we have discussed above, because their members adopted the Evangelical faith after arriving in the New World. All three Churches began among Italian immigrants as the results of the missionary efforts of Louis Francescon, an Italian-American who carried the Pentecostal message from the United States to South America in 1909-1910 (Read 1965: 22). Since that time these Churches have followed separate courses.

The Congregação Cristã has become thoroughly Brazilian; one sees nothing to remind him that this Church began among Italian immigrants. The superficial similarities to the Italian Pentecostals in the United States do not obscure the Brazilian nature of the Church. The music, preaching, and testimonies are thoroughly Brazilian. We met many elders with Italian names, but the number of these is not out of proportion to the large numbers of Italians present in Brazil's population. The Congregação Cristã has grown to 500,000 members, a development which would have been impossible had it confined itself to holding Italian services and ministering only to Italians. Indeed, the Church would have diminished as the colony became integrated into the community at large. Instead of making the mistake of remaining contained within the Italian colony, the Congregação has moved out into Brazilian society and has become Brazilian in the process, maintaining only those Italian customs which were incorporated as doctrine (the holy kiss, and the veil which the women wear in church).

The two Italian Churches in Argentina have not enjoyed equivalent growth even when we take into account the slower growth rate for all Churches in Argentina in comparison with those in Brazil. Both the Asamblea Cristiana and the Asamblea Cristiana Cultural are still known as Italian Churches, and in both we saw evidence of the kind of tension between generations that arises when the second generation of a foreign church attempts to integrate into national life. Even the Spanish services retain an Italian flavor.

By confining themselves for so long to work among Italians exclusively, these Italian-Argentine Churches have not grown as they might have. If they had been more fully integrated into national life, they would probably now be in organic union with the Church of God (including its former Toba Indian work), and the Slavic Pentecostal Churches. The members of both of these last denominations were originally part of the Asamblea Cristiana. If the three had remained united, they would have had a much stronger base for evangelism.

The Asamblea Cristiana Cultural, the original Italian Pentecostal Church in Argentina, also has confined its efforts to providing spiritual care for its own members. It has produced few other congregations and has at present only about 2,000 members. The Asamblea Cristiana, an early split, has been more effective in planting churches and has grown to 22,000 despite other schisms. Both of these Churches could have done better had they followed the lead of the Congregação Cristã in Brazil and broken out of their Italian ethnocentrism.

All three Churches began (although in different cultural settings) by evangelizing Italian immigrants from the same part of Italy and in many cases from the same family group. The dramatic difference of size in these three Churches presents an object lesson in the dynamics of church growth. One Church has 2,000 members, one 22,000, and one 500,000. Students of mission would do well to make a study of this situation and of the reasons for such varied rates of growth. The resistance to the Evangelical message on the part of the Italians in southern Brazil can be explained in part by the difference in the cultural setting from that in Argentina. These in southern Brazil are winegrowers who originally came from northern Italy. The similarity of their present existence to the life they lived in Italy partly accounts for their resistance to change. Their situation contrasts sharply to that of the southern Italians and Sicilians who made their way to the developing cities of São Paulo and Buenos Aires and found themselves in a completely different world.

Indian Churches

Much greater diversity is present among the Indian Churches of Latin America than among other Evangelical Churches. They range from indigenous movements which have arisen spontaneously and without outside aid, such as the Otomí Church in Mexico (McGavran 1963: 98-103), to the carefully cultivated, mission-directed denominations such as the Anglican work among the Araucanian Indians of Chile (Pytches 1967: 114-128).

In considering the Indian Churches we must differentiate between the few scattered aboriginal tribes who, like the Indians of the Amazon Basin, live in complete isolation from the rest of society and the majority who are less isolated and are sometimes even well integrated into the mixed rural population. Of the 35 million pureblood Indians in Latin America, the aboriginal tribes constitute less than one-fourth, so that they form less than 3 per cent of the total population.

Some of the most heroic efforts to evangelize the Indians have been among isolated tribes, the case of the Auca Indians of Ecuador certainly being the best known. This kind of effort has caught the imagination of North American Christians, who have given their unquestioning, enthusiastic support. Many do not realize that this type of Indian constitutes a very small portion of the winnable people in Latin America. The Auca tribe, for example, numbers under 100 persons. While definitely they must be reached with the gospel, a realistic emphasis must be given to this work. Among these aboriginal tribes only the acculturating fringes are open to the gospel as yet. Bennett mentions that the Lacanja group of the Lancandon Indians (of Chiapas, Mexico), which has been exposed to the outside influence of the alligator and *chicle* hunters, is more responsive to the gospel than the conservative Naja group (1967: 50).

The Evangelical Church in an Indian-Mestizo Community

Although the small, vanishing tribes have received a disproportionate amount of attention and effort from Evangelicals, the major part of actual Indian evangelism has been conducted among the larger Indian cultures, which are a viable part of society and which constitute a large part of the rural population of Latin America. Paraguay, Bolivia, Peru, Ecuador, Colombia, Venezuela, Mexico, and all of the Central American countries except Costa Rica have large Indian populations in this category (Beals 1965: 345). Exactly what part of the population in each country can be said to be Indian depends to a large extent on the definition of the word. In deciding who is or who is not an Indian, "on the whole, social and cultural factors are more significant than descent and physical appearance" (Pitt-Rivers 1965: 42). Furthermore, since many of the Indians live among the *mestizo* population, the question of their identity and relationship to the rest of society becomes important.

The distinction must also be made between Indians who speak only their own languages and those who also speak Spanish or Portuguese. Most Indians have some European patterns superimposed in varying degrees upon their own indigenous forms. Some of these patterns were forcibly introduced by their conquerors or by legal and social pressures of later times; other patterns are elements of the European culture which the Indians themselves have adopted. For example, the "native" dress by which some tribes can be distinguished is often based on modified European styles. Such acculturation has produced subcultures, all of which share a common cultural heritage but which differ according to local environment and history (Wagley and Harris 1965: 43).

Early efforts to evangelize the Indians in Spanish and Portuguese produced little growth. Today many Indians speak Spanish and many more understand it. Nevertheless, even in Indian communities where Spanish has become the language of the market place, social communication is still restricted to the Indian language, and the *mestizo* minority often finds it has to learn the language of the Indian majority.

The problem, however, lies not so much with language differences as with different thought patterns. Dr. Jacob Loewen, speaking in the Third Evangelical Communications Congress at Lima in September, 1967, said, "An Indian once complained that the missionary scratches where it does not itch" (Perrow 1967: 24). The Church or mission which does not take into account the differences of thought patterns between the Spanish and the Indian or between tribes and other subcultures is in danger of obstructing church growth. As Latin America succeeds in assimilating and integrating into many different cultural elements, tribal and subcultural differences will decrease. The Evangelical Church is often a catalyst in promoting integration; at the same time, she cannot disregard the real differences that exist. The cultural antipathies are so great between some subcultures or tribes that it is necessary to reach, win, and, in some cases, administer churches separately in each.

We saw many examples of the effects of these cultural antipathies. Many Spanish-speaking Panamanians felt that the Evangelical faith was only for English-speaking peoples because of the West Indian Churches and the North American Protestant Colony in their midst. Similarly, the *ladino (mestizo)* population of at least one area of Guatemala was reluctant to become Evangelical because they thought that the gospel was only for the Indians, whom they considered inferior. The *mestizo* population has seldom been a good bridge of communication with the Indians. In Cuzco, Peru, the Regions-Beyond

Missionary Union planned to begin churches among the Quechuas. With this end in view, the *mestizo* converts formed the Inca Evangelical Society with the purpose of evangelizing the Indians of surrounding communities. They found, however, that being identified as *mestizos* closed the door to the suspicious Indians (Kessler 1967: 160-164).

The Assemblies of God in Bolivia attempted to administer the *mestizo* churches in the eastern jungle of Santa Cruz together with the Indian ones of the *altiplano*. The resulting tensions stymied church growth and brought the work to a standstill. When the church administrators realized the nature of the problem and then began to administer each region separately, they saw increased growth in both regions.

The Presbyterian Church of Guatemala solved some of the problems of cultural antipathies by organizing one of its presbyteries along ethnic lines. The Quiché Indian pastors, although able to express themselves in Spanish, had not felt free to speak out in presbytery meetings. The Church wisely decided to form a separate presbytery made up of Quiché churches. Since then, these churches have forged ahead with new liberty and confidence. The same phenomenon exists on the level of the local congregation. In Olintepeque, Guatemala, the Presbyterian Church was growing in a healthy manner under the direction of a Quiché pastor. When a *ladino* *(mestizo)* bilingual minister came to pastor the church, the growth rate declined. Spanish-speaking people became the influential elements in the church because they were more articulate. Consequently, the Indians became more introverted as the number of *ladinos* increased. The solution was to divide the church on the basis of the languages. Now there are two growing churches of different presbyteries in the same town.

There seems to be more of a tendency for church growth to take place where the Indians either have great self-respect and perhaps even racial pride, or where they are isolated from the overbearing Iberian influence. A quite widespread and puzzling situation exists where the Indians are clearly dominated by the Iberian culture. The Indians recognize that they must adapt to the national language and culture and that their future, their hopes, and the interesting gadgets of modern society all belong to the Iberian or *mestizo* world. They are thus not content to be Indians in an Indian congregation, second class citizens at best. Yet, they are quite unfitted linguistically and culturally to profit by the Iberian mode of worship and to flourish within an Iberian or *mestizo* congregation. The possibility of dual membership in both an Indian congregation and a larger city *mestizo* one is yet to be more fully explored. A comparable situation exists in regard to the possibility of an autonomous sub-presbytery or convention that is run by Indians but which is nevertheless also part of a larger mixed group. The pattern is greatly complicated by the fact that it is quite possible for Indians to become *mestizos* since the racial barrier is not as prominent as the cultural one. Where many *mestizos* are very nearly fullblooded Indians who have merely adopted the ways of the Iberian world, the problem of working in separate homogeneous units becomes considerably more complex. This is not to deny the necessity of the Indians to worship and to work in their own mother tongue. It is merely to point out the tyranny of a dominant culture that quite effectively steals away the Indians' own cultural self-respect.

The Evangelical Church in a Monocultural Indian Community

Of the Amerindians, the Quechuas are the largest integrated ethnic group in Latin America, numbering between eight and ten million. These heirs of the now eclipsed Inca Empires inhabit three countries in South America: Ecuador, Peru, and Bolivia. Their small towns cling to the mountainsides or dot the vast *altiplano* of the Andean range, manifesting a continuing resistance to the pressures of the Spanish and European cultures.

At one time the Quechua held himself high, assured of his status and personality within the structure of the Inca Empire. This was the world of the *chasqui* (the fleet postal runner) and of powerful fortresses — a realm of great men with high moral character who worshipped the spirit that moved the sun. But the modern descendant of the Inca no longer holds his head high. Five centuries of Spanish tyranny have broken his spirit.

> He is the victim of many abuses and has no share whatsoever in the social-political life of the country. The Highland Indian has a double personality: that which he shows when he is surrounded by his own people and is in his environment — when he is gay, talkative, teasing, frank and generous — and the personality he has when he is among strangers and away from his milieu, when he feels he is being exploited or despised (Blomberg 1952: 136).

In the eyes of the world he has accepted Christianity, but underneath he still worships *Pacha Mama* (Mother Earth).

> It is difficult to separate the heritage of Inca myths and rites from the beliefs and rituals brought up by the Spanish missionaries. The Indian, from fear of the hail storms, carries the "saint" up and down the rows and across the field. He carries a stone to the top of each high pass to toss in a mound with a cross to appease the mountain spirits (Dilworth 1967: 45).

To underestimate the silent and introverted temperament of the Indian is a mistake, for underneath he has a strong desire to break his bonds and once more govern and lead his people. This ambition is revealed clearly in his fiesta, when "his suppressed desires to lord it over others come to the fore and he will act as *mayor-domo*" (Dilworth 1967: 45). It is inevitable that these silent Indian masses, who outnumber the white and *mestizo* population in all three Andean countries, will some day arise and recover their rightful heritage. A liberating revolution swept Bolivia in 1952 and is spreading to Ecuador and Peru. Will the Quechuas be swallowed up by the secularistic and materialistic approaches of Marxism, or will they be a spiritual revolutionary force in this vast continent?

Missionaries must understand the nature of the Indian culture: its intricate family patterns, its group conscience, and its mechanism for the reception of new ideas. The thin end of the wedge of Christianity has barely entered among the Quechua Indians. Perhaps 5 per cent of this population has been won to Christ, although missionaries have been working among them for well over half a century. Although a pioneer mission station was founded in Ecuador as early as 1902, the Indians were unresponsive. In 1930, however, an extended family was converted under the leadership of the Christian and Missionary Alliance. Within two years, seventeen families were involved in an active church in that district. Today in Ecuador about 1,500 Quechua Indians are believers.

In Peru we can allude to only two instances of church growth among Indians. When John Ritchie observed that on purchasing a book a Peruvian would immediately sit down and read aloud its contents to an eager audience, he published a free evangelistic flyer as the preliminary step to the evangelism of Peru through literature. Literate *mestizos,* and on rare occasions literate Indians, became the leaders of small groups that sprang up in central Peru. Churches emerged in mining towns, and these in turn fanned out into the small Indian villages. Many Quechuas would seek temporary work in the large mining settlements and there find Christ. Upon returning to their villages, they would lead their families and sometimes their entire communities to Christ. Today in central Peru there are close to 6,000 believers in the Iglésia Evangélica Peruana, who are ethnically of the Quechua Indian culture.

In southern Peru two missionaries reacted against the mission compound concept and moved out to live in Indian communities. Len Herniman went to Huantura and there was responsible for the initial translation of the Quechua New Testament. At the same time Alex Jardine moved to Ayaviri in the *altiplano,* some 13,000 feet in altitude. Throughout the region new churches were established whose vision encompassed the whole *altiplano.* Unfortunately, church growth was retarded because of the lack of adequate leadership.

Although today there are some 150 churches and groups ministering in the area, their estimated membership altogether is only 1,500 — the majority of which are monolingual Quechua speakers.

In Bolivia the Quechua Indians comprise over 50 per cent of the population. In 1907 George Allen founded the Bolivia Indian Mission (now the Andes Evangelical Mission), centering its work in San Pedro de Buena Vista. This area proved to be rather unresponsive, but when another work began in Aiquile in 1923, both groups founded churches which ministered to the surrounding villages. The training of Quechua Indian leaders was initiated in 1936 by Leslie Shedd. Today, Quechua Indians in Bolivia account for some 65 per cent of the more than seven thousand members of the Unión Cristiana Evangélica.

Potentially, the Quechua Church can grow to include many millions. There seems to be a breakthrough under the leadership of the Assemblies of God in the Callejón of Huaylas region of Ancash, Peru, where some 6,000 Indians have come to Christ in the last few months. This would suggest the beginnings of a people movement.

Hamilton stresses that churches expand best along lines of relationship within the Quechua community and that group conscience plays a vital role. The idea of a strong group conscience seems to suggest a weakness of personality to those reared in individualistic Western society.

> But to the highland Indians, deciding by one's self looks careless — and in addition a betrayal of the interests of the whole group. . . . Indians rebel with an indignant sense of injustice at precisely the individualistic approach used by the missionary. They say, "How can we really decide anything unless we talk it over with our folk, listen to those who have had more experience than we, and come to a decision which will benefit all concerned?" (Hamilton 1962: 120-121).

The Indian feels inherently bound to his community and constantly demonstrates allegiance and submission to it. Such complete identity with the group is quite foreign to a North American.

The Aymara tribe constitutes 10 per cent of the population of Bolivia. So strong-willed and ethnocentric were the early Aymaras that they never yielded fully to the power of the Incas. As a result, they have retained their own language even though Quechua is spoken all around them. The Aymaras constitute the fastest-growing segment of the Evangelical Churches in Bolivia. As part of the Evangelism-in-Depth program in 1965, 7,000 Aymaras gathered in La Paz for the first Aymara Evangelical Congress. For some time an interdenominational Aymara committee has been working in La Paz with notable success in the fields of literature, hymnology, and literacy.

Wycliffe Bible Translators and Church Growth

Since the avenue of social interchange is still the indigenous language, the communication of the gospel is best accomplished in the Indian's native tongue. The vision of Cameron Townsend to evangelize the Indians in their mother tongue arose from his own experience in trying to reach with the gospel the Cakchiquel Indians of Guatemala (Wallis and Bennett 1959: 5). His vision led to the founding of the Wycliffe Bible Translators. Although Townsend was not the first to translate the Scriptures into Indian languages (Grubb 1927: 143), he was instrumental in changing the pattern of Indian evangelization. Three examples of Wycliffe work in Mexico will throw some light on the value of the work it is conducting.

The Chols of North-Central Chiapas

Of the 54,761 Chols, 15,700 speak Spanish and the remaining numbers speak one of two dialects: the Tumbala and the Tila. The gospel was first preached to the Chols in 1922 when two Presbyterian ministers from Tabasco, Eligio Granados and José Coffin, made a missionary journey into the Chiapas mountains. On that trip they baptized a number of *mestizo* coffee growers near Tumbala and apparently also some of their Chol servants. These new believers were left unattended for twenty years except for a few visits by Coffin and John Kempers. Nevertheless, the little group of Chol believers remained faithful and established congregations in at least two additional villages.

Linguists of the Wycliffe Bible Translators eventually went to live among the Chols, learned their language, reduced it to writing, and translated the New Testament. Mr. and Mrs. John Beekman and Mr. and Mrs. Wilbur Aulie did the bulk of the translation, with others helping for shorter periods. The New Testament in the Tumbala dialect was dedicated in 1957 and a new edition is now being printed. Even before the New Testament was finished, Wycliffe workers gave the Chols portions of Scripture in their own language and gave instruction in reading and using the Bible.

The tiny Church began to expand rapidly, with a community of 8,171 in 1964 (including adherents and children). Two years later the community had grown to 9,291 persons (Figure 68), or about 16.8 per cent of all Chol speakers. All but a handful of the Chol Evangelicals speak the Tumbala dialect, since the Tila speakers (an estimated 24,000) remain strongly Christo-pagan and highly resistant to the gospel. Thus, Evangelicals constitute about 30 per cent of the total population in the Tumbala dialect. This is one of the highest percentages of Evangelicals for an area of similar size in all Latin America. The field of the Chol Church is divided as follows:

Figure 68

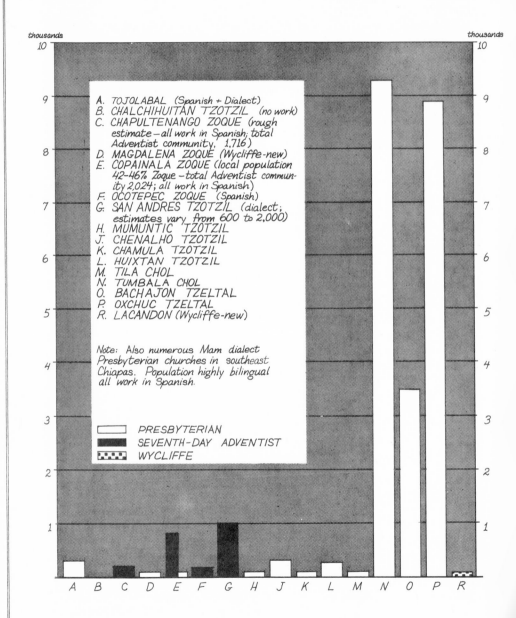

INDIAN PROTESTANT CHURCHES IN CHIAPAS, MEXICO, 1966

A. *TOJOLABAL* (Spanish + Dialect)
B. *CHALCHIHUITAN TZOTZIL* (no work)
C. *CHAPULTENANGO ZOQUE* (rough estimate — all work in Spanish; total Adventist community, 1,716)
D. *MAGDALENA ZOQUE* (Wycliffe-new)
E. *COPAINALA ZOQUE* (local population 42-46% Zoque — total Adventist community 2,024; all work in Spanish)
F. *OCOTEPEC ZOQUE* (Spanish)
G. *SAN ANDRES TZOTZIL* (dialect; estimates vary from 600 to 2,000)
H. *MUMUNTIC TZOTZIL*
J. *CHENALHO TZOTZIL*
K. *CHAMULA TZOTZIL*
L. *HUIXTAN TZOTZIL*
M. *TILA CHOL*
N. *TUMBALA CHOL*
O. *BACHAJON TZELTAL*
P. *OXCHUC TZELTAL*
R. *LACANDON* (Wycliffe-new)

Note: Also numerous Mam dialect Presbyterian churches in southeast Chiapas. Population highly bilingual all work in Spanish.

PRESBYTERIAN
SEVENTH-DAY ADVENTIST
WYCLIFFE

Church	Congregations	Families	Baptized Members	Community 1964	1966
Tumbala	21	407	690	2,306	2,128
Carranza	13	427	724	2,036	2,203
Jerusalem	29	670	1,077	3,829	3,571
Sta. María	8	239	499		1,389
	71	1,743	2,990	8,171	9,291

Only three ordained ministers pastor the Chol field and no new candidates for the ministry as yet have been selected. Ordained elders and deacons do the bulk of pastoral and evangelistic work. The Carranza Church, for example, has fourteen elders, sixteen deacons, and thirteen presidents of local congregations. The Jerusalem Church has more than twenty elders. The three ordained ministers itinerate among the congregations to administer the sacraments and mediate problems. In varying degrees they also give instruction to the elders and lay leaders.

The Tzeltal of Chiapas

The Tzeltal Indians number approximately 95,200 (67,100 monolingual and 28,100 bilingual). The Tzeltal language is of Maya extraction and is closely related to the Tzotzil dialects of the Chiapas central highlands. Like Chol, this language is divided into two main dialects, commonly known as Oxchuc and Bachajon.

The story of the beginning of the Tzeltal Church has been widely publicized. William Bentley of the Wycliffe Bible Translators went to live among the Bachajon Tzotzils in 1940. He returned to the United States to be married but died suddenly just six days before the wedding date. His fiancée, Mariana Slocum, asked to take his place among the Tzeltals. Unable to enter the highly resistant Bachajon area, she began study of the Oxchuc dialect, and for several years she and her partners met suspicion and resistance. Then in about 1948, a disillusioned young Tzeltal who had served as helper to a Catholic priest came to Mariana for instruction. After his conversion, and with a minimum of training, he began to evangelize in surrounding communities with the aid of records and a hand-wound phonograph. In the little valley of Corralito his message was accepted. As a result, the local residents invited Mariana and her partner, Florence Gerdel, to move there and even built a house for them. The medical services of Miss Gerdel complemented the Bible teaching of Miss Slocum.

The Corralito congregation grew rapidly and the gospel soon spread to other communities. Before long a majority of the residents of the area were professing believers, and witchcraft and alcoholism all but disappeared. Schools were established and several Evangelicals were trained by the government as bilingual teachers.

In 1955, having finished the translation of the New Testament in the Oxchuc dialect, the two women moved to the Bachajon dis-

trict where a few families had already been converted through contact with the Corralito Church. Because of the determined opposition,
the women were hidden for a time by the believers. As the number
of Bachajon believers increased, the translators were able to live and
work openly. By 1963 the New Testament was finished and in the
Bachajon dialect, and the two women moved to South America to
begin other work.

In 1966 the Tzeltal churches numbered 12,446 persons, of which
only 1,464 were adult baptized members. More would have been
baptized except for the infrequent visits of an ordained minister.
Believers make up 13.4 per cent of the total Tzeltal population.
Evangelical congregations are now spread evenly over those regions
where a majority of the inhabitants speak only Tzeltal. Among
Tzeltals who are entirely monolingual, Evangelicals number about
20 per cent. In those areas where the Tzeltals are predominantly
bilingual and are intermingled with *mestizos,* the Church has scarcely
even a foothold (i.e., the Ocosingo, Altamiranoa, and El Real
Valleys; the *municipios* of Amagenango, Villa Rosas, and Venustiano
Carranza near the Pan American Highway). From 1964 to 1966 the
Tzeltal Church increased by 2,253 persons, an average of 11 per cent
annual increase.

Church	Congre-gations	Families	Baptized Members	Community 1964	1966
Corralito	30	920	656	4,592	5,105
Pacbilna*	38	877	296	2,635	3,350
Bahtshibiltic	47	887	512	2,964	3,991
	115	2,684	1,464	10,191	12,446

*In 1967 the center of this church was changed from Pacbilna to Palestina.

In total numbers, the Tzeltal Church is one of the largest Evangelical
Churches among Amerindians anywhere in the Western Hemisphere.
It is made up of two separate, though parallel and related, movements.
Neither of the two Tzeltal dialect churches has yet won as large a
number or as high a percentage of its people as the Tumbala Chol
Church. In spite of certain problems in organization and discipline,
healthy growth among the Tzeltals continues.

While Wycliffe workers have enjoyed success in the two cases
cited, they also employ a third and much more common pattern.
The official policy of Wycliffe, also known as the Summer Institute
of Linguistics, is to reduce the language to writing, to translate portions of the Bible, and to leave the people themselves responsible
for the form of Christian fellowship which may develop among them.
If a recognizable Christian Church develops, all is well and good;
if not, Wycliffe does not feel responsible. Most frequently, if a new
church arises, the denominational position of the linguist will be
reflected in it. When no church is planted during the time of trans-

lating, one of two results occurs in some cases, as among the Chontal, the area is left without a church; in others, as among the Huichol, missionaries of another society step in to fill the gap.

The Huichol of Central Mexico

According to the 1960 census, 3,897 monolingual Huichol were living in the States of Jalisco and Nayarit. Another three or four thousand were bilingual. The Huichol have practiced their own religion in which the sun, moon, and ocean are worshipped as deities. The use of peyote has been an integral part of their worship along with Christian elements characterizing the folk religions of nearby Mexican tribes. The Wycliffe men who began the translation work did not establish a church among the first converts. Nevertheless, one arose, but it was not shepherded.

Fortunately, two "free-lance" missionaries befriended the infant church and Ramón Diaz, one of the early converts, became pastor of the Huichols. Ramón moved out of the pagan village with some of his family who had become Evangelicals. Others soon followed. The early growth of the church followed the lines of family relationships. From 18 baptisms in 1961 the total climbed each year until there were about 120 in 1965. There are now more than 400 baptized Evangelicals, who constitute about 5 per cent of the Huichol population.

It is difficult to determine how many congregations Wycliffe Translators have left in their wake. Nevertheless, some systematic provision for church-planting would add a great deal of muscle to their work. Because they fear a possible conflict with governments which are willing to cooperate with Wycliffe as an educational organization but not as a Protestant mission, the translators have a definite reservation about formally establishing churches. But if the discipling of nations is to be taken seriously in our day, a solution to their dilemma should be sought diligently. The Swiss Indian Mission in Peru makes a strong effort to plant churches among tribes where Wycliffe Translators are at work. Similar organized efforts in other parts of Latin America would help to capitalize on the specialized contribution that Wycliffe is making to the Evangelical cause.

Chapter Fourteen

SOCIAL CLASSES

The Evangelical Church presents a cross-section of Latin America in which almost all social strata are included. Furthermore, class distinctions in Latin America, both within the Evangelical Church and in society at large, directly affect church growth. The reality of class differences is reflected in the choice of church leadership, the methodology of evangelism, the type and location of church buildings, the music employed in services, and the materials used in Christian education.

In Latin America, social stratification is not merely an interpretive tool by which scientists measure social phenomena. As Whiteford (1964: 243) has pointed out, Latin Americans themselves are keenly aware of class distinctions in their everyday social relationships. Though the nature of these distinctions is changing rapidly they continue to exist.

Following the pattern of North American sociologists, Latin America has been divided arbitrarily by some scholars into six social classes: upper and lower upper; upper and lower middle; and upper and lower lower (Nida 1958: 104-105). This division is not adequate, however, in analyzing the social makeup of Latin America and much less the Evangelical Church. If the problem consisted only in the variations from one country to another, it would be possible to use modifications of these six classifications, but the problem is much more complex.

Besides the vertical gradations of social class recognized above, Latin America may also be said to contain horizontal ones. The many different ethnic groups in themselves constitute distinct social classes — for example, the *cholo* "class" of the Andean highlands. Within each country the radical differences between rural and urban people and between those of different geographical regions make another type of classification necessary (Adams 1965: 264). Beals (1965: 342-360) has illustrated some of these differences for Brazil, Peru, Guatemala, and Mexico. The variations in the ethnic makeup of each class in each of the four countries and the basic differences of class values from one country to another in even this small sample show the difficulty of defining social class for all of Latin America. *Two Cities of Latin America* (Whiteford 1964) demonstrates that class categories may not even match in two cities. Class distinctions seem to be much more distinct in conservative Popayan than in the more acculturated society of Queretaro. This does not mean that the comparison of the two is not valid. On the contrary, the value of the study is enhanced, but Whiteford does not try to force his categories by relating dissimilar things.

At least three classes (upper, middle, and lower) can be observed in most cases. While this simple a classification is not entirely satisfactory for a complete analysis, we will employ it, limiting our description to the lower and middle classes from which most Evangelicals come.

The Middle Class

Evangelical leaders, in general, want their Churches to be known as middle class, yet their definition of class structure is not sociologically valid. The membership of the Churches that are known as middle class ranges all the way from the upper middle class radical party member in Chile to the upper lower class working man in Buenos Aires. Many times we heard of churches described as middle class merely because their members were regular wage earners. Within this wide "middle class" live most of the non-Pentecostal Evangelicals of Latin America.

Economists, sociologists, and anthropologists also sharply disagree on the definition of the middle class and its role in Latin America. Their discussion is not merely of academic interest to Evangelicals. Evangelicals have tended to identify themselves deliberately or accidentally with the fortunes of the middle class, possibly because most of them were born into the lower class.

The traditional view of the middle class is best expressed by John J. Johnson in *Political Change in Latin America: The Emergence of the Middle Sectors* (1958). He associates technological change and the support of the industrial proletariat with the emergence of the middle sectors. The composition of the middle class was static until the beginning of the twentieth century, and it was not until after World War I that its numbers began to swell. Social mobility, particularly of naturalized citizens and their children and of old rural families, has also caused an increase in the middle classes.

The middle sectors do not constitute a class as such, but include persons of every cultural and economic range who belong for reasons as varied as intellectual achievements and wealth. Their disparity, however, has prevented them from forming a solid political block, although large segments do unite for political advantage.

To the extent that middle sectors have had political cohesiveness and a continuity of common interests, this cohesiveness and continuity seems to have been due to six characteristics they hold in common. They are overwhelmingly urban. They not only have well above average educations themselves but they also believe in universal public education. They are convinced that the future of their countries is inextricably tied to industrialization. They are nationalistic. They believe that the State should actively intrude in the social and economic areas while it carries on the normal functions of government. They recognize that the family has weakened as a political unit in the urban centers, and they have consequently lent their support to the development of organized political parties (Johnson 1958:5).

The role of the liberal professions in influencing the political thought of the middle sectors has declined as other groups have begun to compete for the rewards of political power. The role of the Roman Catholic clergy in politics has also declined as the place of the Church in society has changed and the popular political base has broadened.

The principal point of Johnson's view is that the importance and influence of the middle sectors will grow in the future.

> Past and present developments directly affecting the middle sectors themselves offer abundant evidence that the future holds considerable political promise for them. . . . As the shift of wealth toward the urban economies develops the voice of the commercial and industrial elements in decision-making will become firmer. If it does, they may in the years ahead be up to the herculean task of providing the type of leadership requisite to advance before the fires they themselves lighted overtake them (1958:193-195).

If this view were valid, then the Evangelical Church ought to concentrate on the middle classes, for here would be the future of the Church. It would be necessary for the Church to develop new methods of reaching the middle classes since the old ones have not worked very well. If the Church could win these sectors, the battle for Latin America would be won, because these people would be the decision-makers, the innovators, the wielders of power and influence.

There are alternative explanations, however, for the middle class phenomena. One major objection to Johnson's thesis is that some Latin American societies have large middle classes and yet continue to be stagnant. In fact, the two metropolitan areas with the largest middle classes, Buenos Aires and Montevideo, have existed in the state of unrelieved stagnation for several years. Instead of innovating, the middle classes may actually exert a conservative influence. They often wish to maintain traditional values as a stabilizing force, because the members of the class are so transitional. Although "in one sense, the middle class is more of a process than a stable structural entity" (Adams 1965: 269), its lack of homogeneity forces the members to find a place in the traditional order.

> The degree of dissatisfaction in the middle classes depends largely upon the opportunities open to them for improving, or preserving the positions they have gained. If the system provides a reasonable degree of satisfaction for such aspirations, the middle classes tend to model their behavior and standards on those of the traditional social elite (Ratinoff 1967: 69).

The drive by which the newer members of the middle class have achieved their position is tempered by the opportunities that the new situation presents. As they come to enjoy and appreciate the prerogatives of their status, they often become defensive of their hard-earned standing. They may fear slipping back to lower class standing and thus emphasize the external symbols of middle class identification.

These considerations are significant for the Evangelical Church. If it is not the middle class as such that is moving, then the Church should concentrate not on the middle classes but on those elements of the lower classes that are moving upward in the social scale toward middle class status.

MIDDLE CLASS CHURCHES

What kind of Church is the middle class Evangelical Church? How does it relate to other Churches and to the rest of the middle class? Of whom is it composed? By and large the middle class within the Evangelical Church is homegrown. That is, its members were won to the Evangelical faith while in the lower classes. Through education, improved standards of living, a wider understanding of the world, and the redemptive effect of the gospel, they have moved up the social scale into the middle class. This social advance may occur in the first generation, or it may take longer enough that only the sons or grandsons of Evangelicals reach the middle class.

As long ago as 1930, Webster E. Browning saw the tendency of the Protestant Churches to move up into the middle class.

> The older organizations like the Methodists and Presbyterians who established their work more than fifty years ago, have, in great part due to their schools and educational ideals, grown away from the most illiterate classes of society, among whom the Pentecostals now have their greatest successes. The older churches have gradually built up a following of the people who, while still of the humbler classes of society, are considerably in advance of the poorest and most illiterate (1930:48).

This tendency described by Browning has increased with the years and now constitutes a major problem for many Latin American Churches.

Middle class churches are often isolated from the rest of society.

According to Nida, "the tendency is for such churches to lose touch with the very classes from which most of the members originally came" (1958: 102). We visited dozens of such congregations in Latin America. The pattern seemed to be that a few families were won in the beginning and over a period of time their relatives would also be brought into the church. Yet the congregation has never grown beyond the original circle of relatives — it is as if the old enmities and alliances of pre-Evangelical days are still maintained. At the same time other values have changed so that these Evangelicals are no longer concerned about the kind of life the lower class lives.

On the other hand, middle class churches are also often cut off from the rest of the class of which they long to be a part. They are what Walter Goldschmidt (1950: 483-498) has called a self-identified class, i.e., they conceive of themselves as being a class not fully accepted by other sectors of the middle class because their Protestant views and values contrast sharply with traditional Latin American middle class attitudes.

Isolation prevents church growth: cut off from the lower classes and withdrawn from their own [middle] class, members of these churches live as a minority, not enjoying the influence and power they might have had. The result is an Evangelical ghetto with a minority mentality.

Many missionaries have tended to emphasize the middle classes because of their own cultural bias and middle class background which makes them feel more at home with middle class persons with whom they find more points of similarity and common interest. They fail to understand the values of the lower classes and naturally feel that the middle class is more stable and dependable. Having come from the middle class, they are embarrassed by the lack of social graces among the lower classes and detect in uncouth lower class behavior an undisciplined energy that they consider dangerous. How much more comfortable it is to concentrate on the predictable, familiar middle class!

At the same time, however, the missionary is willing to go to work in the most backward conditions. He is puzzled as to why the national pastor may not be as willing. He fails to see that his own middle class status is not in jeopardy when he works with a lower class because he is a foreigner. But the national pastor is in a much different position (Nida 1958: 120-121).

Preparation of the Ministry

"The leadership within the churches has seemed to come primarily from the families of independent tradesmen and merchants, e.g., carpenters, shoemakers, blacksmiths, and shopkeepers" (Nida 1958: 102). Unfortunately if these leaders are sent to seminaries, they are educated out of their class into the middle class, gaining a middle class standard of living and middle class values that give them a disdain for the life of the class from which they came. The only kind of church they are prepared to pastor is a ghetto church of the middle class.

Another unfortunate fact is that Evangelicals have confused a high academic level with cultural values of the upper classes. What is needed to prepare men to minister among rural people or among people of the lower social classes is not necessarily training on a lower level, but specialized training which will equip them to minister successfully under special conditions.

Education

To a great extent the Churches which are identified as middle class have depended for their growth on the educational systems which the missions have developed. With a few notable exceptions, such as the schools maintained by the Seventh-Day Adventists, Evangelical schools in Latin America have not been effectively evangelistic. Many of the church-related schools we visited have been effective only in educating second generation Evangelicals, while others have failed to maintain an evangelical witness at all. These schools, however, have helped to produce that strange class of people known in Latin America as *friends of the gospel*. These friends are ex-students of Evangelical schools who many times have been "inoculated" against the gospel. They are friendly to Evangelicals but have no intention of ever becoming Evangelicals themselves.

Rural and Urban Congregations

The awkward relationship of rural and urban dwellers is a problem unique to middle class urban Churches. The rural orientation of the lower class urban dwellers is so dominant that the lower class Churches tend to be able to minister equally well in both rural and urban environments. But the transition of a rural middle class dweller to an urban middle class church is much more difficult.

The case of a Brazilian Presbyterian shopkeeper illustrates the disparity between the urban middle class and the rural middle class. This Evangelical had owned a shop in one of the small towns in the interior of the State of Pernambuco. Because rural areas in Latin America usually do not have secondary schools, when his children reached that level he decided to relocate in the capital city of Recife so that they could continue their education. He sold his shop and invested all his capital in a similar one in the city. In the small town he had been a leading social and political figure and was an active layman in the church. He had shared in the political patronage that the winning party gained from time to time and had friends even among the politicians who controlled the state from Recife.

Figure 69

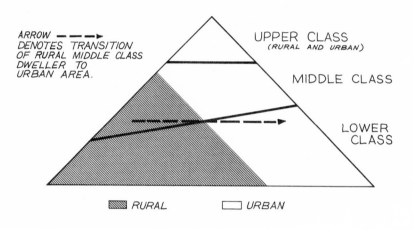

MIGRATION TO THE CITY

ARROW ▬ ▬ ▬►
DENOTES TRANSITION
OF RURAL MIDDLE CLASS
DWELLER TO
URBAN AREA.

UPPER CLASS
(RURAL AND URBAN)

MIDDLE CLASS

LOWER
CLASS

▨ RURAL   ☐ URBAN

His prestige had strengthened the influence of the Evangelical community in the town.

Suddenly everything was different. In Recife, he was just another little shopkeeper and his political friends no longer needed him. Even in the church, there were many whose shops were much larger than his, and whose manner of speaking and conduct showed a level of sophistication that was far above his own. He was bewildered and frustrated by suddenly finding himself an unimportant person, even in the church.

What happened to the shopkeeper and others like him can be shown graphically. The diagram (Figure 69) does not try to depict precisely the relative sizes of the social classes nor the areas of greatest social mobility. When the shopkeeper (represented by the broken arrow) moved from the rural town to the city, although his social values remained constant, at least to begin with, he found himself in a lower social class in *relation to the rest of society* than that to which he was accustomed.

This rural-urban class distinction has hindered the middle class churches in effective rural evangelism. They have depended on a kind of home missionary program which makes the urban middle class responsible for nothing beyond footing the bill for rural evangelism. Consequently the middle class churches are deficient in evangelism skills but high in social prestige. The growth they show is more likely due to their winning an Evangelical to a higher social level rather than to winning a non-Evangelical to the gospel.

THE LOWER CLASSES

In spite of the phenomenal growth of the middle classes in the past half century, most of Latin American society still falls within the huge lower classes. The upper and middle classes might be likened to the small tip of the iceberg that shows above the water, with the great weight of the lower classes remaining out of sight.

The visible manifestations of Latin American culture, with its signs of strong Iberian influence, are expressions of the genius of the upper and middle classes. The lower classes are presumed to share the same value system. Actually, these classes have been the invisible, submerged base on which Latin American society has been built, although exploited by the oppressors, manipulated by demagogues, and kept in fear by ignorance and superstitions. Even the disdain for manual labor which has unfortunately characterized Latin America has depended for its persistence on a lower class forced by sheer economic necessity to do this work.

The dramatic social upheavals and the accompanying phenomenon of Evangelical church growth among the lower classes are simply signs that the iceberg refuses to remain submerged. The new role of the Bolivian Indian since the 1952 revolution; the integration of Guatemalan Indians into national life; the political vigor of Perón's "shirtless ones"; the success of Castro in Cuba; and the sporadic guerilla campaigns in Colombia, Venezuela, and Guatemala are all signals of the great change that is taking place, which will continue to increase in strength in the future. The pained surprise with which Mexico received Oscar Lewis' *Five Families* (1959) and the excited response in Brazil to Maria Carolina de Jesus' *Child of the Dark* (1962) show that Latin America is becoming self-consciously aware of the needs and problems of the lower classes.

This is the segment of society that needs most to be studied systematically, not just in terms of the social services they need, but also in terms of their own cultural values. The excellent typology of Latin American subcultures developed by Wagley and Harris (1965: 42-69) needs a further breakdown of the subculture which they have called the urban proletariat. It is necessary to differentiate between the lower class regularly employed though perhaps unskilled, and the huge number of marginal persons underemployed and perhaps unemployable, who share in none of the fruits of social betterment and are not necessarily of the unassimilated rural persons flocking to the cities. There are immense differences between these groups, differences of material culture and of value systems. To lump them together is to ignore some of the most significant cultural differences in all of Latin America. These are differences which church-planters dare not ignore.

Lower Class Churches

The main growth of the Evangelical Church has been among the lower classes, principally in Churches which have concentrated on winning them. The most typical growth example is that of the Pentecostal Churches. Some of the reasons for Pentecostal growth have been spelled out by McGavran (1963: 113-124), Read (1965), and Johnson (1967a: 8-9, 1967b: 8-9). Many old-line denominations are now overcoming their reluctance to study the growth of the Pentecostal Churches and are beginning to analyze the dynamic factors involved.

Chilean Pentecostals

One of the outstanding cases of Evangelical church growth among the lower classes is that of the Chilean Pentecostal movement which resulted from a revival movement in the Methodist Church. Since this earlier Methodist growth (c. 1890) had been among the lower classes, it was only natural that the lower class Pentecostal Christians breaking away from the Methodist Church should reach out to win the class closest to themselves. From the beginning these Pentecostals have found remarkable response to their message from the lower class Chileans.

Avoided by other Pentecostals because of doctrinal differences, and recently wooed by both the World Council of Churches and the World Evangelical Fellowship, the Chilean Pentecostals have continued to carry on their work in their own distinctive way among the masses. Since before 1930 they have maintained an average annual growth rate of 6.5 per cent. They deliberately concentrate on winning the lower classes, saying that these are the people who have proved to be winnable and that therefore it would be a mistake to try to win other classes. One earnest young Chilean Pentecostal told us, "The other churches are trying to win the upper classes. If it is possible to win these other classes, let the other churches win them, as they do not appear winnable to us. We do not want to cut ourselves off from the people we know are winnable and whom we are bringing to Christian faith."

The people of the Chilean lower classes move often, sometimes to hunt for jobs and sometimes to follow those who have found work. Their mobility has resulted in the spreading of the gospel wherever the Pentecostals have gone. It is significant that the growth of the Chilean Pentecostal Churches has been almost entirely confined to the area of greatest population concentration and economic opportunity. The growth of the Pentecostals in the far North and South is recent and has only followed economic development resulting from the establishment of adequate communications and transportation (Lalive d'Epinay 1965-66: 35).

Other Lower Class Evangelical Churches

It is not true that only indigenous Churches such as the Chilean Pentecostals can multiply among the masses. Mission-related Churches have been equally fruitful. The Mennonite Brethren and the New Tribes Mission in the Choco of Panama are experiencing similar growth, as are the Assemblies of God in Bogotá, Colombia, the Foursquare in Guayaquil, Ecuador, the Methodists in the industrial towns around Concepción, Chile, and the Baptists around Torreón, Mexico.

In one Mexican city we found an independent Methodist missionary operating an old-fashioned rescue mission. His effective evangelism rehabilitated men both spiritually and socially and directed them to established local congregations or churches near their homes. It was easy to think of him as being Pentecostal, but he denied this. He simply felt that it was the lower class, the "down and outs," who presented the mission challenge.

The lower classes will probably continue to be the best target for evangelism for some time to come. They are the most open to innovation if the new idea is presented in terms that are meaningful in their environment. They have the least to lose by becoming Evangelicals. They are demonstrating their openness to the gospel: millions of them have come into the Evangelical Church in the last generation.

The receptivity of the lower classes also has significance for ministerial and leadership training. It is not enough to train men for serving the middle class and elite. New levels of training must be geared to the common people (see Chapter Twenty-two on Ministerial Training). At this point we disagree with the widespread emphasis on training men only on the highest academic level for the ministry in Latin America (Scopes 1962).

Certainly the greatest harvest fields in Latin America today are among the lower classes, but this does not presuppose a lack of other ripe fields. One of our research team attended a middle class Methodist Church in Mexico City where, in spite of a heavy migration to the suburbs, the congregation was maintained by middle class conversions from the world. We also visited other Churches which minister to predominantly university people and men in positions of leadership within the communities. Yet, while opportunities to reach the upper and middle classes must not be overlooked, the great open door is that of the lower classes.

Chapter Fifteen

CULTURAL ENVIRONMENT

The nature and rate of the social changes rapidly occurring in Latin America vary within as well as between countries. Whole populations and social institutions are being transformed. It is, however, outside the scope of this report to consider social changes from the viewpoint of justice. We recognize the significance of the changes which are taking place and agree that grave social inequities require just solutions; yet, our task is to observe, record, analyze, and understand church growth.

We have studied the cultural environment primarily in order to discover ways in which it helps or hinders the salvation of men and their incorporation into the Church of Jesus Christ, the Lord. We are concerned with the influences of the social environment on the penetration of the gospel in society. We have also endeavored to interpret the effect of social change on church growth and to discern some of the ways in which the growth of the Evangelical Church relates to this change.

POPULATION INCREASE AND URBANIZATION

In mid-1968 the estimated population of Mexico, Central America, and South America stood at 240.4 million. The current average annual rate of population increase for Latin America is 3.0 per cent, ranging from 1.2 per cent in Uruguay to 3.7 per cent in El Salvador, as shown in the following table.

POPULATION OF LATIN AMERICA

Country	Population Mid-1967 (millions)	Current Annual Rate of Increase
El Salvador	3.3	3.7%
Venezuela	9.7	3.6
Costa Rica	1.6	3.5
Honduras	2.5	3.5
Mexico	47.3	3.5
Nicaragua	1.8	3.5
Ecuador	5.7	3.4
Brazil	88.3	3.2

Country	Population Mid-1967 (millions)	Current Annual Rate of Increase
Colombia	19.7	3.2
Panama	1.4	3.2
Paraguay	2.2	3.2
Guatemala	4.9	3.1
Peru	12.8	3.1
Bolivia	3.9	2.4
Chile	9.1	2.2
Argentina	23.4	1.5
Uruguay	2.8	1.2
Total Latin America	240.4	3.0%

(Population Reference Bureau 1968)

This phenomenal growth, which promises to double the population of Latin America in the next twenty-six years, poses for the Evangelical Church several problems, of which we stress two.

First, the growth rate of the Church must exceed the population growth rate in order to accomplish the task of evangelism. What might be considered an adequate rate of growth of Churches in Argentina and Uruguay, whose populations are increasing by less than 2 per cent annually, would be inadequate in Guatemala and Costa Rica, whose populations are increasing at 3.1 and 3.5 per cent, respectively. The Church which only matches the growth rate of the population among which it works is merely conserving the children of members or winning enough from the world to replace those who drop away.

Second, a static methodology and an attitude of defeat cannot cope with this burgeoning situation. Imaginative, creative thinking, rather, is needed to plan successful utilization of the opportunity presented by the population surge. Every member of the Church must be mobilized for the task of evangelism. Building expectations of church increase on the foundations of past poor performance is self-defeating. Adequate expectations must be built on the growth achievements which God has granted to some Churches.

The acceleration of population growth creates related social problems, even though the population density of Latin America compares favorably with that of East Asia or Europe, and the percentage of waste land is much lower than that of the Far East or Africa. Yet, Latin America is confronted by problems which arise from the increasing concentration of population in relatively few urban centers.

Urbanization and Church Growth

The resolution of the present social crisis, we believe, will occur in the cities, where the present shift of population results in increas-

Figure 70

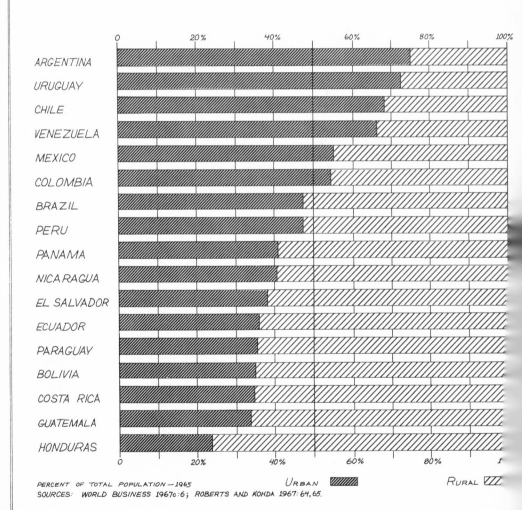

DISTRIBUTION OF POPULATION: URBAN AND RURAL

PERCENT OF TOTAL POPULATION—1965   URBAN   RURAL

SOURCES: WORLD BUSINESS 1967c:6; ROBERTS AND KOHDA 1967:64,65.

ing numbers of social problems, inequities, and injustices. Historically, the demographic pattern in most Latin American countries was characterized by one large capital city which enjoyed a cosmopolitan, essentially European life, and a surrounding hinterland where life

Figure 71

URBAN AREAS OF LATIN AMERICA

○ over 1 million
● 500 thousand to 1 million
● 100 to 500 thousand
· 50 to 100 thousand

was almost primitive and thoroughly rural. The present influx of rural people to the cities and the acculturating effect of modern communications have made the cities somewhat less cosmopolitan and the rest of the country far less provincial in orientation.

As suggested by Ratinoff, "large cities require new organizational functions, which to some extent influence the distribution of power, prestige, and wealth" (1967:61). The new power structure that emerges creates disequilibrium. Old solutions are rejected as no longer adequate, and all of society passes through a series of shuddering adjustments in an effort to reintegrate.

New Freedoms

One important result of urbanization is the exchange of previous social and economic pressures for new pressures of a different kind. The man who heard the gospel before he migrated to the city but felt unable to accept it because of family pressures, finds in the city a social anonymity and economic independence which enable him now to accept the gospel and identify himself as an Evangelical.

This freedom manifests itself in interesting ways. The man who is unwilling in his own community to accept a job involving menial labor for fear of what his peers might think of him, *feels free* to accept any job when he moves to the city. In the new social setting he *is free* from the social restraint which has limited his former choice of employment. If friends have preceded him in moving to the city, he finds that they have already adopted some urban values. If he is the first from his community, he may have acquired enough of the symbols of financial success by the time his friends and relatives follow him that he will not be ashamed of the kind of work he is doing.

He is also free to vote as he chooses. The elaborate schemes to control votes in smaller communities do not work in the city. Although the urban populations may still be deceived by demagogues, they have at least a chance to elect their candidates. The development of an urban proletariat has produced the beginnings of a free electorate.

Pressures which previously determined his religious life have also changed. Gone is the overt pressure from landowner, priest, or political boss who discriminated against nonconforming Evangelicals. Mitigated is the more subtle pressure of friends and family which obligated him to consecrate his marriage before the priest, baptize his children in the Roman Catholic Church, participate in religious ceremonies, and get drunk in village fiestas. If he continues in his former religion in the new secular setting, it is out of personal conviction or deep-seated habit. "The conference of Latin American bishops in June, 1958, concluded that Sunday observance on the continent amounted to 3.5 per cent of the men and 9.5 per cent of the women" (Houtart and Pin 1965:166). The new freedom of the proletariat doubtless augments the defection.

The Role of the Individual

The acculturation which characterizes Latin American urbanization provides a good opportunity for church growth based on personal conversion. The old structured nature of family life gives way to a more open stance toward life, which, in turn, necessitates new values of discipline, education, family relationships, and social contacts. Marriage patterns along with modes of courting change. The introduction of these new elements is altering the old fabric of Latin American life. In the midst of this cultural crisis, which threatens to wed the worst of foreign cultural elements (mostly North American) to the worst remnants of old values, some Latin Americans are engaged in a heroic effort toward an integration that will incorporate the best of the new elements into the noble and worthy values of the Hispanic spirit.

As the role of the individual changes in the new urban environment, so does the Latin's concept of himself. He may resent the social imbalances that persist, and he may feel that only a violent clash will change social structures, but he no longer feels himself to be the helpless victim of an inexorable fate. He revels in a new sense of social and political power.

The fast-growing, indigenous Churches, with their urban bases and lay orientations, have particular appeal to the new urban dweller. In them he finds an opportunity to belong to a group whose activism fits his new-found sense of personal power. The positive Evangelical message helps answer his questions concerning the new society in which he finds himself. He sees that his peers in his Church enjoy responsibility, authority, and status, and he is encouraged to enhance his own status.

Out of this new cultural context, new leaders emerge. Former nonentities find, or are given, new opportunities in which to develop latent capacities. The qualities of leadership necessary in a rural environment are not necessarily those which meet the needs of the new situation. The problems posed by city life call for leaders with new solutions. In those Churches which utilize natural abilities within the group, this new kind of leadership from within is already making itself known.

The noted sociologist Emilio Willems deals expressly with the development of Protestantism in Brazil and Chile in his recent study, *Followers of the New Faith.* He comes much to the same conclusion as we have stated:

> Heavy concentrations of Protestants are correlated with changes strongly affecting the traditional structure of the society; ...

Protestantism may be expected to be relatively weak in areas that have had little or no exposure to such changes (1967a:13).

Evangelization and Mission

The rural background of the urban Church provides a ready-made mission field. The urban Churches are being fed by the rural Churches and at the same time are carrying the gospel back to rural areas. We found many congregations in the interior of Brazil which had no official connection with any denomination but had been started by someone who had become an Evangelical in São Paulo or Rio de Janeiro and had gone back as a spontaneous church-planter.

Urban-based Churches also have the economic capacity for evangelization and mission. Wage earners provide regular *budgetable* income, concomitant with powerful congregations and systematic missions. Without this economic capacity, Churches are limited to providing personnel who must be supported by overseas mission money; or alternatively, they must use the method of the Chilean Pentecostals who provide one-way tickets for their missionaries, leaving them to support themselves in their mission fields as best they can.

Planned campaigns for evangelization of surrounding rural areas are characteristic of some urban Churches. Many Churches struggling toward self-support may never achieve this goal until they succeed in establishing strong urban congregations which can subsidize rural work. Large segments of the Latin American population are outside the money economy, and it is doubtful that they will be integrated into the national life within the foreseeable future. As long as such conditions obtain, the rural Churches (if they continue to function along North American lines) will depend on infusions of capital from overseas missions or urban Churches.

For the first decade, or perhaps a little longer, the rural and therefore group orientation of new city dwellers provides, in itself, a bridge by which they may be reached with the gospel. As they endeavor to cope with their new environment they look for something which will provide continuity, which will answer the puzzling questions which city life poses, and which will give a new sense of community. This they can find in the Evangelical Church — *if the Evangelical Church speaks in terms relevant to their new situation.*

The development of huge apartment complexes occupied by the lower middle classes has complicated the task of evangelism for the Latin American Evangelicals. Some kind of cell movement within these large apartment buildings could reach the apartment dwellers with the gospel. In Mexico City and Caracas we found the beginning of such efforts. These must be multiplied many times over to begin to reach the masses in the anonymity of their isolated apartment existence.

Urbanization in Latin America is continuing at an increasing rate.

> The projected growth rates for urban populations between 1960 and 1975 are three times those for rural populations; for the South American countries these rates are 67 and 22 per cent respectively; for Mexico and Central America, 85 and 26 per cent. Latin America will be predominantly urban by 1970 (Bonilla 1964:186).

As urbanization increases, so the opportunities for Evangelical church growth also increase. As the Evangelical Churches multiply themselves in the opportunities presented by social change stemming from urbanization, they can influence the direction that the urban masses will follow. *Only as they multiply themselves, however, will they have any such influence.*

ECONOMIC DEVELOPMENT

Thirty years ago Merle Davis wrote with prophetic insight concerning the relationship of an economic base to church development (1939). While many of his specific suggestions have been corrected by time, his thesis still remains valid. As the standard of living rises, as laborers get a fairer wage, as minimum wage laws go into effect and labor unions force a fairer distribution of the enormous wealth which machines make possible, biblical churches can thrive — provided, of course, that they are established.

Economic Development and Population Increase

The acceleration of population growth and the concentration of this population in the urban centers are taxing the facilities of the cities beyond their limits. The result is a wide gap between the *haves* and the *have-nots*. Economic development of the Latin countries will not necessarily close the widening gap.

The average annual per capita income in Latin America is $325, which is about one-tenth of that in the United States. (The figure for Latin America is higher than comparable figures for Asia and Africa and is quite similar to that for the Middle East.) In the countries showing the highest rates of population increase, the yearly economic growth is offset by the large number of people in the developing society.

The level of life expectancy has risen sharply through the use of antibiotics, yet cultural pockets exist where the people cannot expect to live more than thirty-five years. The child mortality rate has also decreased in the last fifteen years, but an unending cycle of parasites, vitamin deficiency, and malnutrition keeps this rate higher than it ought to be. Sanitation, hospitalization, professional medical service, medicine, and other aspects of health care are out of the reach of the masses in Latin America.

Educational opportunities are theoretically within the reach of

Figure 72

HEALTH, EDUCATION, AND INCOME IN LATIN AMERICA

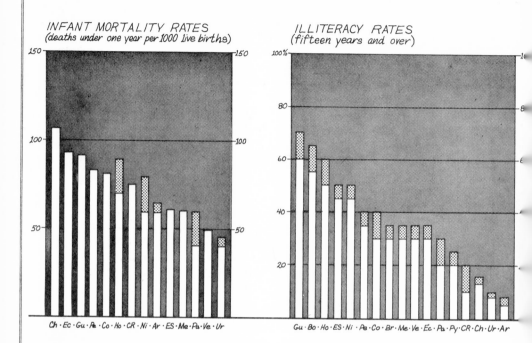

INFANT MORTALITY RATES
(deaths under one year per 1000 live births)

ILLITERACY RATES
(fifteen years and over)

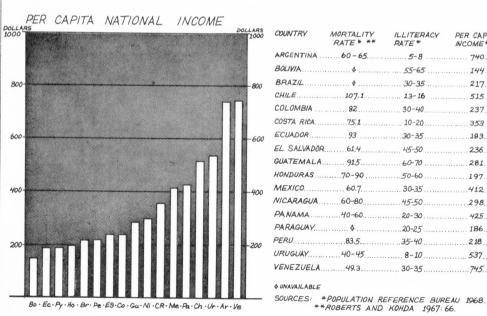

PER CAPITA NATIONAL INCOME

COUNTRY	MORTALITY RATE* **	ILLITERACY RATE*	PER CAPITA INCOME*
ARGENTINA	60 – 65	5 – 8	740
BOLIVIA	◊	55–65	144
BRAZIL	◊	30–35	217
CHILE	107.1	13–16	515
COLOMBIA	82	30–40	237
COSTA RICA	75.1	10–20	353
ECUADOR	93	30–35	183
EL SALVADOR	61.4	45–50	236
GUATEMALA	91.5	60–70	281
HONDURAS	70–90	50–60	197
MEXICO	60.7	30–35	412
NICARAGUA	60–80	45–50	298
PANAMA	40–60	20–30	425
PARAGUAY	◊	20–25	186
PERU	83.5	35–40	218
URUGUAY	40–45	8–10	537
VENEZUELA	49.3	30–35	745

◊ UNAVAILABLE

SOURCES: *POPULATION REFERENCE BUREAU 1968.
**ROBERTS AND KOHDA 1967: 66.

all, but the availability of schools is another matter. Millions of Latins do not know how to read, write, or even sign their names. Government leaders are formulating literacy and educational programs, even in those countries which presently have the lowest rates.

Inflation

Rampant inflation is plaguing most of South America, hindering economic progress and discouraging productive investment. Wage increases lag behind price increases — and wage earners are bearing the brunt of inflation. The problem is particularly grave since the annual inflation rate from 1960 to 1966 in Brazil was 60.5 per cent; in Uruguay, 35.4 per cent; in Chile, 26.3 per cent; and in Argentina, 24.5 per cent (*World Business* 1967a.7:8).

Inflation has been especially damaging to the administration of Churches modeled after North American norms. One congregation we visited in Brazil had saved $4,000 toward the construction of a new sanctuary. At the suggestion of the missionary the members were trying to save another $4,000, an amount that would be matched dollar for dollar by the mission. Within a year they saw inflation whittle their savings to a value of less than $2,000. The new sanctuary is still a dream. Fixed subsidies are also a problem for mission-related Churches. Budgets are in terms of national currencies, but inequities arise as currency values drop.

The same inflationary pattern, however, has provided the opportunity for extensive building programs by the indigenous Churches. Adopting the "anti-savings" mentality which accompanies uncontrolled inflation, they strain their resources to take advantage of the situation. They can charge construction materials this month and make payments with cheaper money next month! In many cases the exorbitant interest rates have been less than the rate of inflation.

A Changing Economic Position

In the midst of the crisis created by inflation, men seek new solutions. While their search is economic, it can have spiritual implications. Some have alleged that Evangelicals seek an escape from the reality of their situation into an "other worldliness." Without hope of changing anything in the secular life, they attempt to live only for the life to come. In general, however, this has not been true of Latin American Evangelicals. As economic conditions have tightened and as change has become a necessity, Evangelicals have become more involved in the solution of personal, social, and economic problems.

The gospel has also improved the social and economic lot of many Latin American Evangelicals. A typical example of this change is the case of a Brazilian who had become a *crente* (believer). The morning after he had made this decision, he also borrowed a ladder to fix his roof. It had leaked for months, but only now with his newly found enthusiasm was the man concerned about fixing it. Within a few months he had built a fence around his property, painted his house, and added a room. When we asked how he could afford to make these improvements he said that he had been spending more than that on women, liquor, and cigarettes. As soon as he could, he also found a place where his children could study. He had not had the opportunity to attend school, but he felt that the future demanded that everyone from the next generation go to school to become something better.

It was as if the experience of salvation had opened his eyes to much more than spiritual truths. For the first time in his life he thought of himself as a son of God, one of Christ's redeemed. The dramatic spiritual results of his action gave him courage to believe that he could improve his own social and economic position. Such a man will not be victimized by demagoguery, nor will he be satisfied with the status quo.

Depersonalization of life, alteration of family relationships, and modification of cultural values accompany modern technological advances in Latin America as elsewhere. The old Iberian pattern of family life is disintegrating under the impact of industrialized society. Everywhere we traveled, parents were puzzled as to how to deal with multiple incomes, unchaperoned children away from home, changed buying patterns, new styles of clothing, and new attitudes toward authority.

The attempt to find norms of behavior in this new order opens the door to the Evangelical Churches. The establishment of a new inner authority which will take the place of the vanishing subordination by family pressures, helps create stability in the midst of change. The Evangelical finds in the gospel a raison d'être in the depersonalized society of factory and city. The sense of community, purpose, direction, hope for betterment, responsibility, and authority found within the Evangelical Church have remade life for him. He becomes aware of his own role in this new force — the biblical Church — which is changing Latin America.

It is not by accident that the largest Evangelical Churches of Latin America are growing in this new, industrialized social order in the urban centers. Over thirty years ago Kenneth Grubb foresaw the move to the cities as unfavorable to church growth (1932:99-100), as did mission leaders in other parts of the world. Yet, the rural-based, mission-related Churches have suffered to the extent that in the cities they have not multiplied churches which minister to their rural members who move to the industrial centers. Comity arrangements aggravated the problem by limiting the work of these same missions. The indigenous Churches led by laymen, not bound by the comity agreements of missions, have tended to fare much better. An analysis of

Chilean Pentecostal growth, for instance, shows a direct relationship between the growth of an urban proletariat and church growth (Lalive d'Epinay 1965-66:35).

Urban industrial development, however, does not in itself guarantee church growth. Caracas, Venezuela, and Buenos Aires, Argentina, are examples. The opportunity for growth that new development presents must be met by Churches which are spiritually and emotionally prepared to serve through multiplying congregations in the growing city. A Church oriented to North America, spending its energies in philanthropic ventures pleasing to North Americans, cannot multiply churches in Latin American cities, no matter how responsive the city dwellers may be.

THE GROWTH OF OTHER RELIGIONS

The fact that Latin Americans have unmet needs of a social, material, and spiritual nature is seen in the increasing rate of growth of other religions. This openness to change implies that if these unmet needs are recognized and analyzed, and if the gospel is preached in such a way as to meet these needs, then the people who are ready for change will come into the Evangelical Church.

By observing which segments of society are responding to these other religions, as well as the nature of their motivation, Evangelicals can better understand their own task. Evangelicals need also to become aware of the methods of propagation used by these religions, the type of indoctrination given, the kind of cultural elements carried over into the new religions (and how these provide for continuity of leadership), and the *kind* of growth which results.

Irreligion

One of the most significant changes has been the marked increase in the number of persons who profess no religion at all. Some of these have been reared in a non-religious environment, and others have become disenchanted with the Roman Catholic Church or with nominal Protestantism. The scope of this phenomenon varies widely in Latin America. The percentage of the population which professes no religion at all ranges from 0.6 per cent in Mexico (Mexican census 1962: 283) to 38.8 per cent in rural Uruguay (CLEH 1963:432).

Anticlericalism in Latin America is neither antireligious nor antichurch. It is directed against the clergy and the Roman Catholic hierarchy as such. Everyone who lives in Latin America is acquainted with the type of persons who have no use for priests but love the Roman Catholic Church. Nevertheless the irreligious do not come from this group.

Neither do the irreligious come from the vociferous group of Comtian positivists, avowed agnostics among the cultured elite, which has never included more than a very small part of the population.

The growing number of religionless persons arise in the secular-ized elements of society, which no longer look to religion to solve the great questions of the day. The social reality of the religionless is pervading Latin America, a proof that the religious liberty of Latin America is real. Men are rejecting a Christianity which is merely superstitious, formal, or nominal.

The fact that people are leaving both inherited Roman Catholi-cism and inherited Protestantism suggests that the Churches have been remiss in teaching and living the truth. An adequate com-munication of the gospel would hold in the Church most of those who leave and at the same time win those who have inherited religion as a way of life.

Syncretistic Christianity

Some forms of syncretism (the blending of opposing principles or practices to make something new) are as old as the Spanish civili-zation in the New World, and others are as new as today's newspaper. Irrelevant elements which have been added to Christianity in Latin America range from the worship of volcanoes in Peru to political philosophies such as Peronism (which includes worship of Eva Perón).

Since the "message" of the gospel consists not only of the original communication but also of everything which is later given to supple-ment it, the original proclamation and the subsequent teaching as understood by the hearer must together be adequate. If the message is incomplete, he is forced to fill in the gaps by supplying non-Christian elements from his experiences and environment. The mis-sionary is particularly vulnerable at this point. He may preach a message "based on the Bible," but it is also based on the presupposi-tions of his foreign culture. The hearer, who has his own presupposi-tions, interprets the message in the only way he can — out of his own knowledge. One result may be syncretism. The missionary may be quite unaware of the problem he has created. An example is the magical use of psalms in southern Mexico. What probably began as respect for the Scriptures as the Word of God has degenerated into a sub-Christian practice of using psalms for magical incantations.

Another form of syncretism results when the form of Christian-ity communicated is itself syncretistic. The Roman Catholic Church brought unchanged to the New World European syncretisms in the form of superstitious elements of European folk religion. This pro-duced a distorted, unbiblical Christianity. Protestants have brought their own lesser varieties of syncretism.

Whenever the complete gospel is not preached and learned there is real danger of syncretism. Only systematic, thorough teaching in culturally relevant terms will safeguard the purity of the gospel message and maintain the genuineness of experience. If the expression of Christianity which people find in the Evangelical Church does not minister to their spiritual needs, they will adulterate their experience with syncretistic elements in their efforts to supply what is lacking.

Luzbetak (1963: 244-248) has defined this religious hybridization as a form of undirected or misdirected reinterpretation, selection, and ramification. The principles he has outlined for overcoming this problem are as valid for Evangelicals as for Roman Catholics: (1) It is necessary to study the particular case of syncretism historically, with the historian's sense of detail and proportion and with his habit of interrelating events. (2) The missionary task consists not only in communicating the Word but also in directing the selection that unavoidably accompanies innovation. (3) The reinterpretation of the message by the hearers must be directed. (4) To displace existing syncretistic beliefs and practices it is necessary to analyze their functions and then find ways to fill the corresponding needs with theologically tenable patterns. (5) The segment of society which is the main current of communication must be reached to avoid the type of uneven social acceptance of Christian ways and values which encourages syncretism. (6) A culturally sound catechistic approach is an excellent antidote against syncretism.

The emergence of syncretism is always a danger signal for the Church. It is an indication that the Church has failed at some point. Whether it takes the form of messianism or other types of nativistic movements; whether it is an admixture of foreign elements with Christianity as an overemphasized aspect of truth; or whether it confuses democracy, communism, or any other political ideology with Christianity, syncretism reminds the Church that she should be teaching in relevant terms the clear, orthodox teachings of the New Testament.

Spiritism

One of the most conspicuous religious manifestations in Latin America at the present time is spiritism, which has its roots in Indian and African animism, as well as European superstitions. It has found wide acceptance throughout Latin America; in fact, many believe it to be the fastest-growing religious movement there today. It is necessary, however, to clarify several points in order to evaluate this claim.

Kinds of Spiritism

The more sophisticated form is known as Kardecism, named after Allan Kardec, pseudonym of Hyppolyte Leon Denisard Rivail, who originated the term spiritism in the middle of the nineteenth century. Kardec's *Le Livre des Esprits contenant les Principes de la Doctrine Spirite* (Rivail 1922) is regarded as the definitive statement of spiritistic doctrines. Kardecism has had particular appeal to the middle and upper classes.

Umbanda is much more widespread than Kardecism in Brazil. It is a more primitive expression of spiritism and is also much older, including elements of Amerindian animism (Menezes 1958) and elements of African religions brought by slaves in colonial times (Carneiro 1948:131). It is impossible to determine how many Umbanda spiritists exist, since it is unnecessary to be a member of a formally organized group. Most spiritists of this type continue to count themselves as Roman Catholic in spite of vigorous efforts on the part of the Roman Catholic Church to stamp out spiritistic practices among her adherents. Roman Catholic saints have been given the names of African deities by these spiritists, so that it becomes impossible to know whether the worshipper is praying to the Catholic saint or to the African god (Herskovits 1965: 541-546).

In 1884 the various spiritist groups of Brazil formed a federation. These are the societies which, for the most part, appear in the Brazilian religious census. In 1940, the general census showed 463,000 spiritists in Brazil. The 1950 census showed 824,553. The religious census of 1960 gives a total of only 636,212, which does not mean that membership has dropped. The 1960 religious census includes only organized groups which filed census forms.

Inadequate Definition of Spiritism

If only registered members of organized spiritistic groups are counted, the percentage of the population included would be quite small. The common claim that there are 12 million spiritists in Brazil is evidently based on a rough calculation of 15 per cent of the population. There is no empirical evidence to support this claim. Kloppenburg suggests that spiritism is

> ... understood as a pretentiously evoked, perceptible communication with spirits from the beyond, whether to receive news from them, to consult them (necromancy), or to place them at the service of men (magic); either to do good (white magic) or to perform some evil (black magic). To be a spiritist, therefore, it suffices to accept this minimum doctrine: that spirits exist; that these spirits are ardently interested in communicating with us in order to instruct us or help us; that we men can evoke perceptible communication with these spirits (1966: 77-78).

Incidence of Spiritism

The rate of occurrence of spiritism is certainly much lower in most other parts of Latin America than it is in Brazil. The Christopaganism of Mexico and Central America is definitely spiritistic though its motif is Indian animism rather than the African animism of the Caribbean and Brazil. This spiritism, whether African or Amerindian, is not confined to the Negroes and Indians but is just as prevalent among *mestizos.*

Growth of Spiritism

The increasing tendency of spiritists to identify with formally organized spiritist groups partly explains the "growth" of spiritism. The Roman Catholic Church has been carrying on a systematic campaign against spiritistic practices among Roman Catholics. The first result has been to induce many who were nominal Roman Catholics to declare themselves as spiritists. This is one of the calculated risks that the Roman Catholic hierarchy took in the beginning of the campaign. In time their efforts will produce Roman Catholics who understand the basic contradictions between Catholic and spiritist teaching.

A large part of the population of Latin America practices some form of spiritism. This has been true for generations. There is no conclusive evidence at the present time that spiritism as such is increasing. If Brazil may be considered as typical, Latin American spiritism will probably become more sophisticated and more formalized.

Lessons for Church Growth

All Protestant Churches have been aware of the dangers of spiritism and have mounted a two-pronged attack against it: one aimed at protecting the church member from heresy and the other aimed at winning the spiritist. Not all Churches have been equally successful in dealing with the problem. The Churches which have attempted to deal with it by exposing the frauds and trickery that accompany spiritism and which by implication deny the reality of the forces with which the spiritists wrestle, have been singularly ineffective in safeguarding their own members and in winning others from spiritism. In the tracts and booklets these Churches have prepared as the means of evangelizing spiritists as well as in the Sunday School literature and other studies for their constituency, they take the view that there is nothing to spiritism and that civilized people need not fear the superstitions of the spiritists. Even if the average church member gives mental assent to this, subconscious fears make him unable totally to disbelieve in spiritism. The Baptist and Presbyterian missionaries who stoutly maintain that spiritism has no effect on their churches would be deeply disturbed if they knew how many of their members go to the *curandero* (healer) when they get sick, live in fear of evil spells and incantations, and are not convinced that Christianity represents a greater power than the spirits.

North American cultural preconceptions of the Churches and missions at this point have hindered them in communicating the gospel to the spiritists. This is particularly unfortunate in view of the fact that spiritists are not otherwise closed to communication. They call all Christians "brothers" because of Christianity's belief in God as a spirit.

The Pentecostals have been much more effective than other Churches in winning spiritists. This is not only because they are willing to allow worship norms that express the cultural dynamics of the people, but also because they grant the spiritists their first premise — that spirits do exist. They preach a positive message of a superior power that can deliver from evil spirits. The man who lives tormented by fears of what witchcraft can do to him, to his business, and to his family, does not want to be told that his fears are irrational. He looks for a power that can free him from the power of this mysterious spirit world that surrounds him. The Pentecostal tells him, "I used to live with the same fears until Christ set me free. You can enjoy the same victory if you become a believer." In effect, the Pentecostal message demythologizes a world with which the spiritist has been unable to cope.

The prevalence of spiritistic practices all over Latin America demonstrates the need for Evangelicals to develop methods and emphases which will win the spiritists. As Tippett (1967:7) has shown, no mere dialogue is sufficient. Nothing less than a power encounter will do.

In the very same way, the best safeguard against spiritism creeping into the Church is an adequate expression of Christianity. No negative polemic can be as effective in combating error as a positive demonstration of spiritual dynamic.

North American Cults

Most of the cults that have gained popularity in other parts of the Western world are also present in Latin America. In general they have not grown as much as elsewhere. Two exceptions to this general observation are the Mormons and the Jehovah's Witnesses.

Mormons

The greatest area of growth for the Mormons has been in southern South America. Since Negroes cannot belong to their priesthood they have almost been forced to rule out large areas of Latin America as sites for their missionary activity. In northern Brazil we were approached by Mormon missionaries on several occasions. We got the impression that they were trying to single out individuals who were pure whites. In the integrated sections of Latin America, this drastically reduces the number of potential contacts.

Thus far, the Indians have not been very responsive to the Mormons in spite of the fact that Mormon teaching makes the Indians a part of God's chosen people. Perhaps this is because the Mormons depend on young people who volunteer two years of their lives for service in missionary work. These young people have no training in cross-cultural communication and lack the technical skills to gain acceptance among the tribespeople.

Even in southern South America we found their missionary work was quite superficial. Some of these young missionaries baptized fantastic numbers of converts. We spoke with some who had been baptized but had no idea what Mormon teachings are or what was the significance of their baptism. Apparently, they had been abandoned since the missionary had gone back to the United States when his time was over. Despite this their metropolitan churches demonstrate vigorous growth and active programs. At the present time the Mormons claim to have 42,917 members in Latin America. It is difficult to tell how many of these are actually practicing Mormons.

Jehovah's Witnesses

Latin America is not the best mission field for the Jehovah's Witnesses. The Latin Americans are very patriotic and strongly loyal. The *Watchtower* teaching, which condemns the economic system, the religious system, and the political system as being the enemies of Jehovah God, sounds like anarchism to the Latin American. The Latin American mentality tends toward more organization in the system instead of less.

In 1942, 807 "ministers" were working in South America. In the following decade that figure rose to 11,795 — an increase of 1,360 per cent for the ten years. Between 1952 and 1962 they increased by 400 per cent. The slower rate of the second decade does not necessarily indicate any marked decrease in the vitality of the movement. It is always easier for a smaller group to achieve a high percentage of growth. The crucial decade will be the present one, from 1962 to 1972. This decade will show whether the Jehovah's Witnesses maintain the same growth pattern.

We talked with many Evangelicals for whom the Jehovah's Witnesses had provided an intermediate step on their way into the Evangelical Church. Some had dabbled in other religions before trying the Jehovah's Witnesses, which then served the function of setting them free from former religious alliances. In this frame of mind they were ready to listen to the positive message of the gospel. It was as if they had had to react against religion in order to accept the new faith. Jehovah's Witnesses could help them to break down their former fears and prejudices but were unable to provide adequate functional substitutes.

Modern Political Movements

The contemporary political movements must be included in the consideration of "other religions" in that they demand personal commitment to an ideology and require participation that is definitely religious in character. They do not have the "foreign" character which hinders the advance of other religions, but deal with familiar concepts in attractive ways and are couched in terms which appeal to the present political needs of Latin America. The appeal of these movements is very subtle, because all are trying to solve man's spiritual problems by apparently non-religious means. Unregenerate man naturally responds to such an approach.

We do not attempt to pass judgment on the relative worth of these political movements. Our argument is that, to the extent that they try to meet the spiritual needs of the people, they are religious in nature. The easy labels which we use to describe political thinking in a North American context are next to meaningless as a means of describing the forces of politics in Latin America. The terms nationalism, Marxism, democracy, totalitarianism, and egalitarianism do not adequately describe the political movements of Latin America. Each of these is a force, but in a manner which is uniquely Latin American.

The success of the twentieth-century political movements of Latin America is significant for the Evangelical Church, because their methodology in seeking member participation utilizes social dynamics — very similar to the methods which the indigenous Pentecostal Churches have employed with such success.

The relationship of the Evangelical Churches to the political movements of Latin America is one aspect of Evangelical church growth which will require further study. Such a study must perhaps await a general study of politization of Latin America (Goldrich 1965: 361). The effect of political movements on the Evangelical Churches, and vice versa, is undeniable. The exact nature of this interrelationship is unclear at present. One of the gravest problems which the Church faces is her responsibility in political life. No simplistic answer will suffice.

A PATTERN OF CHANGE

In great movements born out of visions of justice and peace, men of Latin America are seeking to determine their own future. Although they dream of social betterment and economic opportunity, essentially their openness to change arises out of spiritual needs.

The Evangelical Church as a *community* is a force for change. If it grows greatly, the Evangelical Church will help determine the future of Latin America. In an effort to meet the spiritual needs of Latin Americans, the Church is inevitably a part of the revolution and is itself a reform movement. The Church can obstruct change and miss a glorious opportunity; it can overlook the unique opportunities and fail to capitalize on the situation; or the Evangelical Church can itself be changed and then effect change, thereby fulfilling its mission.

The Church, however, cannot rely merely on the hopes of getting enough changed men to transform society. These redeemed men are themselves the agents of Christ, first as proclaimers of the gospel, and then as improvers of society. Evangelicals who are local leaders, elected government officials, teachers, doctors, social workers, health officers, community-development technicians, and those active in the reform movements are already actively involved. Some missionaries express their fears of such participation. Yet, many of the freedoms enjoyed today by Latin Americans were won by the Evangelical Church. The power of the Church cannot be limited to a mere example of the godly life. She must not be silent in the face of existing injustices.

Furthermore, the fact that people are ready to change religious allegiance places the responsibility for growth squarely on the Evangelical Church. If people are changing — why not to the truth? The *kind* of religious growth demonstrates what elements have been lacking in the former religious situation — a clear indication of what the emphasis of the Evangelical message should be. The Evangelical Church must minister to every spiritual need, but it must begin with those spiritual needs of which people are aware. The class of society which shows itself to be open to religious change, the locality of occurring change, and the kind and extent of religious growth together delineate the field of activity for Christian Churches and their assisting missions. As the Church fulfills its prophetic ministry, it stands over and against all that is unjust and corrupt and shares in the accomplishment of the will of God.

Chapter Sixteen

ROMAN CATHOLIC RESURGENCE

Evangelical church growth in Latin America can best be under-stood in contrast with the dominance of the Roman Catholic Church. In spite of phenomenal Protestant growth in the twentieth century, the Evangelical Church is still only a small minority in the Latin American religious picture.

HISTORICAL ROOTS

For several decades during the pioneer stage of Protestant mis-sions, the principal thrust of the Evangelical message was an anti-Catholic effort directed against Catholic theology and methodology. It was·not that the early missionaries did not preach the gospel. On the contrary, they felt very strongly that what Latin America needed was the message of salvation by faith. However, they overestimated the extent to which the Latin Americans understood and embraced Catholic teachings. They felt that the only way to win men was to combat the errors of Rome. The result was to stir up opposition and persecution from Roman Catholics whose allegiance to their Church was primarily emotional.

The tendency for Evangelicals to be anti-Catholic in their em-phasis was strengthened by the fact that Protestantism was used by the Latin American republican governments as one weapon against the Roman Catholic Church in the politico-religious conflicts of the last century and the early years of this century (Damboriena 1962.1: 12).

Robert Ricard (1966: 3) suggests that the subsequent develop-ment of the Roman Catholic Church in Mexico was but the out-working of principles that were laid down in the sixteenth century. The same could be said for the rest of Latin America. Apart from a few notable instances, the establishing of the Roman Catholic Church in the New World met with little opposition. "The very ease with which the Indian seemed to accept the Roman Catholic religion meant that for him it was both meaningless and sterile" (Rycroft 1958: 108). Even though syncretism was not one of the principles adopted historically by the Roman Catholic Churches, nevertheless it was the immediate result of a foreign religion being superimposed upon a strong native culture by a conquering few.

> When the early missionaries preached Christianity, they expected the people to adopt all of the practices inherent with it, as they were known and carried out in Europe. This meant not only a change in belief, but also in the long-established customs and traditions of the people. Often the only reason for the change was that it was the only way that the missionaries themselves knew. The people, however, rooted in the habits of a lifetime, never really made the new practices (and often the beliefs) a real part of their thinking and acting, and the result was syncretism — a mixture of Christian and pagan practices still to be found in many parts of Latin America today (Wood 1964: 25).

Among these are the identification of African deities with Catholic saints in Brazil and the Caribbean (Herskovits 1965: 541-546), the sacred mushroom in southern Mexico (Luzbetak 1963: 242), the Christo-paganism among Guatemalan (Nida 1961. a: 1-14) and Mexican Indians (Wonderly 1958: 197-202), and the common customs of feast days, shrines, saints, miracles, which closely coincide with pre-Hispanic religious phenomena.

Christianity never really took root.

> Latin America was never "Christian" in the sense that Europe or even North America can be said to be so. What took place here was a colossal transplantation — the basic ecclesiastical structures, disciplines, and ministries were brought wholesale from Spain, and were expected to function as a Christian order: a tremendous form without substance (Miguez Bonino 1964: 168).

Christianity became an isolated religious ceremony, quite divorced from life's activities. The nominal Christianity of the Latin American Catholic is generally recognized by Roman Catholic, Protestant, and secular writers. It is a problem which continues to plague the Roman Catholic Church even today. Most persons in Latin America are only nominally Catholic. Only a small percentage of Catholics in Latin America attend mass as often as once a year. According to Vergara, in Chile, for example, 70 per cent of the population practice no religion whatever. He says that it is in such areas that Protestantism advances (1962: 227). We found this to be true all over Latin America. The percentage of merely nominal Catholics in other Latin American countries is certainly no less than in Chile, and is probably more in many cases. "The fact of the existence of this nominal Catholicism is undeniable" (Damboriena 1962.1:36).

About 90 per cent of the population of Latin America is baptized in the Catholic Church; a much smaller percentage takes first communion; religious marriages represent a still smaller percentage; and Sunday observance is as low as 3.5 per cent among the men and

9.5 per cent among the women. In large cities and rural areas only a very small proportion of the population regularly attends mass. The highest rates for Sunday observances are found in the small cities (Houtart and Pin 1965: 166).

Another serious problem with historical roots which faces the Catholic Church in Latin America is her early association with the conquerors and hence with the oppressors. The Spanish idea of religion as patriotism, and patriotism as religion, was carried to the New World. The *conquistadores* had as an objective the enlarging of the territory of Christianity (Houtart and Pin 1965: 4). The *patronato de Indias,* which gave the Spanish kings ecclesiastical powers, strengthened this view (Mecham 1966: 4).

> The approach to the New World of the west was always marked by three considerations — conquest, settlement, and evangelization. The peoples of these unknown lands were to be brought permanently under the dominion of the Christian kings, to whom God through the Pope has given sovereignty (Neill 1964: 168).

This equating of patriotism and religion brought about an interrelationship between Church and State which has continued to this day to complicate the relationship of the Catholic Church to the republican governments.

The *encomienda* system was another expression of Roman Catholic identification with the oppressor class and proved to be a hindrance to the Christianization of the Indian populations. Under this system, a colonist was given authority over a group of Indians who were to work for him. In return, he assumed responsibility for their material and spiritual well-being. Although priests such as Las Casas and Montesinos raised their voices in protest against the ensuing evils, a pattern of cruelty and violence was established which took centuries to modify. All too often the Catholic Church participated as "colonists," acquiring huge tracts of land and reaping the benefit of free Indian labor under the *encomienda* system.

As the economy of Latin America evolved toward a more viable base and as large estates developed, the landed classes came to think of the Church as their own. Many priests served as private chaplains to wealthy landowners and as the defenders of the status quo. From the upper class the church hierarchy emerged. Therefore, so long as the upper class controlled everything, the Roman Catholic Church enjoyed a favored position. But when the political picture began to change, and the disinherited masses began to seize control, the precarious nature of the Church's position became evident.

Despite legal efforts to control the acquisition of land, the Roman Catholic Church came to be the principal landholder in many parts of Latin America. Because land ownership was equated with political power, the Catholic Church, by virtue of her landholdings alone, became one of the strongest political forces in Latin America.

The independence movements created special problems for the Roman Catholic Church. Religion, as such, was not a factor in causing the revolt. The leaders were all Roman Catholics, although all had been influenced to some extent by French revolutionary thought.

The problem arose, rather, over the question of the status and privileges of patronage. The republican governments claimed for themselves the prerogative formerly held by the Spanish crown of nominating the church bishops. The papacy, on the other hand, saw the end of Spanish rule as an opportunity to terminate patronage, and interpreted this delegation of ecclesiastical powers to the king as merely a concession on the part of the Holy See which could be withdrawn at will. The concordats which were signed between the republican governments and the papacy grew out of the conflict concerning patronage.

> It has been suggested, and the explanation is plausible, that the new republics assumed control over the Church to curb its power and prevent as far as possible the interference of the ecclesiastics in the political affairs of the states. This policy was rendered doubly necessary since the higher Church dignitaries were Spanish sympathizers who frowned on the Revolution (Mecham 1966: 49-50).

As political parties developed through the nineteenth century and on into the twentieth, the Roman Catholic Church tended to ally itself with those which were more conservative. As the political influence of the various parties waxed and waned, the relative power of the Church accompanied the fortunes of the parties with which she had identified herself, or which had identified with her. Liberalism with its anticlerical overtones was seen as an enemy to be opposed by every means.

The identification with the status quo hindered the Church from attuning itself to the profound changes which were sweeping Latin America. The rigid local ecclesiastical structures and the lack of meaningful relationship between parishes militated against any flexibility, political, religious, or social.

Another current problem of the Roman Catholic Church, which also has its roots in history, is her lack of priests. The lack of candidates for the ministry is a danger sign for any Church, but especially for one which permits only the clergy to perform certain rites and administer the means of grace.

In a colonial situation the Roman Catholic Church was especially vulnerable. No serious attempt was made to build up an indigenous ministry (Neill 1964: 173). Very few were ordained who were not of pure European stock. Theoretically the ordination of *mestizos* and Indians was possible, but in practice it was not done. Latin America has never fully recovered.

> Did the fathers of the Sixteenth Century miscalculate? Would the history of the Church in Latin America have been different, and more edifying, if they had from the start shown greater courage, and greater belief in the power of the Holy Spirit to raise up a national Christian leadership from among the people of South and Central America? (Neill 1964: 176).

The problem reached emergency proportions with the expulsion of the Jesuits in the eighteenth century. This left a dangerous vacuum which no one was prepared to fill.

The crisis following independence was even more grave. Bishops who had been loyal to Spain were exiled. For many years the Pope refused to accept any nominations from the republican governments, so sees that were vacated remained unfilled. Even after the signing of the concordats, the consecration of bishops continued to be a long drawn-out process. Without bishops there could be no ordination of priests. The very continuity of the Church was at stake. The liberal-conservative political controversy all over Latin America prevented the structural development of theological institutions which could have helped in the solution of the problem.

As a temporary expedient, the Latin American Church came to depend on foreign personnel. The Catholic Church has not yet solved this problem.

NUMBER OF INHABITANTS PER PRIEST IN LATIN AMERICA:
1912 to 1960
(Houtart and Pin 1965: 146)

Year	Inhabitants/Priest
1912	4,480
1945	5,770
1950	5,720
1955	5,530
1960	5,410

The recent improvement can be attributed to even greater numbers of foreign priests.

Meanwhile, the number of adherents to other religions as well as those professing no religion at all has been climbing steadily, particularly in the twentieth century. Though Protestant missions arrived in force in the nineteenth century, the growth of the Protestant Church is essentially a twentieth-century phenomenon. At least in part, this growth must be attributed to a general drift from the Roman Catholic Church, a drift toward new forms of syncretism, toward the secular religions, and toward a more dynamic expression of religious faith. Protestant growth cannot be attributed solely to the success of Protestant missions but also to a real failure on the part of the Catholic Church to hold its own.

Signs of Roman Catholic Renewal

Dramatic changes are taking place both within the Roman Catholic Church in Latin America and in its relationship to society. It is too early to judge the implications of the patterns that are beginning to emerge. Some reflect worldwide trends within the Church but others are unique to Latin America.

We do not overemphasize the significance of these promised changes. We have no way to know how many are only dreams of a small minority who lack the power to bring them to fruition. What we have seen and known first-hand of the Latin American Roman Catholic Church leads us to believe that it will be a long time before the new things of which we write will become an integral part of Roman Catholic practice there.

We do not know if the forces of reaction will be allowed to stifle the initiative of the avant-garde. We trust not.

Since its present situation is so grave, it will take many years for the Roman Catholic Church to overcome its handicaps. At the same time we recognize that the steps that are being taken are in the right direction.

The most conspicuous changes are those in the area of theological renewal. The redefinition of the Church and its mission and of the nature of revelation, the changes in the liturgy, the new concept of the role of the laity, and the declaration on religious freedom as expressed by the Second Vatican Council have had and will continue to have widespread repercussions in Latin America. If allowed to develop to their logical conclusions, this re-thinking will produce a renewed Roman Catholic Church, even if the process takes many decades. It is for this reason that we describe some of them at length.

Role of the Laity

The emphasis on the apostolate of the laity is particularly important.

> One third of all baptized Catholics in the world now live in Latin America. At present, many of them have no effective contact with the Church, because of a lack of priests, Brothers, Sisters and above all, trained apostolic laymen. Therefore, an already serious situation threatens to become critical, unless the effort of the Church is supported without delay by an impressive increase in apostolic workers, religious and lay (Verhoeven 1966: 127).

Even the problem of an adequate number of candidates for the priesthood depends for its solution on an aroused, involved, participant laity. Vallier has pointed out (1967: 195-197) that both of the radical movements, leftist political and Pentecostal, that have arisen in Latin America in the twentieth century, have been essentially lay movements that have given status, responsibility, and solidarity to their adherents. Neither of these movements has ever lacked leaders. Within the Roman Catholic laity there is a vast reservoir of potential leaders that is just beginning to be tapped.

Because by definition Latin America is Roman Catholic, the Church has lacked a missionary urgency. All of society has been so permeated with Roman Catholic values that the need for spiritual change was not evident until recently. Historically the Christianization of Indian tribes was left to professional missionaries. Also the political and religious systems were so intertwined that it became difficult to say which was supporting which, and in the increasing general disenchantment, the Latin American tended to turn his capacity for missionary zeal in secular directions.

At the same time, the Catholic Church was making almost no effort to utilize the layman in the work of his Church. The sacristan was unusual in that he was interested in church matters, and though a layman, played a certain role. The great majority of Catholic laymen, however, felt neither responsibility nor concern for the religious organization as such. Catholic Action groups were understood to be the secular arm of the Church, answerable to and under the control of the hierarchy. The religious role of the layman was confined to a preoccupation with his own spiritual condition. The only way he could serve his Church as a layman was by his activity in temporal matters.

New emphases in the Roman Catholic Church in Latin America promise to change all this. Long before Vatican II, the Latin American bishops were trying to find a more meaningful role for the faithful. Even though this effort was largely directed toward the upper and middle classes (Considine 1964: 128), it has spilled over to include many from the lower classes. Far more important than any single change of policy has been the general feeling that the layman has a stake in what the Church is doing.

The emphasis of the Second Vatican Council on the layman's *spiritual* responsibilities as stressed by recent encyclicals has served to strengthen this sense of participation in Latin America. The following references to the Documents of Vatican II are based on the unofficial English translation edited by Walter M. Abbott, S.J. (1966: 491-512):

> The laity, too, share in the priestly, prophetic, and royal office of Christ and therefore have their own role to play in the mission of the whole People of God in the Church and in the world.

The Decree on the Apostolate of the Laity speaks of the life, works, and words of the laity as having the power to make the gospel known.

> The hierarchy entrusts to the laity some functions which are more

closely connected with pastoral duties such as the teaching of Christian doctrine, certain liturgical actions, and the care of souls.

The extent and nature of lay participation will be determined by the specific action that Latin American church authorities take to implement the guidelines of Vatican II. The present climate is creating a reserve of good will on which the Roman Catholic Church must capitalize if it wishes to reintegrate the huge masses of nominal Roman Catholics into active, vital participation in the Church. We feel that this is the most crucial area at the present time for the Roman Catholic Church in Latin America.

Place of the Bible

Another area of change in the Catholic Church of Latin America that has been of particular importance to Protestants has been the emphasis on the study and use of the Bible. As has been described in the chapter on the historical development of Latin American Protestantism, the Bible has been the principal evangelistic tool of the *evangelicos*. Naturally enough, Latin American Evangelicals interpret the biblical emphasis by Roman Catholics as the vindication of their own message and methodology.

The "biblical renewal," as the Catholics are calling it, is not primarily a reaction to Protestant success, however. Following the papal encyclical *Divino afflante Spiritu* of Pius XII in 1943, the Pontifical Biblical Commission began to shape the activities of biblical studies. The stress on these studies in Latin America resulted from reforms in the area of pastoral action.

> It aims primarily to restore the living Word of God to its proper place in the daily life of the Church.... What is intended is to bring to the common people, whether educated or not, the riches of the Word of God (Mejia 1966: 209).

If this emphasis continues, it will change Latin American Roman Catholicism beyond recognition.

> Bible services should be encouraged.... They are particularly to be commended in places where no priest is available; when this is so, a deacon or some other person authorized by the bishop should preside over the celebration (Abbott 1966: 150).

Experiments of family and community Bible services, as suggested by Vatican II, have already been successfully carried out in Latin America. Notable among these are the biblical observances in the diocese of Misiones, Argentina (Mejia 1966: 209).

Rise of the Liberals

Many of the changes taking place in Latin America have resulted from a change of mentality in Latin American Roman Catholicism with the emergence of liberals. We need to differentiate between political and theological liberals in the Roman Catholic elite. Some are liberal politically while conservative theologically, or vice versa. This has created shifting alliances in the efforts that are being made to solve social and spiritual problems.

One big gain from the liberal influence has been a healthy identification with the forces of reform. The old image of the conservative reactionary Church opposed to all change is slowly changing. While politically conservative forces still have a strong voice in the Latin American Roman Catholic Church, the Church as a whole has taken a liberal stance. In some places elements of the Roman Catholic Church are in the vanguard of the forces for radical change. It is not an accident that this new phase exactly coincides with renewed biblical emphasis.

Pastoral Plans

An important aspect of the change of mentality in the Latin American Roman Catholic Church has been the development of comprehensive "pastoral plans" on the national, regional, diocesan, and parochial level. The first step in the forming of these pastoral plans was a painful process of self-evaluation. On the basis of the initial inventory of all the resources available and of the external factors that affect the Church and its activities, precise aims can be defined (Houtart 1964. b: 53).

The idea behind the master plan is that the *coordination* of resources is not enough. Nothing less than the *integration* of resources will adequately deal with the problem. This implies radical departures from traditional ways of doing things. More important, it means the combination of resources in new, dynamic ways.

The "pastoral plans" have utilized the hierarchy, the clergy, existing social institutions, lay organizations both national and local, all the means of mass communication, and the talents of interested individuals. A good example is the Natal Movement in northern Brazil, which has supplemented religious education and spiritual guidance with primary education by radio schools, cooperatives, motherhood clinics, and other community improvement projects. The whole of the Northeast, the poorest section of Brazil, has felt the impact of this movement, which has multiplied its limited resources by utilizing them to their fullest. Some of the other "pastoral plans" have even more dramatically achieved stated goals. All of the comprehensive pastoral plans are proving to Latin America that the Catholic Church is in the process of renewal from within and without, and that it is now possible to look to the church as a true ally in the struggle for social justice.

Missionary Effort

In the midst of these various trends toward renewal, another factor presents itself. This is the accelerated foreign missionary effort in Latin America, much of it originating in North America. Responding to pleas from the Holy See, North American bishops have sent hundreds of diocesan priests and religious to Latin America as missionaries.

Evangelicals can learn many lessons from the Roman Catholic missionary effort in Latin America. We face the same problems in trying to communicate cross-culturally. One of the positive lessons that Evangelical missions can learn is the enthusiastic response of missionary candidates when the appeal for personnel is imaginatively couched in terms that realistically describe the need and opportunity.

One of the serious problems of the North American Roman Catholic missionary enterprise in Latin America has been on the basis of private agreements between North American and Latin American bishops. This has created a curious alliance of theologically liberal and politically conservative American bishops with politically and theologically conservative Latin American bishops and has thus tended to support the status quo.

As Ivan Illich pointed out in a controversial article in *America,* this alliance has concerned itself with the search for techniques and well-coordinated programs rather than looking for new ideas or solutions to problems (1967: 88-91). Also, since the agreement between sending and receiving bishops is essentially personal, aid is sent indiscriminately with no consideration of priority of need.

At the same time, the new missionary effort has been strongly institutional. In much the same way that Protestant missionaries have been sidetracked from their main purposes by the time and effort they have had to give to institutions, the Roman Catholic mission effort has been diverted to the administration and maintenance of institutions of every kind. These institutions have absorbed so much money and time that the missionaries have not been able to dedicate themselves to the reintegration of nominal and marginal Roman Catholics into the life of the Church. Worse yet, these very institutions help to keep alive old, inefficient programs that sap the vitality of the new Church.

A foreign clergy is never adequate for proper pastoral care. The foreign priests have the same problems in cross-cultural communication experienced by Protestant missionaries. Celebration of the sacraments is no problem for foreign priests, but the Roman Catholic Church in Latin America — at least the more progressive element — has moved beyond the point where pastoral care is confined to the sacraments. Meaningful pastoral care necessitates a thorough understanding of cultural values.

Many, if not most, of the new missionaries are from missionary orders and are not accustomed to being pastors to 4,000 flesh and blood Latins. They are not prepared to give the kind of pastoral assistance that Latin America needs. Their activities in institutions further tend to isolate them from parish life. The Roman Catholics to whom they minister in the institutions feel the same sense of isolation from the parish and from other Roman Catholics. One of the purposes of the "pastoral plans" all over Latin America is to relate these missionaries more closely to the Roman Catholic community.

The problems of paternalism and cultural imposition are very real. Foreign aid, even in the Catholic Church, has reached such proportions that by its very weight it determines policy. Latin America does not need North American solutions to its problems, but aid in finding its own solutions.

The workshop conducted in 1962 in Rio de Janeiro by the Conference of the Religious of the United States and Canada outlined four principles for the deployment of missionary resources (Houtart and Pin 1965: 247-249).

(1) Selectivity. The need for outside aid is so great that the giving of assistance in any form must be directed to meet the most urgent needs first and to choose those activities which will be most effective. If all 225,000 priests, brothers and sisters in the United States were to go to Latin America immediately, only the present need for priests would be supplied. Since this is impossible, it is necessary to choose what will be done now and what will not be done.

> Selectivity supposes the working out of a hierarchy of choices. First consideration should be given to the relative importance of the different types of action, then to the circle of influence each activity would have (Houtart and Pin 1965: 247).

(2) Pastoral planning. Aid should be directed to activities that are an integral part of the various pastoral plans. Only in this way will there be any guarantee that action is according to need.

(3) Subsidiary action. Foreign missionary personnel should be utilized for those jobs which they as outsiders are able to do. This would free Latin Americans for those specialized jobs which only an insider is equipped to do. Instead of assuming the role of the expert around whom everything revolves, the foreigner thus finds that place in the local picture which his particular talents and skill make for him.

(4) Training. Foreign personnel must be trained in cross-cultural communication. Missionaries have special difficulty in this regard partly because of the external similarity of worship forms. Their training must not only include language skills but also education in the cultural values and social institutions of the people among whom they are to work. Most important of all, they must be taught how to approach a different culture.

Many missionaries are assigned for only two years. To spend

an adequate time of preparation would mean that no time would be left for missionary activity. Therefore most new missionaries have only a few months of "crash" schooling before going to Latin America.

RELEVANCE FOR EVANGELICALS

What are the implications for the Evangelical Church in the current developments in the Roman Catholic Church? We rejoice at the nascent evangelical influences as evidenced by its spiritual renewal and biblical emphases. We await with great interest the results of these trends. If carried to their logical conclusion these emphases will produce a Church that is at once relevant and spiritual. We do not minimize what we consider grave errors in Roman Catholic belief and practice, but we are grateful that the doors and windows of the musty old cathedral are now open and that the fresh winds of spiritual change are allowed to blow. We particularly rejoice in the unchaining of the Bible and will rejoice even more when the use of Scripture leads to more biblical doctrines.

The first visible results of the ecumenical emphasis on the part of the Roman Catholic Church has been greater Evangelical church growth. All over Latin America we met the same phenomenon. Many who had never felt free to visit an Evangelical church before are now attending Protestant services, and some are becoming Evangelicals. Formerly many had been prevented by fear and ignorance from even trying to find out what Protestants believe. Sermons by priests encouraging Roman Catholics to emulate Protestant faithfulness and enthusiasm helped to overcome this fear and reluctance. Pope John's use of the expression "separated brethren" was interpreted by many as an open encouragement to seek closer fellowship with Protestant Churches.

Protestant groups are beginning to lose their minority complex because of the new tolerance expressed by the Roman Catholic Church. Its recognition that Latin America is a pluralistic society has encouraged the Protestants to see themselves in a new light. These Evangelicals are now ready to make themselves heard. It will be interesting to see if they can overcome the ingrained habits of a century of minority status.

The religious situation in Latin America can best be described as a continuum made up of people who are more or less Roman Catholic. Rather than arbitrarily divide them into distinct categories, as can be done for some populations, we have made a diagram based on statistics for mass attendance which produces the type of representation shown in Figure 73.

At one end of the continuum we show those who are the most faithful Roman Catholics. At the other end we show those who are nominal Roman Catholics and are the least committed to the

Roman Catholic Church. The gains that the Roman Catholic Church is making in reintegrating persons into the Church are from that end of the continuum which is already most Roman Catholic. The accessions of the Evangelical Church are from the opposite end of the continuum for the most part. The few exceptions to this rule always receive widespread attention among Evangelicals because of their comparative rarity.

The only Evangelical Church which is making inroads at the Roman Catholic end of the continuum is the Seventh-Day Adventist Church. The reasons for the success of the Adventists in this segment of society would be a profitable matter for all Evangelicals to study.

Since, for the most part, Roman Catholics and Protestants are advancing on opposite ends of the continuum, it will be a long time before they begin to reach the same segments of society. The fact that the Roman Catholic Church is in some ways approximating Evangelical methodology and the Evangelical message would certainly tend to confirm the legitimacy for Evangelicals to press ahead establishing churches.

The best thing for Latin America, and for the Roman Catholic Church, would be for a large segment of the population to become Evangelical. These redeemed men would so change Latin America that the Roman Catholic Church would be far more able to achieve its own goals both in internal structural revisions and in her message and methods relating to the rest of society.

Figure   73

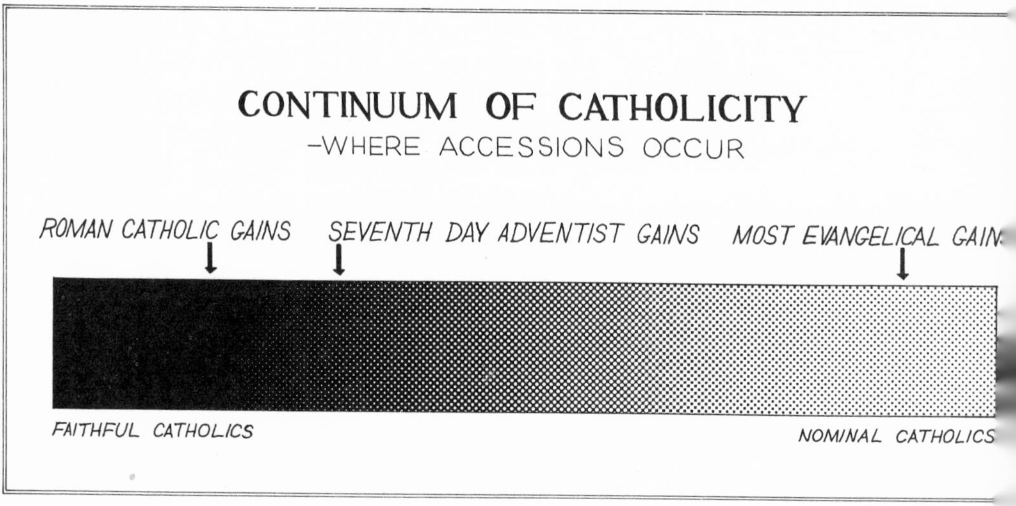

CONTINUUM OF CATHOLICITY
–WHERE ACCESSIONS OCCUR

ROMAN CATHOLIC GAINS   SEVENTH DAY ADVENTIST GAINS   MOST EVANGELICAL GAIN

FAITHFUL CATHOLICS   NOMINAL CATHOLICS

Chapter Seventeen

GROWTH OF THE URBAN CHURCHES

Mass movement of the Latin American population to the cities is rapidly changing the already heterogeneous natures of urban centers such as Monterrey, Guadalajara, Bogotá, Cali, Medellín, Córdoba, Rosário, Pôrto Alegre, Curitiba, Salvador, and Recife — to say nothing of the giants — Mexico City, Buenos Aires, São Paulo, and Rio de Janeiro. According to T. Lynn Smith, "Today most Latin American cities resemble much more closely the cities in other parts of the western world than they do the centers they themselves were only a quarter of a century ago" (1961: 64).

Today the Evangelical Church faces the responsibility of establishing and developing dynamic, relevant churches which can minister the word of reconciliation to the emerging city classes. Wonderly refers to this responsibility as meeting these "culturally 'displaced persons' in their place of need." He poses several questions for the Evangelical Churches in relation to the urban centers:

> How can the church restore to a people in transition to urban life that concept of human dignity which is so important to the Latin American, and at the same time reinterpret this concept in a fully Christian way? What is the place of the so-called "protestant ethic" with relation to the emerging industrial society in Latin America? Which areas of family and economic life have *not* been successfully influenced by Christian concepts? (1960: 209).

Church growth in every metropolitan area demands extensive and creative analysis. The limitations of space and purpose obviously prevent us from discussing the many urban complexes in the countries covered by this survey. Each has unique characteristics, yet all share common factors which enable us to present one urban complex as a case study. The Brazilian urban triangle formed by Rio de Janeiro, São Paulo, and Belo Horizonte represents a significant part of the Latin American scene. A study of the area reveals in general the implications of urban development for the growth of the Evangelical Churches. Even so, the study of the three urban centers is only a small beginning.

269

Figure 74

THE BRAZILIAN TRIANGLE

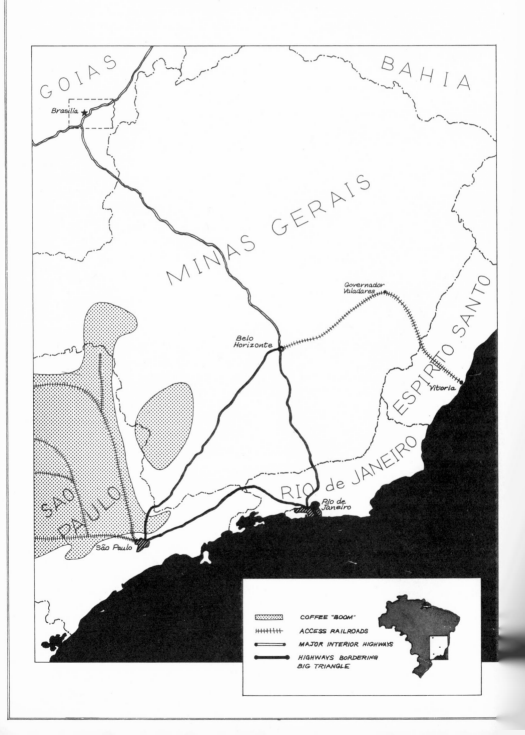

GOIAS

BAHIA

Brasília

MINAS GERAIS

Governador
Valadares

ESPIRITO SANTO

Belo
Horizonte

Vitoria

RIO de JANEIRO

Rio de
Janeiro

SAO PAULO

São Paulo

COFFEE "BOOM"

ACCESS RAILROADS

MAJOR INTERIOR HIGHWAYS

HIGHWAYS BORDERING
BIG TRIANGLE

Brazil's Triangle of Urbanism

The Evangelical Church of Brazil finds herself on the threshold of a new day. In 1960 almost 39 per cent of the Brazilian population lived in urban centers of more than 5,000 inhabitants. By 1970 the percentage living in urban centers will exceed 57 per cent of the total population (Browning 1958: 112). Brazil has been predominantly agricultural, yet "depopulation" of many rural areas is currently in progress (Smith 1963: 598). More than ten large urban networks, including the gigantic metropolitan areas of Rio de Janeiro and São Paulo, are emerging.

Rio de Janeiro and São Paulo, together with the small urban center, Belo Horizonte, constitute a triangle which embraces the highest per capita income of South America and which forms the center of all significant future development of Brazil. Furthermore, these cities of different ages include most of the kinds of cultures and subcultures found in Brazil.

Rio de Janeiro, Cidade Maravilhosa

Known among Brazilians as the Marvelous City, Rio de Janeiro sprawls along a natural border between the mountains and the sea. Yet the beauty of its surroundings does not hide the ugliness found within; its slums are some of the worst in the world, and the clear air that blows in from the sea is quickly polluted by the black smoke of the diesel buses.

In 1760 the arrival of coffee plants in Rio had signaled the beginning of the development of Brazil's natural resources. The Brazilian climate and soil were ideal for the growth of coffee, and by the early 1800's the coffee boom was underway. The center for export remained in Rio de Janeiro until the 1880's when the boom spread to the States of São Paulo, Espirito Santo, and Minas Gerais. Wealthy entrepreneurs formed a new class of investors and developed other industries with the money earned from coffee, and as a result the Brazilian economy was revolutionized. The cultural development of Brazil can also be traced from Rio de Janeiro along the roads that opened the country for the coffee industry (Lamego 1963: 397).

Early Evangelical Growth

Evangelical growth accompanied the expansion of the coffee boom areas. Baptists, Methodists, Presbyterians, and a few other Evangelical denominations prospered here. Because of the link caused by the coffee industry, three centuries of regionalism ended, and Protestant investment and participation were welcomed.

If we could construct a chart of church growth for the Rio de Janeiro area, it would begin in 1869 during the reign of Emperor Dom Pedro II and then take its first upward turn during the era

Figure 75

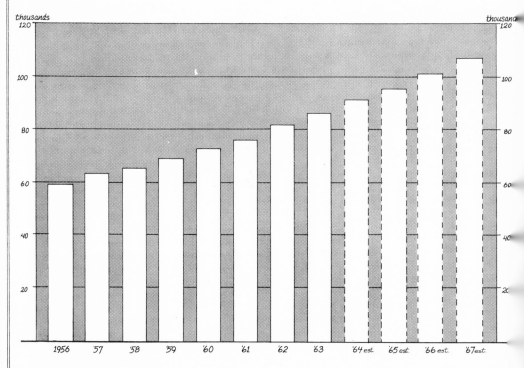

COMMUNICANT MEMBERSHIP OF RIO DE JANEIRO
1958-1963

EVANGELICAL COMMUNICANTS IN RIO DE JANEIRO WERE 2.4% OF TOTAL POPULATION IN 1963.
SOURCE: BRAZILIAN CENSUS, PROTESTANT, 1957, 1959, 1961, 1963.

of the Brazilian empire builder, Ireneu Evangelista de Souza. Souza, the first Brazilian financial magnate, built the railroads, ports, canals, shipping lines, and telegraph lines. The Republic began with the freeing of the slaves in 1888 and President Fonseca's decree of universal suffrage, separation of Church and State, freedom of religion, and a new civil code. Evangelical growth was assured.

Between 1860 and 1900 the Baptist Church grew steadily. Brazilian church leaders were not handicapped by feelings of inferiority to their overseas partners, but rather filled their natural roles with grace and established scores of churches. By 1890 the Presbyterian Church of Brazil had organized its first synod with four presbyteries. Although several waves of persecution beat upon the young Church, it grew substantially. Dedicated pastors and lay leaders enabled it to flourish in an era when economic and cultural life was developing rapidly.

The coffee boom had begun the process of the tri-city expansion. Eventually millions of immigrants — Italians, Germans, Lebanese, Portuguese, and rural Brazilians — made their homes here. In the early twentieth century the Pentecostals joined the historical denominations, and after World War II missions from North American and European Pentecostal Churches established work in the area.

Recent Evangelical Growth

Since 1950 a large influx of people has occurred in the metropolis. Urban developments have replaced orange groves. Many churches have been established in the suburban areas, such as Nova Iguaçu, São João de Meriti, and Duque de Caxias. A recent sociological study of internal migration to the Brazilian cities made by Hutchinson indicates that about 25 per cent of the population in Rio de Janeiro had come from rural areas between 1950 and 1960. In the city of Juiz de Fora the index of rural migration was 50 per cent, and in Volta Redonda 80 per cent. Rio de Janeiro is now less influenced by these migratory movements than in former decades, however, and the unusually high rates of migrational urban growth are found in new suburban areas such as Duque de Caxias, São João de Meriti, and Nova Iguaçu. Between 1950 and 1960 these areas grew by 61,800, 37,400, and 46,700 rural migrants, respectively (1963: 43-45). The Evangelical growth for Rio de Janeiro is seen in Figure 75.

Even though Rio de Janeiro itself is not attracting the large numbers of immigrants it once did, migration continues to certain areas of the metropolis. These are the areas where we must focus our attention. Do areas of high rural-to-urban migration afford a particular opportunity for Evangelicals to establish churches? Having been established, do these churches then have a high potential for growth?

The highest growth rates for Evangelicals in the Rio area (Figure 76) are found in Duque de Caxias, São João de Meriti, Nova Iguaçu, and Volta Redonda. These towns have also been the terminal points for much immigration from the State of Rio de Janeiro and other states since 1950. When growth of the population is compared with the growth of the churches, it would indicate that there is a relationship between Evangelical church growth and the high

Figure 76

GROWTH RATES IN RIO DE JANEIRO,
1958-1963

CITY	EVANGELICAL COMMUNICANTS		NET GROWTH	GROWTH RATE
	1958	1963		-ANNUAL
RIO DE JANEIRO	65,550	86,031	20,481	6.3 %
NITEROI	8,368	10,444	2,076	4.9
DUQUE DE CAXIAS	8,566	13,519	4,953	11.4
SÃO JOÃO DE MERITI	1,444	2,611	1,167	16.1
NILOPOLIS	2,192	2,412	220	2.0
NOVA IGUACU	10,048	18,573	8,525	17.0
VOLTA REDONDA	1,981	3,720	1,739	17.6
BARRA MANSA	1,026	836	(-190)	(-3.7)
BARRA DO PIRAI	951	1,082	131	2.8
PETROPOLIS	6,597	7,137	540	1.6 %

SOURCE: BRAZILIAN CENSUS, PROTESTANT. 1958, 1963.

percentage of rural-to-urban migration. In these same four towns the total net increase of Evangelicals was 16,384 communicants. This is also significant in that perhaps thousands more must be added to the membership of these churches in order to obtain this *net* increase.

The period during which the Evangelical Churches can grow in an immigrant situation is brief. Specific cases of urban church growth in Mexico City, Bogotá, and Belo Horizonte indicate that it takes a rural migrant a decade or two to adjust to the new urban situation. During such a period of adjustment, he is responsive; we must act quickly if we are to act effectively.

Rio de Janeiro to São Paulo — the Paraíba Valley

Once covered with coffee trees, the Paraíba Valley is now dairy land providing dairy products for the industrial cities. This high valley has marked advantages: its proximity to the coastal plain below (a sudden drop of one thousand feet or more) provides potential hydroelectric power. With the establishment of a large steel mill at Volta Redonda in the 1950's the industrial development of the Paraíba Valley began. Electrical power is available for the factories of the Valley, and the prosperity which comes with the Volta Redonda steel complex has made the valley blossom.

The cities of Moji das Cruzes, Caçapava, Taubaté, Guaratinguetá, Cruzeiro Resende, Barra Mansa, Barra do Piraí, and São José dos

Figure 77

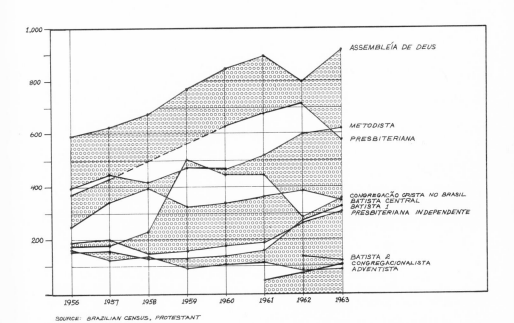

EVANGELICAL GROWTH IN VOLTA REDONDA,
A VALLEY INDUSTRIAL TOWN

SOURCE: BRAZILIAN CENSUS, PROTESTANT

Campos are growing as their industrial activities begin to strike the
candenzas of a developing economy. Eighty-eight towns and cities
in the Valley will eventually become part of an industrial network.
Traveling through the Paraíba Valley we ask, "Where have these
factories come from? We didn't see them the last time we passed
through!" The Paraíba is only one of the many areas touched by a
historical sequence of Brazilian development: the era of exploration,
colonization and settlement; the era of agriculture; the period of
cattle-pasture economy, and the current period of industrialization.

The growth of the Evangelical Churches in Volta Redonda from
1956 to 1963 is illustrated in Figure 77; the high rate of growth
is typical for these new industrial areas of the Valley. According
to Hutchinson, Volta Redonda received 80 per cent of the population
growth between 1950 and 1960 by rural-to-urban migration (1963:
45). The population increase of Volta Redonda has been as follows:

1940	6,000 residents
1950	32,000 residents
1960	83,000 residents
1970 (estimate)	130,000 residents

Such population growth results from the development of the steel
industry that has lifted Volta Redonda to nationwide prominence.

If church-planting is to take place in the industrial cities of the
Paraíba Valley, then the best planning of all Evangelicals in Brazil
must be applied. Only thus can the Church develop so as to take
advantage of the opportunities of these new communities.

São Paulo, the Industrial Capital

Traveling up the Valley of the Paraíba and entering the metropolitan colossus of São Paulo, we follow the route of the coffee boom
which passed this way in the late 1880's and then extended north
and west of the city to the banks of the Paraná River. The location
of São Paulo as the center of influence for the coffee barons became
extremely favorable to its development. The coffee barons invested
profits from the "brown gold" in an emerging industrial complex,
and large immigrations from Europe supplied the manpower for these
industries. São Paulo has now become the industrial capital of Latin
America.

São Paulo presently has the fastest rate of population growth
in Latin America — over 300 per cent since 1940 (Chase Manhattan
Bank 1967:6); its metropolitan population of more than five million
surpasses even that of Greater Rio de Janeiro. In 1964 the Brazilian
Protestant Religious Census registered 1,801 Evangelical churches in
the State of São Paulo; these churches reported 463,320 communicant
members. During 1963 the churches reported 60,000 additions in São
Paulo — an increase of 12 per cent for that year! The director of

the census suggests adding another 30 per cent to the total number of communicants to account for those unreported.

The industrial development of São Paulo, with its accompanying tensions of social transition, presents dramatic opportunities to the Evangelical Churches. If it can be said that the State of São Paulo is the locomotive pulling the rest of the states, then it can also be said that the Evangelical Churches in São Paulo are leading the way for the rest of Brazil. The city of São Paulo has more Pentecostal Christians than any other city in North and South America, and possibly in the whole world. Furthermore, most other Protestant Churches in São Paulo, except those recently arrived, have had a similar growth pattern.

The Apex of the Triangle, Belo Horizonte

The youngest city of the three, Belo Horizonte is only sixty-five years old; yet it has a tremendous beginning. Its population has already passed the million mark and the city is continuing to grow. Studies made by the Census Bureau in the State of Minas Gerais in 1964 (Pinto 1966) indicated that city leaders in Belo Horizonte knew more about the exact location of the *favelas* (slums) and the conditions of the citizens within them than leaders of any other city in Brazil at that time.

The huge deposits of high-grade iron ore which lie to the east of the city will soon make it the steel-producing capital of South America. Belo Horizonte also supplies the major lifelines of transportation to the whole interior, including Brasília and Belém. Plans for Brasília, in fact, were formulated in Belo Horizonte by its former governor, who dreamed that a capital in Brasília would open up the untouched lands of the frontier. The "Road of the Century," the BR-14, is an artery connecting Brasília with the northern city of Belém at the mouth of the Amazon. Already towns are springing up along this and similar roads on the frontier; it will take only a few years to determine the growth of the Evangelical Churches along these roads — a fact which calls into action Evangelical pioneers to plant churches.

Already a network of Evangelical Churches has been established in Belo Horizonte, the largest segment of which is Pentecostal. The traditional Churches are also very strong and most Churches are growing rapidly (see Figure 78). One Evangelical told us about his five children, all of whom had graduated from the university. One is a school administrator, one a lawyer, one a doctor, one an engineer, and the other an Evangelical pastor — a family typical of Evangelical leaders who move in influential circles in Belo Horizonte.

Stretching to the east from Belo Horizonte lies the Valley of the Rio Doce, an area which may soon rival the industrial capacity of the Paraíba Valley to the south. The cities within the valley

area are significant for their growth potential. The Evangelical
Churches have grown here, and probably much greater growth will
accompany the economic expansion of the area.

Coronel Fabriciano is located at a fork of the Rio Doce. City
planners have laid out a large area along the river for a new industrial
park, and hydroelectric facilities are being completed to augment
steel production here. A complex of steel plants is already operating,

Figure 78

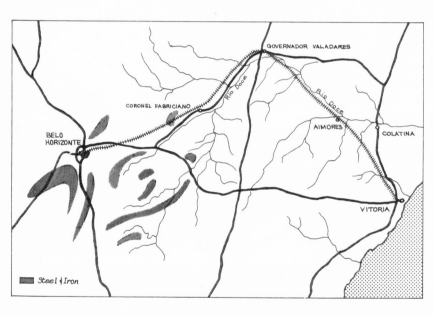

BELO HORIZONTE
AND THE VALE DO RIO DOCE

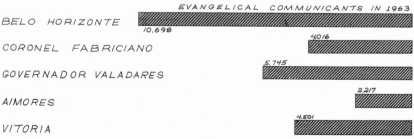

EVANGELICAL COMMUNICANTS IN 1963

BELO HORIZONTE — 10,698

CORONEL FABRICIANO — 4016

GOVERNADOR VALADARES — 5,745

AIMORES — 2,217

VITORIA — 4,501

SOURCE: BRAZILIAN CENSUS, PROTESTANT, 1963

the largest of which is the famous USIMINAS (Minas Steel Plant).
Eight new residential towns are already springing up around the
steel mills. These satellite cities are owned by the steel companies,
which means that property for future church sites must be purchased
within a very short time to insure church establishment. Some of
the Evangelical Churches are already looking ahead and buying now.

Governador Valadares is also located on the Rio Doce, and with
a railroad and federal highway, it is a trade center for the whole
region. This is one town, however, where the Evangelicals lead in
commerce, politics, and social action. The land where the city now
stands was at one time the pasture of a ranch owned by a well-
known Presbyterian. Of course, the Presbyterian Church started
on his ranch; now nine Presbyterian churches are established in
this town of more than 100,000 population. The Baptists, Assemblies
of God, and the Methodists have also grown extensively here. The
prosperity of the area linked to vigorous church-planting could give
the Evangelical Churches a new type of ministry permeating every
aspect of society.

The region surrounding Aimores and Colatina encompasses parts
of Minas Gerais and Espirito Santo, including sections that until
recently were in dispute and noted for their lawlessness. Before
Evangelical Churches were established in Mantenha, thirty were killed
in one five-week period. When Evangelicals began to evangelize the
community, random murder disappeared and it finally became safe
to walk in the streets. Evangelical Churches first grew at an accelerated
rate but have since lost some of the initial thrust partly because
of emigration. Industrial development also planned for the area
would indicate new opportunities for Evangelicals to plant churches
and spark new emphases on social action.

The city of Vitória, capital of the State of Espirito Santo, is
one of the oldest cities in Brazil. Recent development and growth
have resulted from a new port facility for the iron ore hauled by
rail from the fields around Belo Horizonte. Numerous Evangelists
were among those who moved into the area in the early 1900's, and
they met more recent settlers with a spontaneous witness. Always
pressing into the frontier regions, lay leaders organized regular
Evangelical meetings in homes. The first pioneer pastors took the
oversight of the Rio Doce Valley, which has since become the area
of greatest Presbyterian concentration. The few congregations in the
1900's have grown into the Synod of Minas-Espirito Santo with more
than 30,000 communicant members. Similar growth has occurred
among Baptists, and to a lesser degree among the Methodists. Pentecostal churches, starting at a later date, have grown into three or

four large regional ministries in the Valley; their total communicant membership probably numbers more than 50,000.

Site for Mission

Brazil's big triangle includes Evangelical Churches of every type. Some are stagnant, sidetracked, self-contained, withdrawn, and introspective. We wonder what will happen to them in the days of urbanization ahead. They certainly can experience revitalization and renewal, but whether or not they will is another matter. Other churches are dynamic, vibrant, and alive with a variety of ministries that makes bridges into society. These churches, if they remain open to the guidance of the Spirit of God, will find themselves moving into new avenues of service to meet needs at every level of society.

The Brazilian triangle of urbanism, although the most advanced, is typical of several similar dynamic socio-economic situations in other regions of Latin America. The current, widespread migration to the city, with concomitant changes in labor and wage patterns, is more likely to render people responsive to the gospel than to make them resistant. The areas of urban expansion throughout Latin America are uniquely open to the Evangelical message.

PART V
FOCAL POINTS OF GROWTH

The attention and energies of the Evangelical Churches of Latin America are currently concentrated on the frustrations, problems, and opportunities that present growth patterns indicate. Among the crucial issues involved are the problems of the Churches which are not growing, the phenomenon of Pentecostal growth, the areas of cooperation between Churches and missions and between nationals and missionaries, the nature of interchurch cooperation, and the nature and method of ministerial training.

The list of problems facing the Evangelical Churches could be extended indefinitely, but it is significant that the issues which occupy most time and attention on the part of the Churches are those which are most directly involved in growth. Other important areas such as theological and denominational differences are not discussed here. The reaction of the Latin American Churches to the possibilities of today's situation will affect growth potential.

Chapter Eighteen

THE INTEGRATION OF
CHURCH AND MISSION

Some Churches in Latin America grow so slowly that it takes years, even decades, to move from one developmental stage to another. Such slow growth is lamentable and, when it occurs, the problems of missionary domination are concentrated and aggravated. Some of the worst strife and the most devastating divisions within the younger Churches in Latin America have occurred when the disease of slow growth has kept the Church small and weak. Control and authority then tend to remain in the hands of the mission. The alternative is to nationalize the mission, but this is an expedient far different from that of building a strong national Church. Indeed, nationalization of the mission may even militate against the growth of a healthy Church.

Normal growth presents a different developmental pattern. A healthy index of growth, which begins early and sets in motion vigorous step-by-step progression, allows the Church to achieve selfhood and autonomy with much less anguish and with fewer complications. Although in this healthier pattern problems may occur, they are neither so great nor so insoluble as those which accompany slow growth.

When a Church experiences a rapid rate of increase, many things can happen further to aid or to hinder her growth and autonomy. Few studies are available to show the dynamics of rapid growth and its meaning for a young Church. But it is obvious that when growth is accelerated many developmental stages are reached by a rapid succession of ecclesiastical "forced marches." The most important factor in these instances is not the problem of missionary dominance or influence, but provision of necessary resources to guarantee adequate shepherding and continuation of this rapid growth.

It may be necessary to restructure in order to maintain the enthusiasm, energy and activity of the developing churches. Any such restructuring must be carefully worked out as to fit the physical and cultural environment of that church. The new structure that one church adopts may not fit the needs of another. Each church must analyze the needs in view of its own environment and its own growth potential.

Let us take, for example, the Assemblies of God Church in Brazil. The early Pentecostal pioneers, Vingren and Berg, had introduced a form of church polity that represented their Swedish Baptist background. The Swedish missionaries who came to work with them brought the Swedish Pentecostal pattern which had developed out of the same background. But the pattern which evolved in Brazil was something quite different. From the very beginning the Assembly of God in Brazil was indigenous. The first national pastors were ordained within three years of the beginning of the work. As the Church grew, it gradually developed into an autonomous structure with a strong leadership. The pattern which evolved was characteristically Brazilian, quite divorced from the Swedish structures that had been introduced by the missionaries. The Brazilian mother church, which continues to administer daughter congregations, is essentially an episcopal see, with pastor-president fulfilling the functions of a bishop. This system requires a strong, personal leadership — a very common Latin American pattern — which provides continuity and equilibrium in the midst of rapid growth. A more complex structure develops only as the Church becomes larger.

A Church that maintains a healthy pattern of growth by-passes many thorny problems. A number of valuable case studies reveal the dangers inherent in an inadequate and slow pattern of growth. This pattern is often a creeping paralysis caused by a combination of bad habits, a philosophy of missionary logistics based on wishful theological thinking, and a hollow spiritual dynamic which cannot motivate and enliven the Church.

THE INFLUENCE OF PIONEER MISSIONARIES

Are foreign personnel and organizational factors an aid or an obstruction to the growth of Evangelical Churches in Latin America?

The influence of pioneer missionaries is still felt in the Evangelical community. Some Evangelical Churches are commemorating their centennial, and recount the accomplishments, adventures, and ministries of their founders. Other newer Churches still have their founders with them. Churches long founded still may have pioneers in certain aspects of their work, especially if they are opening new fields in frontier areas.

The early pioneers reached their fields with a strong call and a sense of commitment to the task. With optimism they faced the uncertainties of a hostile environment because God had granted man the overpowering assurance of ultimate victory. They fulfilled their roles as courageous communicators of the gospel in cross-cultural situations, and their dedication often produced bountiful results.

Essentially, they were evangelists who did not stay too long in one place. The typical image of the Evangelical pioneer, which we have described in Chapter One, is that of a church-planter: a man of God proclaiming Christ, organizing churches, assisting new believers in the first steps of congregational life, and then moving on to other fields.

These gifted pioneer missionaries exercised an influence still felt today in various forms. In some areas of Latin America they taught whole generations of Latin leaders and led entire Churches through difficult periods and problems to gallant achievements. What exciting stories could be told! What a help their experiences could be to present-day church-planters.

Many pioneers were giants. After they had given long years of service on the field, the strong imprint of their personalities and influence continued in policies, procedures, and strategy followed by succeeding generations. Our research team observed the influence of many creative men of the past, and spoke with many others who are pioneering in the modern setting. The benevolent dominance of such men is at the same time both commendable and dangerous! National leaders, as they emerged, are often confronted with many negative factors in the patterns of influence set up by such pioneers.

Everywhere we went, we saw younger Churches in various stages of development. The missionary-national relationship in mission and Church is a critical one, and church growth is drastically hindered if the dominance of the missionary during the developmental period is not overcome during successive stages of church development.

MISSION-CHURCH RELATIONSHIPS

In order better to understand missionary-national tensions, it may be helpful to discuss the various functional relationships between the mission and the Church.

The functional patterns of mission-church relationships which we observed in Latin America have been described in an article by Harmon Johnson in the *Evangelical Missions Quarterly* (1968: 75-78) as follows.

Functional Patterns

The first step in the establishing of guidelines for measuring mission-church relationships must be the outlining of the functional patterns involved. This preliminary classification *is not a description of formal organization but of functional relationships.*

Generally, the beginning of a mission's work in a field is pioneer. The functional relationship may be outlined as follows (F — funds, P — personnel, I — institutions, C — local churches).

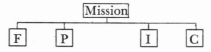

No organizational structure is necessarily implied by the diagram, although such a structure may exist. The idea is that the mission administers, officially or unofficially, funds, personnel, institutions, and local churches.

Eventually, as the national Church evolves, it begins to have a part in administration. This may be an almost immediate step (ideally), or may come at the end of a long struggle between Church and mission in which the mission reluctantly retreats.

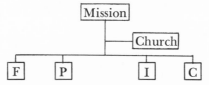

Again, no organizational structure is necessarily implied. This diagram would represent a stage at which the national Church serves as an adjunct of mission. In the various expressions of this phase, the national Church may have authority over some aspects of the work such as responsibility for local churches.

One other common pattern:

The mission still administers the work, but *through* the national Church. This pattern may or may not involve corresponding organizational structure. The mission may administer some aspects of the work, such as institutions, independently of the Church; the Church may have sole authority over other aspects, but the essential relationship is a pattern of mission control.

The development of the Church toward autonomy may take one of two paths. Under the one pattern, the mission becomes an adjunct of the Church.

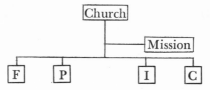

Effective control has passed to the hands of the Church. This is usually formalized by some change in structure. The various aspects of the Church are now administered by the national Church. The role of the mission is to serve the Church in such aspects as are mutually agreed upon by the Church and mission. This pattern may evolve to the eventual assimilation of the mission by the Church or the withdrawal of the mission in recognition of the Church's maturity.

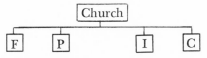

The relationship between Church and mission would then be one of sister Churches sharing cooperative ministries.

The other pattern would be the simultaneous development of Church and mission in the same field.

Each may be responsible for similar, even overlapping or conflicting ministries. This can come as the result of an explosion stemming from unresolved national-missionary tensions. On the other hand, this simultaneous development may result in complementary ministries in which Church and mission cooperate in their joint task.

By whatever patterns these relationships evolve, our goal is to see viable, autonomous Churches which themselves have a sense of mission.

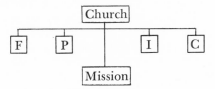

On the basis of this preliminary classification, we may analyze the effectiveness of our own mission-church relationships. The only adequate basis of evaluation is the Church that is produced on the field. If this development can come only at the expense of mission prerogatives, ... God give us grace to do His will. The question of polity or formal organizational structure is not nearly as important as the functional interaction of mission-church relationships (1968: 80-82).

Form of Church Government

In the above model of functional mission-church relationships we have illustrated a few changes that take place when the authority of a mission is transferred to a Church. In our graphs no consideration has been given to the form of church government or to the focus of authority in the various ecclesiastical structures.

The form of ecclesiastical government will not determine the decisions which are made concerning the essential functions of the Church. Such functions include evangelism, formulation of doctrines and creeds, Christian education, finances and stewardship, discipline, leadership and ordination. The ecclesiastical structure becomes only the vehicle which must carry the activity and the dynamic which creates — or hinders — church growth. The Spirit must be given freedom to work within any type of ecclesiastical structure. Many forms of church government have been instituted by the missions. There are times when, for cultural reasons, a Church does not welcome forms imported by the mission, but the modifications which are made are usually minor.

How does a particular form of church government affect church growth? There is no single answer to this question. Some independent Evangelical Churches have a hybrid form of government, including variations of several of the classical forms rearranged to suit their specific organizational needs. These mixtures allow the business of the Church to be done "decently and in order" within the social milieu of Latin America. The team does not feel that any particular form of government need obstruct growth, as long as it allows freedom of worship, freedom for witness, and freedom from dead formalism. However, any form of government will obstruct growth when it becomes a complicated, top-heavy mass of protocol and administrative procedures, stifling initiative and personal enterprise, or dampening the creative ministries which God wants to manifest through His people.

A list of the ten largest Evangelical denominations in Latin America would represent every type of church government, with certain Latin American modifications. Each member of our research team, for instance, belongs to a denomination having a different type of government. We believe that all forms of church government in Latin America have, under some conditions, given rise to growing, dynamic Churches, and, under others, fallen prey to the disease of slow growth or even non-growth.

The Pentecostal Churches in Latin America enjoy the fastest growth, yet have considerable diversity in forms of government. Every type can be found among the Pentecostal Churches. Their congregations seem to thrive on whatever form of government they may have adopted as the vehicle to carry their spiritual dynamic.

The key to their growth is this dynamic, incorporated in an adequate ecclesiastical structure *at the local level*. A Church with a weak spiritual life can do without a heavy organizational structure, though it may actually develop a *more* complex structure to compensate for lack of spiritual vigor.

A Church with a strong spiritual life can support a heavier structure, but the ideal for maximum growth is a strong spiritual life operating through a minimum of structure. Churches strong in spiritual dynamic and light in organizational structure have an initial advantage in being more free to devote themselves to the task of reconciling men to God. A heavy weight of ecclesiastical machinery can slow and hinder church growth. This is a subtle influence, hard to examine objectively. Each Evangelical Church in Latin America must scrutinize the organizational framework it has set up around itself, in order to determine its mobility and flexibility. Does this framework easily carry work loads essential to the growth and development of the Church?

In the final analysis it is not so much the form of church government that determines the effectiveness of the Church. Rather, it is upon the shoulders of those in authority — those who are the decision-makers in the different structures — that the responsibility to inspire, influence and orient the entire Church rests. In the last analysis, decisions on matters of priorities and proper deployment of resources come from those who occupy places of authority. It makes little difference whether these men are missionaries or nationals, whether the office of authority is shared, and whether the form of government under which they work is of one type or another.

THE COMMUNICATIONS TRIANGLE

Even our short consideration of the historical perspectives of Church and mission would be incomplete without mention of a further dimension of foreign influence which affects, both directly and indirectly, the growth of Churches in Latin America. This is the role of the sending Church and the mission board which represents it. The board must interpret what is happening on the field to the churches at home. In order to do this there is usually a triangle relationship of board, mission on the field, and national Church. Each side of this triangle acts as a channel for communication and contact between the different organizations involved.

In the case of larger denominations, each corner on the triangle represents a complex organizational structure. Each organization has its own policy, procedure, historical precedent, and distinct personality. Speed in administration becomes less and less attainable as organizations become larger, the flow of paper heavier, and administrative procedures more sophisticated.

Figure 79

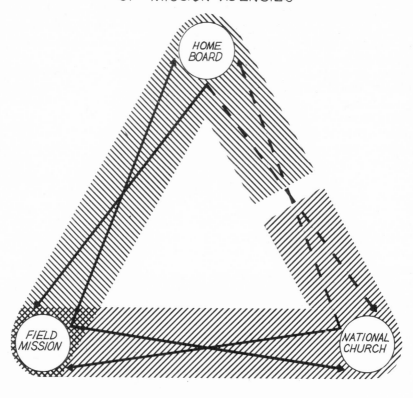

THE COMMUNICATIONS TRIANGLE
OF MISSION AGENCIES

Sides A, B, and C (Figure 79) of this ecclesiastical triangle become channels of different types of communications among the three entities. Most of these communications deal with *personnel, funds, local churches,* and *institutions.* However, the thinking done in relationship to these by the board is not the same kind of thinking that is done on the field. It is even further removed from the thinking of the national Church. As all three organizations think and talk about the need and deployment of the above resources, the whole circuit of communications in this triangle becomes very complex.

Another communication gap exists along the sides of the triangle. Each group has a concept of the role its members must fulfill in their particular situation, and often this self-image and concept of function diametrically opposes the view of function held by those on another side of the triangle. Frequently communication fails between board and Church. We encountered this lamentable situation all over Latin America. Radically different points of view between board and mission and between mission and Church not only cause failure in communication, but also form one of the biggest obstructions to church growth in Latin America. For maximum church growth the vital network of resources and communications between board, mission, and Church must function without short circuits!

Failure in communication has many causes, but a most common one is uncertainty about the paramount aim. If all are agreed on the chief goal, communication becomes much more efficient. A new recognition of and emphasis on the priority and urgency of church growth in all of its ramifications by churches, boards, and missionaries will repair many of the present breaks in the line along the sides of the triangle and dispel doubts and questions lingering in the minds of national leaders. These doubts often have arisen because of past board and mission policies which substituted something else "just as good" for the essential task committed to the Church by the Master — His mandate to preach, disciple, and teach.

THE ROLE OF THE MISSIONARY

When all factors are considered and the innumerable relationships between mission and national Church are seen, the question is immediately asked: What is the role of the missionary in such a confusing, fluid situation? At one time he set the stage for the development of the Evangelical Church in Latin America. His control and influence on the churches stood out clearly in the early stages of their development. Things have changed radically. What now lies ahead for the missionary and his mission? What influence will missionaries have on the development of Evangelical Churches in Latin America in the future?

If all the ripe fields of Latin America had been harvested, and Evangelicals formed the overwhelming majority in these countries, the answer would be plain. It would be easy to see that the day of missionary activity in Latin America was over. But what do we see? The task is only beginning, and innumerable pioneer situations will not be touched by the overburdened, struggling Latin American churches in the next decade or two. The day of the church-planting missionary is really only beginning. Today, however, he must learn from the past. It is essential for him to arrive on the field forearmed with knowledge, know-how, and cultural aptitudes his forebears did not have.

He has several options open to him. (1) He may still work under the jurisdiction of a mission. In time he may be privileged to see his efforts culminate in the establishment of a congregation or a cluster of congregations. If this happens, his role could change in succeeding terms of service. (2) He may work under the jurisdiction of the younger Church which he and his forebears were instrumental in establishing and developing. Later his role could change to that of a missionary specialist who would have a specific

Figure 80

TYPOLOGY OF MISSIONARY ROLES

Mission Relationship to Church	Stage of Church Development				
	PIONEER	EMERGING CHURCH	COOPER-ATION	BEGINNING AUTONOMY	FINAL AUTONOMY
OUTSIDER	APOSTOLATE				
OUTSIDE CONTROL		ADMINI-STRATOR			
INTEGRAL PART OF NATIONAL CHURCH			PARTNER		
INVITED MINISTRY				SERVANT	
AGENT OF INTER-CHURCH MINISTRY					CONSULTANT

job to do, demanding some definite training or talent. This ministry would probably be in response to an expressed need of the young Church. It could mean that his period of service would be shortened to accomplish short-term objectives. Subsequent terms of services might then involve assignments of different natures requiring different spiritual gifts. In the future the gifts which the missionary brings to the Church will determine his role and are bound to increase in importance as an essential part of his call and preparation.

What gifts are needed in the pioneer period of church establishment and development? Does a pioneer missionary in a growing urban situation require those gifts exercised by the pioneer of yesterday as he traveled widely in rural areas ministering to small, isolated groups of interested believers? Figure 80 shows different roles missionaries will be called to fulfill in the days ahead. The talents and gifts needed at each stage of development are manifold, and a positive, creative use of these gifts under the guidance of God's Spirit will assure proper growth and development in the life of the Church.

A proper understanding of the roles that missions and missionaries will play in tomorrow's Church in Latin America may require drastic changes in the recruitment, preparation, and orientation of missionary candidates. Church growth specialists are needed as never before. There is room for the high risk — high gain candidate, meaning one with exceptional qualities, but who also has inherent characteristics that could be disastrous were he placed in certain situations, under certain limitations, and with certain people. The Church in Latin America needs the gifts of such high risk — high gain people who have placed themselves under God's orders for their lives. The risk must be taken in order that the potential gain and blessing may become a reality. Often the influence of such persons is one of the factors that win larger gains at the growing edge of the Church. Missionaries of this type, given experience and orientation, can be a major factor in establishing growing churches, but they will have to minister according to their spiritual gifts and graces and fit in where these will help the Church to fulfill her God-given destiny.

Chapter Nineteen

MISSIONARY-NATIONAL TENSIONS

The crucial level of interaction between Church and mission is the working relationship of missionaries and nationals, since it is at this level that theory becomes practice. The personal relationships involved affect church growth far more directly than the theoretical relationship of the mission to the Church. Even the Church which has no structure of mission distinct from the Church itself is affected if missionaries cooperate in any phase of the ministry of that Church.

The fact that tensions develop is not surprising, since missionaries and nationals are usually working together in situations where the missionaries have seniority but remain outsiders. The contradictions inherent in this relationship can create grave misunderstandings and conflicts which naturally obstruct the growth of the Church.

The tensions which continue to exist and the resulting expressions of resentment are sharpest in the smaller Churches of a few hundred or even a few thousand members assisted by many missionaries. Such tension is much less common in the large, vigorous Churches. When a Church reaches the point where it can muster sufficient resources of personnel and money to make its own way, then the missionary can only continue to work with national leaders at the request, or at the expense, of the Church.

LEADERSHIP TRANSFER

In the Churches which they have helped to found, some missionaries have a unique position as fathers in the faith and as such have assumed dominant roles in establishing church norms. The Churches have, then, developed along the lines set down by the pioneering missionaries. In some cases, even the personal idiosyncracies of the strong missionaries tended to be adopted as the norms of the church, and the national leaders have been obliged to follow the early pattern. Missionaries involved in the life of very young Churches also have greater financial and academic resources than an infant Church can command. In the first phase of work, this disparity

294

does not create any particular problem and the pioneer rightfully enjoys an almost apostolic authority.

In many cases, however, the missionary has conceived of his mission to the young Church as reproducing the North American Church of which he is a part. Forms, structures, and functions have been transported *in toto* to a Latin American setting, not as an expression of theological imperialism but as a sincere effort to produce a Church that is biblical and orthodox. Perhaps this reasoning lies behind the tendency of some missionaries to superimpose their thinking (consciously or otherwise) on matters of policy, administration, and development. This type of action implies, whether or not it is true, that nationals are neither capable of undertaking responsibility nor wise enough in their immaturity to discern what is the correct path for the future of their Church.

These presuppositions, mixed with genuine fatherly love and concern as well as personal anxieties, have resulted in an overprotection of the smaller Churches from the beginning. Their leaders are not permitted to analyze their own situations, much less to make their own decisions, lest they take the wrong direction. Some have suggested that a wave of *nationalism* is sweeping over the Evangelical Church, but this is not so. The case is simply that nationals do not particularly appreciate being relegated to second place concerning the vital matters of mission and Church. The junior role of the national in the early stage of church development creates resentment on his part when the Church evolves to higher levels of maturity. The nationals naturally begin to seek a larger role.

The problem grows more complex as the Church evolves to new stages in its development. New missionaries who are less experienced do not have a "father" relationship to the Church, since many of the national pastors are older than the missionary in terms of Christian service as well as age. Some may even be educated to a higher level than the missionary. Therefore, the new missionary does not necessarily enjoy the confidence and respect of the nationals just because he is a missionary and is expected to demonstrate ability and spiritual authority if he is to be fully accepted.

In some church-mission relationships, the tension has become so great that the only resolution, as far as the national is concerned, has been to reject missionary counsel and direction, thereby demonstrating to his peers and to the missionary his ability to make his own way. If the autonomy of the national Church is real, then it must include the right to make mistakes. Until he has proved himself, the national remains defensive and restive. Once autonomy is established, new relationships can grow between missionary and national. The transition may be abrupt and result in a rift between mission and Church, or the process may be gradual, taking several years to complete.

CULTURAL DIFFERENCES

In most cases, we found the missionary to be more aware of the nature of cultural differences than the national. At least the missionary has lived in both cultures and can see some of the basic dissimilarities. He may not appreciate Latin American values, but he knows that these values exist — an important first step toward understanding. Consequently, training for the mission field hopefully provides the missionary with some anthropological insights.

Communication is hindered by the missionary who concentrates on helping the nationals to understand the North American point of view, rather than finding the best way to express himself in ways that are meaningful to the people among whom he works. He may be in a position of authority and consequently must make value judgments in matters that involve Latin American thought patterns. Furthermore, the national leaders are not always aware of the causes behind tensions. Except for the few who have lived and studied in North America and have seen that culture for themselves, nationals tend to evaluate North Americans in terms of the Latin American culture.

The problem of authority is aggravated in that both missionaries and nationals understand it differently. To North Americans, authority is essentially impersonal and is usually understood in economic terms. To Latin Americans, authority is intensely personal and economic factors are secondary. Nationals and North Americans both interpret their situation in terms of their own background, yet nothing could be more destructive for the Church.

As missionaries gain an understanding of the people among whom they work, they themselves become Latinized. To varying degrees, the veteran missionaries with whom we spoke had adopted (consciously or unconsciously) some features of Latin American life. If the missionaries understand these patterns of behavior, they will find and utilize Latin American ideas for the work of the Church.

LEADERSHIP ROLES

If missionaries conceive of their task in static terms, concerned primarily with conserving the work at its present level, the nationals who rise to leadership will seek similar roles. The result may be a struggle for primacy in a static situation which does not need more leaders. Then either the missionaries are forced out or the nationals lose leadership incentive.

If, however, the missionaries see their task as providing a dynamic force in an expanding Church and they are concerned with outreach and development, they transmit their ideas to the emerging national leadership, and the responsibility and authority of both nationals and missionaries increase as the Church grows.

The nature of missionary responsibility, since missionary training is essentially theological, is a problem in the area of administration. A man may have proved his ability in the ministry before ever coming to the field, but this does not guarantee that he knows anything about the kind of administrative responsibility he will assume as a missionary. He may even be unaccustomed to delegating authority or to the nuances of interpersonal communication which administration involves. A man who has never had any larger responsibility than a small North American pastorate is suddenly expected to administer a large enterprise involving a huge budget and authority over many people. His obvious inexperience is evident to those with whom he works, and his qualifications for authority are not at all clear to them. Success in administration might also become an end in itself, sacrificing the objectives of the mission for a smoothly administered operation.

Ulterior motives may prompt some missionaries to prefer that the nationals be dependent on them for direction, policy, methodology, and government. This seems to be the exception rather than the rule, but the problem is a real one.

Expression of this preference may take the form of controlling the nature and extent of the education of their national leaders. Some missionaries would admit openly that their motive in such control is that once nationals get some education the mission cannot use them, since they refuse to go back to their village churches and also begin to demand bigger salaries. Other missionaries have their own Bible institutes in order to maintain the purity of their doctrine. They assume that the national can receive in the institute all the preparation he needs for their work, and there is no reason for him to go to another school. Others are afraid of losing the nationals to other churches, denominations, or even other countries as so often happens when they are sent to other Bible schools.

In some Bible institutes and seminaries, furthermore, students cannot help but feel that some theological arguments are carefully omitted or are presented in a fashion so as not to confuse the young student. It is the task of the missionary, presumably, to deal with these theological problems at high levels, to digest them, to reach final conclusions, and then merely to pass them down to the national brethren for their mechanical acceptance and communication to the rest of the Church. As a result, "sometimes the Latin American Protestant . . . has the impression that the real conversation is going on over his head. The solutions appear to come ready-made and duly classified, without any possibility of creative work on his part" (Scopes 1962: 173). Perhaps this is because the missionary tends to reproduce the educational philosophy of his alma mater back home.

The natural outcome is that the really promising leaders (both young and old), those who have both the brains and the courage, usually break through such an oppressive barrier and go on to higher education. Yet once a national gains an education against the wishes of his mission, he is seldom welcomed back to that particular fellowship. Many who have innocently tried to resume their previous Christian activities have been mistreated and humiliated economically and socially, sometimes by missionaries whose education has now become inferior to that of the national.

We must give proper credit at this point to many missions for their earnest efforts to raise the level of education for national leaders to that set for missionaries. This is commendable in that their motive in so doing is to educate the nationals specifically in order to turn over to them the direction of the Church. Indeed, some missions anticipate the complete Latinization of their work.

Furthermore, there are indeed financial problems in educating all who want to obtain as much education as they can. Because the financial resources in these cases usually come from the mission, to say that the withholding of funds is wrong is not always fair. It may not be that the missionary wants to keep the nationals dependent, but that he must distribute the limited funds he does have wisely enough that leaders will be trained and remain in the Church, not leave it.

THE NECESSITY OF INTERACTION

For the sake of the Church, there is a need for more interaction in missionary-national relationships, even at the level of theological discussion. The shared goal of winning a continent for God through the gospel demands changes on the part of both. The energy already wasted, the money expended, the fruits thus gathered, and the resulting atmosphere all indicate that we need a cooperative attitude on all levels between the various co-workers in the Church. The interaction of missionaries and nationals can be a positive influence in strengthening the Church. We noted a number of advantages already accruing to the Latin American Churches.

1. Cooperation between missionaries and nationals can save both from cultural blindness, since each group helps the other to see different ways of approaching problems.

2. Cooperation between missionaries and nationals minimizes provincialism. The fanaticism and strangeness which isolation produces are much less a danger in the Churches in which missionaries and nationals share responsibility. Cooperation is a safeguard against irrelevance.

3. Cooperation between missionaries and nationals can help to

relate each Church to sister Churches in the same country and in other countries. As a younger Church reaches higher levels of development and maturity, the relationship to the Church sending missionaries becomes more and more important.

4. Cooperation between missionaries and nationals can have a broadening effect on the Church socially, intellectually, spiritually, and practically. This is due not only to the material resources which each contributes, but also to the far more significant intellectual and spiritual resources of both groups.

We dare not suggest simplistic answers to profound problems; wishful thinking will not heal the breaches nor restore broken fellowships. Nothing less than constant vigilance and faithfulness will safeguard the Churches from misunderstanding. Yet misunderstandings do occur. With this in mind, then, fathers must become brothers. Paternalism with its implied foreign supremacy must disappear. Missionaries must discern carefully how and when to surrender authority. The infant Church must not be left to flounder, nor the mature Church be hindered in development. By the same token, the sons must show themselves to be men. Mature, capable leadership can come to grips with problems that might never be solved on the level of the mission.

Perhaps dynamic church-planting activity would do more to resolve missionary-national tensions than any arbitrary policy, no matter how satisfactory. In the small, struggling Church strong leaders find no adequate means of expression. They spend their energies competing with one another for position. Yet, in the growing Church, energies of both national and missionary leaders are channeled into constructive functions that are not necessarily competitive. Shared activity in an effective church-planting ministry will teach the missionary to appreciate the special gifts of the national, and the national to appreciate the sincerity of the missionary.

Chapter Twenty

ZEAL AND FUTILITY

A hasty glance at the Evangelical Churches of Latin America gives the impression of phenomenal growth for all. Careful inspection, however, reveals that a very large part of the Evangelical communicant membership in Latin America is made up of the members of just a few Churches. The Assemblies of God of Brazil (1,400,000 communicants), the Congregação Cristã of Brazil (500,000), the German Evangelical Lutheran Church of Brazil (324,000), the Presbyterian Church of Brazil (124,000), the Baptist Convention of Brazil (257,000), the Pentecostal Methodist Church in Chile (141,000), and the Pentecostal Evangelical Church, also of Chile (113,000), together constitute over 2,850,000 of the 4,800,000 communicant members of Evangelical Churches in Latin America. Of these seven Churches, the Presbyterians and Baptists of Brazil are the only ones which have sizable missionary participation.

If the membership of the indigenous and non-mission-oriented Churches, such as the Independent Evangelical Churches in Mexico, the Iglésia Apostólica de la Fé en Cristo Jesus in Mexico, the Venezuelan churches under the leadership of Aristides Diaz, O Brasil Para Cristo, and the indigenous Pentecostal Churches in Chile, is added to the 2,850,000, the grand total would be about 3,200,000 — or two-thirds of all Evangelical communicants in Latin America. It is evident that many other Churches and missions are achieving little — and sometimes very little — church growth.

The plight of these smaller missions and Churches is one of the perplexing problems which faces the whole Evangelical Church. If they can diagnose their situation and take whatever corrective measures are necessary, these presently slowly growing missions and Churches can begin to see effective results. If they were working far from other Evangelicals, or among culturally dissimilar peoples, they might attribute their failures to "resistance," to the "need to prepare the people," to the need of more time for "sowing the seed," or to other reasons sometimes given for slow growth. The fact is, however, that most of these missions and Churches are ministering

300

Figure 81

PRINCIPAL CHURCHES IN LATIN AMERICA

KEY:
1. ASSEMBLÉIAS DE DEUS, BRAZIL   1,400,000
2. CONGREGAÇÃO CRISTÃ, BRAZIL   500,000
3. GERMAN LUTHERAN CHURCH, BRAZIL   324,000
4. BAPTIST CONVENTION, BRAZIL   257,000
5. PENTECOSTAL METHODIST,   CHILE   141,000
6. PRESBYTERIAN CHURCH, BRAZIL   124,000
7. EVANGELICAL PENTECOSTAL, CHILE   113,000

TOTAL COMMUNICANTS: 49 Million
TOTAL, 7 CHURCHES: 2.85 Million

REPRESENTS 40,000
COMMUNICANTS

unsuccessfully in the very same communities where some Churches are enjoying rapid growth.

In most cases the lack of response in terms of numbers cannot be attributed to lack of diligence on the part of the missionaries or pastors. As we traveled we found many disappointed missionaries and pastors who are certainly dedicated, sincere workers. Deeply concerned about the apparent futility of their labors, they prayerfully seek some way to be more productive. They are hard at work but have little to show for their labors.

Any marked change in the proportions of total growth achieved by these Evangelical Churches will depend on their willingness to change to modes of mission which do bring men to Christ and which form them into churches. Unless they develop an inner dynamic and an outer contact with the winnable, there is little prospect that their ingrown, closed congregations and frustrated missions will add many to the Lord.

It is paradoxical that those Churches and missions which are trying to reach out and win men but are not achieving results commensurate with the effort expended, represent the greatest potential for increased church growth. Their success would make the present uneven, spotty growth of the Latin American Evangelical Church much more consistent and general.

These Churches and missions represent the bulk of the Evangelical missionary effort in Latin America in terms of money and personnel. Their effectiveness — or lack of it — directly concerns the whole Evangelical Church. The expenditure and utilization of foreign resources can and should be expected to produce more church growth.

THE RIGHT LOCATION

What hinders the growth of these Churches and missions? In part, the answer lies in the location of their work. The sacrificial spirit, which has characterized the missionary movement since its inception, has encouraged missions to seek out the "hard places" — usually meaning the most resistant populations. Resistant segments of society in Latin America are easy to find, but there are also many responsive peoples to whom little or no gospel witness is available. Perhaps a holding action would be adequate in nonresponsive populations until the time when they, in turn, become open to the gospel and someone finds the key to their hearts. Where traditional methods are not bringing men to faith and obedience, it is futile to think that more of the same will somehow change things.

Binding Comity Arrangements

Some missions have been confined to nonresponsive areas by old comity agreements which have, in other cases, also kept out more

vigorous missions that might have grown. What was designed originally as an aid to effective occupation has become, in some places, a
hindrance to church growth.

Even more frustrating under comity arrangements is the effect
of population mobility on church growth. Often, those who have
risen to leadership in the rural congregations are best able to take
advantage of greater economic opportunities elsewhere and thus
leave their homes. While the rural church's loss should be the urban
church's gain, it seldom works out that way in practice. Differences
of church customs, of polity, and even of doctrine constitute such a
problem for the one who moves that he is often unable to find his
church (or at any rate, a suitable church) in his new surroundings.
He may not leave the Church, but often he ceases attending or fails
to reassume the leadership responsibility he was exercising in his
home congregation. We saw an example of this in eastern Venezuela.
The leadership drain to the western part of the country has left
many churches decimated. The loss of the leaders themselves and of
their stabilizing influence which would have given continuity to their
programs was keenly felt by the local churches.

Concentration on Small Tribes

Some missions have deprived themselves of the opportunity of
establishing self-sustaining churches by concentrating on small tribes.
It is difficult for us to defend the size and scope of the missions'
investment of men and money among dozens of tiny tribes far from
national life. We are not speaking of large Indian populations which
constitute viable societies and whose tribal languages will continue to
be their principal means of communication for generations to come.
We refer, rather, to those small and vanishing tribes hidden away
in remote jungles.

In the whole Amazon Basin, for example, there are only 136,000
uncivilized tribespeople, most of whom live in small tribes and
speak mutually unintelligible languages. Most assuredly, these tribes
need to hear the gospel, but their evangelization must not be understood as the sum of mission. More than 250 missionaries work among
these tribes, more than are working in the States of Santa Catarina
and Rio Grande do Sul, which have a combined population of over
nine million. A comparable investment in any of the large cities of
Latin America devoted to the effective communication of the gospel
could produce more church growth in six months than would result
from the evangelization of every member of dozens of jungle tribes.

Outside the Money Economy

Working among small segments of society located outside the
money economy has also made it more difficult to produce self-sustaining churches. Many missions establish churches patterned along

Figure 82

GROWTH OF TWO COLOMBIAN CHURCHES

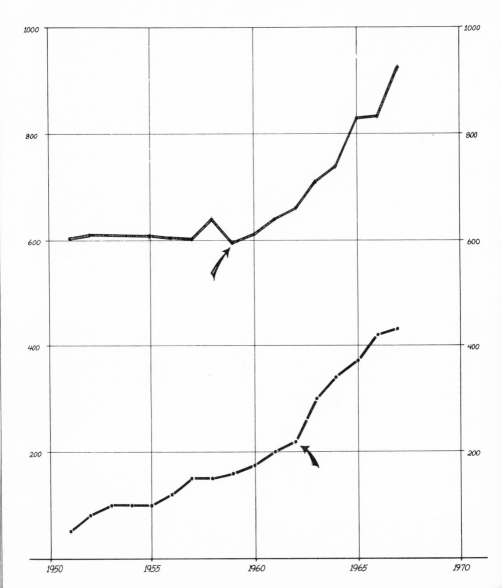

NOTE: ARROW DENOTES CHANGE IN MISSION POLICY IN THAT YEAR

European or North American lines. This creates ecclesiastical structures which are expensive to maintain. Unless urban-based churches
with a wage earner economy can subsidize them, these rural churches
organized and administered after a foreign pattern are doomed to
depend on perpetual mission subsidies with the attendant evils of
domination and paternalism.

Merle Davis in *How the Church Grows in Brazil* (1943:84) describes the difficulty such a church has in supporting a trained middle
class minister. It is not just a matter of expecting the man to deny
himself and live on the level of the people. Built-in foreign forms
and structures require capital expenditure for buildings and equipment, literature, schooling, attendance at denominational conventions
and assemblies, and for all the other "props" of a professional
ministry.

We are not suggesting that the countryside be abandoned, but
that mission in the rural areas be *linked* to mission in the *cities*. If,
instead of *confining* their ministry to rural areas, these missions would
establish a broader base, their situation would change. The Mennonite Brethren and the Cumberland Presbyterians in Colombia have
proven the value of such a change of emphasis. Both can date their
increased growth and a new pattern of support and stewardship
from the decision to emphasize urban church-planting. Note the
striking increase of membership (Figure 82) after they started
church-planting evangelism in the city.

Some of the newer missions consider the localities having the
fewest Evangelicals as the best place to start churches. The fallacy in
relying on this supposition as the sole criterion is that the area may
have the smallest percentage of Evangelicals because it is the poorest
site for mission — it is the most resistant to the gospel. If missions
would choose areas where Evangelicals have already won large numbers they might do better. Were they to seek areas in which 10 per
cent of the population were Evangelical, they would still encounter a
large receptive and unsaved population. Most cities can absorb much
more evangelistic effort before growth rates will level. Huge populations must still have the gospel proclaimed to them.

The Right Place at the Wrong Time

In 1932, Erasmo Braga and Kenneth Grubb envisioned the great
potential of the interior of Brazil for the Evangelical Church. They
called for great missionary efforts (1932:105) in the frontier areas.
However, they spoke thirty years too soon; it is only now that the
vast hinterland is being developed on a large scale. Missions which
rushed in thirty years ago have spent hundreds of man-years and
millions of dollars with only small churches to show for it. Even
worse, these small congregations are made up of "old-timers" who

resent newcomers. This seals them off from effective evangelism among the new settlers who come from other parts of Brazil.

To be "too late" has proven just as bad. The Methodist revival in the 1890's around Temuco, Chile, was one of the early examples of evangelistic success in Latin America (Kessler 1967:102). The Methodist success acted as a magnet to attract other Evangelical missions. Long after the frontier conditions (which had created the right environment for the Methodist Church to grow) had passed, other missions were still flocking to begin church work in Temuco. Their efforts made Temuco the Evangelical capital of Chile, but none of them enjoyed the same measure of success as the Methodists.

A Changing Environment

A locality becomes or ceases to be "the right place for mission" according to other factors, too. The Baptist seminary in Torreón, Mexico, is a case in point. The area around Torreón has provided an ideal laboratory for training pastors in effective evangelism. The efforts of the students have also produced a number of successful churches. Environmental factors, however, are about to change all this. Torreón depends on irrigation and the whole area is currently declining as the water table falls. When irrigation is prohibitively expensive or no longer possible, the region will revert to its previous arid state, and most people will move elsewhere.

If the seminary stays where it is, it will find itself in a stagnant, backward region, far from the dynamism of the national life of Mexico. If the seminary is to continue to produce pastors who are productive, experienced church-planters, it must find a new "laboratory" in some developing area of Mexico. It is always unwise for missions to allow their investment in buildings to tie them to low-potential areas.

THE RIGHT MESSAGE

The disappointment and frustration of the Churches and missions who are not seeing appreciable church growth may also be attributable to a wrong emphasis in presenting the message. The gospel itself cannot change: "The heart of the gospel is in eternal and unchanging categories.... Either we have the gospel whole and given or we have no gospel at all" (Webster 1965:5). At the same time, the emphasis of the message (or the vehicle of the gospel) will vary with time, person, and circumstance.

North American Accretions to the Gospel

Many of the missionaries in Latin America, instead of preaching the gospel, are proclaiming how they heard and responded to the gospel. They come from North American backgrounds and have had similar religious experiences. The pattern was usually one of dramatic change. Some had been rebellious children of strongly religious parents and had returned to their parents' Church following some personal crisis. Others were from a secular materialistic background, and had been introduced to Evangelical Christianity in a time of similar crisis.

Crisis experiences color their presentation of the gospel more than they realize. Unfortunately for these missionaries, Latin Americans experience personal crises arising from their own environment and social values, which are quite different from the typical psychological crises North Americans experience. When a missionary ties the gospel to an emotional crisis which is foreign to the Latin American mentality, he seriously hinders the communication of the gospel. Naturally, the effective evangelists in Latin America have utilized the opportunities presented in times of human turmoil, but they instinctively use the natural crises of Latin American life and mentality. They do not attempt to separate man from his society, but deal with him in his cultural context.

The North American accretions to the gospel, which often render it ineffective in North America, cannot but hinder the task of church-planting in Latin America. The forms, structures, concepts, and procedures which hamper the North American Church at home are no more helpful on the mission field.

Furthermore, if there ever was a time when the negative message of legalistic anti-Catholicism served the needs of Latin America, that time is long *past*. Everyone in Latin America can learn from the example given by the Churches who never speak publicly in a vindictive and condemnatory way against any religion and always emphasize the positive elements of the gospel.

Indigeneity of Church Practices and Speech

The autochthonous worship norms, church architecture, and church music that Latin American Churches are developing are obvious indications of the vitality and maturity of the indigenous Evangelicals. The direct relationship between the growth rate of the Church and the indigeneity of church practices is significant.

Missions have often imposed their own figures of speech on the field. We remember the perplexed expression with which a Brazilian congregation sang a missionary's translation of "Heavenly Sunshine." In their tropical environment they could not imagine what was heavenly about sunshine. To them, the "Shadow of a Rock in a Weary Land" would have been much more appropriate.

Becoming fluent in Spanish and Portuguese is essential. The gospel is not commended by marring these beautiful tongues. God's messenger must not only say the right words and deliver the biblical message, but he must speak it in the language that the people know.

THE RIGHT SUPPOSITIONS

The third major hindrance for the Churches and missions which are not growing is the lack of right suppositions. Missionaries are usually deployed on the basis of unquestioned, inherited assumptions as to priorities. They carry on their work without questioning the relevance of these suppositions to their chief goal, the real growth of the Church. Methodology that is correct in one population would be incorrect in another; that which may have been correct in 1940 is often inadequate in later decades.

The Place of Institutions

Many missions and missionaries work under the assumption that the best way to commend the gospel to unbelievers is through philanthropic institutions: schools, hospitals, and orphanages. This may have been true in 1900, but the evidence against it today is so overwhelming that no mission or Church should assume it true without testing it rigorously under current conditions.

Hundreds of missionaries are assigned to institutional work which, *in populations where churches can be planted,* effectively removes them from responsibility for church-planting. This continues for generation after generation of missionaries, simply because the institutional program is so great that the churches cannot maintain it. Therefore, a large part of the missionary force must be located at the institutions.

We fear that too often institutions represent nothing more than an opportunity to exercise the particular skills of the missionaries. Kessler recounts how a school was started in Peru by a missionary because he happened to have a daughter who was a trained teacher (1967:38). While this may be an extreme example, many times missionaries do start institutional "works" which they feel they can carry on well.

Other mission institutions have been begun by those whose efforts at church-planting had proved futile. Unable to progress in church-planting, they turned to less frustrating tasks. These missionaries feel more at ease with a regular program in which they have defined duties with people seeking their help for specific ailments, than with the uncertainties of evangelism where they constantly have to seek people to whom to impart their message.

In sharp contrast to institutions run with mission money from abroad are those maintained by the indigenous Churches. The day schools and orphanages of the Brazilian Assemblies of God are specifically church related. They are born out of the social concern of the churches and serve real local needs. They may not be evangelistic in nature, but they are used evangelistically and are kept subservient to the Church's mission to evangelize its community. How unfortunate it is that the mission-related Churches have often been deprived of the privilege of developing their own institutions in response to the social needs of their environment. Taught to rely on outside help, they never really develop an adequate social conscience.

Evangelical institutions under mission management such as the Baptist hospital in Guadalajara, Mexico, which maintains a strong evangelistic witness and has served a church-planting function, prove that mission institutions *need not hinder* church growth. We gladly pay tribute to mission institutions of this sort. They have helped and are helping in the evangelization of the land. Nevertheless, we urge that this supposition be regularly tested.

The Nature of Institutions

In regard to the schools, many presuppose that once a school is established, it will be flamingly Evangelical and will serve the Evangelical community, thus contributing, unquestionably, to the welfare of the Church. Where the mission is large and wealthy and the Church remains small and dependent, it usually happens that all Evangelical children attend the mission school. Latin America, however, is full of mission schools which are not flamingly Evangelical and which do not greatly serve the Evangelical community. Frequently many teachers are non-Evangelicals, and frequently the fees charged by the school are so high that only well-to-do people can enroll their children.

Consequently, mission schools which directly affect the advance of the gospel or nurture the new members to make their congregations self-propagating are justified. Otherwise, assignment of missionary personnel to these schools is poor methodology.

North American Ecclesiastical Structures

North American mission and church structures have tended to discourage the new patterns and forms which the changing scene in Latin America require, on the assumption that the only ones biblically defensible are the North American ecclesiastical structures. The separation of North American culture from essential gospel is never easy, but it must be done if the potential of the three or four thousand (or more) missionaries who are seeing little church growth is to be realized. Yet, indigenous Churches have taken every type of polity, ecclesiastical structure, church architecture, method of evangelism, leadership training, and church administration and, without departing from the authority of the Bible, have "Latinized" them to meet their needs. One of the marks of these greatly growing Churches is that as circumstances change, they are flexible and free to change with them.

On the other hand, the missions and mission-related Churches have not found change easy. Their capital investments in property and equipment act as a great weight around their necks. The care and upkeep of property becomes an end in itself rather than a means by which the mission fulfills its calling. Missionaries see themselves ideally as servants rather than masters; however, their desire to have their fledgling churches follow the right course often makes it difficult for them to relinquish control and accept a secondary place.

QUESTIONS THAT MUST BE ASKED

The first step toward reversing current growth trends for the non-growing Churches and missions is self-examination. Evangelical leaders need to ask themselves several questions, some of which may be very painful.

Is their location just a matter of historical accident? Did they just "happen" to choose this place? Is their location based on obsolete comity agreements which should be changed? Did they choose a site for mission because it was known as a hard field? Are they carrying on the personal project of a former missionary even though the original need for the project has been met?

Should they continue to work where they are? Is it possible to sacrifice the capital investment that such a change might involve? Are their reasons for continuing emotional rather than objective? Are the prospects for church growth better somewhere else? Would their special ministries be more effective in another situation? Would some other Church or mission be more successful in their place?

If they are to move, where will they go? Where is there *proved* openness to the gospel? Do the Evangelical Churches that are already in such a new place need assistance? Would they welcome help? Should the present area be abandoned or is a holding action in order? Should they consolidate efforts by leaving unproductive areas and concentrating on those places which show more promise?

How culturally relevant is the emphasis of their message? How positive is the message? How Latin American are the worship norms and structures? How successful is present methodology? Can they take advantage of the opportunities that present themselves?

Obviously these questions are much easier asked than answered. At the same time, the Church or mission which asks itself such questions and endeavors to answer them objectively is engaged in a constructive task which could change its growth pattern. We believe that sincere efforts of evaluation will reveal many areas in which change can and will produce greater growth.

NEW POLICIES

Nothing less than new policies will result from the painful, prayerful self-examination for which we have called. Not all of these new policies will produce church growth, as some efforts will prove abortive. Furthermore, we are not speaking of the changes which all missions and Churches institute from time to time to meet new situations, without deliberately planning for greater church growth. Some of these may even favorably affect church growth patterns; however, it would be foolish to rely on this kind of change to produce growth.

In some unusual cases nothing less than the ministry of a "maverick" may be needed to initiate church growth. Where traditional methods have failed, the unorthodox and even eccentric ideas of one who cannot or will not "go by the book" may provide the means for successful evangelization. The history of the Evangelical Church in Latin America is replete with examples of these iconoclasts who have shocked and dismayed their more traditional colleagues, but who also have been instrumental in some of the most dramatic breakthroughs in areas thought to be resistant.

Such action ought not to surprise us. New situations call for new solutions. The problem is to recognize the contribution that the unconventional pioneer can make and encourage him to find a place in which his individuality can express itself positively in new church-plantings rather than negatively in conflict with his colleagues.

Above all else, single solutions for all of Latin America must be rejected. The basic unity of Latin America, which permits us to speak of it as an entity, must not blind us to the real differences of every piece of its vast mosaic and the varied approaches required. These differences can create problems even within a country. The Methodist pastor from São Paulo who tries to minister in the northwest of Brazil is puzzled by the customs and habits of the people, as is the Presbyterian pastor from Mexico City who goes to Chiapas.

International problems present more serious problems, as illustrated by the translators of the Spanish Bible who must find terms that mean essentially the same thing all over Spanish America. Visual aids for Christian education present a similar problem, as does the choice of music from country to country.

PROGNOSIS

Zealous Churches and missions, although plagued by futility, have within their power under God to change their own growth patterns. This will not happen unless ruthless action is taken and some radical changes are made in philosophy and methodology of mission, but it *can be done*. Between the recklessness of change for change's sake and the obstinate conservatism that rejects anything new, lies a course of action that will change the defeats of the past into future victories. Such action will demand the utilization of every spiritual, anthropological, and psychological insight, as well as reliance on spiritual and material resources.

These Churches and missions dare not rationalize any lack of success and they must not be defeated by defeat. Out of painful lessons can come glorious successes. As God gives the increase in Latin America, everyone who is preaching the gospel can enjoy the kind of church growth that God desires.

Chapter Twenty-one

PENTECOSTAL GROWTH

The growth of the Pentecostal Churches of Latin America is one of the significant aspects of the general Evangelical advance. As was shown in Chapter Two, Pentecostal members now comprise 63.3 per cent of the total Evangelical membership. To understand the growth of the Evangelical Churches in Latin America it is now necessary to understand the reasons for Pentecostal growth. Since their beginning in the first decade of the twentieth century, the Pentecostal Churches of Latin America have grown more rapidly than sister Churches in other parts of the world.

Although the movement is over sixty years old in Latin America, it is only in the last few decades that the multitudes have been won. It took the Iglésia Metodista Pentecostal twenty years to win the first 10,000 members. Similarly, after thirty years of growth the Assemblies of God of Brazil had only 25,000 members.

SOME IMPORTANT DISTINCTIONS

It is not possible to speak of *the* Pentecostal Church of Latin America. There are many kinds of Pentecostal Churches, of which some are growing and some are not. There is no organic union between the various Churches except for those who belong to North American Pentecostal denominations.

The Pentecostal Churches present a wide variety of church polity, theological base and orientation. The Pentecostal movement did not develop out of one particular background. It was rather a revivalist movement which drew men from every type of Church. These differences of background have tended to become institutionalized. Though Pentecostals tend to be congregational, Arminian, and baptistic, there are so many exceptions that it is impossible to make blanket statements about their theological position.

The Chilean Pentecostals, for example, isolated themselves from the rest of the Pentecostal movement over the question of the mode of baptism. The Chilean Pentecostal Churches began as a revival movement within the Methodist Church. Their leader for the first twenty years was Willis Hoover, a Methodist missionary who left

Figure 83

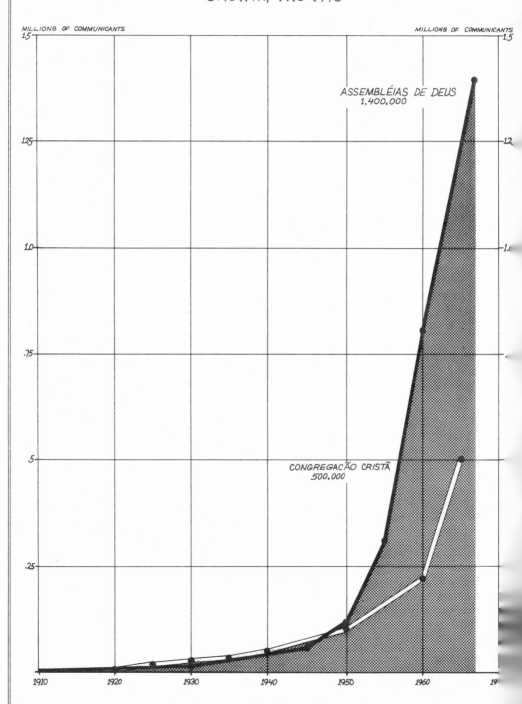

THE ASSEMBLÉIAS DE DEUS AND CONGREGACÃO CRISTÃ:
GROWTH, 1910–1970

ASSEMBLÉIAS DE DEUS
1,400,000

CONGREGACÃO CRISTÃ
500,000

with them. In his early contacts with Pentecostal leaders elsewhere the matter of water baptism became an issue. The Church in Chile took the name Iglésia Metodista Pentecostal (The Pentecostal Methodist Church). Hoover maintained that they were true Methodists and would not abandon the Methodist practice of infant baptism. The ensuing disagreement effectively sealed off the Chilean Church from the mainstream of Pentecostalism. While other Pentecostal Churches elsewhere began to define the theological base for their position the Chilean Pentecostals carefully avoided specific formulations of doctrine.

PENTECOSTAL WORSHIP

One characteristic which all Pentecostals share is their belief in an existential Pentecost. They believe that the ecstatic phenomenon of the day of Pentecost can be the experience of every Christian today. They speak of this as the "baptism with the Spirit." Most Pentecostal Churches in Latin America (with the notable exception of the Chilean Pentecostals, who make up almost 12 per cent of the Pentecostals in Latin America) teach that speaking in tongues is *the* initial evidence of the experience of the baptism with the Spirit.

It is in their pattern of worship that Pentecostals differ most from other Evangelicals. The worship is uninhibited and spontaneous. Among more extreme groups, the spontaneity degenerates into disorder and excess, and their fanaticism has sullied the reputation of all Pentecostals. The Pentecostal belief that God speaks today creates in their worship an attitude of expectancy. Life and enthusiasm characterize even the more formal Pentecostal Churches.

In a literal interpretation of First Corinthians they allow freedom of expression so that anyone who has a song to sing, a message in tongues or an interpretation, or a testimony to give, has opportunity to edify the church. In contrast to the North American Pentecostal pattern in which such manifestations are formalized under the strict control of the pastor in charge, the Latin American Pentecostal Churches treat such manifestations for the most part as an informal means of praise to God.

While some Pentecostals consider spiritual manifestations as man's reaction to the moving of the Holy Spirit upon him, and others consider the manifestation as a direct operation of the Spirit, all Pentecostal Churches exhibit similar manifestations.

Latin Americans feel at home in the exuberance of Pentecostal worship. In part, this may be a reaction against the extreme formalism of their former religion. Everyone is able to participate in the happy singing, the united prayer and shouts of praise. The Pentecostals have not been given a foreign form of worship which they must try to fill with meaning. They have, rather, an experience which may take whatever form the content requires.

Thus, the Pentecostal worship pattern is in harmony with the cultural dynamics of the people. That this is not just an expression of Latin temperament but is a profound expression of all of life, is shown by the vigorous growth of the Pentecostals among the descendants of Northern Europeans in southern Brazil.

INCORPORATION

The Pentecostal Churches incorporate converts into a community of faith. The spontaneous expression of spiritual life is shared with other believers. "God's presence and gifts are looked for — not exclusively but basically and typically — in the fellowship of the believers, not in individualistic seclusion" (Roberts 1963: 32).

Each Pentecostal Church has its own way of making converts a part of the fellowship of the church. Some few baptize immediately upon confession of faith. Others enroll the converts at once in learners' classes.

The two predominant patterns are those of the Assemblies of God in Brazil and the Chilean national Pentecostals. The differences in the two reflect the basic theological differences that exist.

The unconverted are not allowed in the prayer meetings and Bible studies of the Assemblies of Brazil. The idea is that Christian nurture ought to be restricted to believers. Before a man can understand spiritual truth he must experience regeneration. The unregenerate must hear the gospel and be given the opportunity to accept or reject.

The biblical metaphors of catching fish and feeding sheep are used frequently. They say, "Do not feed the fish. If we teach men all about the life of faith and grant everyone the privileges which should be reserved for those who are believers, they will never accept the gospel. We will feed the flock of God only."

The new convert who is allowed to participate in the prayer meetings and Bible studies is made to feel that now he belongs. It may be several months before he can be baptized, but he already has a visible sign of belonging. In the anonymity of collective prayer and praise the convert learns to pray. The warm, friendly fellowship of the church encourages him to stand firm in his new faith.

The Chilean pattern utilizes other means to demonstrate incorporation. New converts are encouraged to give immediate expression to their faith by preaching on the street corner. This method gives the new believer an immediate sense of community. He is not kept in an interminable limbo of probation. At once he is a brother. His cooperation is appreciated and utilized. He feels he belongs. By verbalizing his faith he makes his commitment more secure. By public testimony he identifies himself as an Evangelical. This public identification makes it more difficult for him to recant or return to the world.

In the Pentecostal fellowship, people of many different temperaments gain confidence, courage for witness, a sense of spiritual obligation and personal responsibility. This creates an exciting sense of urgency and an immediacy of mission.

The Pentecostals are known for their energetic, forceful, and persistent efforts in proclaiming the gospel. One Evangelical missionary, speaking of the Chilean Pentecostals, said, "They act as if their salvation depends on their preaching the gospel on street corners." The missionary spoke perhaps more truly than he knew. Their life has depended on preaching the gospel. If the Chilean Pentecostals had not carried the gospel to the streets they would have been no more effective than other Evangelicals in winning the Chileans. Without mission subsidies to support them, they probably would have long since disappeared if it had not been for the economic support given by converts of their street preaching. In spite of serious internal strain, the evangelistic emphasis of the Chilean Pentecostal Churches has been responsible for their sustained growth and continued dynamic health.

The Pentecostal conceives of regular church services as the time when Christians gather for worship, mutual encouragement, and an opportunity to meet God. Though they do preach the gospel in the church services, the Chilean Pentecostals make little effort inside the church to convert unbelievers. The place where they persuade men is out where men are — on the street corners, in the jails, in the parks and plazas. The other Evangelicals in Chile have reacted strongly against their techniques, and in order not to be identified with the Pentecostals whom they feel to be socially and spiritually inferior, they have neglected open-air evangelism. Non-Pentecostal Evangelicals do their evangelistic preaching inside the church buildings where the unsaved are seldom seen.

Pentecostal evangelistic effort is not the professional activity of the ministers but rather the responsibility and privilege of every believer. The newest convert is encouraged to declare his faith publicly in a street corner testimony. The present leading ministers describe how they began their life of Christian witness in this manner.

When asked why their Churches continued to grow, they said, "We grow because we preach in the open air. We do not wait until men are interested in going to church. We go to them to interest them. Anyone who would try this same method would also grow. Men are interested in what we say on the street corner because we are not talking about cold theories but about what we ourselves have experienced. We tell them of how God has helped us and healed us. We talk of a victorious life and describe the joy we feel. We sing happy music that confirms our words. When we show men how God has promised to do the same for anyone who will ask him, many of them meet God. By the next service they are with us to give their testimonies."

The most obvious benefit of this method is that an inexhaustible supply of working personnel is provided. The only requirements for service are knowing the Lord, a public declaration of faith in Him, and courage to speak up. With every convert the working force grows.

One difficulty is that it is impossible to control what will be said and done in these open-air services. Strangely enough, due no doubt to the work of the Holy Spirit, this has not created as grave problems as could be feared. We heard many examples of amusing things said by inexperienced and ignorant new Christians, but these new believers nevertheless have glorified Christ and communicated the gospel.

New converts have tended to pattern their testimonies after those of the older believers, but underneath all witnessing is a genuine personal experience. God has touched them and they tell of His power according to their own understanding and ability.

The Chilean Pentecostals owe much to their Methodist antecedents. Their "Articles of Faith" are taken from the Articles of the Methodist Church. They describe their street preaching as being a continuation of the Wesleyan method of evangelism. They consider themselves to be true Methodists, because they represent the moralizing influence of early Methodism and as such are a movement of the people. Vergara (1962: 127) has described Chilean Pentecostalism as Methodism carried to its ultimate conclusion.

The Chileans who have migrated to Argentina have taken the Pentecostal message with them. The Chilean Pentecostal Churches have also sent missionaries who are expected to support themselves. All that the Church gives them is a one-way ticket! Their major responsibility is to care for the Chilean Christians in Argentina. They have not confined their activities to this, however. These missionaries explained to us that they have been able to win other migrant Chileans as well as Bolivian and Paraguayan settlers in Argentina. They have also succeeded in winning some of the very lowest segment of Argentine society, a group hitherto completely neglected by Evangelicals.

PATTERN OF PENTECOSTAL GROWTH

Country	Percentage of Evangelicals Who Are Pentecostal	Communicant Membership of Pentecostal Churches	Index of Relative Size
Chile	82.8	365,781	478
El Salvador	69.1	24,725	112
Brazil	66.3	2,234,788	385
Mexico	62.5	268,712	94
Venezuela	42.6	19,995	50

Country	Percentage of Evangelicals Who Are Pentecostal	Communicant Membership of Pentecostal Churches	Index of Relative Size
Panama	40.7	15,280	296
Argentina	39.3	96,806	108
Guatemala	32.8	25,347	168
Colombia	31.4	23,195	39
Ecuador	28.0	3,511	23
Costa Rica	24.2	2,952	91
Uruguay	23.5	5,115	81
Honduras	23.1	4,335	75
Paraguay	14.1	1,474	49
Nicaragua	13.4	2,649	106
Peru	10.4	6,464	50
Bolivia	7.5	3,406	105

It is noteworthy that in the countries where the Evangelical Churches have grown most, the Pentecostals have had their greatest growth. Approximately 93 per cent of the Pentecostals are found in the four countries having the highest percentage of Evangelicals. The Pentecostals in these four countries alone make up 60 per cent of the total Evangelical communicant membership for all of Latin America.

MINISTERIAL TRAINING

Few similarities exist between the national Pentecostal Churches of Chile and the Assemblies of God of Brazil except that both are Pentecostal. The greatest similarity between these two rapidly growing movements has been their theology of the ministry. Mission-related Pentecostals have tended to adopt patterns modeled after the traditional Churches, but indigenous Churches such as the Brazilian Assemblies and the Chilean Pentecostals have been free to develop their own patterns. It is significant that these two movements, with no interaction and no known cross-fertilization of ideas, and rising from quite dissimilar backgrounds, have developed almost identical patterns of selecting and training ministers.

They are not the only Churches to use this approach, but non-Pentecostal Churches in general could easily learn from them. Their main premise is that qualifications for the ministry are spiritual rather than academic (McGavran 1963: 119). Certainly no Evangelical can argue with that! The man who shows the capacity for spiritual leadership is chosen for the ministry. Therefore, any member of a church is a potential minister.

The man who in this way is recognized by the Church as a minister, and is assigned to a field, now has a direct financial stake in his own work. His income varies directly with the result of his efforts. "A community will have no pastor unless it is able to support him, and the candidates for the ministry have to father a large flock in order to carry out their vocation" (Lalive d'Epinay 1967: 189).

The obvious difficulty under this system is that it does not provide for a sophisticated degree of theological knowledge but is concerned with certain leadership gifts involved in what is an empirical ability to evangelize. The two Pentecostal Churches deal with this problem differently. The Chileans emphasize the charismatic nature of spiritual leadership and feel that the growth of the church is in itself a demonstration of divine blessing. Success is not measured so much in theological correctness as in effective communication of the gospel. The Brazilian Assemblies have attempted to maintain doctrinal correctness and to preserve the theological dimension by bringing their ministers together for biblical instruction at regular intervals.

Kessler (1967: 341-342) has outlined three conditions which are necessary to make the apprenticeship system practicable. (1) Volunteers must have something to communicate beyond intellectual knowledge. (2) The apprenticeship system is possible only where each church is subdivided into cells so the inexperienced can gain experience as part of a greater whole. (3) The inexperienced worker must be given authority commensurate with his responsibility.

The process of becoming a pastor is not a rapid one. To pass through each stage of development usually takes many years. By the time a man is recognized as full pastor he is a mature, experienced leader. Novices are given the type of opportunity that gives them a sense of belonging (e.g., participation in public meetings, recognition as an Evangelical), but are never given authority over the work.

The pastors who emerge from the apprenticeship system are *men of the people*. They are not separated from those to whom they minister by any social distance nor by cultural barriers. Moreover, since they have never lived in isolation from the people, they are less apt to try the impossible, continue with that which is unimportant, or to stress the irrelevant. Their system "produces pastors who are the genuine expression of the congregation, since they do not differ from them either socially or culturally" (Lalive d'Epinay 1967: 190).

Arno Enns has pointed out that the Pentecostal system has redefined the role of the generations (1967: 117). Instead of sending a young man to compete with the leaders of an older generation, the apprenticeship system sends him out to pioneer new territory, where he is utilized in a role befitting his age and temperament. As an evangelist or missionary he can express his youthful rebellion and enthusiasm in attacking the status quo. As a pioneer in new areas, he can express himself creatively. By the time he reaches the point in his ministry where he is a part of the power structure, he is no longer quite as youthful. Experience has broadened him, made him more aware of others, and equipped him to fulfill a pastoral function. Also an inexhaustible vein of leadership potential has been tapped that has enriched the Church.

As described in Chapter Twenty-two, Pentecostals develop pastoral leaders from among the laity. They depend on God's effectual call. Leaders emerge from among the converts through in-service training at the level of the local congregation. Here pastoral and spiritual gifts and personal consecration are tested and developed. Calling to the ministry is verified by success in communicating the faith and multiplying churches. Finally ministers are accepted or rejected by the approval or disapproval of the members of the church.

The Pentecostal system leads to involvement and self-propagation. The Pentecostals work to involve all their members in the various aspects of their work in a vital grass-roots system of witness and evangelism. By means of open-air services on street corners and in public places, by house services, by myriad preaching points and congregations, the Pentecostals approach a near total level of lay participation.

The growing Pentecostals are intensely indigenous. Whether or not their participation in politics is overt or not, the Pentecostal Churches are caught up in the inexorable forces of change that are operating on existing power structures. They freely adopt and adapt practices and procedures in church life which reflect their cultural background and heritage.

Ecclesiastical structures are modified to suit Latin American patterns. Whether polity is officially congregational, presbyterian, or episcopal (and all three types are present), the structure always seems to evolve to a pattern of strong personal leadership, which is the pattern most understandable to Latin America. Authoritarian control is still acceptable to Latin Americans. Pentecostals seek to govern and support their members, leaders, and their programs through a light, flexible ecclesiastical structure which deals with discipline, delegates authority in matters of faith and practice, and fixes spiritual responsibility for pastoral oversight of all church activities. This organizational pattern, *on the economic level of the people,* displays a functional efficiency in enlisting loyal support by the members through a mandatory system of tithes and offerings.

SENSE OF MISSION

The sense of mission which characterizes the growing Churches of Latin America (Monterroso 1967: 6-8) is particularly marked among the growing Pentecostal Churches. Without exception, they believe that their message is exactly what men need. *Christus Victor* is the Savior they present. The Pentecostal believers themselves have experienced the reality of freedom from the old fears of supernatural evil and the new fears of modern technological society.

No problem is too difficult to solve, no obstacle too great to overcome to these intrepid men. Their own experience of a personal Pentecost makes them to believe that the Great Commission which the book of Acts ties to the promise of the Holy Spirit has been given to them personally. Conscious of the presence of the Lord and firmly convinced of the truth of their message, they are ready to carry it anywhere and everywhere.

The Pentecostal Churches do not feel themselves to be a part of the tradition of church history. Ignoring the centuries of church evolution since apostolic times they attempt to return to the simplicity and power of the early Church. Whatever they recognize as the leading of the Spirit they are free to follow. Sometimes their methods are highly unconventional. Sometimes they are shocking to other Evangelicals who are more self-conscious about their methodology.

Some Roman Catholics say, "Let the Pentecostals increase. It is better for the masses to become Pentecostal than communist. In the end they will come back to Rome." This is only wishful thinking on their part. There is no evidence even to suggest that the Pentecostals will follow such a course; in fact, every bit of evidence shows a strong trend in the opposite direction. In the 1964 Chilean elections in which the Christian Democratic Party came to power, the Pentecostals voted for the Socialist candidate rather than identify with the Catholic Church. To the lower class Chileans, the traditional identification of the Catholic Church with the forces of reaction and oppression is too recent and too real to be offset by the liberal tendencies of some contemporary Roman Catholics.

The antipathy, however, is more than political. The lay-orientation of the Pentecostals sets them at permanent variance with the Roman Catholic system, which is hierarchically structured and which leaves to a professional clergy all responsibility and authority. The Pentecostal Chuches will move toward greater interaction with other Evangelicals rather than union with Rome. Their emphasis on a personal encounter with God, and on the authority of Scripture, places them solidly within the Evangelical camp.

In their sense of mission, the Pentecostals are not hindered by some of the activities that distract others from evangelism. Their institutions are always on a level which the local church can support and administer. They have not been saddled with all of the machinery which North Americans and Europeans seem to feel are an essential part of the life of the Church.

Neither do they have a fear of bringing the "wrong" people into the Church. They have no social prerogatives to protect nor social standings to lose. They are busy winning their relatives, their friends, and their neighbors. They understand their own people's spiritual and social needs.

Autochthonous musical expression, architecture, festivals, symbols, and art forms are adapted by the Churches. This is a natural development of the indigenous Church in its true meaning. Such adaptations assume new meaning and serve as functional substitutes for old patterns.

HEALING CAMPAIGNS

Campaigns patterned on the North American healing evangelists of the 1950's have played a large part in Pentecostal growth in Latin America in the last two decades. Without making any value judgment as to the validity of this approach, Evangelical leaders recognize that mass campaigns emphasizing prayer for physical healing have changed the attitude of society toward Evangelicals.

The Tommy Hicks campaign in Argentina in 1952, which is described in Chapter Four, created an atmosphere of openness which has benefited all Evangelical Churches there. The spectacle of hundreds of thousands of people gathered under Evangelical auspices changed the Argentine Evangelical's image of himself and gave him standing with the government. Since then, hundreds of smaller campaigns have had similar impact in the provincial capitals.

In Venezuela, the campaigns of A. A. Allen, though they split Evangelical Churches, served to awaken the country to the existence of those churches. Similarly, in Brazil, Mexico, and Chile, mass healing campaigns have moved the Pentecostals to the forefront of the Evangelical scene. In Uruguay the rapid growth of the Pentecostals dates from the first campaign of Morris Cerullo in 1964. The tent campaigns of the Church of the Foursquare Gospel in Brazil were the beginning of their churches in that country. In Ecuador, their strong church in Guayaquil is the result of a healing campaign.

In all of these campaigns, the principal element is the preaching of the gospel. Healing is presented as just one of the blessings that God provided in Christ and His saving work. A people who live in fear of supernatural powers and blame most sickness on evil powers do not find it difficult to believe that God can and will help them. The message of physical as well as spiritual deliverance suits their world view.

Pentecostals commonly speak of their message as the gospel of power. The preaching of divine healing is far more than a gimmick to get people to listen to the gospel. The Old Testament idea of soundness or wholeness is bound up in their presentation of the gospel.

PENTECOSTAL CHURCHES WHICH HAVE NOT GROWN

Not all Pentecostal Churches in Latin America are growing. The name "Pentecostal" is no magical guarantee of growth. In fact, some of the Pentecostal Churches of Latin America are as frustrated and impotent as any of the Churches and missions described in Chapter Twenty.

Some of the indigenous Pentecostal Churches are not growing. Of the dozens of groups which have broken away from the Pentecostal Methodist Church and the Pentecostal Evangelical Church in Chile, for example, only a few have demonstrated sufficient vitality to grow and thrive. The few who have, have exceeded the growth rate of the two principal Churches, but those who have not had the necessary leadership and evangelistic thrust have lagged far behind. Most of these splits last only a few years until yet another Church begins or the members return to their former Churches.

Freedom from foreign domination will not, in itself, influence growth. It is only as freedom is used that it is meaningful. When Latin Americans use their freedom from foreign patterns to assert their native genius under divine inspiration in finding new ways to reach men, the Churches will grow.

The Pentecostal Churches which have been most plagued by lack of growth have been the mission-related Churches. The same dissipation of energy spent in missionary-national squabbles and the same preoccupation with form without regard for function, have hindered some of the Pentecostal Churches. There seems to be a feeling among some Pentecostal missionaries that it is enough to be Pentecostal. They are content to use the same methods as other missionaries and rely on "Pentecostal power" to make them effective. The sad truth is that this does not work. Ineffective methods cannot be sanctified by the dedication or sincerity of anyone. The genius of Pentecost is to be free to find new methods.

The Pentecostal missionary in São Paulo who has thirty members in his congregation after twelve years of hard work, or the Pentecostal missions which have been able to grow only by taking over indigenous churches, prove the need for something more than a Pentecostal label.

The growth patterns of the Assemblies of God in Venezuela and Colombia changed radically after old missionary methods had been rejected. The successful Pentecostal pattern which Melvin Hodges pioneered in El Salvador was introduced by newer missionaries. Static churches began to grow. From a total of two organized churches, one national worker, and eighty-three members in 1955 after twenty years work, the Assemblies of God in Colombia had nineteen organized churches, approximately eighty preaching points, thirty-two national workers, and 800 members in 1966.

One other hindrance to growth among Pentecostals has been

the use of irrelevant cultural patterns. The history of Pentecostal work in Peru, for example, has been a series of abortive attempts. When an apparent break occurs, it quickly stops. The essentially *mestizo* type of worship which is so effective elsewhere in Latin America does not meet the needs of the Indians. They welcome the message of deliverance, but later find the pattern of life in the church to be incomprehensible.

What produces church growth in Buenos Aires may be useless in Corrientes. What helps the Church to reproduce itself in Tabasco does not work in Monterrey. Only as the Church is truly Pentecostal, existentially experiencing the leading of the Holy Spirit, is it free to do whatever is necessary to proclaim the gospel effectively.

Chapter Twenty-two

MINISTERIAL TRAINING

The Church grows at the level of the local congregation, the local leader being the key figure in that growth. His effectiveness, in turn, depends to a great extent on the kind of preparation he has had. Thus the training of the minister directly affects all other factors of church growth.

PROBLEMS UNDER THE PRESENT SYSTEM

Some of the problems found in Latin America are those faced by seminaries everywhere, but others are unique to Latin America. For the Evangelical Church to be the force that God intends, she must meet and solve these problems.

The Foreign Nature of Existent Training

Protestant Evangelical ministerial training programs in Latin America are usually a deliberate imitation of the European or the North American systems. This imitation is not necessarily the result of imperialistic ambitions on the part of the missions, but rather the desire to initiate a training system of the highest caliber. Consequently the missionaries have reproduced the only system they know. The Latin American system is an imitation, in that most seminaries, Bible institutes, and Bible schools have copied foreign curricula, foreign faculties, and foreign methods of student selection, following North American patterns without seriously attempting to adapt educational essentials to Latin American needs.

Lack of Sufficient Leaders

We estimate that there are 75,000 Evangelical congregations in Latin America. Most of these are not under the pastoral care of ministers trained in theological institutions. Furthermore, at the present rate of growth, approximately 5,000 new congregations are formed each year. If all the students of the 360 existing theological training institutions were to become pastors after graduation, there still would be an insufficient supply of pastors for the new congregations alone, to say nothing of those already existing. Since only a fraction of the graduates actually enter the ministry, there is little hope that the present system will provide enough trained leaders to meet the need.

Static Training in a Changing Situation

Latin American Churches are in a state of dynamic flux. Growth is so accelerated that the Churches are hard pressed to keep pace with the changes. In this dynamic state, training for a static situation is irrelevant and dangerous. A man whose traning is exclusively academic, whose courses in "practical" theology do not extend beyond sermon preparation, and who is taught to think of the Church only as an institution to be preserved, is ill equipped to minister to the contemporary Evangelical Church. If he has been cloistered for three years in the isolated environment of a seminary whose values are foreign to those of the community, he cannot begin to understand and appreciate the problems with which most of his countrymen struggle. What is more, if he has been trained to think of himself as a professional whose personal responsibility is to do the work of the "ministry," then he will soon be overwhelmed by a task too large for one man; he is appalled and frustrated when he attempts to do what he has been taught is his responsibility as an ordained minister.

Poor Library Facilities

One of the most glaring weaknesses of the schools we visited was their very poor library facilities. One Bible institute in the capital of a country which has a literacy rate of over 80 per cent had a total of twenty-four books in the library, of which six were duplicates. This is an extreme example; yet few of the schools had adequate libraries. The Survey Commission on the Christian Ministry in Latin America and the Caribbean reported that 40 per cent of the schools which responded had fewer than 500 volumes in their libraries and 68 per cent had fewer than 2,000 (Scopes 1962:230). If the institutions which did not respond were included, the former percentage would have been much higher.

Ineffective Faculties

The favorable ratio of teachers to students in existing theological institutions (Scopes 1962:231) is deceptive. Most of the teachers are men who are not academically prepared to teach. Because of this, the opportunity and educational potential of seminars, reading courses, and workshops, which such a ratio should permit, are never really utilized.

CONSIDERATIONS IN PLANNING A MINISTERIAL TRAINING PROGRAM

When discussing changes in ministerial training programs, missions are almost always hampered by the fact that they cannot begin at the beginning, but must try somehow to overcome the momentum of ongoing programs sufficiently to make whatever changes are both necessary and possible. But partial success of those programs so often clouds the picture that it is almost impossible even to know what changes are necessary and possible. In such a situation it is sometimes helpful to pretend that no institution now exists, and from that premise to study the needs of the national Church, the cultural and economic situation in which it finds itself, and the resources available for ministerial training. From this study irrefutable facts emerge, and on the basis of these considerations the ideal training program may then be planned.

But an institution usually exists already and cannot be dreamed into non-existence. Given the ideal program resulting from the study, what changes now are both necessary and possible in the present institution?

How Should Men Be Trained?

How should men in Latin America be trained for the ministry? Should they all be trained alike? Perhaps different Churches have different educational needs for their leadership. Perhaps even within a Church one type of ministerial training will not suffice. How can we be sure that we are not merely transplanting foreign successes or mistakes into a Latin American situation?

Levels of Training

One recommendation of the Survey Commission mentioned previously is that standards of ministerial training should be raised to a university level because of the rising general educational levels (Scopes 1962:231). In part, this recommendation is another expression of mission influence on theological thinking. The missionaries may conceive of pastors as well-educated men who are accepted as leaders because of academic achievement. However, this is not in accord with the attitudes and values of most Latin Americans. Education may provide access to a higher social level but does not automatically earn leadership status. Leadership is, to an important extent, charismatic and depends very little on social standing or educational achievement.

It is generally accepted that a minister should be the social and intellectual peer of the people to whom he ministers. However, since the largest segments of Latin American society belong to the lower classes, to upgrade the ministry to higher social and academic levels would confine the Church's ministry to a very small segment of society. Because the uneducated masses do not readily follow the highly educated but want leaders from their own ranks, university-trained men often find themselves unable to minister to the greater proportion of Latin American Evangelicals.

Throughout Latin America, in every kind of church, we met

Evangelical pastors who had been educated out of the class from which they had originally come. After three years of isolation from the community they returned to it with middle class tastes, middle class values, and a middle class mentality. They were, as a result, unwilling or unable to identify with church members who had not been through the same acculturation to another subculture.

The income level of the educated national pastor creates problems for him in his relationship to the church and to the missionary. Anyone with better than secondary education in Latin America can earn much more than the amount an average worker can earn. The graduate of the seminary or Bible institute can demand the same salary for secular work as the graduates of the other institutions of higher learning. Some of those who choose to enter the ministry after completing their schooling are dedicated leaders for whom financial advantages are unimportant. Many are able to subsist on the low salary they earn as pastors, until their families begin to grow. On the other hand, there are other graduates not possessing leadership potential, nor are they intellectually gifted, who continue in the ministry chiefly because they are unable to compete with their peers for secular employment.

Tension with missionaries may also result from the disparity of pay scales. We met many highly educated nationals who were the academic equals or superiors of missionary colleagues. One national pastor with whom we spoke had earned the degree of Master of Theology from a North American seminary. The missionary with whom he was working had earned a Bachelor of Divinity degree from the same institution. The national pastor was earning one-seventh as much as the missionary. Whether the missionary pay scale should be cut or the national pastor's salary raised is not the question. The significant factor is the responsibility for the support of highly trained men that the national Church has been forced to assume. To pay these men commensurate with their training would strain the resources of the Church beyond limit if all ministers were educated to the same high level.

Because of the manner in which the Evangelical Churches have grown, it is beyond question that some highly trained men are needed at the level of denominational administration or to serve as theological scholars. For the former, it may be that training in techniques of administration rather than higher theological studies would be more appropriate. Unfortunately no such practical training is generally available in Latin America. Only a small proportion of Evangelical leaders, however, are needed for scholarship or administrative posts. The type of leader the Latin American Churches need most of all is the pastor who can minister to the common people in their cultural milieu.

The Churches must determine what level or levels of training will produce enough men who are socially, intellectually, and spiritually capable of pastoring existing churches and of planting new ones. The simplistic formula, "higher is better," will not suffice. Training on every level must be of the highest quality. Even to train men for a high school level of ministerial education, many of the existing institutions must upgrade the quality of instruction.

Subcultures

The national who ministers within his own country, yet to a subculture foreign to him, is seldom prepared to adjust to the fundamental differences he encounters. He often lacks the anthropological insights which could enable him to appreciate the people with whom he works and to communicate effectively across cultural barriers. As a result, he may feel their cultural values to be an aberration of the norms of his own culture, and as part of his pastoral task he may fight these differences or try to correct them. Failing in this, he is often reduced to the position of one who scorns the culture of those he is seeking to win.

While many pastors may be able to bridge the gap between cultures and communicate adequately, not all can make the transition. Such men are doomed to frustration in their ministry unless fortunately they are called to a church within their own subculture. Most congregations are composed of the common people, but most ministerial candidates are trained only for urban middle class pastorates. The result is that often the majority of ministerial candidates may be misfits in the ministry or may be driven by their frustration and failures to leave the ministry.

The Evangelical Churches of Latin America must seek to develop ministerial training programs within the numerous subcultures which are currently receptive and where churches are multiplying. What is at stake is not the prestige of the Evangelical Churches, but the very spiritual welfare of Latin America. Nothing less will do than training which is specifically aimed at each level of subculture within the Church. Evangelicals must end their slavery to an educational system designed to honor and glorify the culture of the classes presently in control. An education which emasculates the preacher and makes him ineffective among the common people cannot be described as education on a high level. "Lower standards" which, nevertheless, enable men to win others and shepherd the flock are a much more effective education. Therefore, theological training in Latin America must emphasize the *practical* aspects of the ministerial calling by means of a multi-level program.

Curriculum

To attain a multi-level training program, each Church must develop its own curriculum which prepares men for the various levels of society within, or potentially within, its membership.

The curriculum for theological study in Latin America ought to emphasize the need for a ministry to the unconverted and to new converts. Most of the members of the churches are first generation Evangelicals. They do not have the background of biblical knowledge or ethical values that ought to characterize Evangelicals of the second and third generations. The pastor must concentrate his efforts, rather, on teaching basic principles. He cannot presuppose a store of knowledge on the part of his parishioners that could enable them to grasp anything but direct, specific instruction.

Preparation for evangelism is of even greater importance. It seems to us that most theological institutions in Latin America teach evangelism in terms of techniques or methods rather than in terms of theological principles. Yet the gimmicks of North American evangelism are often ineffective in Latin American settings. Even if other techniques could be developed that would be more effective, they would not take the place of men trained in the spirit of evangelism. The successful evangelists of Latin America are not as concerned with methods as they are concerned with the tremendous need of the people for vital spiritual life.

Both effectiveness in evangelism and ministering to first generation Evangelicals imply training that is more practical than theoretical or academic. The specific curriculum should be Bible-centered and be tailored to meet the needs of the specific subculture in which the student is to minister. Those courses which provide an understanding of man, which open the treasures of the Scriptures, and which enrich the experience of the student must become the core of the program. It is not necessary that such training be within the framework of the traditional seminary education.

Theological study for pastors should reflect the situation of the Evangelical Church today. Not all the theological controversies of other eras of church history are relevant today in Latin America. Theological arguments that are cogent and pertinent elsewhere may be significant only to the Latin American Christian scholar.

Which Men Should Be Trained?

The shortage of candidates for the ministry and the failure of many Bible institute and seminary graduates to enter the pastorate have led many missionaries and national pastors to decry the lack of leadership material in the Church. Church and mission leaders have despaired of ever solving the problem.

How can the Evangelical Churches of Latin America continue to grow and maintain their spiritual equilibrium in the face of this dearth of ordained pastors? Are the right men being trained? How can more of the right type of candidates be found? In the answer

to these burning questions lies the solution to the present impasse
in the training of the ministry.

Young Men

In almost every reference to theological training since the beginning of Evangelical missions in Latin America, specific emphasis is
given to the training of *young* men. The presupposition has been that
dedicated young men will present themselves as candidates for the
ministry. Churches and mission, in addition, have offered subsidies
and the opportunity for advanced education to induce young men
to enter the ministry. This pattern has produced the present generation of leaders of the Evangelical Churches. No more capable
group of men can be found anywhere. The training institutions of
Latin America have clearly demonstrated that they can produce the
top-level leaders that the Churches require. When these men go
abroad for further study, they more than hold their own with men
who come from other parts of the world.

On other levels, though, this system of training has been less
successful. Present methods have not yet produced enough pastors.
Only a small percentage of Bible institute and seminary graduates
actually enter the ministry, as the majority choose secular careers.

At the heart of the problem lies the status of the graduate. On
the basis of his education he is ordained a pastor. After three years
or more of theory and academic exercise, he has the opportunity to
put into practice what he believes the church needs. He may even
emerge from his educational training as an iconoclast. He takes the
pastorate of an established congregation. Immediately he must interact with the existing power structure of the group. As an outsider,
he asserts his authority by appealing to his status. In the personality
clash that ensues, he may emerge victorious, with an exalted opinion
of his own importance, and may thereafter refuse to consider the
opinions and ideas of his church members. If he is defeated in the
struggle, he may leave the ministry or resign himself to staying on as
the puppet of the powerful members of the church.

For many of these young men, their only hope of success in the
ministry is to bring enough new converts into the church to change
the existing power structure. These new members naturally look for
spiritual counsel and direction to their pastor, who is their father in
the faith. Unfortunately many, perhaps most, of the young pastors
have not received the kind of training that equips them for this
kind of evangelism. Too often, they are busy defending the faith in
theological arguments, or are sidetracked into such a preoccupation
with secular issues that they lack spiritual dynamic.

Natural Leaders

Most congregations are now under the care, not of highly educated pastors, but of earnest laymen. Responsibility has fallen to them almost by default in the absence of ordained pastors. As a rule these men have no official status in the Church. In most Churches, because of their lack of formal training, they are held to be ineligible for ordination. Often they have neither voice nor vote in church assemblies.

Yet these men may be the true natural leaders of their congregations. Their status within the congregations is not arbitrary nor does it result from outside influence. Whatever leadership they exercise depends completely on the confidence and respect they command from their peers.

Thus, these lay pastors are the men who must be trained if we are to maintain the present momentum of growth, renew non-growing churches, and safeguard the Evangelical Church against slipping into heresy. *The need is not to find and train potential leaders but to train leaders who are already functioning.*

In summary, then, we suggest a general revision of priorities of leadership training to insure the type of indigenous preparation which is essential for the Evangelical Churches in Latin America. The 360 existing theological training schools need to adapt their curricula, faculties, and facilities to meet the needs of the new day in Latin America.

PATTERNS TO STUDY

In the new Latin America many experiments are taking place. Some of these are political, some social, and others religious. Ministerial training programs are not exempt from experimentation. Several new patterns are emerging, some of which have already proved successful. Others are still in their first few years of trial. For the Church which is examining her leadership problems, each of these patterns is worthy of study.

Successful Patterns

Several Latin American Churches have been unusually successful in training leaders who already exist within the congregations. Two of these are Churches unhampered by superimposed foreign patterns because they have arisen independent of foreign mission effort. The third pattern we present has been the result of a dramatic restructuring of an existing institution having foreign ties and foreign personnel on its staff. In spite of the differences among these examples, each seems to take into account the needs of a growing, widely diversified Latin American Church.

The Pentecostal System

The Chilean Pentecostal pattern described by Lalive d'Epinay (1967:185-192) is essentially that of the Brazilian Assemblies. The new member is given opportunity to testify publicly to his faith. The man who develops the ability to express himself, who enjoys the respect of fellow members, and who proves himself in whatever test is put to him, achieves the status of a recognized lay helper. Through the successful handling of increasing responsibilities, he may arrive at the point where he is ready to assume the leadership of a preaching point under the tutelage of another layman. At each stage he is answerable to the leadership of the Church.

If a man proves his ability, he is asked to open a new congregation. He still has no financial stake in the church work he is conducting. Even the costs of transportation and supplies are his own responsibility. If he is able to plant a congregation, he has demonstrated his qualifications to be a minister. Only after establishing a new church will he be accepted as a minister, but he is still not ordained. The Church sends him to a new field where he must again prove his ministerial gifts. Only then will he finally be ordained to the ministry. Thus, all ministers are proven church-planters. Let it be noted that in this arrangement being a church-planter involves being a successful shepherd of souls.

Both the Brazilian Assemblies of God and the Chilean Pentecostals are seeking new dimensions in ministerial training. We trust that neither will lose sight of the positive values of their present systems. Real danger exists that the Bible institutes presently beginning in Brazil will adopt the professional-class mentality which has hindered the effectiveness of the traditional Churches. The Comunidad Teológica (Theological Community) in Chile, which was designed to train Pentecostal pastors in their own environment, has not enjoyed the full confidence of the Pentecostal Churches, partly because it failed to conserve the values of the present apprenticeship system.

Whatever form the training of pastors of the Brazilian Assemblies and the Chilean Pentecostals may take, it is imperative that this form preserve the essential characteristics which allow for the recognition and selection of natural leaders within the group. By systematizing the subject matter of the short-term institutes and providing supplementary correspondence studies, the Brazilian Assemblies can also produce theologically trained pastors for their multiplying congregations. A modified form of the same system ought to serve well in Chile.

The Guatemalan Seminary

The Presbyterian Seminary in Guatemala has proved that an extension system of training is practical and valid for non-Pentecostals as well. For many years the seminary was located in Guatemala City to be as close as possible to the center of the cultural and intellectual life of the country. In an effort to get closer to the bulk of the people to whom the Church was ministering, the seminary was moved to a rural area.

Finally, discovering that most of the proven natural leaders in the congregations still could not attend school full time, the whole program of the seminary was decentralized and an extension program began. As a result, seminary enrollment has risen from an average of 10 to 15 yearly to over 140 in 1966. The Faculty is developing courses which utilize programmed instruction. Without leaving their families, employment, or churches, men are able to complete their seminary work, advancing at their own pace. The seminary starts on the level where these men live and work, and helps them to become able ministers. It sacrifices nothing essential in their training. A built-in screening process helps to guarantee that only the right kind of candidate will persevere and complete the course. Meanwhile, the Church is not deprived of their services. Working on four academic levels, the seminary is also reaching up to university graduates in a professional class for which the Church never before had a properly trained ministry. This illustrates the necessity of training a ministry from within the subcultures at every level.

The Gran Colombia Experiment

Plans were launched at the World Vision Pastors' Conference in Colombia in April, 1967, for a similar theological training extension system for Colombia, Ecuador, Panama, and Venezuela. A "pre-theological" level of the program will provide the equivalent of a sixth-grade education for rural pastors. The lowest level of theological education will then provide a complete ministerial course (Winter 1967:12). This program relies heavily on specially designed "Inter-texts" which will be the work of teachers in the seminaries and Bible institutes throughout Latin America, and which will be available to those in other countries as well. As the plan achieves its goals on these levels, higher levels will be added.

Since this represents the cooperative effort of many denominations and missions, it may provide the answer to the pressing problem of training Evangelical ministers in *Gran Colombia* and elsewhere, especially if Evangelism-in-Depth continues officially to sponsor this kind of local leader training as it moves to other countries. If existing institutions recognize this program as a valuable supplement to their own efforts, they are apt to see their resident programs grow also as churches multiply and more upper-level leaders are needed.

The basic plan of these extension programs is that the students cover the material at home using semi-programmed texts. Once a week they meet with the professor for a half-day conference. Once a month all students meet at the sponsoring institution for one or two days of seminars. Fewer professors can handle a much larger number of students than in resident schooling. Most important is the fact that the natural leader is not excluded. It is a type of continuing education for pastors, but it also reaches men who have never been to seminary at all.

Emerging Patterns

No simplistic answer will serve for the problems of training the ministry in Latin America. Several methods already in practice in limited ways can be used to much greater effectiveness if applied more widely. Huge additional expenditures of capital are not needed, however. The Evangelical Church already has the resources to train an effective ministry. Modifications of both old and new patterns are worthy of experiment. Several patterns of such experimentation are emerging in widely separated areas of Latin America.

In-Service Training

In addition to the apprenticeship and extension programs already mentioned, there are many other kinds of on-the-job training which have been tried and have proved effective in Latin America. One of these is the internship plan, whereby the candidate completes his theological training under the guidance of an ordained minister acting as a tutor. This method is being employed increasingly to aid in the transition from the ivory tower seminary to the harsh reality of life in the larger world. Its success depends on the wisdom, vision, and capacity of the man who serves as mentor.

The "practical work" in which theological students are required to participate has often been an exercise in futility which has failed to prepare men for actual ministerial life. That practical work can mean far more has been demonstrated by the Baptist seminary in Torreón, Mexico, where students have planted self-supporting churches all over the adjoining area. The man who has planted a church before finishing his training is far more apt to be successful in the ministry than one who has not.

Short-Term Courses

Originally designed for rural areas, short-term courses are also being accepted in the cities as a means by which ministerial students can be kept in contact with the world. Students continue in secular employment, and their course of study is spread over a period of several years. The drop-out rate may be high, but the dedication required automatically eliminates less capable leaders and raises the quality of those who persevere. These courses can be made to serve whatever level the Church finds necessary or appropriate. If properly designed they can also provide continuing educational opportunities that keep already ordained ministers informed and aware.

Night Schools

In order to train mature men who are prevented by family responsibilities from a full-time study program, special night courses have been prepared. These are usually not lower-level courses designed for laymen, but are the equivalent of daytime courses. Hopewell (1967:162) points out that the night school program can attract even superior students.

Such phenomena as the growing professional class in the Pentecostal Churches, the development of the Evangelical University in Guatemala, and the growing numbers of Evangelicals with theological and other professional degrees from European and North American schools indicate the need for some Latin American theological training for men who will minister to congregations of the highly educated. At the same time, the gap between this high level and the level of the rest of the Church is so alarming and so great that drastic measures must be taken.

Night schools can be very effective in training professional and highly educated men for the pastoral ministry. Or, on the other hand, less educated people may also be trained by this method. It is possible to have at the same time and in the same place one seminary class for doctors, lawyers, and engineers, and another class for high school or junior high school graduates. Both, on completion of their courses, may be ordained, but each group will find its own level of society to which to minister.

In effect, night and short-term courses take theological training to the student. By concentrating on students who are part of the secular world, the seminary keeps its trainees aware of the world. Indeed, the courses themselves are shaped by their context and made more relevant to the needs of men.

EVALUATION

The arguments that rage over the respective merits of Bible institute versus seminary, three-year versus five-year training, denominational versus interdenominational seminary, and secondary versus university level, are not of primary importance. The theological training of pastors can be evaluated only in terms of its service to the Church. How well do graduates serve the Church? How effective are they as evangelists, pastors, administrators, or church-planters? These are the crucial questions today. Questions of curriculum, level of studies, entrance requirements, length of course, and even seminary location can be resolved only in the light of the larger issues of purpose and function. Theological education must be conducted *in context,* taking into account existing kinds of churches, the levels of culture concerned, and the real growth potential of a given segment of the population.

There is a danger that theological education may become an end in itself rather than the means by which men are prepared for service (Scanlon 1962:25). Internal institutional changes are significant only to the extent that they are vitally related to the production of men who are more effective in the ministry.

The majority of theological institutes will probably not change their emphases, except perhaps to move toward even higher standards. The drive to upgrade standards has been used to raise funds and elicit sponsor interest. To emphasize other levels of training at this juncture might threaten budgets, since other types of training might not require the present facilities nor the existing teaching staff.

It was encouraging to notice the reaction of those who took part in a workshop on extension methods and theological textbooks held at Armenia, Colombia, in September of 1967 (ALET 1967). At that workshop the vast majority of the Bible institutes and seminaries in Colombia committed themselves to a serious trial of the extension training for the local, natural leaders in their respective church movements. Since then, many theological institutions around the world have requested detailed explanations of the extension system which uses programmed textbooks.

Perhaps our fears are ill founded. What a victory it would be for the Latin American Evangelical Church if seminaries and Bible institutes were to broaden their approach and begin to develop training programs on the many levels needed by the Church! If the response to the demand for multi-level, relevant training is general and genuinely interdenominational, the expanded program need not become an intolerable burden for any one denomination or mission. If basic materials are developed on a cooperative basis and are of a type that they can be used by all denominations, each Church and mission will be able to deploy its resources more creatively.

Training ministers and leaders for rapidly growing Churches requires a multi-level emphasis. Theological training on the highest academic level must not be slighted, but we have devoted most of our attention in this chapter to the other end of the spectrum, which *is* being slighted by most Churches and missions. Theological training must produce not only Christian scholars and administrators, but also preachers, ministers, pastors, and elders who are skilled in communicating the gospel to the multitudinous subcultures of Latin America, with special attention given to the enormous numbers of common people who make up the masses representing 160 of the more than 200 million people in Latin America.

Chapter Twenty-three

COOPERATION

As part of our preparation for the study of Evangelical church growth, we corresponded with the board secretaries of most of the missions at work in Latin America concerning those aspects of church growth which they felt were most crucial. Among their suggestions which helped shape the course of our study were questions and comments concerning Evangelical cooperation.

Some were concerned about the relationship of faith missions to denominational missions, others about the effects of competition; some noted the scandal of division and schism, and others the positive and negative effects of comity. All of these matters directly influence the growth rates of the Churches and are part of the larger question of Christian unity which all Churches face today.

It is outside the scope of this study to describe the theological and philosophical bases of Christian fellowship. This chapter deals, rather, with the practical expressions of Christian cooperation among Evangelicals. The question of the relationship of Evangelicals to the Roman Catholic Church is dealt with separately in Chapter Sixteen.

The minority status of Evangelicals and the magnitude of the task yet undone demand close cooperation in the sharing of responsibility. We do not speak of unity for unity's sake, desirable as that may be, but of united obedience in the task of evangelism.

EARLY EFFORTS

The statement of the 1916 Panama Congress on the subject of cooperation (Missionary Education Movement 1917.3: 11-160) was a weak declaration as compared with the action taken by missions in other parts of the world. Beaver explains that since this was the first cooperative conference in Latin America, the delegates were afraid of taking more positive steps which might limit the missions in their freedom to act (1962: 150).

The history of the Evangelical Church in Latin America suggests that even as early as 1916 the Evangelicals often worked cooperatively and thus were not troubled by many of the problems perplexing missions elsewhere. Although denominational lines have usually been

339

tightly drawn among Latin American Evangelicals, this has not prevented cooperation on the functional level.

The Panama Congress was itself an expression of cooperation. Previously, in 1913 the Foreign Missions Conference of North America had convened in New York to discuss the Latin American situation. Delegates had named a continuing committee to be designated as the Committee on Cooperation in Latin America (Missionary Education Movement 1917.3: 9). It was this Committee on Cooperation which had planned and convened the Panama Congress.

THE COMMITTEE ON COOPERATION IN LATIN AMERICA

For fifty years, the Committee on Cooperation in Latin America (CCLA) served the Evangelical Churches and missions. Most of the Churches and missions of the traditional denominations in Latin America participated in CCLA. For several decades, this included almost all Evangelicals of Latin America until the arrival of the newer faith missions and the rapid growth of the Pentecostals after World War II.

Immediately following the Panama Congress, the Committee on Cooperation sponsored seven regional conferences at San Juan, Santiago (Chile), Rio de Janeiro, Lima, Havana, Barranquilla (Colombia), and Buenos Aires, whose purpose was to encourage cooperation at the national level and to implement the areas discussed at Panama most relevant to each local situation.

These regional conferences outlined the broad cooperative policies by which missionaries would govern their activities for decades to come. One result of the conferences was the formation of national councils of Churches in several Latin American countries. The activities of the Committee in relation to the national councils were coordinated at five regional centers.

Dr. Samuel Guy Inman, a missionary of the Christian Churches, recognized by authorities as an expert on Latin American affairs, served as secretary of the Committee on Cooperation from its inception. During the many years he served, the Committee sponsored several inter-American congresses, the largest of which were patterned after the Panama Congress of 1916. The Montevideo Congress in 1925, which confined its deliberations to Evangelical work in South America, and the Havana Congress in 1929 were landmarks in the development of the Evangelical Churches of Latin America.

A comparison of these three major congresses (Panama, Montevideo, and Havana) reveals two important factors. First, in each succeeding congress, the role of the Latin American nationals is much more conspicuous and the relative importance of missionary participation much less. Second, the priorities of missionary endeavor changed. The emphasis on pioneer evangelism at Panama gave way to a preoccupation with the institutional programs of the Churches and missions.

The Committee on Cooperation in Latin America was a stroke of genius in a day when the administration of most Churches was carried on by missionaries. Originally, the *cooperation* referred to in the title was cooperation between missions. As the Evangelical Churches of Latin America evolved and developed, the role of the Committee changed because the role of the missions was changing. Eventually, the questions of cooperation between Churches and mission and between Churches became much more important than questions of inter-mission relationships.

Thirty-five missionary agencies were members of the Committee. Although the Committee included several boards which did not belong to the Federal Council of Churches (later the National Council of Churches) in the United States, the Committee always maintained a close relationship with the NCCC.

The Committee on Cooperation in Latin America addressed itself to those areas of work beyond the capacity of any one Church or mission. A major area of effort, for example, was in Christian literature. The Committee made possible cooperative publishing houses, literacy programs, development of Christian education curricula, Sunday School materials, other literature, and colportage. Later, CCLA aided the Churches in developing the ability to utilize the capacities of mass media in the proclamation of the gospel.

The Evangelical student and youth movements of Latin America were helped in their development by the Committee on Cooperation. Many of the outstanding Evangelical spokesmen of Latin America are products of these youth movements.

The Committee on Cooperation in Latin America provided opportunities for promising students to further their education in Latin America and abroad. Scholarships and fellowships have enabled hundreds of potential leaders to prepare themselves for service in the Church.

Theological training in Latin America was another area in which the Committee directly helped the Evangelical Churches. The present accreditation associations resulted from the work of the Committee on Cooperation in this area.

The marked effectiveness of the Committee on Cooperation may be attributed to its own concept of itself and its work. The purpose of the Committee was not cooperation as an end in itself. Rather, the Committee understood cooperation as a means by which the Churches and missions of Latin America would be able to accomplish their tasks. This pragmatic approach enabled the Committee to avoid many of the pitfalls which troubled cooperative efforts in other parts of the world. By concentrating on specific tasks, the Committee evaded the perplexing question as to the nature of the basis for cooperation. Churches and mission united to carry out projects about which they agreed.

During its last fifteen years, Dr. Howard Yoder, a Methodist missionary, served as secretary of the CCLA. By 1964, the Committee had fulfilled its original purpose. The Churches of Latin America by that time had begun to develop their own structures for dealing with the areas of concern of the old Committee.

In its place, the National Council of Churches of Christ in the United States of America organized a Latin American area department of its Division of Overseas Ministries. This area department serves those missions and Churches which cooperate with the NCCC and guides them in directions which seem good to it. It considers a large part of its work the interpretation of Latin America and its problems to the North American Churches. Part of the problem of cooperation among Evangelical Churches in Latin America is that, in the new climate of today, they are seeking ways to relate to each other as sister Churches.

Furthermore, the rapid growth of other Churches and the proliferation of other missions which do not belong to the NCCC and its organizations, mean that the Latin America department is no longer widely representative. If cooperation between all Evangelicals is sought, it will have to be projected on a broader base than an organization to which many of them do not belong. It may be impossible, in the near future, to regain the near complete cooperation of the early twenties. Nevertheless, far more cooperation is being achieved now than then, although in several different orbits. Evangelicals need to use their several means of cooperation more and more as one of the keys to greater church growth.

COMITY

Although formal comity agreements were late in developing, unwritten arrangements of the same type were in effect from the beginnings of the Evangelical Church in Latin America. Perhaps such arrangements were necessary because of the vastness of the field and the contrasting smallness of the missionary force. Each Church had room for expansion without intruding on another's field. It was not until much later, with the arrival of many newer missions, that conflicts over territory became a problem. As in other parts of the world, early efforts to assign territorial responsibility formally, emphasized the positive element of occupying the whole field rather than the negative aspect of avoiding competition. Division of territory was recognized as an important first step in cooperation (Missionary Education Movement 1917.3:21).

As early as 1888 the first effort had been made toward a territorial division of Mexico, but it was not until 1914 in Cincinnati that the missions which had worked in Mexico prior to the 1910 Revolution adopted a plan assigning territories to each. Sometime before 1916 a similar comity arrangement was agreed upon for the Methodists, Presbyterians, and Episcopalians in Brazil.

At the regional conferences following the Panama Congress, a remarkable spirit of cooperation prevailed. Most cases of overlapping and competition were amicably resolved without resorting to written agreements (Beaver 1962: 140-159).

A look at the kinds of comity which developed will help us to understand the nature of Evangelical cooperation. We will not attempt to describe all of the comity agreements in Latin America but will simply review a few representative areas.

Mexico

The best-known comity agreement is the Cincinnati Plan for Mexico to which we have already referred. The Cincinnati meeting was convened by the newly formed Committee on Cooperation for the purpose of reorganizing the work after the ravages of the Revolution. Most of the missionaries to Mexico happened to be in the United States at the time (Missionary Education Movement 1917.3). This conference did not purport to be a meeting of the Churches of Mexico as such, although it was the Churches which would be most affected by the decisions made. The delegates recognized that all recommendations and decisions could be advisory only, and would be binding neither on the missions nor on the Churches. Plans were made for cooperation in the preparation and distribution of literature, the standardization of education, the establishment of a union seminary, and the division of territory.

We must not judge these missionaries, however, by present-day standards. At the time there were less than 25,000 communicant members in all Evangelical Churches in Mexico. Since these Churches were weak and dependent, the missions felt it necessary to solve the problems for the Mexican Church.

The whole situation seems, however, a bit anomalous. The conference report ends with the statement, "It was recognized by all that it was indispensable that the plans should have the approval and support of the leaders, both men and women, in the Mexican Churches" (Missionary Education Movement 1917.3: 120). Nevertheless, the conference delegates deliberately planned to present the Mexican Churches with a *fait accompli* — a comity agreement which the missionaries believed was needed. From beginning to end the national Churches had no voice in the sweeping changes that were to be made. A committee of five missionaries was asked to prepare a paper entitled "A Message to the Mexican People," to be distributed in Mexico. The only part the nationals were asked to play was to translate the paper into good Spanish.

The distribution of territory was based on the ratio of missionaries to population. The number of national pastors was not considered, even though national workers outnumbered foreign missionaries by more than 2.5 to 1. A more equitable decision could have
been made by concentrating missionary resources at the points of
greater potential growth or, on the other hand, by assigning missionaries where the fewest national workers were employed.

Two years later in Panama the Cincinnati Plan was said to have
the "hearty support of many of the native workers" (Missionary Education Movement 1917.3:26). Nevertheless the formal approval and
support for which the report had called were never actually sought.

Kenneth Grubb (1935:104-105) suggested three reasons why the
Cincinnati Plan was not able to accomplish its aims: (1) the plan
gave the impression that the mission boards were trying to impose
their own desires on the nationals; (2) the plan gave the impression
that the object was to save money for the missions rather than to
occupy the field; and (3) the speed with which the plan was applied
gave the impression of precipitate action by the mission boards. The
CGRILA team, on visiting Mexico in 1966, was surprised to find
that after fifty years national church leaders still resented arbitrary
assignment of congregations to other denominations.

The Cincinnati Plan did not produce the desired results. Rather,
it effected a division into cooperating or non-cooperating Churches.
Missions who arrived later or who had not participated in the
comity agreement had to bear the stigma of interlopers or prose-
lytizers. Although these accusations may have been true in some cases,
many missions came to Mexico because they saw fields where their
own ministry would complement the work of the existing Churches
and missions. As the growth of indigenous Churches surged ahead
of the growth of most traditional Churches, the discussions about
cooperators or non-cooperators became irrelevant.

Mexico has never been "occupied" in the sense in which the
missions intended the term. It is pointless to conjecture as to what
would have happened had Mexican Churches participated in formulating the Cincinnati Plan, or had "non-cooperating" Churches cooperated. "The Cincinnati Plan may perhaps be said to have interrupted the spontaneous development of a cooperation which time
and patience would ultimately have achieved" (Báez Camargo 1935:
105). The early promise of Evangelical growth in Mexico was not
fulfilled until much later, and then quite apart from inter-mission
cooperation.

Peru

The outworking of the comity agreement for Peru was more
successful than in Mexico. The arrival of the Pentecostals interrupted
this, however, and their disregard for comity encouraged other

missions also to move into territory already assigned. Following the Panama Congress, the Peruvian regional committee on cooperation had devised a comity plan based on the natural divisions of the country, particularly taking into account communication developments. Lima was set aside as the common base for all missions. The Evangelical Union of South America was responsible for the southern part of the country. The Methodist Episcopal Church was assigned the central region with the exception of a central highland town where the Evangelical Union already had established itself. The Free Church of Scotland took responsibility for the North, but later divided its territory with the Nazarene and the Pilgrim Holiness Churches. According to Kessler (1967: 92), John Ritchie, as chairman of the Peruvian committee on cooperation, tended to interpret comity as referring exclusively to missions. He felt that local congregations should be free to affiliate with any denomination they chose. The result was an undercutting of the Methodists in the highland towns.

A number of factors in the development of the Peruvian Evangelical Church tended to minimize the importance of comity as an expression of cooperation. Among these were the cooperation of the Evangelical Union of South America and the Christian and Missionary Alliance in the Iglésia Evangélica Peruana, early experiments at joint theological education, Ritchie's strong role as *the* Evangelical leader in Peru at the time, and the general spirit of cooperation which finally resulted in the formation of the National Evangelical Council in 1940.

Once Churches and missions began to disregard comity agreements, those which were more aggressively evangelistic began to establish churches without consideration of any prior claim in that field. In 1925 there were only eight missions working in Peru (Beaver 1962: 296); at present there are at least thirty-five. The varied ecclesiastical and theological positions they represent have made comity impossible.

Venezuela

The comity agreement for Venezuela came much later. Venezuela was one of the last countries of Latin America to be evangelized. Most of the missions arrived at the same time, that is, around the turn of the century. When church growth made necessary some delineation of territorial responsibility, an agreement was drawn up which followed the pattern of mission penetration within the country. There had been little overlap of effort.

Since then, the comity agreement has affected the growth of the Church in its relationship to both migrants and immigrants. The economic development of Venezuela has created geographic mobility within the country, and at the same time has acted as a magnet to attract foreign settlers. Many of the ambitious, capable persons who want to get ahead have moved to the more developed areas of the country. Consequently, the less developed areas have sufferd from leadership strain. Their churches have provided churches in the more prosperous areas with top-level leaders.

Furthermore, some churches have only a very tenuous connection with their mission through an association of churches. This is true of the Evangelical Alliance Mission, the Orinoco River Mission, the Baptist Mid-Missions, and the Evangelical Free Church, all of which are all strongly congregational in polity. Many times such missions were unable to tell us how many churches were related to them. Since all their congregations are independent by definition, there is an absence of denominational loyalties. At the same time, since there are no close ties between these churches and their denominations, congregations which may splinter off may either affiliate with other denominations not observing comity or become isolated independents.

As Latin American society has become more complex, and as the Evangelical Church has grown and matured, the fortunes of all Evangelicals have become so intertwined that no mere geographical division is an adequate base for cooperation.

Service Missions

Through popular misuse, the term "service mission" has become ambiguous and is often understood to mean any mission which does not plant churches. This is a distortion of the intended purpose of a service mission, which is actually to supplement the ministries of other missions.

Service missions are not a new development in Latin America. The Latin America Mission, which was one of the earliest, was organized in Costa Rica in 1921 as the Latin America Evangelization Campaign. The relative importance of service missions has increased since then, particularly in the last decade.

At the same time, many groups begun as endeavors to serve other missions have eventually founded new denominations. For example, the Latin America Mission has founded churches in Costa Rica and Colombia which have grown into the Association of Biblical Churches of Costa Rica and the Association of Evangelical Churches of the Caribbean, respectively. Some service missions which have accidentally founded churches wisely decided to provide leadership for them, even though the stated purpose of those missions was not to found new denominations.

It is difficult to understand the sense in which some missions use the term "service mission" to describe themselves. Highly distrustful of other missions, isolated from the national Churches, and preoccupied with their own activities, they sometimes follow a course far removed from the mainstream of Evangelical life. For example, the stated purpose of one "service mission" we studied is to provide films for Evangelical church use. But when the Brazilian churches rejected this offer, the mission showed the films anyway in rented school auditoriums. If such missions cannot or will not serve the Church, according to their stated functions, then their projects become ends in themselves and often have no influence whatsoever on church growth or evangelical outreach.

However, true service missions, such as the Overseas Crusades and the Latin America Mission, are serving the Evangelical Churches in ways that will continue to bless Latin America for generations. They act as catalysts to stimulate inter-mission and interdenominational cooperation. No one mission or Church can provide every ministry that is needed. The principle of cooperation implies that the Churches need and invite the assistance of the service missions. It is on such a basis that service missions such as the Overseas Crusades have attempted to serve the Latin American Evangelical Church.

Overseas Crusades

In four major ways Overseas Crusades has provided valuable assistance to denominational and faith missions alike. (1) It has provided competent technical assistance for specialized ministries using modern mass media. (2) It has coordinated pastors' retreats, short-term Bible courses, and training institutes for all denominations. (3) It has instigated a number of cooperative inter-mission projects. (4) It has organized and coordinated evangelistic campaigns, both denominational and interdenominational in sponsorship, local and national in scope. In trying to cooperate with all groups, however, it has met with some difficulties. The conservative theological position of Overseas Crusades has estranged some of the more liberal elements in the Evangelical movement. At the other end of the spectrum are those who are offended that Overseas Crusades does not require a doctrinal statement from every denomination that it serves.

The response of other missions to the efforts of a good service mission is cumulative. As Evangelicals learn to work together under the leadership of such an organization, they are better able to take advantage of other available ministries even outside those organizations with which they have previously cooperated. Overseas Crusades emphasizes its own cooperative nature and thereby becomes a catalyst for cooperative efforts between all other Churches and mission organizations.

Latin America Mission

Following almost four decades of meritorious service to the Evangelical Churches of Latin America in such areas as literature, radio, theological education, and evangelistic campaigns, the Latin America

Mission in 1959 launched a new type of endeavor which grew to be the largest ministry of the mission. Evangelism-in-Depth is more than a new method of evangelism. Indeed, when other missions have tried to copy only its methodology, the results have been singularly discouraging. Evangelism-in-Depth is rather a philosophy or, if you will, a theology of evangelism which revolves around two foci. One is the thesis set forth by Kenneth Strachan:

> The successful expansion of any movement is in direct proportion to its success in mobilizing and occupying its total membership in constant propagation of its beliefs (1961: 25).

The other is a burning conviction that every man should find salvation through placing his faith in Jesus Christ and becoming His confessed follower.

The plan as developed (Strachan 1961: 27-29) consists of five major points. (1) The plan for evangelism should be in terms of a specific national or regional territory. (2) Individual believers must be trained and mobilized for continuous and effective witness to the saving power of Jesus Christ. (3) The local church is the normal unit for witness and evangelism, and provides the necessary leadership for this. (4) Interdenominational and inter-mission cooperation is necessary. (5) The activity of the individual believer, the local churches, and the denominations must be coordinated in one over-all strategy for total evangelization.

The first Evangelism-in-Depth campaign was held in Nicaragua in 1959. Because of its success, similar campaigns were later held in Costa Rica, the Dominican Republic, Venezuela, and Bolivia. Evangelism-in-Depth is now a major department of the mission and has expanded its activities to include other parts of the world as well as Latin America.

Within the framework of Evangelism-in-Depth, there is room for evangelistic campaigns of the traditional type, but the mobilization of the whole Church and the emphasis on cooperation at every level have made the program both unique and far more effective than previous efforts. Even Churches which usually do not cooperate with others because of doctrinal differences have shared in this type of evangelism. Neither the integrity nor the autonomy of any church is compromised. The kind of cooperation that Evangelism-in-Depth engenders is designed to continue after the campaign is over. By cooperating in evangelism, the Churches establish new relationships to each other that facilitate further cooperative efforts.

Even the kind of opposition to cooperation that arose in Bolivia and Venezuela after the Evangelism-in-Depth campaigns could not destroy the basic sense of oneness that had been created by the unified effort. Artificial denominational differences had lessened as men began to see beyond their own small part of the work of the Church and to realize that they were but part of a much larger effort.

The practical effect of Evangelism-in-Depth has been to show many groups which had never experienced growth that growth was possible. They came to recognize more fully their own leadership resources and discovered that they could cooperate with other groups without compromising themselves or their principles. Consequently they began to believe and work for greater things for God.

HINDRANCES TO COOPERATION

Theological Polarization

The efforts to cooperate in evangelism have highlighted the differences and similarities within the Latin American Evangelical Church. One of the problems, however, is the matter of identification with foreign organizations with the resulting importation of foreign theological problems irrelevant to Latin America.

The particular affiliation of a mission and its consequent commitment to a particular theological position are almost meaningless issues in Latin America so far as the related Churches are concerned. Instead there is an overwhelming general agreement among Evangelicals on theological issues. For missionaries, though, North American and European affiliations are very important, and to the extent that the Churches of Latin America are still dependent on the missions, they are inevitably influenced by such affiliations.

Until recently, these foreign connections only indirectly affected the Churches. The Confederation of Brazil and the Councils of Chile and Peru, for example, were made up of Churches affiliated with conservative faith missions and denominational mission boards which were members of the National Association of Evangelicals (U.S.A.) or the World Council of Churches. Agencies of both the World Council and the National Association of Evangelicals were involved in helping the Latin American Churches to provide literature and other materials for Christian education, social services, and theological training. Each agency endeavored to serve the whole Church and not merely a section of it.

Amicable relationships have not been allowed to continue in this manner, however, since pressure from both groups is forcing an artificial polarization of the Latin American Evangelical Church. This polarizing influence certainly does not represent the majority opinion of either side. It is regrettable, therefore, that the agencies of cooperation have thus become the unwilling instruments of power politics.

Whichever side is victorious in this struggle, the Evangelicals of Latin America will suffer. Although neither stance has more than minority support, most of the Churches will eventually be driven to one or the other extreme. Because of the generally conservative position of the Churches, that element which seeks to align Latin American Evangelicals with North American conservatives is more likely to win. To those who claim that such is a natural alliance, it is necessary to point out that its realization would permanently estrange Churches which are theologically orthodox but which are related to denominations belonging to the World Council of Churches.

CGRILA believes that the Churches in Latin America must be allowed to remain unaligned except as their consciences and their own needs indicate a distinctive Latin American position.

Denominationalism

Besides the question of international affiliations, other problems hinder any effort of a cooperative nature. Elsewhere in this study we have considered ethnic and social differences and their effects on cooperation. In addition to these, there are many problems created by denominationalism, which is as strong in Latin America as anywhere else in the world. Unfortunately, the sectarian spirit tends to exaggerate theological differences and to create distrust. Few denominations in Latin America have a theology that excludes other Churches from the body of Christ, but because of denominational separatism an atmosphere of ignorance and fear is created which precludes fellowship with others.

The same spirit manifests itself as denominational pride in which denominational projects become more important than any other consideration. Such preoccupation with denominational aggrandizement can lead to overt proselytism and to ethnic disregard for the brethren of other Churches. What was formerly "healthy competition" then becomes sheep-stealing.

THE POSITIVE SIDE

Despite such very real problems there is tangible solidarity among Latin American Evangelicals as a whole. Their sense of brotherhood encourages every objective student of Latin America to believe that there already exists a spiritual unity which transcends any human attempt at organic union. For many years Evangelicals have functioned together as a minority group. Now that the Evangelicals are sufficiently numerous to be a recognized social force, even more concerted efforts can be directed toward evangelism of the whole society.

The growing ability of Latin Americans to withstand outside pressures is another indication of the strength and vitality of the Church. The Evangelicals are not willing to conform to foreign patterns. The freedom of the Churches to make their own decisions will grow as they become increasingly independent financially. If the Evangelicals insist on remaining self-sufficient, and resist outside efforts forcing polarization, the spirit of cooperation will become stronger.

Successful past cooperative efforts encourage the Churches to work together now in new areas. Because they are becoming aware of their own resources, from now on they will tend to supplement local ministries by reciprocal assistance, rather than to rely unilaterally on their own particular missions. It is this cooperative process that some missions seem unwilling to face realistically.

In the final analysis it may well be that the question of ecclesiastical affiliation will determine the future role of missions. If the Churches can meet their own needs by a cooperative sharing of ministries, the role of the missions, at least in their present form, may be threatened.

PROSPECTS FOR THE FUTURE

Improved means of communications have made all Latin Americans neighbors. Interchurch cooperation will tend to increase as the continent develops. Every cooperative venture in theological education, in evangelism, or in literature ties the Churches more closely together. Again and again as we went from country to country we were reminded of how distances have become insignificant and how every part of Latin America is accessible.

Cross-Fertilization

An encouraging sign of possible cooperation is the "cross-fertilization" of resources and personnel. Colombian pastors in Venezuela, Brazilians in Chile, Argentines in Uruguay, Colombia and Mexico, Puerto Ricans in Central America — are all able to stimulate new kinds of cooperation. These men who have studied in interdenominational or union seminaries welcome fellowship with other Churches.

Theological Consensus

A Latin American theological consensus will doubtless emerge which will reflect the realities of Latin culture and will by-pass foreign theological squabbles. Even the Latin American use of the term *Evangelical* rather than *Protestant* indicates that the Church wishes to make its own way on its own terms regardless of what outsiders might feel about the Church.

European and North American theological emphases concerning secularized Christianity find little echo in Latin America, where the Evangelical Church is too busy fulfilling its mission to be troubled by these theological issues. The crucial issues in Latin America relate, rather, to the effective communication of the gospel. Only to the fringes of the far right and the far left is irrelevance of the gospel a problem.

If a theological consensus does emerge, it will unite Evangelicals in a common cause. Together they will face the problems of social injustice and the Church's role in effecting social change. Together they will work to multiply viable churches all over Latin America.

Interchurch Cooperation

The report on the Panama Congress of 1916 shows clearly that cooperation was understood to be between missions, merely serving as an example to the Churches. Some missions have attempted to maintain this state of affairs to the present time. Happily, however, in most cases authority and responsibility for interdenominational cooperation have developed in the Churches.

Future cooperation will probably further this trend. Cooperation in Christian service will be primarily between Churches rather than between missions. The cooperative efforts of the missions will be in relation to the Churches with which they work. It will be the Churches, not the missions, which will determine the kind and extent of cooperation. A test of the effectiveness of the missions in establishing vigorous Churches will be the nature of cooperation sought by these Churches independently of their missions.

Cooperation can minimize the duplication of church efforts in every field and can multiply the resources available for church-planting. Through cooperation on these practical, functional levels, the Evangelicals of Latin America can present to the world a united testimony of their essential unity in Christ.

PART VI
EVANGELICAL PROSPECTS

What can Protestants in Latin America expect to happen during the next decade? The answer to this question depends on developing trends in many areas of life in Latin America as a whole as well as within the Evangelical Church. One of the functions of this research project has been to investigate church growth factors in the light of the total Latin American situation, with an eye to the future. The decade ahead is extremely important to the Evangelical Churches ministering in Latin America and, therefore, also to the leaders engaged in church-planning.

Chapter Twenty-four

GUIDELINES FOR STRATEGY

At every level of the Evangelical community the formulation of plans for church-planting mission is crucial. Everyone wants answers to the question, "What must be done by Evangelicals in Latin America now?" Some basic considerations are presented in this chapter — which should be brought to the attention of every leader of Church and mission responsible for administering any part of the program of mission.

DEFINING THE MANDATE

The lively discussion between the few who are on the extreme left and right of the Protestant theological spectrum in Latin America is mounting in intensity. The discussion revolves around the question, "What is the contemporary mandate for the Protestant Church in Latin America?"

The one extreme calls for a new generation of leaders who will be active in all types of social action, even to the point of using violence. The other extreme calls for a new isolation from the social struggle in Latin America and a concentration on conservatism. During the days ahead, while this debate rages, Latin American Evangelicals, who for the most part are not on the side of either extreme, must define for themselves what is their mandate from Christ. The Department of Missionary Studies of the World Council of Churches meeting at Iberville, Quebec, formulated a statement which serves to focus attention on the fundamental task of the Church today:

> The Church of Jesus Christ has been commanded by her Lord to proclaim the Gospel to men and women in every human situation. Her mandate is nothing less than the making of all nations His disciples. In her inner life, the Church offers herself daily to God; in the world she is to live for those who have not yet heard or received the Gospel. It is her very nature to be an outward-looking fellowship of witness. "That which we have seen and heard we proclaim also to you, so that you may fellowship with us" (I John 1:3). The Church must therefore seek to be ever growing in num-

bers, as well as in grace and knowledge of her Lord and Saviour — not for reasons of self-aggrandizement, but in pursuance of God's desire that all men should be saved. So great a commission requires a total dedication of the Church's resources, a working recognition of the unity of God's people and of the unity of the task, and, above all, complete dependence upon and obedience to the Holy Spirit. It calls for a constant, self-forgetful concern for the world for which Christ died (WCC 1964: 1).

This statement is clear enough to be understood by all, yet broad enough to include the whole concern of God for both His world and His Church. This divine concern for men and women entangled in our changing world should be mirrored by all God's children and given concrete expression in His Church. Out of a clear understanding of our mandate and resulting concern comes a renewal of our obedience to Christ. "So great a commission requires a total dedication of the Church's resources" (WCC 1964: 1).

BACKGROUND CONSIDERATIONS

At every ecclesiastical level, in order to devise realistic policies, an awareness of background factors is essential. Let us consider some of these.

Rising nationalism is bound to affect Evangelical activity in both positive and negative ways. Waves of national feelings are legitimate expressions of awakening self-consciousness in Latin Americans. They can be utilized by church-planters or, if disregarded, can work powerfully against the spread of the knowledge of Christ.

While the Church is, of course, dedicated to reaching all men, regardless of their class or position, she should concentrate special attention on the masses who are receptive. The future of the Church lies with the common people.

The ministry of reconciliation which has been given to the Latin American Evangelical Church is set in a social context of rapid changes moving toward revolutionary explosion. The revolutionary mood is increasing in its appeal to the minds of men and women. With this in mind, the Church must prepare for the uncertain days ahead.

Evangelicals in Latin America must be relevant to their generation. They must always be the growing edge of the Church. Churches which lack the necessary spiritual dynamic cannot fully understand the present opportunities until they are awakened to the dangers of self-containment, self-interest, and self-destruction. Evangelicals must strive consciously to become aware of God's action in human history and to remember the urgency of their common task.

In some countries in Latin America, Evangelicals have grown sufficiently in numbers to be heard in various political arenas. They must develop the conviction that God calls them to use their political power to secure honest government, social justice, and — to be specific — streets and sewers.

Evangelicals must be aware of the significance of Roman Catholic renewal in each country. God has given Latin America a new freedom for each individual to read and study the Bible. Evangelicals can now speak openly about the claims of the Bible concerning the Savior and His desire that all become new creatures in Him.

STRATEGIC APPROACHES

During the current social upheaval, planning for several decades ahead is impractical. The day of a long-range strategy aimed at fifty years hence is past. Plans cannot be formulated for each Church or mission, but we would suggest seven approaches which Churches and missions can apply to their own particular needs.

Select the Course of Highest Priority

From many alternatives the church-planter must select the one course which fits his circumstances. To decide priorities and to plan a sequence of activities is not easy. Such decisions require that we seek the divine will and discern the signs of the times. Proper timing is crucial. Church leaders must discover when to continue with older methods and when to launch daring experiments. Making decisions of this sort requires knowledge, courage, honesty, and faith. Decisions affecting church-planting often raise controversy. Areas given priority by one Church may seem of only marginal importance to another. Furthermore, vested interests, "pet projects," party lines, and dominant personalities may prevent creative thinking where it is most needed.

Understand Positive and Negative Dynamics of Church Growth

The widespread distribution and use of the Bible has been a means whereby countless numbers of individuals have been regenerated. Reading of the Bible has led many to Christ, and these in turn have been instrumental in establishing congregations and churches, a process which still continues in Latin America.

The fight for religious liberty in Latin America has made it possible for Protestants to enjoy freedom to proclaim their faith openly. There are still pockets of persecution, but God is granting Evangelicals the right to live and proclaim the gospel. All Christians should, therefore, press for religious liberty.

Evangelical schools have been instrumental in breaking down walls of prejudice and in educating generations of believers' children, but today the value of these schools is changing.

Pioneer church-planters usually have gone to receptive rural areas. Now church-planters should turn to the rapidly developing urban areas.

Early use of voluntary lay leaders as preachers and teachers has enabled large fields to be served by one ordained minister. This lay leadership has grown to great proportions in some Evangelical Churches and constitutes one of the most promising elements for the future growth of many more Churches in Latin America.

Networks of family relationships have provided pathways for acceptance of the gospel. Entire families have been won through the spontaneous and personal witness of one member of the family to another. We can document many cases of conversion through relationships either of blood or marriage.

The Latin American personality has great capacity for profound religious experience. As Christ indwells, He releases an unlimited supply of native enthusiasm, oratory, aggressive friendliness, courageous witness, and propensity for growth in the religious life.

The Presbyterian churches in Salvador, Bahia, Brazil, analyzed the situation in their city of almost one million people. The following factors, which they found had been obstructing their growth for several years, will serve to illustrate negative factors which hinder other denominations and missions in similar situations.

Presbyterians tried to plant churches among the middle class. Very few middle class people live in Salvador, Bahia. Only the rich and the poor are found in sizable numbers. Yet it is usually among the middle class that the Presbyterians attempt to plant churches.

Presbyterians paid little attention to spiritists. Yet very large numbers of *umbanda-candomble* (low spiritism) and the Centros Espiritas (spirit centers — more than 900 in 1960) multiply in the rapidly expanding low class districts of Salvador and around the whole Bay area.

Presbyterians met a brick wall in entrenched Roman Catholicism, as Salvador is a Roman Catholic stronghold. There are at least 365 Roman Catholic churches and a vast army of officials of the Roman Catholic Church. Papers, radios, and other public organs have been tightly controlled by them.

Excessive numbers of common-law marriages and much sexual promiscuity cause many young people to drift away from the Presbyterian churches. Only a small portion return after middle life.

The Presbyterian missionaries turned the city over to the Presbyterian Church and left Salvador forty-five years ago when the Brazil Plan was adopted as the *modus operandi* between missions and Church. At the same time the Baptists and Pentecostals — missionaries and Churches — came into Salvador to liberate many into the freedom of Christ. (In the early 1960's the Presbyterian Church invited its assisting missionaries to return to work in Salvador and some growth has begun.)

Presbyterian churches have misunderstood the concept of a

"mother church." They have considered groups of new converts as belonging to the mother church, rather than to send out members and finances in order to form new churches. Even in sections of the city where there were enough Presbyterians to insure the establishment of separate, growing congregations, the mother church has maintained control and inhibited increase.

Rural fields have been too large for one pastor to care for adequately. An example of this is the Feira, Cabeça, Cachoeira field. Stewardship can help, but drastic measures must be taken to insure adequate pastoral support.

Part-time ministry among pastors permits them to hold other part-time jobs in teaching, law, politics, and other fields. This leaves little time for an effective pastoral ministry. New congregations arising in the outlying districts suffer from the lack of good and consistent pastoral oversight.

During long decades, lack of aggressive evangelistic campaigns has meant that very few new converts were brought into the churches to encourage and enliven the older members. Presbyterian churches here emphasized education in Salvador to the virtual exclusion of missionary activities connected with church-planting.

Prepare for Growth

Churches and missions should initiate responsible membership accounting in order to learn the manner of collecting essential statistics with respect to all phases of their church life. They will thereby come to understand their individual growth opportunities and problems in depth. Church growth surveys, and the procedures involved in making them, can be learned by local leaders.

Every Church and mission should use all available means to understand how God is multiplying churches. Of necessity this will include the best insights from completed church growth studies and from the research of sociologists, anthropologists, and other social scientists. A deeper understanding of the Latin cultures and subcultures, with their intricate values and customs, is important to all who formulate policies for Evangelical Churches.

Missions should prepare workers for communicating the gospel. Changes in the social environment and the rapid growth of Evangelical Churches necessitate a new kind of preparation for all personnel, national and foreign, who will be involved in church extension. Every worker must grow in his understanding of interpersonal relationships. Many Protestant missions have concentrated so heavily on their own fields of endeavor that each knows very little about the other's work — even though they may have lived in close proximity to one another for years. Evangelicals must become better acquainted with one another if they are to cooperate in their common task.

Now that church growth research methodology is available, any missionary or church leader can better understand the total Evangelical enterprise. Strategy for Evangelical advance, at whatever level, can be based on a scientific understanding of facts and insights. There is no excuse for coming to the conference table without understanding how, where, and why the Church has grown and is likely to grow.

Deploy Evangelical Resources Adequately

Once the facts are understood, resources can be better utilized and correct decisions be made concerning priorities. The freedom that the Church or mission has in making such decisions also plays a part in correct deployment. True, some missions either do not have resources available, or cannot bring together those which are available, so as to take advantage of the opportunities which loudly proclaim the high-potential areas. Many missions, though, have the resources and could deploy them better, if they would.

In order to win battles, an army must have adequate logistics — that complicated operation which brings together adequate supplies and the right people at the proper time in order to accomplish the desired objective. The Church is God's instrument for reconciliation in the world and, therefore, He is the great master of logistics. His objectives must become the objectives of His people. The Church must be disentangled from the secondary objectives and free to move into areas God has prepared for receptivity. The situation in Latin America clearly indicates that God wants His people to concentrate their activity in those areas of society where exists the greatest potential for spiritual and moral change. Evangelicals all over Latin America ought to evaluate their work in the light of the real receptivities of various populations. Let each Church and mission ask itself, Have we attempted to evangelize receptive areas? Have we concentrated sufficient resources there? Have we learned productive patterns?

Recognize Fruitful Areas

Many of the high-potential areas of modern Latin America have been pointed out in previous chapters. It may be helpful by way of illustration to mention a few of these again. A word of caution, however: a responsive area by itself does not guarantee a growing Church. In high-potential areas churches must be established by high-potential Churches or missions. Only then shall we see churches multiply.

Colombia

After the shaking of *La Violencia*, Colombia has emerged as a land of great opportunity. Especially receptive are urban areas such as Cali, part of the Cauca Valley, the developing heartland of Colombia found within the triangle between Bogotá, Medellin, and Cali and areas surrounding Bucaramanga.

Mexico

The area inhabited by descendants of the Maya Indians offers much growth potential. This region stretches across the States of Yucatán, Campeche, Quintana Roo, Tabasco, and Chiapas, to the border of Guatemala. Northwest Mexico is another area of Evangelical opportunity, now benefiting from the vast network of irrigation canals in the fertile plain region below Guaymas reaching as far as Mazatlán. Mexico City and the Federal District are also open to the gospel.

Guatemala

Northeastern Guatemala is a new land frontier being developed through accelerated immigration of Indian tribes and *mestizos* from both sides of the border.

Brazil

The northeastern part of the State of Paraná is the center of a new land development that moves west from the historic coffee boom area. Another new settlement area is the southern part of the Amazon Basin, which will be bisected by roads from Brasília to Belém and from Brasília to Pôrto Velho.

Argentina

An area of development is the Camahua region of the Province of Rio Negro. Here are found tremendous resources of iron ore, coal, and petroleum. Hydroelectric power is being harnessed, and a vast area of irrigated agricultural land around Neuquén is opening up.

Mining Development Areas

Iron ore, mineral, and petroleum areas are developing in Brazil (the Valley of the Rio Doce between Belo Horizonte and Vitória and in Amapá, above the mouth of the Amazon) and Venezuela (the industrial complex at Ciudad Bolivar in the Guiana Highlands).

Roads

New roads lead to frontier development: the Transversal, from Curitiba, Brazil, through Asunción, Paraguay, and on to Lima, Peru; Brasília to San Gabriel, Rio Grande do Sul; Brasília to Fortaleza; Brasília to Vitória; La Marginal which is being cut along the eastern side of the Andes in Ecuador, Peru, and Bolivia, and will open up the inner Amazon Basin.

Metropolitan Areas

Growing cities have a high potential for church growth (see Chapter Seventeen). We list the largest here:

Greater Buenos Aires and Federal District	7,000,000
Greater Mexico City and Federal District	5,500,000
Greater São Paulo and the cities of Santo	
André, São Bernardo, and São Caetano	5,500,000
Rio de Janeiro and Niterói	3,500,000
Greater Lima, Peru	2,000,000
Greater Caracas, Venezuela, and the strip	
which extends to Valencia	2,500,000
Greater Santiago, Chile	2,500,000
Greater Montevideo, Uruguay	1,500,000
Bogotá, Colombia	1,350,000
Recife, Brazil	1,110,000
Belo Horizonte, Brazil	1,080,000
Salvador, Brazil	1,000,000
Guadalajara, Mexico	992,000
Pôrto Alegre, Brazil	980,000
Monterrey, Mexico	914,000
Rosário, Argentina	890,000
Cali, Colombia	805,000
Córdoba, Argentina	784,000
Barranquilla, Venezuela	750,000
Maracaibo, Venezuela	750,000

Border Areas

Both the northern and southern borders of Mexico offer unique opportunities; as well as the border between Brazil, Argentina, and Paraguay, known as the territory of Misiones.

Evaluate Quality and Quantity of Church Growth

Strategy formulation is incomplete unless there is some way to measure the results of our efforts. Recently one Evangelical Church in Brazil, facing a great opportunity in a large metropolitan area, formulated good strategy: (a) placing a team of four pastors in the city, and (b) spelling out the criteria for evaluating the success of the ministry of these men. Merely placing the men in the city was not enough, though it involved costly decisions about priorities. In addition they provided for an analysis of the work.

Answer Thorny Questions

Serious questions face those who have the responsibility for formulating strategy — questions which arise time and again all over Latin America. Although the following questions are not exhaustive, they are representative and certainly demand immediate consideration.

1. How to Identify with the People?

Since there are thousands of foreign missionaries working in Latin America, the problem of identification with the people is crucial. North Americans face a number of cultural adjustments, but so also do Argentines called to work in Colombia and Brazilians called to work in Chile. The process of adjustment usually involves serious cultural shock. Even a Brazilian pastor from Rio Grande do Norte feels this shock when he accepts a pastorate in Rio Grande do Sul, 2,000 miles farther south. In order to cross barriers of this kind, God's people must become a servant people, making themselves available for work in relationships which are conducive to the highest utilization of personal and material resources. The spiritual and material resources of all outside missionary endeavor in Latin America must be welded into viable partnership plans for Evangelical advance.

2. Shall Church and Mission Pay Pastors and Evangelists?

It is the unusual churchman who can use subsidy to aid the church-planting process without simultaneously hindering the initiative or destroying autonomy. The classic discussion of mission subsidy by J. Merle Davis (1947: 77-85) contains the best available summary of the negative effects of subsidy.

The unfortunate effects of subsidy administration are felt throughout Latin America. In many countries employment of subsidy has seriously handicapped whole denominations. Many who have made ill-advised distribution of foreign money, upon realizing their error, have then taken stern measures to eliminate subsidy entirely. When subsidy cuts are made suddenly without proper preparation, however, growing Churches may cease to develop. Some never recover from the blow. Davis' observation applies to most mission-related Churches in Latin America today:

> Where a policy of gradual reduction of foreign aid was applied, there was a measure of adjustment among Younger Churches, but where the cut was sudden and arbitrary and without a preparatory period, there resulted a shrinkage in churches, leadership, and members from which some fields have scarcely yet recovered (1947: 83).

Strategists, however, are challenged to face the dilemma of subsidy in creative ways appropriate to their particular situation, so that the fullest benefit inherent in well-planned subsidy may be realized.

> The partial interpretation of the indigenous church principle ought to disappear. It should have a new interpretation, but this time a complete one. A self-propagating church does not mean fewer workers in the untouched field, and much less does it mean that we should relate our national or foreign workers solely with the

existing church. This is only a tiny edge of the coin. Those who limit these principles to the visible church alone are perhaps doing something wonderful in the eyes of a world which responds to trends of publicity, but they are failing in their true apostolic responsibility. In order for indigenous principles to have their full value, they should be practiced both inside and out of the present church. They should not signify a slackening of forces, but rather an increase; not retirement of funds, but relocation of them. Today more than ever we need men from every nation who are moved, not by the flow of publicity, but by the cosmic passion of the Great Commission (Isais 1966: 256-57).

The implementation of indigenous church principles must be reviewed in the light of the challenges of the present unpredictable situation.

3. In What Sense Is the Church Exclusive?

Many Churches in Latin America are bound by a sterile exclusivism which hinders growth. Some Churches are so hampered that they are able neither to function adequately nor to express their God-given compassion, concern, and charity. When a Church establishes laws so rigorous that it becomes exclusive and loses its freedom to witness in its own cultural and social environment, it is time to look once more to the gospel of the grace of God. Such a Church is usually self-contained, introspective, self-satisfied, and self-righteous and lives in a ghetto of its own making. Freedom to move into new opportunities of witness, to innovate, and to function as an alert pilgrim people is therefore stultified. The result is a separated people — separated from involvement in God's great concern for all mankind.

A Church may speak of good works, but when these are generated by exclusivism only still-born works will result. Churches caught in this vicious cycle fail to grow in a manner commensurate with their opportunities. God's free people share a spirit of contagious liberty which enables them to become a creative force in the world. Fresh infusions of grace and spiritual vitality will energize God's obedient people and make possible a daring dedication to total evangelism aimed at redeeming men, and, in God's good time, the structures of society.

4. What Can Be Done About Lack of Responsible Participation?

The presence of large numbers of nominal church members undermines efforts to mobilize the resources of local churches. Churches will seldom grow unless individual members feel a sense of obligation to be participants in, rather than spectators of, God's plan. Where genuine gratitude exists, a sense of accountability in the attitudes of individual believers emerges. How can a strategy-planning body deal with non-involvement? First, they must recognize the importance of responsible participation; second, they must seek the enlistment of all believers in the life and work of the Church.

5. How Can the Church Overcome Spiritual Drag?

In Evangelical Churches where advance has decelerated, spiritual drag hinders an active and effective ministry. No vision inspires courageous outreach, and concern for others is minimal.

The time in which we live demands that we recover our spiritual endowments; if Presbyterians, then we must halt our backsliding and realize our election; if Baptists, we must be born again; if Methodists, we must receive a second blessing at the mourner's bench! Churches and Christians can be renewed, reborn, recommissioned. They can begin to perform vital ministries as God's Spirit fied with less than that full spiritual dynamic that is the birthright of the Church of Christ?

6. How Can Evangelical Churches Escape a Minority Mentality?

Evangelicals in Latin America have long been persecuted as a tiny minority which stood out against the cultural Church of the land. This day has not completely left us. The feelings of inferiority shared by many Evangelicals have been detrimental to the growth of the body of Christ. Occasionally these feelings have been overcome — a significant turn from the defensive to the offensive.

Churches of a given denomination which are small and separated by distance would do well to organize periodic conferences in central locations. Such meetings can strengthen believers through shared fellowship as all participate, and as everyone senses the excitement of the essential Christian unity and victory. Those who were once timid and inactive can be inspired by new spiritual expansion to communicate their faith in face-to-face witnessing. When this occurs, Evangelicals are activated and become occupied with new patterns of aggressive outreach. For many Latin American Evangelicals, this is the only way to break the unconscious minority mentality. United efforts in evangelism also help to break down minority mentality and parochial pessimism. A new Evangelical mentality could overcome obstacles past and present.

This dynamic which the Evangelical Churches need is the energizing force behind successful strategy. May God grant us spiritual discernment to gain a better understanding of our task, a better deployment of our resources, and a better evaluation of the results.

Chapter Twenty-five

NEED FOR RESEARCH

Specialized research surveys can be used to correct the common blind spots concerning church growth. Although some leaders already understand certain aspects of the dynamics of church growth on their own fields, it may be helpful to outline the various procedures for gaining such an understanding and for interpreting the data which are gathered. Knowledge of church growth requires a working familiarity with the research that has been completed as well as that which presently is being conducted by Protestants, Roman Catholics, and others. Specific church growth research in Latin America has only begun. Some ideas for a continuing future research program are suggested below.

CHURCH GROWTH RESEARCH ON DIFFERENT LEVELS

In every part of Latin America there is a need for concerned Evangelicals to conduct on-the-job surveys such as can be done by local leaders. This is not impossible if leaders are willing and objective. A research survey should be conducted on all levels of church life.

Level of the Local Congregation

Any church growth survey must begin with adequate statistics of the congregation. When the process of data-collection is complete, a series of line graphs can be constructed showing the development of membership, church school, and finances of the local church in the past five-, ten-, or fifteen-year period. The chart of membership should show the complete history of the number of communicants, against which to study reports of those interviewed. Members within the local church may be aware of fluctuations in membership through the years, but it is difficult to discern with accuracy the growth trends of a local church without the visible means of a graph.

Bar graphs or population pyramids may be used to show the composition of the local congregation on the basis of age, sex, race, and other factors which enable us to analyze membership. These can indicate recent trends in membership affecting the capacity of the congregation for witness and outreach, both now and in the future.

366

Saunders' study of a Methodist congregation in Brazil illustrates the value of such a study of a local church (1960: 415-50). The church he chose to study is located in the State of Guanabara, Brazil, about thirty miles from the city of Rio de Janeiro, in the town of Monte Alegre. In addition to the Methodist church, which had 142 members at the time of the study, there are four other Evangelical Churches in the town. The Baptist church had approximately 500 members, the Congregational church about 200 members, the Pentecostal church (denomination not indicated in the study) about 150 members, and the Presbyterian church about 50 members.

A discussion of the implications of each of Saunders' tabulations is not included here. Rather, the tables are reproduced in order to show the kind of data to be sought and the value of conducting such a study. The uses to which the data can be put depend entirely on the creativity and ingenuity of the researcher.

RACIAL COMPOSITION OF CHURCH MEMBERS

	Number	Percentage
White	68	47.9
Mulatto	42	29.6
Negro	32	22.5
TOTAL:	142	100.0

PLACE OF BIRTH OF CHURCH MEMBERS

Place	Number	Percentage
Rio de Janeiro	38	26.8
Minas Gerais	32	22.5
Bahia	10	7.1
Espirito Santo	2	1.4
Guanabara	59	41.5
Portugal	1	0.7
TOTAL:	142	100.0

AGE DISTRIBUTION OF CHURCH MEMBERS

Age	Number	Percentage
0-5	0	0.0
6-10	2	1.4
11-15	13	9.2
16-20	17	12.0
21-25	24	16.9
26-30	16	11.3
31-35	10	7.0
36-40	12	8.5
41-45	17	12.0
46-50	4	2.8

Age	Number	Percentage
51-55	10	7.0
56-60	10	7.0
61-65	5	3.5
66-70	0	0.0
71-75	1	0.7
76-80	1	0.7
TOTAL:	142	100.0

MARITAL STATUS OF CHURCH MEMBERS

Status	Number	Percentage
Married	89	62.7
Single	45	31.7
Widowed	8	5.6
TOTAL:	142	100.0

OCCUPATION OF CHURCH MEMBERS

Occupation	Number	Percentage
Unskilled manual laborer	13	9.2
Skilled manual laborer	17	12.0
Subsistence farmers	3	2.1
Lower class housewives	90	63.4
Middle class housewives	2	1.4
Office workers	14	9.8
Liberal professions	3	2.1
TOTAL:	142	100.0

MARRIAGE WITHIN OR WITHOUT THE GROUP

Total married or widowed	Percentage of total membership
97	68.3
Total of married or widowed who married within the group	Percentage of total married or widowed
82	84.5
Total of married or widowed who married outside the group	Percentage of total married or widowed
15	15.5

CHURCH ATTENDANCE

Number of members "faithful" in attendance	Percentage of total
	74.0
105	
Number of members "unfaithful" in attendance	Percentage of total
	26.0
37	

PARTICIPATION IN CHURCH SOCIETIES

Number of persons who belong to Percentage of total
   one or more societies   78.2
             111

Number of persons who did not Percentage of total
   belong to any society   21.8
             31

FINANCIAL CONTRIBUTIONS

Number of tithers   Percentage of total
            14   9.9

Number of "systematic" contrib- Percentage of total
   utors   40.8
            58

Number of "irregular" contrib- Percentage of total
   utors   49.3
            70

DISTANCE FROM HOME TO CHURCH

Distance in Kilometers	Number	Percentage of total
0-1	60	42.3
2-5	55	38.8
6-10	15	10.5
11-15	7	4.9
16-20	2	1.4
more than 20	3	2.1
TOTAL:	142	100.0

Such data-recording, even though time consuming, is a valuable measurement of the local congregation. A careful study can help leaders locate weaknesses and neglected areas as well as strong points. Through self-evaluation and continued research a plan of action may be outlined which can stimulate renewal. This type of local study and research in thousands of churches across the continent is urgent and can be conducted by any who are concerned enough (1) to ferret out the necessary facts, (2) to chart the data and make correlations and interpretations, and (3) to take action without delay concerning the findings.

It is staggering to realize that many Evangelicals in church after church in Latin America are not aware of developments in their immediate communities, to say nothing of neighboring communities. Neither are they aware of developments in other Evangelical Churches within their community. One way of remedying this situation is to construct a map for the area which will show where the members of any given church live in relation to that church. The map must be large enough to plot the whole membership, and a colored dot or pin could be used for the home of each member or family. When the map is complete, the boundary lines of the church will emerge, along with the distribution of the membership. Consecutive studies should then build upon new strengths and weaknesses that are revealed by the map.

If the same type of map is used to chart the members of the church school, leaders may discover which part of the community is reached by both the worship services and by the educational program. The location of the leaders both in the church and the church school should be clearly indicated on this same map. Their distribution may help to explain the abundance of, or lack of, leadership: If natural leaders live far from the church, the church school may lack sufficient teachers. New members of both the church and the church school should be charted as to location.

Third, the local study must be done in reference to the larger social context. Urban officials can supply information on city planning, zoning codes, land use, and housing developments. New streets, sewers, water systems, electrical installations, schools, and parks are essential factors in population distribution, and should be included on community maps. Many of the details mentioned here may seem unimportant until they are seen as part of a complete picture. Because extension of electrical lines, water, and sanitation facilities accompany the influx of inhabitants, Evangelicals must become acquainted with the statistics of their installations. Such cities as Córdoba in Argentina; Guadalajara and Monterrey in Mexico; and Goiánia, Maringá, Governador Valadares, and Brasília in Brazil are changing so rapidly that map studies may be outdated in less than a year. It is obvious, therefore, that there is a real need for continuing research. Local city governments, planning boards, and public works departments can supply maps and information. Local commercial associations can indicate locations of industrial developments and factory worker housing. In larger cities, district censuses are available to study comparative growth trends.

In rural congregations or missions church workers would do well to list pertinent facts about the province or county in which the church is located — such as existing work opportunities, the type of economy, the condition of roads and accessibility, climate information, schools, housing, hospitals and medical services, communication and mail services, local newspapers, and any other information necessary to give a total community picture.

A good example of a useful type of chart is one we acquired in Córdoba, Argentina, showing the geographical, economic, and political synthesis of that province. It includes thirteen maps, and a table in the center which condenses all of the factual information. The maps interpret graphically the political divisions, roads, economy, geology, agricultural production, aboriginal populations, altitude, climate, rainfall, tourism, water, type of land, and urban centers. Every Evangelical leader who is responsible for church-planting should have this basic information for his specific area. However, such statistical data and maps are of little value unless we are able to plot against them the distribution of church members and baptisms. It is the *comparison* which tells us the kind of people who are being won to Christ and which throws light on economic and social factors responsible, at least in part, for receptivity.

An example of superb congregational charting has been done by the Rev. R. H. Conerly of the Methodist Church in Mexico City. His maps revealed membership migration because of economic and social advance. Although the growth experienced was basically only transfer growth, the doors for indigenous evangelism were certainly open in the newly developing areas resulting from this migration. Conerly was well aware of the situation and recognized where an evangelistic thrust ought to be made.

Level of Denominational Strategy

If a critical statistical examination of the local church is urgent, how much more urgent it is that a denomination should engage in the same kind of self-evaluation and analysis! Here the research begins to take on larger dimensions, with a larger group of people assuming the responsibility of church growth research. A preliminary series of studies of local congregations should be combined to show the size, distribution, concentration of churches, and membership of the denomination as a whole. The line graphs indicating the growth of individual churches should be plotted on a combined growth chart for the entire denomination. Eventually, if data are available, the growth in each field, community, or subculture within the total denominational context may be charted. The study might also be divided according to rural areas, cities (by sizes), provinces or counties, states, and the entire country. When the statistics have been charted with care and accuracy and compared with corresponding maps, the denomination will better be able to understand its past development. Now it can courageously consider the necessary steps for future growth. Young churches cannot afford to hesitate in initiating such growth surveys. The time has come when we must be familiar with each aspect which aids or hinders the Church in faithfully fulfilling its mandate.

Level of Comparative Denominational Studies

What happens when two or more denominations have done

careful research of the growth of their churches and have then decided
to combine their findings in a cooperative project? We have not yet
seen such joint studies of churches in Latin America, but the potential of this method has been demonstrated when individuals occasionally have gathered church growth data for all denominations
in one particular country and combined them in comparative growth
charts. Results of such comparative studies for other parts of the
world have amazed Evangelical leaders in Latin America, who often
have been so busily occupied with their own fields that they know
nothing of the activities of sister Churches within the same areas.
Many times their suprise is sufficient to awaken these leaders to the
need of careful research, not only of the growth of their own denominations, but also the comparative growth of others.

Other Levels of Needed Research

There are many facets of church growth in Latin America
which should be investigated immediately. For instance, an intensive
study needs to be conducted of rapidly growing Churches and of the
dozen or so outstanding Evangelical Churches in Latin America
which have a membership of over 50,000 communicants. Such a
study could be conducted country by country, church by church, or
denomination by denomination, with special reference to demon-
strable church growth insights learned. It would deal with the
relation of ministerial training to church growth, lay involvement, the
role of the missionary in a growing church, the mission in the process
of becoming a Church, and other related dynamic factors of church
growth. This specific type of survey might be called intensive in that
its focus is one church, one denomination, one country, or one church
growth factor.

Additional themes which require further research are suggested
at the end of this chapter. A wide circulation of the results of such
surveys could initiate great changes among Evangelicals in the
Churches of Latin America and help in winning multitudes to Christ
in the days ahead. If such research could hearten the enlightened
believers, help to break the spirit of pessimism and self-containment
common in many Churches, and involve larger numbers of Evangelicals in planting vigorous churches, then its impact on Latin American society would constitute a moral, social, and spiritual revolution
of considerable magnitude.

In their preparatory investigations, researchers should also utilize
that research which has been completed by other Protestants, the
Roman Catholics, and social scientists of related disciplines.

PROTESTANT RESEARCH IN LATIN AMERICA

The World Dominion Survey Series of Protestant missions, which
included seven volumes on Latin America, was the only descriptive

resource on Latin American Protestantism until the early 1940's, when J. Merle Davis began to publish the International Missionary Council Series of Economic Research in Evangelical Churches in South America. These publications give important historical perspectives and statistical measurements at specific points of time. In 1961 McGavran began the Church Growth Survey publications. These have included *Church Growth in Jamaica* (McGavran 1962) ; *History of Protestantism in Costa Rica* (Nelson 1963); *Church Growth in the High Andes* (Hamilton 1962) ; *God's Messengers to Mexico's Masses* (Taylor 1962) ; *New Patterns of Church Growth in Brazil* (Read 1965) ; *Tinder in Tabasco* (Bennett 1968), and a study of Argentina by Arno Enns which will appear soon.

The Department of Studies of the World Council of Churches in 1962 established a study center in Montevideo under the leadership of Julio de Santa Ana. Similar centers are functioning in Buenos Aires directed by Leopold J. Niilus, and in Brazil under the administration of Julio Andrade Ferreira. These centers perform specific socio-cultural studies, and function as information centers for their areas. Another Protestant center for Hispanic studies, the Hispanic-American Institute, Austin, Texas, is directed by Jorge Lara-Braud. Other small study centers function in some of the Evangelical Confederations of certain South American countries. One service these centers offer for those interested in church growth surveys is a yearly census for their respective countries.

Another valuable aid to those interested in the Latin American Evangelical Church is the recently published *Protestantism in Latin America: A Bibliographical Guide,* compiled by John H. Sinclair (1967) and available from the Hispanic-American Institute at Austin.

The Missions Advanced Research and Communications Center (MARC) of World Vision International and Fuller Theological Seminary will play an important role in future church growth research by using the systems approach to the analysis of data. MARC is currently engaged in a computer study based on the Protestant Census of Brazil (Read 1967a:2-4) .

ROMAN CATHOLIC RESEARCH IN LATIN AMERICA

The Roman Catholic Church maintains a number of study and research centers in Latin America, the best known of which are those in Chile and Mexico. The Center of Intercultural Information in Cuernavaca, Mexico, conducts an extensive program of research and documentation.

Many notable publications by Roman Catholics have appeared recently on themes relevant to the changing ministry of the Roman Catholic Church in Latin America. The FERES series of Latin

American documents and Sociological and Socio-Religious Studies on
Latin America appeared in the early 1960's in a forty-two-volume
set. Two of these volumes contain an excellent religious survey of the
growth of Latin American Protestantism by Prudencio Damboriena
(1962, 1963). This is probably the outstanding statistical study of the
last decade.

The five conferences of the Catholic Inter-American Coopera-
tion Program (CICOP) have been attended by the leading Roman
Catholic missiologists of Latin America. The papers presented at
CICOP conferences should be read by any and all who would be
aware of the dramatic changes presently occurring in the Roman
Catholic Church in Latin America (Considine 1964, 1965, 1966;
Shapiro 1967).

Secular Research

Social scientists have found the subcultures of South America
fertile territory for extended research programs. Recently, C. Wagley
of Columbia University edited a symposium which classifies all significant current research on Latin America (1964). Sociological and
anthropological studies by social scientists have provided a substantial
bank of invaluable information that offers rich insights into many
areas of Latin American society — insights that Evangelicals must not
ignore.

The appended bibliography includes a selection of recent
books on Latin America from Protestant, Roman Catholic, and secular
sources. We recommend that all who are interested in the Latin
American Evangelical Church read as widely as possible in the various
fields of Latin American life and culture.

Future Use of CGRILA Resources

A flow of statistics and other data from field notes, correspondence, and other sources has been accumulating in our files. The
background material collected, however, constitutes no more than
an embryonic stage of the research that should be done in the
seventeen countries included in this study. The statistical bank
which is ready to file on electronic data-processing cards is also only
a beginning. The 30,000 units of church growth data for Brazil recorded on computer storage tapes are currently available to those
who are qualified to study Brazilian church growth at this level.
Yet the records of data are waiting for researchers who can give their
talents and efforts to the time-consuming reading, charting, and
writing demanded by the task. Latin American Protestant leaders
are at least twenty years behind in background research and in
practice of church growth methodology.

The data mentioned should be made available to select, seasoned
missionary and national leaders of Latin America who come to the

School of World Mission and Institute of Church Growth at Fuller Theological Seminary in Pasadena, California. These Latin American scholars could carry forward the main objectives of church growth research, pursuing their investigations across Latin America: (a) by utilizing every opportunity to update the data records; (b) by being educationally well prepared for their task; (c) by using every available means to provide themselves with appropriate scientific research tools and training in the social sciences; (d) by developing further research methodology through new techniques and projects; and (e) by making specific plans for seminars in North and South America to study and implement their findings in every possible way.

Within a few years a number of church growth research specialists would be concentrating on research within their various Churches, but also would be available to participate in short courses, institutes, conferences, and church growth workshops in different regions of Latin America.

A comprehensive church growth atlas should be published, together with a historical outline of the Evangelical Church in Latin America complete enough to be used as a standard reference work. A biannual bulletin of church growth in Latin America should be printed and distributed as widely as possible. A church growth survey of the Caribbean area of Latin America should also be conducted, and periodic revisions of church growth studies in Latin America must be published.

Continuing practical research in the area of church growth will contribute directly to the Evangelical Churches in their task of winning men and women to Jesus Christ, of teaching new converts to win others, and of seeking to involve greater numbers in direct evangelism.

SUGGESTED SURVEYS

The following factors which affect the growth of the Evangelical Churches need immediate research by teams or individuals. Help is available for all who would undertake church growth research in a free booklet, "How to Do a Survey of Church Growth," by Donald A. McGavran (available at the Institute of Church Growth, 135 North Oakland Avenue, Pasadena, California 91101). Additional publications concerning methods of survey are now in preparation and soon will be available from the same address. These will be available in Spanish and Portuguese, as well as English.

Environmental Factors:
1. Geographical advantages or disadvantages.
2. Economic development.
3. External migration and natural increase of population.

4. Internal migration (of individuals or families).
5. Extended family relationships.
6. Relationship of social structure to church-planting, numerical growth, and organic development.
7. Syncretistic religions.
8. Cultural dynamics.
9. Ethnic and racial affinities.
10. The social revolution.
11. Political participation by the Church.
12. Nationalism.
13. Religious freedom.
14. Religious persecution.
15. The new Roman Catholic stance.
16. Rural-urban sociological patterns.

Theological Factors:

17. Theological emphases compared to growth statistics.
18. Content and type of preaching.
19. The use and distribution of the Bible.
20. Indoctrination and discipline.
21. Pre- or post-baptismal catechesis.
22. Emphasis on the work of the Holy Spirit.

Ecclesiological Factors:

23. Autochthonous worship patterns.
24. Church architecture and music.
25. Priority areas for church extension.
26. Membership mobility and membership losses.
27. The self-image of congregation or denomination.
28. Nominal and marginal membership.
29. The nature of persons being incorporated into church membership.
30. Leadership roles and preparation.
31. Lay leadership.
32. Organizational structures.
33. Functional structures.
34. The role of institutions.
35. Roles of missions and missionaries.
36. Deployment of personnel and funds.
37. Stewardship education and promotion.

Chapter Twenty-six

THE DECADE AHEAD: LATIN AMERICA, 1970 TO 1980

Ahead of Evangelicals in Latin America lies a decade of crucial debates, decisions, developments, and possibly dangers. We are optimistic, however, because of the many signs of vitality in the Evangelical Church. Therefore, we would like to recapitulate not only the problem areas ahead but also the prospects, stressing especially the present strengths which should give a solid and positive base for the coming decade.

A DECADE OF DEBATES AND DANGERS

A vociferous minority in the Evangelical Church is attempting to redefine evangelism as participation in every movement which is working for a more just social order. Another minority, equally vocal, is opposed to any such emphasis as a formal action by the Church. The debate between these two groups will continue, and Churches will be induced to adopt one or the other of these extreme positions. In the process some will be sidetracked from biblical evangelism and will lose their prophetic witness by becoming tools of non-Christian ideologies. Others will withdraw from interaction with the world in a mistaken attempt to maintain their separation from the world. They, too, will lose their prophetic witness by becoming irrelevant. It is unfortunate that radical positions at either end of the spectrum seem necessary. That these two needed emphases cannot be set against each other, the Montevideo Congress on Christian Work discovered as far back as 1925 (Speer 1925.2: 45). A proper balance must be maintained. Probably the great majority of the Churches will press forward, emphasizing both evangelism and social action in differing measure as God gives them wisdom to see. It will become increasingly clear that effective evangelism requires participation in a prophetic role of protest against the injustices of an unbalanced social system. More and more sensitive church leaders will cry out against these injustices and will emphasize the need to break down secular power structures, to seize control of communication centers, and to by-pass any hard ecclesiastical structures which seem to be opposed to change. In many places this active Christian social concern will be the spark for a vigorous evangelism which will produce strong churches.

377

As Evangelicals grow in number and voting power, their increasing political weight will be felt all over Latin America. Especially is this true in Brazil and Chile, where the Evangelical Churches are large and undoubtedly will continue to grow. In Brazil thirty Evangelical candidates have already been elected to state and federal offices. In the 4,000 municipalities, almost 400 Evangelicals hold political offices in city or county government. Thus a Protestant holds office in one out of ten municipalities of Brazil. This number probably will be four times as large by 1980. As the number of Evangelicals increases, the political pressure they exert through social legislation may mean significant benefits for the masses. No doubt some Christians will misuse their political power, but God will also achieve righteous ends through many others.

Because of the rapid acceleration of social change in the days ahead, an increasing number of movements doubtful in value will emerge to fill some of the spiritual voids which rapid change creates. Some will be deviations from Christianity; others will be of the religious-science type, theosophic in nature, and led by popular "personality cult" leaders. Since some of these movements will have originated within the churches, factions will be at work within Evangelical Churches as well. Leaders will need great patience, wisdom, and spiritual authority to cope adequately with the attendant problems.

Religious deviations of this type can be checked if the weak ministries of teaching in the Churches are strengthened, and if new emphasis is given to courses which instruct the believers in the historic faith. Churches which emphasize the Bible and teach a solid system of doctrine to every one of their members will be much less vulnerable to deviations than Churches which neglect the Bible and minimize teaching.

We were alarmed at the lack of sound teaching and Bible exposition in many of the churches visited. In the fields of ethics, morals, and social responsibility, we often found clear scriptural teaching to be lacking. This weakness could become one of the biggest dangers to face Evangelicals in the decade ahead. The Bible has played a prime role in the growth and development of the Evangelical Church in Latin America, but there still is a need for campaigns of Bible distribution and Bible teaching to help incorporate basic truths into the lives of all believers.

Another real danger facing the Latin American Church in the near future is that of internal strife. When young Churches in Latin America continue for long periods to experience little growth, other problems are magnified. Most Churches and missions have passed through times of great tension between nationals and missionaries. It would be folly to say that this tension within the ecclesiastical power structures will not continue. Yet, both missionaries and nationals must consider whether or not such emphasis on power politics is necessary. Struggles of this kind always retard growth or even bring it to a standstill. Multitudes which otherwise could have been won, thus are neglected. Is not this one of the greatest dangers of all?

We believe that the modern foreign missionary who dedicates time to evangelizing and who adapts properly in a new relationship "with" or "under" the national Church can see gratifying results in church development. We believe that the national who likewise evangelizes and recognizes his role as being coordinate with or subordinate to the mission will also see gratifying results. Both missionary and nationals have something unique and necessary to contribute to church-building. The gospel which is best understood and appreciated by Latins is that which shines forth through the Latin American personality and culture. On the other hand the missionary's exposure to more than one culture and to new techniques of evangelism often make him a valuable aid in evangelization.

The Methodist Church in Mexico is trying out a new form of partnership which teams up Mexican and Californian leaders for the purpose of planting churches in the high-potential areas of the provinces of Baja California and Sonora. This same partnership emphasis is seen among the Baptists in Argentina, Mexico, and Brazil.

In a day of integration it is imperative that nationals and missionaries work together on an equal basis. It is also necessary that the Church senses its own mission, its own abilities and resources, and the value of its own cultural heritage.

Although in the past two decades many Churches have declared their independence, there is a real danger that some Latin American Churches will continue to depend upon foreign forms and resources and fail to thrust their roots down into the fertile soil of their own continent. The beauty and color of the Latin American culture can greatly enrich the Evangelical Church in its music, literature, architecture, and other integral parts of church life. The Church has already begun to integrate into its services typically Latin music which captures the heights and depths of Latin temperament and religious emotion, demonstrating the new vitality and Christ-consciousness of the recently converted in their various congregations. There is a danger, especially in city churches, that an adaptation of the gospel message and the church's liturgy to indigenous forms will stop here. National leaders as well as missionaries fear that too complete an adaptation will result in heresies. Thus they lean too closely on recognized European or North American systems.

Instead of trusting the mission or the missionaries for guidance in developing a truly Latin American Church, Latin American Evangelicals must learn to place their faith in the Holy Spirit, who makes all things new. If the believer can trust God for his salvation, then he can also trust God to lead him away from formal or foreign church practices into the enjoyment of the spiritual dynamic God grants to His people.

BASES FOR OPTIMISM AND POSSIBILITIES FOR THE FUTURE

One of the most oft-repeated criticisms of Latin American Evangelicalism has been that the Church is fractured into many competing denominations. One group of Churches doesn't respect another whose type of worship service varies from its own, or whose people seem to come from a different cultural background. As we came face to face, however, with the spontaneous enthusiasm and deep dedication of Christians of all denominations, we were forced to change many of our preconceived ideas about certain Churches. We were convinced that it is almost impossible to pin labels on people and/or groups and denominations. We found that Evangelicals who are considered to be liberal in doctrine think of themselves as conservative in every way. Churches we had considered to be isolationist we found to be actively seeking fellowship with Churches in the ecumenical movement, for example. We discovered that forms of worship strange to us may be equally valid means of praising God.

Let us take, for example, the Methodist churches we visited in and around Tomé, Chile. Here the churches are growing faster than their sister churches of the same denomination in other parts of the country. The ten or more Methodist churches around Tomé have an unusual vitality in their worship and maintain an effective outreach by means of a warm, spiritual expression of their faith. Their church music is lively, and their people feel a close relationship with God. These Methodist churches are located in an area where Pentecostal Churches also have made their biggest impact. Here the Methodists accept rather than repel certain "Pentecostal" manifestations.

Quite a controversy exists among many traditional Methodists concerning the way in which these sister Churches have chosen to express their new life. While some Methodist leaders are quite alarmed at the Pentecostal influence within their own denomination, others prefer to support these expressions of joyful witness, active lay participation, lively music, and expressive corporate worship. These men would endorse the friendly pattern of fellowship and community. One influential Methodist leader has gone so far as to suggest that the "Tomé image" of a church is the hope of the Methodist Church in Chile.

Or, let us look at the strange story of a man commissioned by God to go to Argentina as he knelt in prayer in his hotel room in Spokane, Washington. The Reverend Theodore ("Tommy") Hicks went to Argentina when Perón was still at the height of his power.

What happened in Buenos Aires after he had spent only 59 days in evangelistic and healing campaigns is almost beyond belief (*Christian Century* 1954: 814-815).

Many Evangelicals in Argentina, whether or not they agree with Hicks' theology, admit that his meetings broke the back of the rigid Argentine resistance to the Evangelical witness. All of Argentina heard and read about Tommy Hicks. Louis Stokes, field representative for the Assemblies of God, said that the Pentecostals had not grown in Argentina until the Hicks meetings. Afterward, there followed a complete change in the spiritual atmosphere of Argentina. A new generation of preachers were encouraged to enter cities all over Argentina and hold city-wide meetings. All the churches which participated in the evangelistic campaigns and which encouraged the practice of faith healing registered church growth.

Whether or not other campaigns stress healing, one of our greatest hopes for the growth of the Church in Latin America in the next decade is this type of mass evangelistic campaign. Congregations of different churches experience true revival as they learn the joy of working together. By 1980 there will be many nationwide denominational and interdenominational evangelistic endeavors which will probably be patterned after the successful Evangelism-in-Depth campaigns or the Baptist campaign of the Americas planned for 1969-70. Churches will have to make important decisions as they unite at the local level for these campaigns. Many more Evangelicals will be mobilized, and through joint action for mission multitudes will be given the option to accept Jesus Christ. Non-Pentecostals will have to decide whether to unite with Pentecostals in city-wide healing meetings, which will doubtless continue to draw large crowds. More than ever before, Pentecostals will unite with other Evangelical Churches for mass evangelism, benefiting all who participate. Cross-fertilization between old-line and Pentecostal denominations can be beneficial to those Evangelicals who are willing to learn from their Pentecostal brethren and to understand the Pentecostal pattern of growth. Where this happens, new, enthusiastic communities of faith emerge. Emotional worship experiences meet the needs of the members of the congregations and prepare them to return to their work *fired up,* empowered with a new spiritual vitality for witness.

In Brazil we visited many Baptist, Methodist, Congregational, Presbyterian, Mennonite, and other Churches where a warm Christian atmosphere prevailed. Here also corporate prayer, hearty congregational singing, and special services devoted to anointing the sick with oil were part of the life of all of these churches.

It has been the conversion of urban masses that more than anything else has created interdenominational understanding and appreciation. In the city Evangelicals of one group become acquainted with those of another, find their enthusiasm, Christian experience, and even their hymnology to be very similar if not identical, and it is here that they join together in mass evangelistic campaigns which further unite them.

Another basis for optimism for Latin American church growth in the next decade is the strong emphasis that all Churches now place upon youth. It is the youth who are most likely to be able to develop a truly Latin American Evangelical Church. They are the ones who speak of their faith in a new language and with a new idiom.

Many times the new expression of the gospel is characterized by energetic impatience, overabundance of hope, and impractical ideals. A young generation captured for Christ and coming under His control is the finest guarantee that the Church will grow. This is true in spite of the fact that young Evangelicals are very uneasy about what lies ahead. Yet theirs is a divine discontent.

The Church is not only capturing these young people for Christ, but is mobilizing them for evangelism. Special evangelistic campaigns in Argentina (led by men such as Hicks, Oswald Smith, Billy Graham, Aristia) have been the means for the enlistment of many capable and energetic young Argentines who have assisted in church growth. A promising group of young Evangelical nationals, trained in an atmosphere of optimism about the future of evangelism, have been sent out to plant churches in Uruguay, Paraguay, as well as other parts of Argentina.

In Bogotá, a lay pastor uses Bible school night students to begin churches in the urban districts. Recent migrants are won and are immediately put to work in their own areas of the city.

The Latin American Church has early learned to utilize its complete membership in evangelism. There are, however, certain other men who are a chosen few committed to more intense preparation for a more specific ministry. This level of training will be one of the great emphases of the next decade.

We have seen previously, for example, that the present system of ministerial training is inadequate throughout Latin America. Not enough leaders are taught, and those now in preparation are often not receiving instruction in what is most vital to their ministry. Leaders must be given more adequate training in church growth principles and procedures. Better preparation is needed for future pastors to face the uncertainties of current social change and effectively to evangelize receptive pockets in the subcultures of Latin society. If in their education the good insights of anthropology, sociology, and other related sciences are not fully utilized, church growth will suffer. All churchmen — nationals and missionaries —

who wish to see rapid and lasting expansion must have available scientific tools to probe, repair, and build the Church.

Developing leadership at every level demands costly decisions. Pentecostal churches feel the need for preparation of leaders on the Bible Institute level and are establishing many more of these schools throughout Latin America. Some Chilean Pentecostals seek a way whereby their ministers can receive a systematic theological education, but others fear that such a training will cool their evangelistic zeal and ardor. The role of the more than 300 Bible institutes and seminaries of all denominations presently training lay leaders and pastors in Latin America will become more crucial. The Guatemalan experiment (see Chapter Twenty-two, Ministerial Training), which is carrying theological training to the unpaid lay leaders of rural churches, will become a model for other training programs.

We may expect a large increase in the number of part-time ministers. We hope that ordained Protestant ministers in Latin America will exceed the total number of Roman Catholic priests by 1975. Despite strategy decisions that channel resources into other activities of supposedly higher priority, Evangelicals must do everything possible to increase the number of trained leaders. This is essential because the emerging ministerial candidates will shape the destiny not only of the Evangelical Churches but of much of Latin America itself.

Evangelization of Indian Tribes

A bright prospect for church growth in Latin America is the evangelization of Indian tribes. The Church will grow more rapidly as linguistic analysis and Scripture translation make the Bible available for the many Indian tribes of Latin America. Pioneer translation work has been done by a number of Wycliffe translators and denominational missionaries who have realized the great value of giving to all men the Word of God in their own tongue.

The Anglicans have done remarkable evangelistic work among the Indians of northern Argentina, doing Bible translation and literacy work as well as giving valuable assistance in the practical fields of agriculture, medicine, and education.

Similarly, in the State of Tabasco, Mexico, the Indian Church has multiplied rapidly. Here in 1932 the Marxist governor clamped down on religious observance, and the Roman Catholic and Protestant clergy were asked to leave. As a result lay people were obliged to "pass the word along." Because of the communistic political domination, the Presbyterian Church here received no ministerial leadership, Mexican or American, for the next seven years. But the underground network of lay witnesses energetically planted churches throughout Tabasco, and in twelve years' time a few hundred communicants grew to more than 10,000, all without a professional ministry (Bennett 1968).

Figure 84

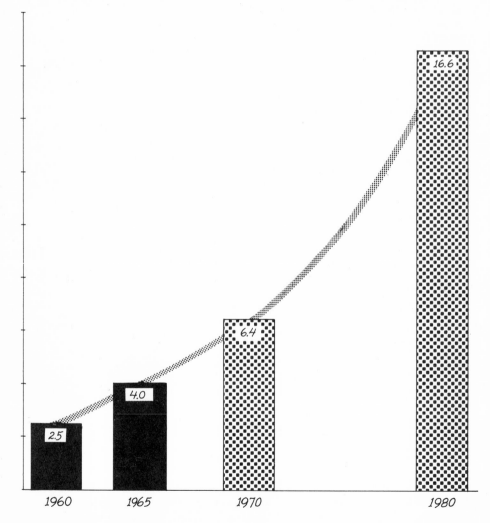

THE DECADE AHEAD: 1970-1980
PROJECTED GROWTH OF COMMUNICANT MEMBERS
OF EVANGELICAL CHURCHES IN LATIN AMERICA

2.5

4.0

6.4

16.6

1960   1965   1970   1980

PROJECTIONS BASED ON AVERAGE ANNUAL GROWTH RATE OF 10%.
FIGURES SHOWN IN MILLIONS.

One of the signs of health of the Otomí Indian Church in the State of Hidalgo in Mexico is the regular routine for teenage girls to collect foodstuffs from house to house for the support of Otomí missionaries to unconverted mountain-dwelling Otomís. The mother church already has forty daughter congregations.

It would be unfair not to recognize the role that missionaries are playing and will play in the next decade in the growth of the Latin American Evangelical Church. Many are concerned about their missionary role and activity in these times of radical change and are now ready to analyze their whole method of working. Some are beginning to use church growth methodology, incorporating new insights into plans and policies.

In the decade from 1970 to 1980, portions of the research techniques perfected by North American industry and commerce will be successfully adapted to the needs of Protestant leaders. New tools available through the social sciences will make it easier to analyze the problems that face Churches in society. These same tools will aid denominational planners in solving problems and planning adequate programs for multiplying churches in every subculture in Latin America. The systems approach of handling data will make possible more effective plans for carrying out the Church's task (MARC 1966: 3). Computers, mass media, and aerospace facilities will open brand-new communications options to Evangelicals in Latin America (Read 1967a:2-4). Unfortunately, not all Evangelical strategists will feel the need for, or be trained to use, these modern and sophisticated techniques. Moreover, these techniques at present are not widely available to assist churches in fulfilling their mandate for Christ. Nevertheless, the possibility of teaching, preaching, and communicating the gospel to millions is one of the liveliest options in Latin America today.

If the current growth rate does not decrease, Evangelical Churches in Latin America will have more than doubled in communicant membership in the ten-year period between 1960 and 1970. There is every reason to expect this to happen again in the decade between 1970 and 1980. If the Church continues to grow at the present rate, there will be over thirteen million communicant members by 1980. This will give the Evangelical community more than twenty-seven million members, or 8 per cent of the population.

*   *   *   *   *   *

A thousand assurances reinforce the conviction that the Evangelical Church has the capacity for growth in spite of the trials and testing of our time. The same conditions which threaten her also bring receptivity to new ideas, and herein lies hope. We believe that in the face of change the Church will surely grow.

BIBLIOGRAPHY

ABBOTT, Walter M., ed.
   1966   *The Documents of Vatican II*. New York, Guild Press, America Press, and Association Press (Angelus Book).
ABREO, Sylvio Fróes
   1957   *O Distrito Federal e seus recursos naturais*. Rio de Janeiro, Instituto Brasileira de Geografia e Estatística.
AB'SABER, Aziz Nacib, and BERNARDOS, Nilo
   1958   *Vale do Paraíba, serra da mantiqueira a arredores de São Paulo*. Rio de Janeiro, Conselho Nacional de Geografia.
ADAMS, Richard N.
   1965   "Social Organization: Introduction," in Heath and Adams (eds.), *Contemporary Cultures and Societies of Latin America*, pp. 257-287.
ADAMS, Richard N., ed.
   1965   See HEATH and ADAMS (eds.), *Contemporary Cultures and Societies of Latin America*.
ADAMS, Richard N., *et al.*
   1960   *Social Change in Latin America Today: Its Implications for United States Policy*. New York, Random House (Vintage Book).
ALET
   1967   "The Extension Seminary and the Programmed Textbook," report of workshop at Armenia, Colombia, Sept. 4-9 (1967). Pasadena, Asociación Latino-Americana de Escuelas Teológicas, Region del Norte.
ALEXANDER, Robert J.
   1962   *Today's Latin America*. Garden City, Doubleday & Company (Anchor Book).
ALLEN, Roland
   1962a *Missionary Methods: St. Paul's or Ours?* Grand Rapids, William B. Eerdmans.
   1962b *The Spontaneous Expansion of the Church*. Grand Rapids, William B. Eerdmans.
   1964   *Missionary Principles*. London, World Dominion Press.
   1965   *The Ministry of the Spirit: Selected Writings of Roland Allen* (David M. Paton, ed.). Grand Rapids, William B. Eerdmans.
ALONSO, Isidoro
   1964   *La Iglesia en America Latina*. Friburgo, FERES.
America
   1967   New York, 116.3 (Jan 21): 88-91.
América Latina
   1963   Rio de Janeiro (Centro Latinoamericano de investigaciones en ciencias sociales), 6.2: 43-45.
American Anthropologist
   1950   Washington, 52: 483-498.
American Journal of Sociology
   1953   Chicago, 59.2 (Sept): 136-143.
Anais do XXXI Congresso Internacional de Americanists
   1955   São Paulo: 357-376.

ANDERSON, Fletcher
1967 Letter to William R. Read (May 29). Buenos Aires, Council of Evangelization of the Methodist Church, Argentina Annual Conference.
ANDERSON, Gerald H., ed.
1961 *The Theology of Christian Mission.* New York, McGraw-Hill.
1967 *Christian Mission in Theological Perspective.* Nashville, Abingdon Press.
ANDERSON, Nels
1964 *Urbanism and Urbanization.* Leiden, Netherlands, E. J. Brill (International Studies in Sociology and Social Anthropology).
ANGELL, Robert
1945 See GOTTSCHALK, KLUCKHORN, and ANGELL, *The Use of Personal Documents in History, Anthropology, and Sociology.*
Annals of the American Academy of Political and Social Science
1958 Philadelphia, 316: 102-110, 111-119.
1961 Philadelphia, 334: 1-9, 10-19.
ANTUNES, Celso
1964 *Geografia do Brasil.* São Paulo, Editôra do Brasil (Third Edition).
ARBIZÚ, Francisco
1932 See WILLIAMS and ARBIZÚ, *Standard of Christian Doctrine and Practice.*
Archives de Sociologie des Religions.
1958 Paris (Groupe de Sociologie des Religions), 3.5 (Jan-June): 3-29, 31-37, 111-120.
ARCINIEGAS, German
1967 *Latin America: A Cultural History.* New York, Alfred A. Knopf.
ARENSBERG, Conrad M., and NIEHOFF, Arthur H.
1964 *Introducing Social Change: A Manual for Americans Overseas.* Chicago, Aldine Publishing Company.
AZEVEDO, Fernando de
1950 *Brazilian Culture: An Introduction to the Study of Culture in Brazil* (W. R. Crawford, trans.). New York, Macmillan.
AZEVEDO, Thales de
1963 *Social Change in Brazil.* Gainesville, University of Florida Press.

BÁEZ CAMARGO, G.
1956 "Church, State and Religious Liberty in Latin America," *World Dominion,* 34 (Jan): 29-32.
1957-58 "Protestantism in Latin America: Mexico," *Religion in Life,* 27.1 (Winter): 35-44.
BÁEZ CAMARGO, G., and GRUBB, Kenneth G.
1935 *Religion in the Republic of Mexico.* London, World Dominion Press (World Dominion Survey Series).
BALDUS, Herbert
1954 *Bibliografía crítica de etnología brasileira.* São Paulo, Comissão do IV centenário da cidadé de São Paulo.
BANTON, Michael, ed.
1966a *Anthropological Approaches to the Study of Religion.* London, Tavistock Publications.
1966b *The Social Anthropology of Complex Societies.* New York, Frederick A. Praeger (Vol. 4, A S A Monographs).
BARBIERI, Sante Uberto
1962 *El Pais de Eldorado* (Adam F. Sosa, trans.). Buenos Aires, Editorial la Aurora.
BARNETT, H. G.
1953 *Innovation: The Basis of Cultural Change.* New York, McGraw-Hill.

BARZINI, Luigi
1964 *The Italians.* New York, Atheneum Publishers (Bantam Book).
BASTIDE, Roger
1958 "Le Messianisme raté," *Archives de Sociologie des Religions,* 3.5 (Jan-June): 31-37.
1960 *Les Religions Afro-Brésiliennes.* Paris, Presses Universitaires de France.
BATES, M. Searle, and PAUCK, Wilhelm, eds.
1964 *The Prospects of Christianity Throughout the World.* New York, Charles Scribner's Sons.
BAVINCK, J. H.
1964 *An Introduction to the Science of Missions.* Philadelphia, Presbyterian and Reformed Publishing Company.
BEACH, Harlan P.
1916 *Renaissant Latin America: An Outline and Interpretation of the Congress on Christian work in Latin America, held at Panama, February 10-19, 1916.* New York, Missionary Education Movement of the United States and Canada.
BEACH, Harlan P., et al.
1900 *Protestant Missions in South America.* Chicago, Missionary Campaign Library.
BEALS, Carleton
1961 *Nomads and Empire Builders: Native Peoples and Cultures of South America.* New York, Citadel Press.
BEALS, Ralph L.
1965 "Social Stratification in Latin America," in Heath and Adams (eds.), *Contemporary Cultures and Societies of Latin America,* pp. 342-360.
BEAVER, R. Pierce
1953 "Theological Education in the Younger Churches." A report prepared for the Committee on Cooperation in Latin America (mimeographed).
1962 *Ecumenical Beginnings In Protestant World Mission: A History of Comity.* New York, Thomas Nelson & Sons.
BENDIX, Reinhard, and LIPSET, Seymour, eds.
1953 *Class, Status and Power.* Glencoe, Ill., The Free Press.
BENNETT, Charles
1967 "The Evangelical Church in Chiapas: A Preliminary Survey." An unpublished report prepared for Church Growth Research in Latin America, Fuller Theological Seminary, Pasadena.
1968 *Tinder in Tabasco.* Grand Rapids, William B. Eerdmans.
BENNETT, Mary A.
1959 See WALLIS and BENNETT, *Two Thousand Tongues to Go.*
BENNETT, Wendell C., and BIRD, Junius B.
1960 *Andean Culture History.* New York, American Museum of Natural History.
BERG, Daniel
n.d. *Enviado por Deus: Memórias do Daniel Berg.* São Paulo, Gráfica São José.
BERNARDES, Nilo
1958 See AB'SABER and BERNARDES, *Vale do Paraíba, serra da mantiqueira e arredores de São Paulo.*
BERNSTEIN, Harry
1942 "Some Inter-American Aspects of the Enlightenment," in Whitaker (ed.), *Latin America and the Enlightenment,* pp. 53-69.
BEYER, Glenn H., ed.
1967 *The Urban Explosion in Latin America: A Continent in Process of Modernization.* Ithaca, Cornell University Press.

BEYERHAUS, Peter, and LEFEVER, Henry
  1964 *The Responsible Church and the Foreign Mission*. Grand Rapids, William B. Eerdmans.
BINGLE, E. J., and GRUBB, Kenneth, eds.
  1952 *World Christian Handbook, 1952 Edition*. London, World Dominion Press.
  1957 *World Christian Handbook, 1957 Edition*. London, World Dominion Press.
BIRD, Junius B.
  1960 See BENNETT and BIRD, *Andean Culture History*.
BISIO, Julian A.
  1960 *La Gracia de Dios*. Buenos Aires, Libreria Editorial Cristiana S.R.L.
BLACK, Donald
  1965 *The Educator In Mission*. New York, United Presbyterian Church in the USA.
BLANKSTEN, George I.
  1961 "The Aspiration for Economic Development," *Annals of the American Academy of Political and Social Science*, 334 (March): 10-19.
BLOMBERG, Rolf
  1952 *Ecuador: Andean Mosaics*. Stockholm, H. Geber.
BOER, Harry R.
  1961 *Pentecost and Missions*. Grand Rapids, William B. Eerdmans.
BOLTON, Herbert Eugene
  1935 *History of the Americas*. Boston, Ginn and Company (New Edition).
BONILLA, Frank
  1964 "The Urban Worker," in Johnson (ed.), *Continuity and Change in Latin America*, pp. 186-205.
BORRIE, W. D.
  1959 *The Cultural Integration of Immigrants*. Paris, UNESCO.
BRAGA, Erasmo, and GRUBB, Kenneth G.
  1932 *The Republic of Brazil*. London, World Dominion Press (World Dominion Survey Series).
Brasil Presbiteriano
  1963 São Paulo, 6.15 (Nov 15-30): 7.
Brazilian Census, Protestant
  1960-67 *Estatística do culto Protestante do Brasil* (1957-1963). Rio de Janeiro, Serviço Gráfico do Instituto Brasileiro de Geografia e Estatística.
Brazilian Census, Roman Catholic
  1958-67 *Estatística do culto Catolico Romano do Brasil* (1955-1964). Rio de Janeiro, Serviço Gráfico do Instituto Brasileiro de Geografia e Estatística.
Brazilian Census, Spiritist
  1962-66 *Estatística do culto Espirita do Brasil* (1959-1963). Rio de Janeiro, Serviço Gráfico do Instituto Brasileiro de Geografia e Estatística.
BREESE, Gerald
  1966 *Urbanization in Newly Developing Countries*. Englewood Cliffs, Prentice-Hall (Modernization of Traditional Societies Series).
BRIGHAM, William T.
  1965 *Guatemala: The Land of the Quetzal*. Gainesville, University of Florida Press.
BROWN, Arthur Judson
  1936 *One Hundred Years*. New York, Fleming H. Revell (Second Edition, Book One).
BROWNING, Harley L.
  1958 "Recent Trends in Latin American Urbanization," *Annals of the American Academy of Political and Social Science*, 316: 111-119.

BROWNING, Webster E.
1925   *New Days in Latin America*. New York, Missionary Education Movement in the United States and Canada.
1928   *The River Plate Republics*. London, World Dominion Press (World Dominion Survey Series).
BROWNING, Webster E., RITCHIE, John, and GRUBB, Kenneth G.
1930   *The West Coast Republics of South America*. London, World Dominion Press (World Dominion Survey Series).
BUCAFUSCO, Luis P.
1955   *Laicos activos: iglésia viva*. Buenos Aires, Libreria La Aurora.
BURGDORF, Aug.
1925   *Dispelling the Spiritual Gloom in South American Forests and Pampas*, Vol. 2 (L. Fuerbringer, ed.), *Men and Missions*. St. Louis, Concordia Publishing House.
BURNS, E. Bradford
1966   *A Documentary History of Brazil*. New York, Alfred A. Knopf.
BURSK, Edward C., and CHAPMAN, John F., eds.
1963   *New Decision-Making Tools for Managers: Mathematical Programming as an Aid in the Solving of Business Problems*. New York, The New American Library.
BUTLAND, Gilbert J.
1960   *Latin America: A Regional Geography*. New York, John Wiley and Sons.
BUTLER, Charles
1964   "Protestant Growth and a Changing Panama: A Study of Foursquare Gospel and Methodist Patterns." An unpublished thesis, Perkins School of Theology, Southern Methodist University, Dallas.

CALDERON, Luis
1963   *Problemas de urbanización en América Latina*. Friburgo, FERES (Estudios sociológicos latino-americanos).
CALLOW, Kathleen
1962   *Ploughing in Hope*. Santa Ana, California, Wycliffe Bible Translators.
CALMAN, Richard, ed.
1966   See LYLE and CALMAN (eds.), *Statistical Abstract of Latin America, 1965*.
CAMARGO, Ferreira de
1961   *Kardecismo e Umbanda*. São Paulo, Livraria Pioneira Editora.
CANDIDO, Antonio
1951   "The Brazilian Family," in Smith and Marchant (eds.), *Brazil, Portrait of a Half Continent*.
CARNEIRO, Edison
1948   *Candombles da Bahia*. Bahia, Brazil, Publicações do Museu do Estado.
1964   *Ladinos e Crioulos: Estudos sobre o negro no Brasil*. Rio de Janeiro, Editôra Civilização Brasileira.
CASCUDO, Luis da Camara
1965   *Made in Africa*. Rio de Janeiro, Editôra Civilização Brasileira.
CASTELLAN, Yvonne
1962   *El Espiritismo*. Buenos Aires, Compañia General Fabril Editora.
CASTRO, Emilio
1963   "Christian Response to the Latin American Revolution," *Christianity and Crisis*, 23.15 (Sept. 16): 160-163.
CCPAL
1963   *La Naturaleza de la Iglésia y su misión en Latinoamérica*. Bogotá, Congreso Continental de Estudios, Comité de Cooperación Presbiteriana de América Latina.

CEDEC
1966   "Censo de la obra evangélica en Colombia: 1966, Parte I: Introducción y membresia, Parte II: Formas de servício y ministério." Bogotá, Colombia, Confederación Evangélica de Colombia.
1967   "Censo de los miembros de la Iglésia Evangélica en Colombia: 1967." Bogotá, Confederación Evangélica de Colombia.

CHAPMAN, John F., ed.
1963   See BURSK and CHAPMAN (eds.), New Decision-Making Tools for Managers.

CHASE MANHATTAN BANK OF N.A.
1967   "Urbanization in Latin America." New York, Economic Research Division, Chase Manhattan Bank (mimeographed).

CHERRY, Thomas James
1957   "A Review of the Indigenous Church Principle in Latin America in the Light of Changing World Conditions." An unpublished Master's thesis, Fuller Theological Seminary, Pasadena.

CHEVALIER, François
1963   Land and Society in Colonial Mexico: The Great Hacienda (Alvin Eustis, trans.). Berkeley, University of California Press.

CHIRGWIN, A. M.
1954   The Bible in World Evangelism. London, SCM Press.

Christian Centufy
1954   "But What About Hicks?" (editorial), Christian Century. Chicago, 71.27 (July 7): 814-815.
1968   "Latin America Today" (special issue), Christian Century. Chicago, 85.3 (Jan 17).

Christianity and Crisis
1963   New York, 23.15: 160-163; 23.21: 224-228.

Christianity Today
1963   "Tempest in Latin America" (special issue). Washington, 7.21 (July 19).

Churchman
1967   London, 81.2 (Summer): 114-128.

CIDOC
1965   Latin America in Maps, Charts and Tables (No. 3, Socio-Educational Data). Cuernavaca, The Center of Intercultural Documentation.

CIF
1963   Latin America in Maps, Charts and Tables (No. 1, Socio-Economic Data; No. 2, Socio-Religious Data). New York, Center of Intercultural Formation (Fordham University).

CIF Reports
1965-66   Cuernavaca, Mexico (Center of Intercultural Documentation—CIDOC), Vols. 4-5.

CLARK, Elmer T.
1949   The Small Sects in America. New York, Abingdon Press.

CLARK, Francis E., and CLARK, Harriet A.
1909   The Gospel in Latin Lands. New York, Macmillan.

CLARK, R. B.
1938   Under the Southern Cross: The Story of Alliance Missions in South America. Harrisburg, Pa., Christian Publications.

CLEH
1963   Situación económica y social del Uruguay rural. Montevideo, Centro Latinoamericana de Economía Humana.

CLEMMER, Myrtle
1961   See RYCROFT and CLEMMER, A Statistical Study of Latin America.

1962 See RYCROFT and CLEMMER, *A Study of Urbanization in Latin America.*

1963 See RYCROFT and CLEMMER, *A Factual Study of Latin America.*

CLISSOLD, Stephen

1966 *Latin America: A Cultural Outline.* New York, Harper & Row (Harper Colophon Book).

COGGINS, Wade T., ed.

1961 See TAYLOR and COGGINS (eds.), *Protestant Missions in Latin America.*

COLLIER, John

1947 *Indians of the Americas.* New York, The New American Library (Mentor Book) (Abridged).

COMMITTEE OF THE ROYAL ANTHROPOLOGICAL INSTITUTE OF GREAT BRITAIN AND IRELAND

1964 *Notes and Queries on Anthropology.* London, Routledge and Kegan Paul.

CONDE, Emílio

1951 *Pentecoste para todos: Doutrina do Espírito Santo.* Rio de Janeiro, Casa Publicadora da Assembléias de Deus.

1960 *História das Assembléias de Deus no Brasil.* Rio de Janeiro, Casa Publicadora das Assembléias de Deus.

CONGREGAÇÃO CRISTÃ NO BRASIL

1957-65 *Relatório e balanço—1956,* 1958, 1961, 1962, 1963, 1964. São Paulo, Congregação Cristã no Brasil.

1962 *Breve história, fé, doutrina e estatutos.* São Paulo, Congregação Cristã no Brasil.

CONN, Charles W.

1959 *Where the Saints Have Trod: A History of the Church of God Missions.* Cleveland, Tenn., Pathway Press.

CONSIDINE, John J., ed.

1964 *The Church in the New Latin America.* Notre Dame, Fides.

1965 *Social Revolution in the New Latin America* (A Catholic Appraisal). Notre Dame, Fides.

1966 *The Religious Dimension in the New Latin America.* Notre Dame, Fides.

Conviction

1967 Los Angeles (Fellowship Press), 5.1: 8-9; 5.7: 8-9.

COOK, Harold R.

1954 *An Introduction to the Study of Christian Missions.* Chicago, Moody Press.

1967 *Highlights of Christian Missions: A History and Survey.* Chicago, Moody Press.

COREY, Stephen J.

1925 *Among South American Friends: The Journal of a Visit to South America.* Cincinnati, Powell & White.

CORREDOR, Berta

1962 *La Familia en America Latina.* Friburgo, FERES (Estudios sociológicos latino-americanos).

CORREDOR, Berta, and TORRES, Sergio

1961 *Transformación en el mundo rural latino-americano.* Friburgo, FERES (Documentos latino-americanos).

COX, Harvey

1966 "Mission In A World Of Cities," *International Review of Missions,* 55 (July): 273-281.

COXILL, H. Wakelin, and GRUBB, Kenneth, eds.

1962 *World Christian Handbook, 1962 Edition.* London, World Dominion Press.

1967   *World Christian Handbook 1968*. London, Lutterworth Press.

CRABTREE, A. R.
   1953   *Baptists in Brazil*. Rio de Janeiro, Baptist Publishing House.

CRANE, James D.
   c1961   "What We Can Learn from the Assemblies of God in El Salvador." An unpublished report to the Foreign Mission Board, Southern Baptist Convention (mimeographed).

Cristianismo y sociedad
   1965-66   Montevideo, 3.9-4.10: 19-43.

DA CUNHA, Euclides
   1944   *Rebellion in the Backlands*. Chicago, University of Chicago Press.

DAMBORIENA, Prudencio
   1962   *El Protestantismo en America Latina: Tomo I, Etapas y metodes del protestantismo latino-americano*. Madrid, FERES (Estudios socio-religiosos latino-americanos).
   1963   *El Protestantismo en America Latina: Tomo II, La situación del protestantismo en los paises latino-americanos*. Friburgo, FERES (Estudios socio-religiosos latino-americanos).

DANIELS, Margarette
   1916   *Makers of South America*. New York, Missionary Education Movement of the United States and Canada.

D'ANTONIO, William V., and PIKE, Frederick B., eds.
   1964   *Religion, Revolution, and Reform: New Forces for Change in Latin America*. New York, Frederick A. Praeger.

DAVIS, J. Merle
   1939   *The Economic and Social Environment of the Younger Churches*. London, Edinburgh House Press.
   1940   *The Economic Basis of the Evangelical Church in Mexico*. London, International Missionary Council.
   1942a   *The Church in Puerto Rico's Dilemma*. New York, International Missionary Council.
   1942b   *The Cuban Church in a Sugar Economy*. New York, International Missionary Council.
   1943   *How The Church Grows In Brazil*. New York, International Missionary Council.
   1947   *New Buildings On Old Foundations*. New York, International Missionary Council.

DAYTON, Edward R.
   1966   "Computerize Evangelism?" *World Vision Magazine*, 10.3: 4-5.

DEBRAY, Régis
   1967   *Revolution in the Revolution? Armed Struggle and Political Struggle in Latin America* (Bobbye Ortiz, trans.). New York, Grove Press.

DEBUYST, Federico
   1961   *La Población en América Latina: Demografía y evolución del empleo*. Friburgo, FERES.

D'ECA, Raul
   1963   See WILGUS and D'ECA, *Latin American History*.

DE JESUS, Carolina Maria
   1962   *Child of the Dark: The Diary of Carolina Maria de Jesus* (David St. Clair, trans.). New York, The New American Library (Signet Book).

DEPARTMENT OF THE ARMY
   1961   *Area Handbook for Colombia*. Washington, U.S. Government Printing Office.

1964   *Area Handbook for Venezuela.* Washington, U.S. Government Printing
       Office.
1966   *Area Handbook for Ecuador.* Washington, U.S. Government Printing
       Office.
DIEGUES, Manuel, Jr.
1960   *Regiões culturais do Brasil.* Rio de Janeiro, Centro Brasileira de Pes-
       quisas Educacionais.
DILWORTH, Donald R.
1967   "The Evangelization of the Quichuas of Ecuador." An unpublished thesis,
       School of World Mission and Institute of Church Growth, Fuller Theo-
       logical Seminary, Pasadena.
DOLESH, Daniel Emeric
n.d.   *The Church in Latin America Today: Its History, Its Crisis, Its Future.*
       Davenport, Iowa, Latin America Bureau, National Catholic Welfare
       Conference.
DORSELAER, Jaime, and GREGORY, Alfonso
1962   *La Urbanización en América Latina: Tomo I, Descripción del fenómeno
       de urbanización en América Latina; Tomo II, Interpretación del fen-
       ómeno de urbanización en América Latina.* Friburgo, FERES (Estudios
       sociológicos latino-americanos).
DOZER, Donald Marquand, ed.
1965   *The Monroe Doctrine: Its Modern Significance.* New York, Alfred A.
       Knopf.
DUEY, Charles J.
1965   *Covenant Missions in Ecuador.* Chicago, Board of Missions of the Evan-
       gelical Covenant Church of America.
du PLESSIS, David J.
1958   "Golden Jubilee of Twentieth-Century Pentecostal Movements," *Inter-
       national Review of Missions,* 47 (April): 193-201.
DWIGHT, Henry Otis
1905   *The Blue Book of Missions for 1905.* New York, Funk & Wagnalls.

Ecumenical Review
1964   Geneva (WCC), 16.2: 195-199.
1968   Geneva (WCC), 20.1: 16-32.
Ekklesia
1960   José C. Paz, Arg., 4.6 (April): 8-20.
1965   José C. Paz, Arg., 9.19 (April): 35-45.
EMERY, James
1963   "The Preparation of Leaders in a Ladino-Indian Church," *Practical
       Anthropology,* 10.3 (May-June): 127-134.
Encounter
1965   London (Spender, Lasky, eds.), 25.3 (Sept): 41-49.
ENNS, Arno W.
1967   "Profiles of Argentine Church Growth." An unpublished thesis, School
       of World Mission and Institute of Church Growth, Fuller Theological
       Seminary, Pasadena.
ESTEP, W. R.
1962   "Church and Culture in Latin America," *Southwestern Journal of The-
       ology,* 4.2 (April): 27-47.
EUDALY, Nathan Hoyt
1959   "A Critical Evaluation of Leadership for Baptist Churches in Spanish
       America." An unpublished thesis, Southwestern Baptist Theological
       Seminary, Forth Worth.

Evangelical Missions Quarterly
1966   Springfield, Pa., 3.1 (Fall): 21-31.
1968   Springfield, Pa., 4.2 (Winter): 75-88.

FARON, Louis C.
1959   See STEWARD and FARON, *Native Peoples of South America*.
1964   *Hawks of the Sun: Mapuche Morality and Its Ritual Attributes*. Pittsburgh, University of Pittsburgh Press.

FEDERACIÓN DE IGLÉSIAS EVANGÉLICAS DEL URUGUAY
1965a *Aspectos religiosos de la sociedad uruguaya*. Montevideo, Centro de Estudios Cristianos de la FIEU.
1965b *Hombre, ideologia y revolución en América Latina*. Montevideo, Iglesia y Sociedad en America Latina de la FIEU.

FIFE, Eric S., and GLASSER, Arthur F.
1961   *Missions in Crisis: Rethinking Missionary Strategy*. Chicago, Inter-Varsity Press.

FISHER, Sydney Nettleton, ed.
1964   See TEPASKE and FISHER (eds.), *Explosive Forces in Latin America*.

FLEMING, Daniel J.
1925   *Whither Bound in Missions?* New York, Association Press.

FREEDMAN, Ronald, ed.
1964   *Population: The Vital Revolution*. Garden City, Doubleday & Company (Anchor Book).

FREITAS, Byron Torres de, and PINTO, Tancredo da Silva
n.d.   *Camba de Umbanda*. Rio de Janeiro, Gráfica Editora Aurora.

FRETZ, Joseph Winfield
1953   *Pilgrims in Paraguay: The Story of Mennonite Colonization in South America*. Scottdale, Pa., Herald Press.

FREYRE, Gilberto
1963   *New World in the Tropics: The Culture of Modern Brazil*. New York, Random House (Vintage Book).
1964   *The Masters and the Slaves: A Study in the Development of Brazilian Civilization* (Samuel Putnam, trans.). New York, Alfred A. Knopf (Borzoi Book).
1966   *The Mansions and the Shanties: The Making of Modern Brazil* (Harriet de Onís, trans.). New York, Alfred A. Knopf (Borzoi Book).

Frontier
1960   London, 3 (Autumn): 214-216, 220-223.

FUNES, D. Gregorio
1910-11 *Ensayo de la historica civil del Paraguay, Buenos Aires y Tucumán* (Vols. 1, 2). Buenos Aires, Talleres Gráficos.

FURTADO, Celso
1963   *The Economic Growth of Brazil: A Survey from Colonial to Modern Times* (Aguiar and Drysdale, trans.). Berkeley, University of California Press.

GALVÃO, Eduardo
1955   *Santos e visagens, um estudo da vida religiosa de Itá, Amazonas*. São Paulo, Companhia Editora Nacional.

GANZ, Emilio H.
1958   See TRON and GANZ, *Historica de la colonias Valdenses Sudamericanas en su primer centenário (1858-1958)*.

GAXIOLA LOPEZ, Maclovio
1964   *Historia de la Iglésia Apostólica de la Fé en Cristo Jesus de Mexico*. Mexico, Libreria Latinoamericana.

GEIGER, Pedro Pinchas
1956 *Urbanização e industrialização na orla oriental da baia de Guanabara.* Rio de Janeiro, Instituto Brasileiro de Geografia e Estatística.
GENSICHEN, Hans-Werner
1966 *Living Mission: The Test of Faith.* Philadelphia, Fortress Press.
GERASSI, John
1965 *The Great Fear in Latin America.* New York, Collier Books (New, Revised Edition).
GIBBONS, William J., ed.
1956 *Basic Ecclesiastical Statistics for Latin America 1956.* Maryknoll, N. Y., World Horizon Reports.
GIBBS, Jack P., ed.
1961 *Urban Research Methods.* Princeton, D. Van Nostrand.
GIL, Federico G.
1966 *The Political System of Chile.* Boston, Houghton Mifflin.
GILL, Clark C.
1966 *Education and Social Change in Chile.* Washington, U.S. Government Printing Office.
GILLIN, John P.
1960 See ADAMS, *et al., Social Change in Latin America Today.*
1965 "Ethos Components in Modern Latin American Culture," in Heath and Adams (eds.), *Contemporary Cultures and Societies of Latin America,* pp. 503-517.
GILLMORE, Maria McIlvaine
1926 See WHEELER, W. Reginald, *et al., Modern Missions in Chile and Brazil.*
GIST, Noel P., and HALBERT, L. A.
1961 *A Cidade e o homen: A Sociedade urbana* (Vols. 1, 2). Rio de Janeiro, Editora Fundo de Cultura.
GLASS, Frederick C.
n.d. *Through Brazilian Jungleland with the Book, or, Revolutionaries Abroad.* London, Pickering & Inglis.
n.d. *Through the Heart of Brazil.* London, Evangelical Union of South America.
1943 *Adventures with the Bible in Brazil.* New York, Loizeaux Brothers.
GLASSER, Arthur F.
1961 See FIFE and GLASSER, *Missions in Crisis.*
GLOVER, Robert Hall
1946 *The Bible Basis of Missions.* Los Angeles, Bible House of Los Angeles.
1960 *The Progress of World-Wide Missions.* New York, Harper & Row.
GODDARD, Burton L., ed.
1967 *The Encyclopedia of Modern Christian Missions.* Camden, N. J., Thomas Nelson & Sons.
GOFF, James E.
1965 "Persecution of Protestants in Colombia." An unpublished dissertation, San Francisco Theological Seminary, San Anselmo.
GOLDRICH, Daniel
1965 "Toward the Comparative Study of Politicization in Latin America," in Heath and Adams (eds.), *Contemporary Cultures and Societies of Latin America,* pp. 361-378.
GOLDSCHMIDT, Walter
1950 "Social Class in America—A Critical Review," *American Anthropologist,* 52: 483-498.
GOODENOUGH, Ward Hunt
1966 *Cooperation in Change: An Anthropological Approach to Community*

Development. New York, John Wiley & Sons (Science Edition).
GOTTSCHALK, Louis, KLUCKHORN, Clyde, and ANGELL, Robert
1945 *The Use of Personal Documents in History, Anthropology, and Sociology.* New York, Social Science Research Council (Bulletin 53).
GREGORY, Alfonso
1962 See DORSELAER and GREGORY, *La Urbanización en América Latina.*
1965 *A Igreja no Brasil.* Lovaina, Colombia, FERES.
GRUBB, Kenneth G.
1927 *The Lowland Indians of Amazonia.* London, World Dominion Press (World Dominion Survey Series).
1930 See BROWNING, RITCHIE, and GRUBB, *The West Coast Republics of South America.*
1931 *The Northern Republics of South America.* London, World Dominion Press (World Dominion Survey Series).
1932 See BRAGA and GRUBB, *The Republic of Brazil.*
1935 See BÁEZ CAMARGO and GRUBB, *Religion in the Republic of Mexico.*
1936 *An Advancing Church in Latin America.* London, World Dominion Press.
1937 *Religion in Central America.* London, World Dominion Press (World Dominion Survey Series).
1939 [Review of Ten Years Evangelical Progress to 1938. Misc. Latin America Supplements to World Dominion Survey Series.] London, World Dominion Press.
1960 "Evangelical Religion in Brazil," *Frontier,* 3 (Autumn): 220-223.
GRUBB, Kenneth, ed.
1949 *World Christian Handbook, 1949 Edition.* London, World Dominion Press.
1952 See BINGLE and GRUBB (eds.), *World Christian Handbook.*
1957 See BINGLE and GRUBB (eds.), *World Christian Handbook.*
1962 See COXILL and GRUBB (eds.), *World Christian Handbook.*
1967 See COXILL and GRUBB (eds.), *World Christian Handbook.*

HADDOX, Benjamin E.
1965 *Sociedad y religion en Colombia.* Bogotá, Antares-Tercer Mundo.
HAHN, Ferdinand
1965 *Mission in the New Testament.* Naperville, Ill., Alec R. Allenson (Studies in Biblical Theology, No. 47).
HALBERT, L. A.
1961 See GIST and HALBERT, *A Cidade e o Homen: A Sociedade urbana.*
HAMILTON, Keith E.
1962 *Church Growth in the High Andes.* Lucknow, India, Lucknow Publishing House (available at the Bookstore, Fuller Theological Seminary, Pasadena).
HANKE, Lewis
1949 *The Spanish Struggle for Justice in the Conquest of America.* Philadelphia, University of Pennsylvania Press.
1964 *Do the Americas Have a Common History? A Critique of the Bolton Theory.* New York, Alfred A. Knopf.
1967a *Mexico and the Caribbean: Modern Latin America Continent in Ferment* (Vol. 1). Princeton, D. Van Nostrand Company (Second Edition).
1967b *South America: Modern Latin America Continent in Ferment* (Vol. 2). Princeton, D. Van Nostrand Company (Second Edition).
HARR, Wilbur C., ed.
1962 *Frontiers of the Christian World Mission Since 1938.* New York, Harper and Brothers.

HARRIS, Marvin
1952 "Race relations in Minas Velhas: a community in the mountain region of Central Brazil," in Wagley (ed.), *Race and Class in Rural Brazil,* pp. 47-81.
1956 *Town and Country in Brazil.* New York, Columbia University Press.
1958 See WAGLEY and HARRIS, *Minorities in the New World.*
1964 *Patterns Of Race In The Americas.* New York, Walker and Company.
1965 See WAGLEY and HARRIS, "A Typology of Latin American Subcultures."
HARRIS, Marvin, and KOTTAK, Conrad
1963 "The Structural Significance of Brazilian Racial Categories," *Sociologia,* 25: 203-209.
HASELDEN, Kyle
1964 *Death of a Myth: New Locus for Spanish American Faith.* New York, Friendship Press.
HASSE, Elemer
1964 *Luz sôbre o fenômeno pentecostal.* São Paulo, Imprensa Metodista.
HAUSER, Philip M., ed.
1964 *Handbook for Social Research in Urban Areas.* Paris, UNESCO.
HEATH, Dwight B., and ADAMS, Richard N., eds.
1965 *Contemporary Cultures and Societies of Latin America.* New York, Random House.
HERRICK, Bruce H.
1965 *Urban Migration and Economic Development in Chile.* Cambridge, Massachusetts Institute of Technology Press.
HERRING, Hubert
1968 *A History of Latin America: From the Beginnings to the Present.* New York, Alfred A. Knopf (Third Edition).
HERSKOVITS, Melville J.
1965 "African Gods and Catholic Saints in New World Religious Belief," in Lessa and Vogt (eds.), *Reader In Comparative Religion,* pp. 541-546.
HIGH, Stanley
1925 *Looking Ahead with Latin America.* New York, Missionary Education Movement of the United States and Canada.
HIRSCHMAN, Albert O.
1963 *Journeys Toward Progress.* Garden City, Doubleday & Company (Anchor Book).
HISPANIC FOUNDATION
1966 *National Directory of Latin Americanists.* Washington, Hispanic Foundation, Reference Department, Library of Congress.
HODGES, Melvin L.
1953 *The Indigenous Church.* Springfield, Mo., Gospel Publishing House.
HOGG, William Richey
1952 *Ecumenical Foundations.* New York, Harper & Brothers.
1960 *One World, One Mission.* New York, Friendship Press.
HOLMBERG, Allan R.
1960 See ADAMS, *et al., Social Change in Latin America Today.*
HOOVER, W. C.
1931 *Historia del Avivamiento Pentecostal en Chile.* Santiago, published by the author.
HOPEWELL, James F.
1967 "Mission and Seminary Structure," *International Review of Missions,* 56 (April): 158-163.
HORNER, Norman A.
1965 *Cross and Crucifix in Mission.* New York, Abingdon Press.

HORTON, Arthur G.
  1966   *An Outline of Latin American History.* Dubuque, Iowa, Wm. C. Brown.
HOUTART, François
  1964a *El Cambio social en América Latina.* Brussels, FERES (Estudios socio-
          lógicos latino-americanos).
  1964b "The Master Plan Arrives in Latin America," in Considine (ed.), *The
          Church in the New Latin America*, pp. 52-63.
HOUTART, François, and PIN, Emile
  1965   *The Church and the Latin American Revolution* (Gilbert Barth, trans.).
          New York, Sheed and Ward.
HOWARD, George P.
  1944   *Religious Liberty in Latin America?* Philadelphia, Westminster Press.
HUDSPITH, Margarita Allan
  1958   *Ripening Fruit: A History of the Bolivian Indian Mission.* Plainfield,
          Bolivian Indian Mission (now Andes Evangelical Mission).
HUEGEL, John
  c1963   "A Bridge into Mexico." An unpublished report of Evangelical Churches
          in Ciudad Juarez, prepared for Disciples of Christ, El Paso, Texas
          (mimeographed).
  1963   See McGAVRAN, HUEGEL, and TAYLOR, *Church Growth In Mexico.*
HULBERT, Winifred
  1935   *Latin American Backgrounds.* New York, Friendship Press.
HUMPHREYS, R. A., and LYNCH, John
  1965   *The Origins of the Latin American Revolutions, 1808—1826.* New York,
          Alfred A. Knopf.
HUTCHINSON, Bertram
  1963   "The Migrant Population of Urban Brazil," *America Latina*, 6.2 (April-
          June): 43-45.
HUTCHINSON, Harry William
  1957   *Village and Plantation Life in Northeastern Brazil.* Seattle, University
          of Washington Press.

IBGE
  1963   *Tipos e aspectos do Brasil.* Rio de Janeiro, Instituto Brasileiro de
          Geografia e Estatística.
IGREJA METODISTA DO BRASIL
  1961-65 *Atas e documentos do concilio da 2ª Região Eclesiástica.*
          Pôrto Alegre, Casa Publicadora Concórdia S.A.
ILLICH, Ivan
  1967   "The Seamy Side of Charity," *America*, 116.3 (Jan 21): 88-91.
IMAZ, Jose Luis de
  1964   *Los que mandan.* Buenos Aires, Editorial Universitaria de Buenos Aires.
International Review of Missions
  1958   London (IMC), 47: 193-201.
  1966   Geneva (WCC), 55: 273-281, 307-312.
  1967   Geneva (WCC), 56: 158-163, 185-192.
ISAIS, Juan M.
  1966   *The Other Side of the Coin.* Grand Rapids, William B. Eerdmans.
ISAL
  1961   *Encuentro y desafio: La Acción Cristiana Evangélica Latinoamericana
          ante la cambiante situación social, política y económica.* Montevideo,
          Iglésia y sociedad en America Latina.

JAMES, Preston E.
1942 *Latin America*. New York, Lothrop, Lee and Shepard.
1964 *Introduction to Latin America: The Geographic Background of Economic and Political Problems*. New York, Odyssey.

JENSEN, Alfredo
1965 "La Congregación de immigrantes como base de la misión," *Ekklesia*, 9.19 (April): 35-45.

JOHNSON, Harmon A.
1967a "Latin America—Background for Revival," *Conviction*, 5.1: 8-9.
1967b "What Is the Secret of the Growth of the Brazilian Church?" *Conviction*, 5.7: 8-9.
1968 "Research Is the Key to Church Development," *Evangelical Missions Quarterly*, 4.2 (Winter): 75-88.

JOHNSON, John J.
1958 *Political Change In Latin America: The Emergence of the Middle Sectors*. Stanford, Stanford University Press.

JOHNSON, John J., ed.
1964 *Continuity and Change in Latin America*. Stanford, Stanford University Press.

JOHNSTON, James, ed.
1888 *Report of the Centenary Conference on the Protestant Missions of the World, London, 1888* (2 vols.). New York, Fleming H. Revell.

JONES, Clarence F.
1930 *South America*. New York, Henry Holt.

JONES, Emrys
1966 *Towns and Cities*. New York, Oxford University Press.

JORDAN, David C.
1966 See WHITAKER and JORDAN, *Nationalism in Contemporary Latin America*.

Journal for the Scientific Study of Religion
1967 Washington (Soc. for the Scientific Study of Religion), 6.2: 253-258.

KEEN, Benjamin, ed.
1967 *Readings in Latin American Civilization: 1492 to the Present*. Boston, Houghton Mifflin.

KESSLER, J. B. A.
1967 *A Study of the Older Protestant Missions and Churches in Peru and Chile*. Goes, The Netherlands, Oosterbaan & le Cointre.

KINGSBURY, Robert C., and SCHNEIDER, Ronald M.
1965 *An Atlas of Latin American Affairs*. New York, Frederick A. Praeger.

KLOPPENBURG, Boaventura
1964 *O Espiritismo no Brasil*. Petropolis, R. J., Editora Vozes Limitada.
1966 "The Prevalence of Spiritism in Brazil," in Considine (ed.), *The Religious Dimension in the New Latin America*, pp. 77-87.

KLUCKHORN, Clyde
1945 See GOTTSCHALK, KLUCKHORN, and ANGELL, *The Use of Personal Documents in History, Anthropology, and Sociology*.

KOHDA, Takako, ed.
1967 See ROBERTS and KOHDA (eds.), *Statistical Abstract of Latin America, 1966*.

KOTTAK, Conrad
1963 See HARRIS and KOTTAK, "The Structural Significance of Brazilian Racial Categories."

LABELLE, Yvan
  1964 See RAMIREZ and LABELLE, El Problema sacerdotal en America
        Latina.
LACY, Creighton, ed.
  1965 Christianity Amid Rising Men and Nations. New York, Association Press.
LALIVE d'EPINAY, Christian
  1965-66 "La Expansion protestante en Chile," Cristianismo y sociedad, 3.9-4.10:
        19-43.
  1967 "The Training of Pastors and Theological Education: The Case of
        Chile," International Review of Missions, 56 (April): 185-192.
  1968 "The Pentecostal 'Conquista' in Chile," Ecumenical Review, 20.1 (Jan):
        16-32.
LAMBERT, Jacques
  1967 Latin America: Social Structure and Political Institutions (Helen Katel,
        trans.). Berkeley, University of California Press.
LAMEGO, Alberto Ribeiro
  1963 O Homen e a serra. Rio de Janeiro, Instituto Brasileiro de Geografia
        e Estatística.
LANTERNARI, Vittorio
  1963 The Religions of the Oppressed (Lisa Sergio, trans.). New York, The
        New American Library (Mentor Book).
LARA-BRAUD, Jorge
  1964 See WONDERLY and LARA-BRAUD, "Los Evangélicos somos así?"
Latin America Evangelist
  1967 Bogota, N. J., 47.3 (May-June): 6-8.
Latin American Digest
  1967 Tempe (Center for Latin American Studies, Arizona State University),
        Vol. 1.
Latin American Research Review
  1966 Austin, Texas (Latin American Research Review Board).
LEBER, Charles T., ed.
  1951 World Faith in Action. Indianapolis, Bobbs-Merrill.
LEFEVER, Henry
  1964 See BEYERHAUS and LEFEVER, The Responsible Church and the
        Foreign Mission.
LÉONARD, Émile G.
  1963 O Protestantismo Brasileiro: Estudo de eclesiologia e história social.
        São Paulo, Asociação de Seminários Teológicas Evangélicas.
LESLIE, Ruth R.
  1923 "The Protestant Movement In Mexico." An unpublished thesis, School
        of Missions, Northwest Christian College, Eugene, Oregon.
LESSA, William A., and VOGT, Evon Z.
  1965 Reader In Comparative Religion: An Anthropological Approach. New
        York, Harper & Row (Second Edition).
LEWIS, Oscar
  1959 Five Families. New York, Basic Books.
  1960 See ADAMS, et al., Social Change in Latin America Today.
  1961 The Children of Sanchez: Autobiography of a Mexican Family. New
        York, Random House (Vintage Book).
  1964 Pedro Martinez: A Mexican Peasant and His Family. New York, Ran-
        dom House.
  1965 "Urbanization Without Breakdown: A Case Study," in Heath and Adams
        (eds.), Contemporary Cultures and Societies of Latin America, pp.
        424-437.

LIEUWEN, Edwin
  1961 *Arms and Politics in Latin America*. New York, Frederick A. Praeger.
LINDSELL, Harold
  1962 "Faith Missions Since 1938," in Harr (ed.), *Frontiers of the Christian World Since 1938*, pp. 189-230.
LINDSELL, Harold, ed.
  1966 *The Church's Worldwide Mission*. Waco, Texas, Word Books.
LIPSET, Seymour, ed.
  1953 See BENDIX and LIPSET (eds.), *Class, Status and Power*.
LIPSET, Seymour Martin, and SOLARI, Aldo, eds.
  1967 *Elites in Latin America*. New York, Oxford University Press (Galaxy Book).
LUZBETAK, Louis J.
  1963 *The Church and Cultures: An Applied Anthropology for the Religious Worker*. Techny, Illinois, Divine Word Publications.
LYLE, Norris B., and CALMAN, Richard A., eds.
  1966 *Statistical Abstract of Latin America, 1965*. Los Angeles, University of California (Ninth Edition).
LYNCH, John
  1965 See HUMPHREYS and LYNCH, *The Origins of the Latin American Revolution, 1808—1826*.
LYRA, Jorge Buarque
  1960 *Orientação evangélica*. São Paulo, Emprêsa Gráfica Carioca S.A.
  c1964 *O Movimento pentecostal no Brasil: Profilaxia cristã dêsse movimento em defesa de "O Brasil para Cristo."* Niterói, Brazil, published by the author.

MACKAY, John A.
  1932 *The Other Spanish Christ*. London, Student Christian Movement Press.
  1961 *The Latin American Churches and the Ecumenical Movement*. New York, Committee on Cooperation in Latin America, NCCC.
MADDOX, James G.
  1956 *Technical Assistance by Religious Agencies in Latin America*. Chicago, University of Chicago Press.
MADSEN, William
  1964 *Mexican-Americans of South Texas*. New York, Holt, Rinehart and Winston.
MAFUD, Julio
  1965 *Psicología de la viveza criolla*. Buenos Aires, Editorial Américalee S.R.L. (Second Edition).
MANNONI, O.
  1964 *Prospero and Caliban: The Psychology of Colonization* (Pamela Powesland (trans.). New York, Frederick A. Praeger.
MARC
  1966 "Summary Report." Pasadena, Missions Advanced Research and Communication Center (available from World Vision International, Monrovia, mimeographed).
MARCHANT, Alexander, ed.
  1951 See SMITH and MARCHANT (eds.), *Brazil, Portrait of a Half Continent*.
MARSHALL, Andrew
  1966 *Brazil*. New York, Walker and Company.
MARYKNOLL FATHERS, ed.
  1964 *The Christian Challenge in Latin America: A Symposium*. Maryknoll, N.Y., Maryknoll Publications.

McCLELLAND, Alice J.
   1960   *Mission to Mexico.* Nashville, Board of World Missions, Presbyterian
          Church in the United States.
McGAVRAN, Donald A.
   1955   *The Bridges of God: A Study in the Strategy of Missions.* New York,
          Friendship Press.
   1962a See PICKETT, *et al., Church Growth and Group Conversion.*
   1962b *Church Growth in Jamaica: A Preview of Things to Come in Many
          Lands.* Lucknow, India, Lucknow Publishing House (available at the
          Bookstore, Fuller Theological Seminary, Pasadena).
McGAVRAN, Donald A., ed.
   1965   *Church Growth and Christian Mission.* New York, Harper & Row.
McGAVRAN, Donald, HUEGEL, John, and TAYLOR, Jack
   1963   *Church Growth In Mexico.* Grand Rapids, William B. Eerdmans.
McGREGOR, Pedro
   1966   *Jesus Of The Spirits.* New York, Stein and Day.
McGREGOR, Robert Gardner
   1926   See WHEELER, W. Reginald, *et al., Modern Missions in Chile and
          Brazil.*
McLEAN, J. H.
   1916   *The Living Christ for Latin America.* New York, The Board of Foreign
          Missions and the Woman's Board of Foreign Missions of the Presbyterian
          Church, USA.
McLEAN, J. M.
   1954   *Historia de la Iglesia Presbiteriana en Chile.* Santiago, Escuela Nacional
          de Artes Gráficas.
McLEAN, Robert, and WILLIAMS, Grace Petrie
   1916   *Old Spain in New America.* New York, Association Press.
MEANS, Frank K.
   1958   "The Mission Boards and the Evangelical Churches in Latin America."
          An address given at the Study Conference of the Committee on Coopera-
          tion in Latin America, November 6-8 (1958). New York, CCLA.
MECHAM, J. Lloyd
   1966   *Church and State in Latin America: A History of Politico-Ecclesiastical
          Relations.* Durham, University of North Carolina Press (Revised Edition).
MEJIA, Jorge
   1966   "Biblical Renewal in Latin America," in Considine (ed.), *The Religious
          Dimension in the New Latin America,* pp. 205-211.
MENEZES, Heraldo
   1958   *Caboclos na Umbanda.* Rio de Janeiro, Coleção Afro-Brasileira.
METHODIST EPISCOPAL CHURCH, SOUTH
   1901a *General Missionary Conference of the Methodist Church in the South:
          New Orleans, April 24-31, 1901.* Nashville, Methodist Church South
          Press.
   1901b *Missionary Issues of the Twentieth Century.* Nashville, Methodist Church
          South Press.
Mexican Census
   1962   *VIII Censo General de Poblacion—1960.* Mexico, D.F., Secretaria de
          Industria y Comercio Dirección General de Estadística, Estados Unidos
          Mexicanos.
MÍGUEZ BONINO, José
   1964   "Latin America," in Bates and Pauck (eds.), *The Prospects of Chris-
          tianity Throughout the World,* pp. 165-182.
MILNES, David
   1960   "Let My People Go," *Frontier,* 3 (Autumn): 214-216.

MINTZ, Sidney
1953 "The Folk-Urban Continuum and the Rural Proletarian Community,"
    American Journal of Sociology, 59.2 (Sept): 136-143.
MISSIONARY EDUCATION MOVEMENT
1917 *Congress on Christian Work in Latin America* (Vols. 1, 2, 3). New
    York, Missionary Education Movement.
MISSIONARY INFORMATION BUREAU
1967 "The Statistical Missionary Image." São Paulo, MIB (Occasional Paper
    10, May).
Missionary Review of the World
1925 "Ancient Inca Civilization in Latin America" (special issue), *Missionary
    Review of the World.* New York, 48.10.
MOENNICH, Martha L.
n.d. *That They May Hear.* Chicago, Chicago Gospel Tabernacle.
MONEY, Herbert
1957-58 "Protestantism in Latin America: Peru," *Religion in Life,* 27.1
    (Winter): 24-34.
MONTERROSO, Victor M.
1967 "Interview: Church Growth in the Americas," *Latin America Evan-
    gelist,* 47.3 (May-June): 6-8.
MOOG, Vianna
1964 *Bandeirantes and Pioneers* (L. L. Barrett, trans.). New York, George
    Braziller.
MOORE, Roberto Cecil
n.d. *Los Evangélicos en marcha... en América Latina.* Santiago, Chile,
    Liberia El Lucero.
MOREL, Edmar
1966 *Padre Cícero—O santo do Juàzeiro.* Rio de Janeiro, Editôra Civili-
    zação Brasileira, S.A.
MORNER, Magnus, ed.
1965 *The Expulsion of the Jesuits from Latin America.* New York, Alfred
    A. Knopf.
MORSE, Richard M.
1965 *The Bandeirantes: The Historical Role of the Brazilian Pathfinders.*
    New York, Alfred A. Knopf.
MULHOLLAND, Dewey M.
1961 "A Curriculum For A Seminary In The Brazilian Hinterland." An
    unpublished thesis, Fuller Theological Seminary, Pasadena.
MYKLEBUST, Olav Guttorm
1951 *An International Institute Of Scientific Missionary Research.* Oslo,
    Egede-Instituttet (Occasional Paper No. 1).

NEEDLER, Martin C., ed.
1964 *Political Systems of Latin America.* Princeton, D. Van Nostrand.
NEELY, Thomas B.
1909 *South America: Its Missionary Problems.* New York, Board of Foreign
    Missions of the Presbyterian Church in the U.S.A.
NEHEMKIS, Peter
1966 *Latin America: Myth and Reality.* New York, The New American
    Library (Mentor Book) (Revised Edition).
NEILL, Stephen
1952 *The Christian Society.* New York, Harper & Brothers.
1964 *A History of Christian Missions.* Baltimore, Penguin Books.
NELSON, Wilton M.
1963 *A History of Protestantism in Costa Rica.* Lucknow, India, Lucknow

Publishing House (available at the Bookstore, Fuller Theological Seminary, Pasadena).

NEWBIGIN, Lesslie
1954 *The Household of God.* New York, Friendship Press.

NICHOL, John Thomas
1966 *Pentecostalism.* New York, Harper & Row.

NIDA, Eugene A.
1954 *Customs and Cultures: Anthropology for Christian Missions.* New York, Harper & Row.
1958 "The Relationship of Social Structure to the Problems of Evangelism in Latin America," *Practical Anthropology,* 5.3 (May-June): 101-124.
1960a *Message and Mission: The Communication of the Christian Faith.* New York, Harper & Row.
1960b "The Roman Catholic, Communist, and Protestant Approach to Social Structure," *Practical Anthropology,* 7 (supp.): 21-26.
1961a "Christo-Paganism," *Practical Anthropology,* 8.1 (Jan-Feb): 1-15.
1961b "Communication of the Gospel to Latin Americans," *Practical Anthropology,* 8.4 (July-Aug): 145-156.
1961c "The Indigenous Churches in Latin America," *Practical Anthropology,* 8.1: 97-105.
1968 *Religion Across Cultures: A Study in the Communication of Christian Faith.* New York, Harper & Row.

NIDA, Eugene A., and WONDERLY, William L.
1963 "Selection, Preparation, and Function of Leaders in Indian Fields," *Practical Anthropology,* 10.1 (Jan-Feb): 6-16.

NIEBUHR, H. Richard, and WILLIAMS, Daniel D., eds.
1956 *The Ministry in Historical Perspectives.* New York, Harper & Row.

NIEHOFF, Arthur H.
1964 See ARENSBERG and NIEHOFF, *Introducing Social Change.*

NIILUS, Leopoldo J.
1967 "The Role of the Church in the Latin American Society." A study paper prepared for the Lutheran World Federation Commission on Stewardship and Evangelism, meeting at Springfield, Ohio, April 9-15 (mimeographed).

NINA RODRIGUES, Raymundo
1945 *Os Africanos no Brasil.* São Paulo, Companhia Editôra Nacional (Third Edition).

Occasional Bulletin
1968 New York (Missionary Research Library), 19.1 (Jan): 1-13.

O'DEA, Thomas F.
1966 *The Sociology of Religion.* Englewood Cliffs, Prentice-Hall.

ORDÓÑEZ, Francisco
n.d. *Historia del Cristianismo Evangélico en Colombia.* Cali, Colombia, La Alianza Cristiana y Misionera.

PARA, Manual
1965 *Realidad social de América Latina.* Montevideo, Iglésia y Sociedad en América Latina.

PARKER, Joseph I., ed.
1938 *Interpretive Statistical Survey of the World Mission of the Christian Church.* New York, International Missionary Council.

PATCH, Richard W.
1960 See ADAMS, *et al., Social Change in Latin America Today.*

PATON, David M., ed.
1960 *The Ministry of the Spirit: Selected Writings of Roland Allen.* Grand Rapids, William B. Eerdmans.
PAUCK, Wilhelm, ed.
1964 See BATES and PAUCK (eds.), *The Prospects of Christianity Throughout the World.*
PAZ, Octavio
1961 *The Labyrinth of Solitude: Life and Thought in Mexico* (Lysander Kemp, trans.). New York, Grove Press.
Pensamiento Cristiana
1963-66 Córdoba (Alejandro Clifford, ed.), Vols. 10-13.
PEREIRA DE QUEIROZ, Maria Isaura
1958a "Classifications des Messianismes bresiliens," *Archives de Sociologie des Religions,* 3.5 (Jan-June): 111-120.
1958b "L' influence du Milieu Social Interne sur les mouvements messianiques bresiliens," *Archives de Sociologie des Religions,* 3.5 (Jan-June): 3-29.
PERROW, Maxwell V.
1967 "Evangelical Communications Congress Searches for Better Strategy in Latin America," *World Vision Magazine,* 11.11 (Dec): 24.
PICKETT, J. W.
1963 *The Dynamics of Church Growth: A Positive Approach for World Missions.* New York, Abingdon Press.
PICKETT, J. W., et al.
1962 *Church Growth and Group Conversion.* Lucknow, India, Lucknow Publishing House (available at the Bookstore, Fuller Theological Seminary, Pasadena).
PIERSON, Donald
1952 *Cruz das Almas: A Brazilian Village.* Washington, Institute of Social Anthropology, Smithsonian Institute (Publication 12).
1967 *Negroes in Brazil: A Study of Race Contact at Bahia.* Carbondale, Southern Illinois University Press.
PIKE, Frederick B., ed.
1964a *The Conflict Between Church and State in Latin America.* New York, Alfred A. Knopf.
1964b See D'ANTONIO and PIKE (eds.), *Religion, Revolution, and Reform.*
PIN, Emile
1963 *Elementos para una sociología del Catolicismo latinoamericano.* Friburgo, FERES.
1965 See HOUTART and PIN, *The Church and the Latin American Revolution.*
PINTO, Magalhães
1966 *Levantamento da população favelada de Belo Horizonte.* Belo Horizonte, Minas Gerais, Secretaria de Estado do Trabalho e Cultura Popular.
PINTO, Tancreda da Silva
n.d. See FREITAS and PINTO, *Camba de Umbanda.*
PITT-RIVERS, Julian
1965 "Who Are The Indians?" *Encounter,* 25.3 (Sept): 41-49.
POHL, Irmgard, and ZEPP, Josef
1967 *Latin America: A Geographical Commentary.* New York, E. P. Dutton (Dutton Paperback).
Polemica, dialogo y misión
Montevideo (Centro de Estúdios Cristianos).

Population Bulletin
1962 Washington (Population Reference Bureau), 18.6.
1965 Washington (PRB), 21.4.
POPULATION REFERENCE BUREAU
1962 "Latin America and Population Growth," *Population Bulletin*, 18.6.
1965 "World Population Projections, 1965–2000," *Population Bulletin*, 21.4.
1966 "World Population Data Sheet—1966." Washington, PRB.
1968 "World Population Data Sheet—1968." Washington, PRB (March).
POZAS, Ricardo
1962 *Juan the Chamula: An Ethnological Re-creation of the Life of a Mexican Indian* (Lysander Kemp, trans.). Berkeley, University of California Press.
Practical Anthropology
1958 Tarrytown, N.Y., 5.3: 101-124; 5.5, 6: 197-202, 228-233.
1959 Tarrytown, 6.2: 55-64.
1960 Tarrytown, 7.5: 205-209; 7 (supp.): 21-26.
1961 Tarrytown, 8.1: 1-15, 97-105; 8.4: 145-156; 8.5: 193-199.
1963 Tarrytown, 10.1: 6-16; 10.3: 127-134.
PRESCOTT, Lyle
n.d. *Luz en la América Latina*. Kansas City, Mo., Nazarene Publication House.
PYTCHES, David
1967 "Anglicanism in Chile Today," *Churchman*, 81.2 (Summer): 114-128.

QUIRING, Wilmer Allan
1957 "The Establishment of Evangelical Christianity in Colombia, South America, 1825–1900." An unpublished thesis, Kennedy School of Missions, Hartford Seminary Foundation, Hartford, Connecticut.

RAMIREZ, Gustavo Perez, and LABELLE, Yvan
1964 *El Problema sacerdotal en América Latina*. Friburgo, FERES.
RAMOS, Jovelino Pereira
1963 "O lugar da Estatística," *Brasil Presbiteriano*, 6.15 (Nov 15-30): 7.
RAPP, Robert S.
c1965 *A Confederação Evangélica do Brasil e o evangelho social*. São Paulo, Missão Bíblica Presbiteriana no Brasil.
RATINOFF, Luis
1967 "The New Urban Groups: The Middle Classes," in Lipset and Solari (eds.), *Elites in Latin America*, pp. 61-93.
READ, William R.
1965 *New Patterns of Church Growth in Brazil*. Grand Rapids, William B. Eerdmans.
1967a "Breakthrough," *World Vision Magazine*, 11.9 (Oct): 2-4.
1967b "Honey On The Border," *World Vision Magazine*, 11.10 (Nov): 2-5.
REDFIELD, Robert
1953 *The Primitive World and Its Transformations*. Ithaca, Cornell University Press (Cornell Paperback).
1956 *The Little Community*. Chicago, University of Chicago Press.
REID, Ann Townsend
1926 See WHEELER, W. Reginald, *et al.*, *Modern Missions in Chile and Brazil*.
Religion in Life
1957-58 Nashville (Abingdon Press), 27.1 (Winter): 5-53.
REMBAO, Alberto
1957-58 "Protestantism in Latin America: The Reformation Comes to Hispanic America," *Religion in Life*, 27.1 (Winter): 45-53.

REX, Eileen E.
1964 "A Functional Philosophy of Missions for the Indian Tribes of Colombia." An unpublished thesis, Fuller Theological Seminary, Pasadena.
REYBURN, William D.
1959 *The Toba Indians of the Argentine Chaco: An Interpretive Report.* Elkhart, Ind., Mennonite Board of Missions & Charities.
RIBEIRO, Domingos
1937 *Origens do evangelismo brasileiro (escôrço histórico).* Rio de Janeiro, Impresso no Est. Grafico "Apollo."
RIBEIRO, René
1952 *Cultos afro-brasileiros do Recife.* Recife, Boletim do Instituto Joaquim Nabuco (Numéro Especial).
1956 *Religião e relações raciais.* Rio de Janeiro, Ministério de Educação e Cultura.
RICARD, Robert
1966 *The Spiritual Conquest of Mexico* (Leslie B. Simpson, trans.). Berkeley, University of California Press.
RITCHIE, John
n.d. *The Indigenous Church in Peru.* London, World Dominion Press.
1930 See BROWNING, RITCHIE, and GRUBB, *The West Coast Republics of South America.*
1945 *Indigenous Church Principles in Theory and Practice.* New York, Revell.
RIVAIL, Hippolyte Leon Denizard
1922 *Philosophie spiritualiste Le Livre des Esprits contenant les Principes de la Doctrine Spirite.* Paris, Librairie des sciences psychiques.
RIVERA, R. Pedro
1962 *Instituciones protestantes en Mexico.* Colonia Guerrero, Mexico, Editorial Jus, S.A.
ROBBINS, Richard
1958 "Myth and Realities of International Migration into Latin America," *Annals of the American Academy of Political and Social Science,* 316: 102-110.
ROBERTS, C. Paul, and KOHDA, Takako, eds.
1967 *Statistical Abstract of Latin America, 1966.* Los Angeles, University of California (Tenth Edition).
ROBERTS, W. Dayton
1963a "Latin America: Challenge of a New Day," *Christianity Today,* 7.21 (July 19): 3-19.
1963b "Pentecost South of the Border," *Christianity Today,* 7.21 (July 19): 32.
1967 *Revolution in Evangelism: The Story of Evangelism-in-Depth in Latin America.* Chicago, Moody Press.
RODRIGUES, José Honório
1967 *The Brazilians: Their Character and Aspirations* (R. E. Dimmick, trans.). Austin, University of Texas Press (Texas Pan American Series).
ROGOFF, Natalie
1953 "Recent Trends in Urban Occupational Mobility," in Bendix and Lipset (eds.), *Class, Status and Power,* pp. 442-454.
RYCROFT, W. Stanley
1942 *On This Foundation: The Evangelical Witness in Latin America.* New York, Friendship Press.
1951 "Latin America Tomorrow," in Leber (ed.), *World Faith in Action,* pp. 263-285.

1955 "A Strategy for the Christian Mission." A study paper for the Conference on Latin America, Hartford Seminary Foundation, May 26-28.
1958 *Religion and Faith in Latin America*. Philadelphia, Westminster Press.
RYCROFT, W. Stanley, and CLEMMER, Myrtle M.
1961 *A Statistical Study of Latin America*. New York, COEMAR, United Presbyterian Church in the USA (bulletin).
1962 *A Study of Urbanization in Latin America*. New York, COEMAR, United Presbyterian Church in the USA.
1963 *A Factual Study of Latin America*. New York, COEMAR, United Presbyterian Church in the USA.

SABANES, Carlos M.
1966 "Urbanization In Latin America," *International Review of Missions*, 55 (July): 307-312.
SABLE, Martin H.
1965 *Master Directory for Latin America*. Los Angeles, Latin American Center, University of California.
SANTA ANA, Julio De
1963 "Argentina and Uruguay at the Crossroads," *Christianity and Crisis*, 23.21 (Dec. 9): 224-228.
SAUNDERS, John
1960 "Organização social de uma congregação protestante no Estado da Guanabara, Brasil," *Sociologia*, 22.4: 415-450.
SCANLON, A. Clark
1962 *Church Growth Th.ough Theological Education (in Guatemala)*. Guatemala, Libreria Bautista.
SCHNEIDER, Ronald M.
1965 See KINGSBURY and SCHNEIDER, *An Atlas of Latin American Affairs*.
SCHNITZLER, Hermann
1924 *The Republic of Mexico*. New York, Nicholas L. Brown.
SCHURZ, William Lytle
1961 *Brazil: The Infinite Country*. London, Robert Hale Limited.
1964 *This New World: The Civilization of Latin America*. New York, E. P. Dutton (Dutton Paperback).
SCIENTIFIC AMERICAN, INC., ed.
1965 *Cities*. New York, Alfred A. Knopf (Borzoi Book).
SCOBIE, James R.
1964 *Argentina: A City and a Nation*. New York, Oxford University Press.
SCOPES, Wilfred, ed.
1962 *The Christian Ministry in Latin America and the Caribbean*. New York, Commission on World Mission and Evangelism, WCC.
SEAMANDS, John T.
1966 "What McGavran's Church Growth Thesis Means," *Evangelical Missions Quarterly*, 3.1 (Fall): 21-31.
SHAPIRO, Samuel, ed.
1967 *Integration of Man and Society in Latin America*. Notre Dame, University of Notre Dame Press.
SHAULL, M. Richard
1957-58 "Protestantism in Latin Amercia: Brazil," *Religion in Life*, 27.1 (Winter): 5-14.
SILVERT, K. H.
1961 "Nationalism in Latin America," *Annals of the American Academy of Political and Social Science*, 334 (March): 1-9.

SILVERT, K. H., ed.
  1963 *Expectant Peoples: Nationalism and Development*. New York, Random
        House (Vintage Book).
SIMPSON, Lesley Byrd
  1967 *Many Mexicos*. Berkeley, University of California Press (Fourth Edi-
        tion, Revised).
SINCLAIR, John H., ed.
  1967 *Protestantism in Latin America: A Bibliographical Guide*. Austin,
        Texas, Hispanic-American Institute. The reader can find further biblio-
        graphical data on subjects related to Protestant history and contem-
        porary church life in Latin America in this *Guide*. It includes an index
        of authors and editors, a list of the location of Protestant mission
        archives, centers of publication on Latin America, and other useful
        bibliographical aids to assist the student and researcher in the general
        field of Latin American studies. The reader will also find in the *Guide*
        annotations on many of the works listed in this bibliography and
        indications of the location of certain books not currently available.
SINGH, G. H.
  1962 See PICKETT, *et al., Church Growth and Group Conversion*.
SJOBERG, Gideon
  1960 *The Preindustrial City: Past and Present*. New York, The Free Press.
SMALLEY, William A.
  1958 "Planting the Church in a Disintegrating Society," *Practical Anthro-
        pology*, 5.5, 6 (Sept-Dec): 228-233.
SMALLEY, William A., ed.
  1967 *Readings in Missionary Anthropology*. Tarrytown, N. Y., Practical
        Anthropology, Inc.
SMITH, Timothy L.
  1957 *Revivalism and Social Reform*. New York, Harper & Row (Harper
        Torchbook).
  1961 *Latin American Population Studies*. Gainesville, University of Florida
        Press.
  1963 *Brazil: People and Institutions*. Baton Rouge, Louisiana State Uni-
        versity Press (Second Edition).
  1964 "Urbanization in Latin America," in Anderson (ed.), *Urbanism and
        Urbanization*, 2: 228-242.
SMITH, T. Lynn, and MARCHANT, Alexander, eds.
  1951 *Brazil, Portrait of a Half Continent*. New York, Dryden Press.
Social Forces
  1953 Chapel Hill (University of North Carolina), 31 (May): 339-342.
Sociologia
  1960 São Paulo (Fundação Escola de Sociologia e Política de São Paulo),
        22.4: 415-450.
  1963 São Paulo, 25: 203-209.
SOLARI, Aldo, ed.
  1967 See LIPSET and SOLARI (eds.), *Elites in Latin America*.
SOLOMON, Victor
  1965 *A Handbook on Conversions to the Religions of the World*. New York,
        Stravon Educational Press.
Southwestern Journal of Theology
  1962 Fort Worth (Southwestern Baptist Theological Seminary), 4.2: 27-47.
SPEER, Robert E.
  1912 *South American Problems*. New York, Student Volunteer Movement.
  1925 *Christian Work in South America*, Vols. I, II. New York, Fleming H.
        Revell.

1926   See WHEELER, W. Reginald, *et al., Modern Missions in Chile and Brazil.*

SPIEGEL, Henry
1949   *The Brazilian Economy: Chronic Inflation and Sporadic Industrialization.* Philadelphia, Blakiston Co.

STEIN, William W.
1961   *Hualcan: Life in the Highlands of Peru.* Ithaca, Cornell University Press.

STEWARD, Julian H.
1950   *Area Research: Theory and Practice.* New York, Social Science Research Council (Bulletin 63).
1963   *Theory of Culture Change: The Methodology of Multilinear Evolution.* Urbana, University of Illinois Press.

STEWARD, Julian H., and FARON, Louis C.
1959   *Native Peoples of South America.* New York, McGraw-Hill.

STOCKWELL, B. Foster
1957-58   "Protestantism in Latin America: Argentina and Uruguay," *Religion in Life,* 27.1 (Winter): 15-23.

STOKES, Louie W.
1968   *Historia del Movimiento Pentecostal en la Argentina.* Buenos Aires, published by the author.

STRACHAN, R. Kenneth
1961   *Evangelism-in-Depth: Experimenting with a New Type of Evangelism.* Chicago, Moody Press.

STUDENT VOLUNTEER MOVEMENT
1906   *Students and the Modern Missionary Crusade.* Nashville, SVM.
1911   *World Atlas of Christian Missions.* New York, SVM.

STUNTZ, Homer C.
1916   *South American Neighbors.* New York, Methodist Book Concern.

STYCOS, J. Mayone
1968   *Human Fertility in Latin America.* Ithaca, Cornell University Press.

SUNDKLER, Bengt
1963   *The World of Mission.* Grand Rapids, William B. Eerdmans.

SVALASTOGA, Kaare
1965   *Social Differentiation.* New York, David McKay (McKay Social Science Series).

SZULC, Tad
1966   *Latin America.* New York, Atheneum (New York Times Byline Book).

TALBOT, Phillips, ed.
1960   *A Select Bibliography: Asia, Africa, Eastern Europe, Latin America.* New York, American Universities Field Staff.

TANNENBAUM, Frank
1946   *Slave and Citizen: The Negro in the Americas.* New York, Random House (Vintage Book).
1960   *Ten Keys to Latin America.* New York, Random House (Vintage Book).

TAVARES de SÁ, Hernane
1947   *The Brazilians: People of Tomorrow.* New York, John Day.

TAWNEY, R. H.
1954   *Religion and the Rise of Capitalism.* New York, The New American Library (Mentor Book).

TAYLOR, Clyde W., and COGGINS, Wade T., eds.
1961   *Protestant Missions in Latin America: A Statistical Survey.* Washington, Evangelical Foreign Missions Association.

TAYLOR, Jack E.
1962 *God's Messengers To Mexico's Masses.* Eugene, Oregon, Institute of Church Growth (available at the Bookstore, Fuller Theological Seminary, Pasadena).
1963 See McGAVRAN, HUEGEL, and TAYLOR, *Church Growth In Mexico.*
TEPASKE, John J., and FISHER, Sydney Nettleton, eds.
1964 *Explosive Forces in Latin America.* Columbus, Ohio State University Press.
TESTA, Michael P.
1963 *O apóstolo da Madeira (Robert Reid Kalley).* Lisbon, Igreja Evangélica Presbiteriana de Portugal.
THEOBALD, Robert
1960 *The Rich and the Poor.* New York, The New American Library (Mentor Book).
THEODORSON, George A., ed.
1967 *Studies in Human Ecology.* Evanston, Harper & Row.
THOMPSON, Augustus C.
1895 *Moravian Missions: Twelve Lectures.* New York, Charles Scribner's Sons.
THOMPSON, Edward Herbert
1960 *People of the Serpent: Life and Adventure Among the Mayas.* New York, Capricorn Books.
THOMPSON, Phyllis
1960 *Faith by Hearing: The Story of Gospel Recordings.* Los Angeles, Gospel Recordings.
THOMSON, James
1827 *Letters on the Moral and Religious State of South America.* London, Nisbet.
TILLY, E. A.
1901 "Brazil: A Survey of the Field," in Methodist Episcopal Church South, *General Missionary Conference of the Methodist Church in the South,* pp. 422-427.
TIPPETT, A. R.
1965 "Mexican Notebook: Report and Evaluation of a Brief Visit to Mexico." An unpublished, confidential report for Church Growth Research in Latin America, Fuller Theological Seminary, Pasadena.
1966 "The Holy Spirit and PERT," *World Vision Magazine,* 10.9: 12-13, 23.
1967 *The Growth of an Indigenous Church.* School of World Mission and Institute of Church Growth, Fuller Theological Seminary, Pasadena (mimeographed).
TOMASEK, Robert D., ed.
1966 *Latin American Politics: 24 Studies of the Contemporary Scene.* Garden City, Doubleday & Company (Anchor Book).
TORRES, Sergio
1961 See CORREDOR and TORRES, *Transformación en el mundo rural latino-americano.*
TRACHSEL, Laura
1961 *Kindled Fires in Latin America.* Marion, Indiana, World Gospel Mission.
TRENCHARD, Alejandro Clifford
1957 *Un hombre bueno.* Buenos Aires, Establecimiento Gráfico Racciatti.
TRON, Ernesto, and GANZ, Emilio H.
1958 *Historia de las colonias Valdenses Sudamericanas en su primer centenario (1858-1958).* Colonia Valdense, Uruguay, Libreria Pastor Miguel Morel.

TUCKER, Hugh C.
1902 *The Bible in Brazil: Colporter Experiences.* New York, Fleming H. Revell.
1925a "The Bible in Latin America," in Turner (ed.), *The Foreign Missions Convention at Washington 1925,* pp. 345-347.
1925b "The Indians in Latin America: The Appeal They Make and the Obligation We Face," in Turner (ed.), *The Foreign Missions Convention at Washington 1925,* pp. 320-323.

TURNER, Fennell P., ed.
1925 *The Foreign Missions Convention at Washington 1925.* New York, Fleming H. Revell.

VAILLANT, G. C.
1951 *The Aztecs of Mexico.* Harmondsworth, Middlesex, U.K., Penguin Books.

VALLIER, Ivan
1967 "Religious Elites: Differentiations and Developments in Roman Catholicism," in Lipset and Solari (eds.), *Elites in Latin America,* pp. 190-232.

VAN DUSEN, Henry P., ed.
1963 *Christianity on the March.* New York, Harper & Row.

VAN LEEUWEN, Arend Th.
1964 *Christianity in World History.* London, Edinburgh House Press..

VERGARA, Ignacio
1962 *El protestantismo en Chile.* Santiago, Editorial del Pacifico, S.A.

VERHOEVEN, Thomas W.
1966 "New Army of Catechists in the Andes," in Considine (ed.), *The Religious Dimension in the New Latin America,* pp. 127-139.

VICEDOM, Georg F.
1965 *The Mission of God: An Introduction to a Theology of Mission* (Thiele and Hilgendorf, trans.). St. Louis, Concordia Publishing House.

VILLALPANDO, Luis
1966 "Misión de cien años." Buenos Aires, Consejo Metodista de Evangelización (mimeographed).

VISSER 't HOOFT, W. A.
1963 *No Other Name: The Choice between Syncretism and Christian Universalism.* Philadelphia, Westminster Press.

VOGT, Evon Z.
1965 See LESSA and VOGT, *Reader In Comparative Religion.*

WACH, Joachim
1944 *Sociology of Religion.* Chicago, University of Chicago Press (Phoenix Book).

WAGLEY, Charles
1955 "Brazilian Community Studies: A Methodological Evaluation," *Anais do XXXI Congresso Internacional de Americanists,* pp. 357-376.
1960 See ADAMS, *et al., Social Change in Latin America Today.*
1963 *An Introduction to Brazil.* New York, Columbia University Press.
1965 "On the Concept of Social Race in the Americas," in Heath and Adams (eds.), *Contemporary Cultures and Societies of Latin America,* pp. 42-69. 531-545.
1968 *The Latin American Tradition: Essays on the Unity and the Diversity of Latin American Culture.* New York, Columbia University Press.

WAGLEY, Charles, ed.
1952 *Race and Class in Rural Brazil.* Paris, UNESCO.
1964 *Social Science Research in Latin America.* New York, Columbia University Press.
WAGLEY, Charles, and HARRIS, Marvin
1958 *Minorities in the New World: Six Case Studies.* New York, Columbia University Press.
1965 "A Typology of Latin American Subcultures," in Heath and Adams (eds.), *Contemporary Cultures and Societies of Latin America,* pp. 42-69.
WALKER, Louise Jeter
1965 *Faculty Training Program For Overseas Bible Schools.* Springfield, Mo., Foreign Missions Department of the Assemblies of God.
WALLIS, Ethel E., and BENNETT, Mary A.
1959 *Two Thousand Tongues to Go.* New York, Harper & Row.
WARNECK, Gustav
1906 *Outline of a History of Protestant Missions from the Reformation to the Present Time.* New York, Fleming H. Revell.
WARNSHUIS, A. L.
1962 See PICKETT, *et al., Church Growth and Group Conversion.*
WATSON, Tom
1965 *T. J. Bach: A Voice for Missions.* Chicago, Moody Press.
WCC
1962 "Latin American Statements on Church and Society." Geneva, World Council of Churches *(Background Information for Church and Society,* No. 30).
WCC, Department of Missionary Studies
1964 "The Growth of the Church" (a Statement drawn up by a Consultation convened at Iberville, Quebec, July 31-August 2, 1963), *Ecumenical Review,* 16.2: 195-199.
WCC, Division of World Mission and Evangelism
1963 "A Tent-Making Ministry: Towards a More Flexible Form of Ministry." Geneva, World Council of Churches.
WEBER, Max
1963 *The Sociology of Religion.* Boston, Beacon Press.
WEBSTER, Douglas
1965 *Unchanging Mission: Biblical and Contemporary.* Philadelphia, Fortress Press.
WENDT, Herbert
1966 *The Red, White, and Black Continent.* Garden City, Doubleday & Company.
WENGER, A. Grace
1961 *God Builds the Church in Latin America.* Scottdale, Pa., Herald Press.
WEYER, Edward, Jr.
1961 *Primitive Peoples Today.* Garden City, Doubleday & Company (Dolphin Book).
WHEELER, W. Reginald, *et al.*
1926 *Modern Missions in Chile and Brazil.* Philadelphia, Westminster Press.
WHITAKER, Arthur P., ed.
1942 *Latin America and the Enlightenment.* New York, Appleton-Century Company.
WHITAKER, Arthur P., and JORDAN, David C.
1966 *Nationalism in Contemporary Latin America.* New York, Free Press.
WHITEFORD, Andrew H.
1964 *Two Cities of Latin America.* Garden City, Doubleday & Company (Anchor Book).

WHITING, John W. M., *et al.*
1966   *Field Guide for a Study of Socialization.* New York, John Wiley and Sons (Vol. 1, Six Cultures Series).
WIESER, Thomas, ed.
1966   *Planning For Mission.* New York, U.S. Conference, WCC.
WILDER, Amos N.
1965   *Kerygma, Eschatology, and Social Ethics.* Philadelphia, Fortress Press (Facet Book).
WILGUS, A. Curtis
1941   *The Development of Hispanic America.* New York, Rinehart.
WILGUS, A. Curtis, ed.
1961   *The Caribbean: The Central American Area.* Gainesville, University of Florida Press.
1962   *The Caribbean: Contemporary Colombia.* Gainesville, University of Florida Press.
WILGUS, A. Curtis, and D'ECA, Raul
1963   *Latin American History: A Summary of Political, Economic, Social, and Cultural Events from 1492 to the Present.* New York, Barnes & Noble.
WILLEMS, Emílio
1947   *Cunha: Tradição e transição em uma cultura rural do Brazil.* São Paulo, Secretaria da Agricultura do Estado de São Paulo.
1953   "The Structure of the Brazilian Family," *Social Forces,* 31 (May): 339-342.
1967a   *Followers Of The New Faith: Culture Change and the Rise of Protestantism in Brazil and Chile.* Nashville, Vanderbilt University Press.
1967b   "Validation of Authority in Pentecostal Sects of Chile and Brazil," *Journal for the Scientific Study of Religion,* 6.2: 253-258.
WILLIAMS, Daniel D., ed.
1956   See NIEBUHR and WILLIAMS, *The Ministry in Historical Perspectives.*
WILLIAMS, Grace Petrie
1916   See McLEAN and WILLIAMS, *Old Spain in New America.*
WILLIAMS, Maude Newell
1918   *The Least of These—In Colombia.* New York, Fleming H. Revell.
WILLIAMS, Ralph D., and ARBIZÚ, Francisco
1932   *Standard of Christian Doctrine and Practice: For the Membership of the Local Assemblies of God.* Santa Ana, El Salvador, Tipografía Lux.
WINER, B. J.
1962   *Statistical Principles in Experimental Design.* New York, McGraw-Hill.
WINTER, Ralph D.
1967   "The Guatemalan Presbyterian Seminary," in ALET (pub.), "The Extension Seminary and the Programmed Textbook," pp. 10-13.
WIPFLER, William L.
1968   "Religious Syncretism in the Caribbean: A Study of the Persistence of African and Indian Belief," *Occasional Bulletin,* 19.1 (Jan): 1-13.
WOLF, Eric
1959   *Sons of the Shaking Earth.* Chicago, University of Chicago Press.
WONDERLY, William L.
1958   "Pagan and Christian Concepts in a Mexican Indian Culture," *Practical Anthropology,* 5.5, 6 (Sept-Dec): 197-202.
1959   "Social Anthropology, Christian Missions, and the Indians of Latin America," *Practical Anthropology,* 6.2 (March-April): 55-64.
1960   "Urbanization: The Challenge of Latin America in Transition," *Practical Anthropology,* 7.5 (Sept-Oct): 205-209.

1961   "Indian Work and Church-Mission Integration," *Practical Anthropology*, 8.5 (Sept-Oct): 193-199.

1963   See NIDA and WONDERLY, "Selection, Preparation, and Function of Leaders in Indian Fields."

WONDERLY, William L., and LARA-BRAUD, Jorge
1964   *"Los Evangélicos somos así?"* Mexico, Casa Unida de Publicaciones, S.A.

WOOD, Robert
1964   *Missionary Crisis and Challenge in Latin America*. St. Louis, B. Herder.

WOOD, Thomas B.
1900   "South America as a Mission Field," in Beach, *et al., Protestant Missions in South America*, pp. 197-215.

WORCESTER, Donald E.
1963   *The Three Worlds of Latin America: Mexico, Central America, and South America*. New York, E. P. Dutton.

World Business
1967a   "Inflation in Latin America," *World Business*. New York (Chase Manhattan Bank, Economic Research Division), 7: 5-9.

1967b   "Perspective on World Business," *World Business*. New York, 4: 5.

1967c   "Urbanization in Latin America," *World Business*. New York, 5: 3.

World Christian Handbook
1949   See GRUBB (ed.).

1952   See BINGLE and GRUBB (eds.).

1957   See BINGLE and GRUBB (eds.).

1962   See COXILL and GRUBB (eds.).

1967   See COXILL and GRUBB (eds.).

World Dominion
1956   London, 34 (Jan): 29-32.

World Vision Magazine
1966   Monrovia, California, 10.3: 4-5; 10.9: 12-13, 23.

1967   Monrovia, 11.9: 2-4; 11.10: 2-5; 11.11: 24.

WYCLIFFE BIBLE TRANSLATORS
1963   *Who Brought the Word*. Santa Ana, California, Wycliffe Bible Translators.

YOCCOU, Raul Caballero
1964   *"Hermanos Libres" ¿Por qué?* Buenos Aires, Dile S. R. L.

YUASA, Key
1967   "Churches in Minority Situation: The Brazilian Case." Cuernavaca, Center of Intercultural Documentation (Document 68/49, Nov).

ZELINSKY, Wilbur
1966   *A Prologue to Population Geography*. Englewood Cliffs, Prentice-Hall (Foundations of Economic Geography Series).

ZEPP, Josef
1967   See POHL and ZEPP, *Latin America*.

ZWIRNER, Walter
1960   "Emigración inmigración y su influencia sobre hombres e iglesias," *Ekklesia*, 4.6 (April): 8-20.

INDEX